Freedom Soldiers

FREEDOM SOLDIERS

The Emancipation of Black Soldiers in Civil War Camps, Courts, and Prisons

JONATHAN LANDE

OXFORD
UNIVERSITY PRESS

OXFORD
UNIVERSITY PRESS

Oxford University Press is a department of the University of Oxford. It furthers
the University's objective of excellence in research, scholarship, and education
by publishing worldwide. Oxford is a registered trade mark of Oxford University
Press in the UK and certain other countries.

Published in the United States of America by Oxford University Press
198 Madison Avenue, New York, NY 10016, United States of America.

© Oxford University Press 2024

All rights reserved. No part of this publication may be reproduced, stored in
a retrieval system, or transmitted, in any form or by any means, without the
prior permission in writing of Oxford University Press, or as expressly permitted
by law, by license, or under terms agreed with the appropriate reproduction
rights organization. Inquiries concerning reproduction outside the scope of the
above should be sent to the Rights Department, Oxford University Press, at the
address above.

You must not circulate this work in any other form
and you must impose this same condition on any acquirer.

Library of Congress Cataloging-in-Publication Data
Names: Lande, Jonathan, author.
Title: Freedom soldiers : the emancipation of black soldiers
in Civil War camps, courts, and prisons / Jonathan Lande.
Other titles: Emancipation of black soldiers in Civil War camps, courts, and prisons
Description: New York, NY : Oxford University Press, 2024. |
Includes bibliographical references and index. |
Identifiers: LCCN 2024020131 (print) | LCCN 2024020132 (ebook) |
ISBN 9780197531754 (hardback) | ISBN 9780197531778 (epub) | ISBN 9780197531785
Subjects: LCSH: United States. Army—History—Civil War, 1861–1865. |
United States. Army—African American troops—History—19th century. |
United States. Colored Troops—History. | African American soldiers—Social conditions—19th century. |
Absence without leave—United States—History—19th century. | Enslaved persons—Emancipation—
United States—History—19th century. | African American soldiers—History—19th century. | Military
offenses—United States—History—19th century. | United States—History—Civil War, 1861–1865—
Participation, African American | United States—History—Civil War, 1861–1865—Social aspects.
Classification: LCC E540.B53 L363 2024 (print) | LCC E540.B53 (ebook) |
DDC 973.7/415—dc23/eng/20240723
LC record available at https://lccn.loc.gov/2024020131
LC ebook record available at https://lccn.loc.gov/2024020132

DOI: 10.1093/oso/9780197531754.001.0001

Printed by Sheridan Books, Inc., United States of America

For Kate

Contents

Introduction: The Long March Out of Slavery in Union Blue   1

PART I *Freedom in Camp*

1. "Bound for Freedom's Light": Enlisting and Emancipating Men in the US Army   15
2. "Parts of the Gigantic Machine of Death": Adapting and Reacting to US Army Discipline   34
3. "No Intention of Deserting": Escaping Camp and Taking Leaves of Freedom   56

PART II *Freedom in the Military Justice System*

4. "Unworthy of Freedom": Policing War Workers and Emancipation in the Courts-Martial   81
5. "Establish My Innocence": Defending Flight and Freedom in the Courts-Martial   109
6. "Ought Not to Be in Prison": Petitioning State Officials for Freedom during Incarceration   132

Conclusion: The War for Liberation within the Ranks   158

Acknowledgments   167
Appendix: Black Soldiers Tried for Desertion during the US Civil War   173
Notes   213
Bibliography   265
Index   301

Freedom Soldiers

Introduction: The Long March Out of Slavery in Union Blue

"I'SE TIRED OF staying here," he told his captain, "and I'se going home." The exhausted, homesick, once-enslaved soldier then headed out of camp. Weeks earlier, as the US Army waged war on Confederates, he had evaded Rebel enslavers and enlisted. Although opposed to arming Black men for most of the first two years of war, US government officials changed course in 1863. To turn the Rebel's enslaved laborers into allies, US Army recruiters promised to free those who volunteered. Yet, while enlistment legally ended their enslavement, it marked only another step in their long march out of slavery. As the soldier explained to his captain, his struggles continued within the ranks. He said that he had grown "weary of war" during his time in the Eleventh Louisiana Infantry (African Descent). He "wanted to see his family" and "concluded to go home." The break was not necessarily permanent, he promised. "If the captain desired it," he said, he "would come back in a little while, but he was going home then." Clarifying the particulars of military discipline, including perhaps that desertion constituted a crime punishable by death, the captain swayed the soldier to grab his gun and gear and return to his duties. But the captain could not persuade all of the soldiers of the Eleventh to stay.[1]

Months after learning US Army regulations and clashing with Confederates, soldiers of the Eleventh continued leaving camp without permission. Since being raised in the summer of 1863, the Eleventh had served laudably in Louisiana at the fortifications on the Mississippi River near Milliken's Bend. War correspondent Thomas Knox surveyed the men and declared that the soldiers made "excellent material for the army." Knox also noticed that, while the men served, their "home ties were very strong" and "their affection for wives and children" was equally powerful.[2] These ties undoubtedly made

Freedom Soldiers. Jonathan Lande, Oxford University Press. © Oxford University Press 2024.
DOI: 10.1093/oso/9780197531754.003.0001

the men superb soldiers. If the enemy attacked, they would fight not only to defend the fort at Milliken's Bend but also for their families' safety.[3] In fact, they did just that. They had shielded the fort against a July 1863 assault. Many fighting in the rags they left slavery wearing rather than in Union blue, the Eleventh repulsed the Rebels with a "genuine bayonet charge" and the help of an ironclad, *Harper's Weekly* reported. In so doing, the soldiers proved their "valor and heroism," Black recruiters in the North proclaimed.[4] But their bonds to kin came to pose a problem. In January 1864, the army moved the Eleventh fifty miles south to Waterproof, Louisiana. Many soldiers became dismayed, even enraged. They "expected to remain at Milliken's Bend" near their families, Knox learned. Desperate to care for their families, the reporter wrote, a few grew "mutinous" while "a half-dozen of the men went out of the lines one night." Commanders caught them walking north, returned them to camp, and likely to train the offenders as well as their compatriots, placed those who decamped within the guardhouse. The punishment did not suffice, however. The soldiers continued leaving for "brief visit[s] to their families," Knox wrote. Officers considered their flight desertion, yet these enlisted freedom seekers saw nothing amiss. Most even "request[ed] their comrades . . . notify their captains that they would be absent a short time," the reporter noted.[5] Knox, as well as officers and high-ranking commanders, thought once-enslaved soldiers would learn that desertion was a problem. But the enlisted freedom seekers continued decamping throughout the war.[6] For men who had long absconded to ameliorate the conditions of slavery, their mobility was not criminal. To them, mobility was a means of pushing back against unacceptable restraints in their daily lives. As they traversed the process of emancipation during their service, these once-enslaved soldiers continued using their mobility to shape their liberation.

Such soldiers' stories differ from those whose gallantry defines the wartime epic of Black soldiers vanquishing Rebels. As early as 1863, Black activists and white allies depicted Black military service as the progression of enslaved men from bedraggled laborers to valiant freedom fighters. For two decades after the war, historians and veterans championed the men and their pluck.[7] Over the next sixty years, the soldiers faded into obscurity. Historians reframed the end of slavery as a tragedy for Black southerners who, in these white scholars' view, had been better off enslaved. After civil rights activists rallied against segregation in the mid-twentieth century, scholars energized by the fight to end racism revived the history of men serving in the United States Colored Troops (USCT). They penned studies of the soldiers' frontline courage and recounted their protests against unequal pay. These histories overturned misconceptions about passive enslaved southerners and Black

Introduction

FIGURE I.1 The US Army enlisted enslaved southerners near the Mississippi River and formed regiments including the Eleventh Louisiana Infantry (African Descent) (later the Forty-Ninth United States Colored Infantry or USCI). The army moved the Eleventh to Milliken's Bend, an outpost supporting Major General Ulysses S. Grant's operations around Vicksburg, Mississippi. On June 7, 1863, the men defended the fort from a Confederate attack with the Ninth Louisiana Infantry (African Descent) (later the Sixty-Third USCI), the Thirteenth Louisiana Infantry (African Descent) (later disbanded), the First Mississippi Infantry (African Descent) (later the Fifty-First USCI), and the Twenty-Third Iowa Infantry. The battle grew bloody. The Federals repulsed the initial Rebel assault. Finally, with the aid of an ironclad that shelled Rebel attackers, the Federals won the day. But in January 1864, men of the Eleventh were transferred far from their families, causing much consternation among the enlisted freedom seekers. "The Battle at Milliken's Bend," *Harper's Weekly*, July 4, 1863. Library of Congress, LC-USZ62-131137.

fighters' absence in the war to raze the Confederacy. The revision culminated with *Glory* (1989), the exceptional Hollywood depiction of the war, which elevated elements of this scholarship for public consumption.[8] As important as these revisions were to acknowledging Black soldiers' mettle and sacrifices, the story of Black Civil War service has other dimensions that have not been captured. Not all Black soldiers abided by army regulations as they struggled for freedom. Soldiers like those in the Eleventh killed Confederates courageously one day and decamped the next. Their stories broaden the history of Black Civil War service to encompass the war for liberation within the army and reveal that the experiences of formerly enslaved soldiers did not all lead, uninterrupted, from slavery to freedom.

Freedom Soldiers shows that, as they fought for the US Army, once-enslaved men continued using their feet and their words to fashion their lives after slavery. Although slavery collapsed suddenly in the United States, historians have shown that, for those who had been enslaved, freedom was multidimensional, and emancipation was not instantaneous. When war erupted, enslaved southerners assiduously worked to dismantle the violently enforced labor system that denied them personhood. In the years that followed, to live freely, once-enslaved men, women, and children strengthened families, attended schools, regulated churches, governed themselves, and worked as they wished.[9]

Tearing down slavery and its many vestiges was a protracted process though. During this process, formerly enslaved civilians traveled over grueling terrain, faced rampant disease, and coped with the whims of officials in Union-run refugee camps. On their journeys, freedom seekers met reversals, too. Those who made dramatic leaps forward one month suffered setbacks the next. They might be reenslaved, lose shelter, or lack sufficient food. Enslaved people also had distinct experiences from one another, as each person's journey was unique to their circumstances and the obstacles they encountered.[10] Thousands on this rocky road of liberation entered the US Army, where they resumed their journeys of emancipation. To actively engage this process and influence their evolving bonds with the US government, the formerly enslaved men examined here took self-granted breaks—or what are called here, "leaves of freedom"— and then defended their actions within the military justice system. They saw mobility as a crucial tool for shaping their lives after slavery. If tried and incarcerated for deserting, they defended their actions, demonstrating that they continued seeing their unauthorized departures as legitimate means of redressing unacceptable restraints in the army.[11]

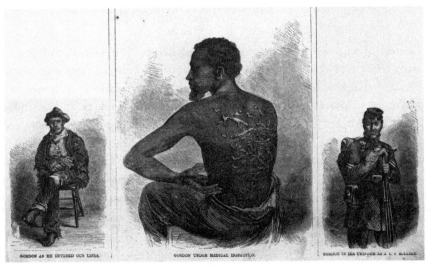

FIGURE 1.2 *Harper's Weekly* published these images of "Gordon," whom the paper called "a typical negro," and constructed a story of an enslaved man's wartime liberation. The images and accompanying article offered a linear account of an enslaved southerner leaving behind bondage, including its brutal enforcement, and becoming a free man. The images also glorified the shift from the work of the field to the work of the soldier. The first image showed a hardscrabble laborer while the third image depicted a proud recruit in Union blue. "A Typical Negro," *Harper's Weekly*, July 4, 1863. Library of Congress, LC-USZ62-98515.

Desertion in the USCT remained low throughout the war, yet flight by formerly enslaved soldiers offers insights into the process of emancipation unfolding in the army. The rate of desertion within the USCT (7 percent) was lower than the overall rate of desertion among white soldiers on either side of the conflict (10 to 15 percent). According to the US government's tally, 12,440 of the 178,975 Black men who served between late 1862 and mid-1865 deserted. (As in calculations of white soldiers, the official number of USCT deserters does not incorporate those who took leaves without permission but were not recorded as deserters.[12]) The army tried at least 653 of those who left and convicted 628 (96 percent) before sending most to prison. The soldiers thus composed a small portion of the USCT.[13] However, scholars agree that, although deserters constituted a subset of armies, their actions stem from political views that cannot be detected when reviewing the accomplishments of crack regiments. Historians have shown that white men ran to recover independence or expressed their dissatisfaction with leaders. Men fearful of the wartime strains on their families also left to feed or shelter kin. These scholars argue that the soldiers' actions are evidence of unspoken rules regulating armies, working-class relationships with the state, and alternative means of exerting masculine duty.[14] Similarly, an analysis of government reports, newspapers, soldiers' diaries and letters, courts-martial transcripts, and imprisoned deserters' letters discloses a history differing from those underscoring Medal of Honor heroics.[15] As such, although those who left were a minority of the USCT, their stories show that some formerly enslaved soldiers performed bravely on the battlefield, yet they pursued freedom within their day-to-day lives working as soldiers, an occupation where combat was the exception, not the norm.

To appreciate the meaning of desertion among the formerly enslaved, it is crucial to recognize that for the men war was work, as well as a chance for glory, and enslaved southerners viewed the transformation of working conditions as essential to their liberation. Military service during the Civil War era conjures up visions of steadfast citizen-soldiers, but war was also work. Because soldiering is associated with combat and death, not productive labor, military historians have been less likely to consider war work and soldiers laborers. Observing why people enlisted and what they did as soldiers, historians have increasingly noted the unmistakable similarities between labor and service. These military workers the world over entered armies with the promise of pay and filled their days chopping trees, cultivating gardens, or building roads.[16] Offering steady wages, the nineteenth-century US Army, likewise, enticed the urban poor and penniless migrants. For these men, days in the ranks were demanding and infrequently led to battlefields. Soldiers composing the modest sixteen-thousand-strong Regular Army were subjected to endless drilling and violent officers before garrisoning outposts and erecting bridges.[17] When the Civil War engulfed the country, men of myriad occupations anxious to defend the nation enlisted. But war remained work. President Abraham Lincoln recognized as much, remarking that "patriotism" motivated lusty youths while the jobless enlisted for "want of employment."[18] Soldiers observed the relationship, too. After logging hours digging trenches and filling sandbags, they grumbled, comparing service to civilian jobs or linking their plight to the most wretched laborers they could imagine: the enslaved.[19]

Black men also experienced military service in the Civil War ranks as work. Many had been forced to labor for Confederates when the war began, undoubtedly giving some a sense that military camps were spaces of drudgery.[20] When Lincoln opened the US Army to Black men with his Emancipation Proclamation, he transformed the military into an opportunity for liberation, yet he stipulated that Black soldiers in the US Army would "garrison forts, positions, and stations," meaning the army intended to hold the men to noncombat roles. For most, it did just that. As Private Alexander Porter, an enslaved Mississippi house waiter who joined the Fifty-Eighth United States Colored Infantry (USCI), explained, "I was not engaged in any actual battles." Although some Black soldiers eventually had the opportunity to attain glory on the battlefield, the majority did not. The US Army kept 100 of the 166 USCT regiments working, not fighting. Officers like the commander of Private Hubbard Pryor and his comrades in the Forty-Fourth USCI thought Black men "had more work in them than I could get out of any other troops," ensuring many of the USCT raised breastworks rather than assault them.[21] Compared to freeborn men, military service for formerly enslaved southerners had an additional labor distinction: enlistment ended their days as enslaved laborers, a point communicated by images of wartime refugees transitioning from scarred laborers into uniformed soldiers. Military service was their first job as free laborers, and this fact informed the men's approach to the work of war.[22]

As formerly enslaved war workers, these Black southern soldiers often responded to poor conditions as despondent employees. Black civilians around the South agitated to define work during the war and to ensure that war work was not akin to slave labor. These efforts mirrored labor activism across the Confederacy. As white southerners scrambled to maintain slavery, enslaved men and women renegotiated labor roles, as such roles were among

FIGURE 1.3 This photograph of Hubbard Pryor was taken shortly after he fled slavery in Georgia and shows him in the garb he wore when he escaped bondage. National Archives, Washington, DC, photo no. 849127.

the defining characteristics of their enslavement.[23] The arrival of Yankees increased enslaved southerners' resistance. As a white southern woman complained, the "negroes, presuming upon the presence of their [US Army] protectors, worked when they pleased." They defied violent, inflexible working conditions. They rejected excessive hours, commanded pay, and insisted on an end to beatings. If concessions were not made or violence reemerged, they went on strike or quit altogether. Many fled to refugee camps, where their activism persisted. Some pursued farm ownership while those who worked for northern reformers disobeyed paternalistic crusaders, rebuffed wage employment, and rebuked cruel managers. If compelled to sign a contract, they reserved the right to renegotiate or resign. In their efforts, they challenged prevailing free-labor ideas and pushed back against undesirable conditions.[24] Formerly enslaved men who entered the US Army contested conditions

FIGURE I.4 This photograph of Hubbard Pryor, now Private Pryor of the Forty-Fourth United States Colored Infantry, shows the formerly enslaved man dressed in his US Army uniform, and shortly before he was captured and reenslaved by Confederates. Hubbard Pryor, Compiled Military Service Record, National Archives, Washington, DC, photo no. 849136.

as well. To do so, they turned to forms of activism popularly used to shape conditions within slavery.

Black southerners in the ranks relied on time-tested modes of resistance. As historians have shown, Black northern soldiers drew on the democratic tools developed before the war. They turned down unequal pay, wrote letters to newspapers and politicians, and peaceably contravened direct orders to dispute racist policies.[25] The emphasis on these political tactics has treated Black soldiers' democratic endeavors as the dominant method (if not the only method) of activism.[26] However, resorting to alternative means to negotiate conditions within the army, formerly enslaved soldiers turned to long-practiced means of southern Black empowerment: mobility politics and legal activism. Enslaved rebels periodically tried to overthrow slavery altogether, but resisters largely empowered themselves within captivity. They reclaimed power over their bodies and challenged oppressive conditions with their feet and words, not with their fists or firepower.[27] They briefly recovered control of their persons in fancy clothes at parties beyond enslavers' surveillance. When hotheaded overseers grew vicious, the enslaved temporarily disappeared into Carolina swamps and Cajun bayous. To be near auctioned-off kin, they subsisted in the backcountry. These efforts were more than breaks from bondage. Travel within the despotic system afforded opportunities for self-expression, a reprieve from tyranny, and chances to nurture families without necessarily procuring liberty.[28] In the southern legal system, they countered enslavers' domination as well. In courts, they claimed protection within communities. Contesting property claims over their bodies, they articulated alternatives to enslavement or racial identity. In freedom suits, they sued for their permanent release from chattelhood. Imprisoned Black southerners, meanwhile, organized within penitentiaries and traded ideas of resistance.[29] Those formerly enslaved soldiers vexed by constraints within the army likewise resisted with such tools.

Certain formerly enslaved men reacted to restraints within the US Army as they had during slavery, revealing that they continued fighting for freedom after enlistment. Although military service furnished tremendous opportunities for the enslaved who volunteered, it also imposed significant limitations. With the exception of slavery, military service was arguably the most taxing job in the Civil War era, explaining why so many white and Black soldiers compared service to bondage. Commanders demanded total subservience and implemented strict routines and corporal punishment to induce recruits to relinquish individuality and independence.[30] While white and Black men faced similar discipline, those within the USCT managed additional constraints. As a result of government officials' racist views, Black men almost exclusively served under white officers who considered it incumbent upon them to guide enslaved men's transition from slavery. Many officers had volunteered for the USCT altruistically, and they sympathized with the rank-and-file. The best of these officers contributed to the impressive battlefield record of the USCT.[31] Yet they considered the formerly enslaved "perfectly childlike," as a colonel leading Black men wrote, and thus, he added, they "are no more responsible for their actions than so many puppies."[32] As a result, USCT officers, many with virtuous intentions, not only imposed demanding discipline prevalent in the era's armies but also thought Black soldiers required lessons in what a high-ranking commander called "the duties and

FIGURE 1.5 Certain commanders of the US Army believed formerly enslaved southerners—including those who entered the ranks—needed an education in the proper habits of freedom. Officials like Adjutant General Lorenzo Thomas went so far as to explain to enlisted and civilian freedom seekers the "duties of freedom" near the Mississippi River. "The War in the Southwest: Adjutant-General Thomas Addressing the Negroes in Louisiana on the Duties of Freedom," *Harper's Weekly*, November 14, 1863. Library of Congress, LC-USZ62-133069.

responsibilities of freedom."[33] Officers hoped to disabuse Black recruits of slavish behaviors that white northerners felt the enslaved had absorbed. Many Black soldiers were aggrieved by such discipline, especially when its enforcement resembled the violence of slavery. To be sure, service was not slavery by another name. But—after having lived under and risked death to escape overseers who savagely enforced hours of toil—some would not countenance the terms of service. Disregarding regulations and officers, they fled camp for temporary breaks to care for their family, to salvage their health, or to escape abusive officers. Those caught, tried, and incarcerated defended their actions and contested their imprisonment. In so doing, they attempted to shape conditions within the army that they found hostile to their bondage-born dreams of liberation.

Observing the men's resistance within the USCT, *Freedom Soldiers* reveals that the once-enslaved used tools wielded during slavery to carry on their struggle against unacceptable restraints and that, as a result, the process of emancipation continued after enlistment. Formerly enslaved men's experiences were not entirely unique compared to their freeborn counterparts. Like white and Black soldiers who were free at enlistment, formerly enslaved troopers often left to help families, receive reliable health care, or escape brutal officers. But the soldiers' political, social, and economic backgrounds shaped their view of flight. When describing why they decamped, the formerly enslaved referenced their prior enslavement, the travails family members held in bondage faced, or the obstacles kin met on the journey to freedom. The formerly enslaved soldiers thus differed from their freeborn counterparts not necessarily in motivation but rather in why the problems emerged necessitating their departure. Whereas white soldiers described demands resulting from their paternal duties they had become accustomed to fulfilling as free men, for instance, enlisted freedom seekers pointed to the demands they imposed on themselves because they wished to be dutiful fathers or husbands after years of forced separation. As is detailed here, the once-enslaved men acted with their experiences in bondage and the ongoing process of emancipation playing pivotal roles in the soldiers' approach to service and reasons for leaving.[34] Factors shaping the contours of each soldier's exodus included obstacles obstructing civilians on their journeys. Like the refugees living within Union camps, soldiers' experiences during the process of emancipation were influenced by government policies, battlefield outcomes, rampant disease, and food shortages. In addition to these factors, enlisted Black southerners also discovered that the institution that furnished weapons and wages could simultaneously stall or upend their advance. A soldier's progress could be impeded by a brigadier general inaugurating a new campaign before breakfast. It could be suspended by a capricious captain irked by the growing sick list in the afternoon. It could be thwarted by a churlish sergeant on a vendetta following taps. Most USCT soldiers fulfilled their duties without incident, but others, despite their commitment to the Union cause, resisted as they had during slavery: with their feet and their words. The men's experiences demonstrate that the difficulties complicating the process of emancipation centered on the constraints instituted by officials and imposed by officers. These enlisted freedom seekers experienced this march out of slavery based upon the restraints they thought acceptable. Their flight and the ensuing clashes over the legitimacy of their flight within the military justice system show that certain battles waged over the extent of liberation in the postemancipation South unfolded first, and in particularly dramatic forms, in the US Army.

By concentrating on resistance within the USCT, *Freedom Soldiers* also yields insights into the burgeoning bond between Black southerners and the state. By entering the army, recruits forged a social contract with the US government. In exchange for their service defending the Union, the men expected officials to support their liberation and listen to their demands. As part 1 demonstrates, formerly enslaved soldiers entered the army anticipating the state would salute their sacrifices and allow them to leave at will. By leaving camp without permission, they tapped the tools employed to ameliorate life during slavery in an attempt to shape not only conditions within the army but also the terms of the social contract they brokered with the state. When tried and incarcerated, part 2 shows, freedom seekers beseeched officials to see that their actions stemmed from their objective of escaping slavery, rather than a flagrant disregard of officers or regulations. As such, they reasoned, they had not violated the terms of their social contract. They instead insisted that their flight was legitimate and incarceration unjust. In camps, courts, and prisons, therefore, Black southerners used political tools forged in slavery to demand that officials acknowledge their sacrifices and support their endeavors toward freedom, even when they undermined military discipline.

In full, this book is not a history of combat-hardened freedom fighters but of enlisted freedom seekers within the highly disciplined world of the US Army. The freedom soldiers of this history were men who nurtured parents during garrison duties only to be ripped from wives when the latest campaign demanded it. Men who escaped tyrants on the cotton fields only to suffer brutal officers in camp. Men who abandoned hours stooped over caldrons of boiling sugarcane only to succumb to diseases sweeping through the South. Men who had evaded provost marshals tasked with ensnaring deserters only to be reenslaved by Confederate pickets. Men who honored their commitments to children only to find themselves on trial for desertion. Men who had recuperated under trusted care at home only to wind up in blighted prison cells. Men, in short, who contributed to the Union cause on their march to freedom yet also reacted to obstacles inhibiting their pursuit with the tools they had brandished to soften the daily tyranny of bondage. Braving death, they ran from camp. Facing censure, they defended their flight in courts. Clamoring for justice from prisons, they appealed to officers. Time and again, these men demanded the state endorse their ongoing fight for freedom and refused to abide by the stringent, violent discipline that limited the horizons of liberation.

PART I

Freedom in Camp

I

"Bound for Freedom's Light": Enlisting and Emancipating Men in the US Army

"WE ARE GOIN' out of slavery," they sang, clad in Union blue.[1] The men had joined the US Army after Republican officials, first reluctant to free and arm enslaved southerners, concluded that victory over the Confederates necessitated an alliance. The US government freed them to encourage loyalty. But this marked only the beginning of the long march out of slavery. Throughout the war, once-enslaved soldiers confronted erupting Rebel cannon and possible reenslavement by their onetime oppressors. They endured separation from hungry children and ailing wives. They weathered cold nights in tents and hot days at drill. To steel themselves, they recited spirituals that had sustained them on cotton fields—but now on battlefields. They added marching songs to their repertoire to guide them through the hard days of war.[2] Many favored "John's Brown's Body," an anthem that resurrected the abolitionist martyr who led a doomed war on slavery. They trumpeted its revolutionary message after joining the army and conquering Rebel cities.[3] Verses from other songs spoke of an ongoing exodus from bondage, not the culmination of their struggle to be free. "I will enlist, gird on my arms, / And fight for liberty," they chanted.[4] Warriors calling themselves "freedom's stalwart legions" lifted their voices, declaring, "Fight we . . . For Freedom and the Right."[5] They assaulted Confederate strongholds, occupied Rebel towns, and navigated the twists and turns on their journey out of slavery, reminding themselves in song, "We are bound for freedom's light."[6] As they attested lyrically, they crusaded for their own liberation as they fought a bloody war to subjugate Rebels. But, as they also made plain in their battle hymns, neither

Freedom Soldiers. Jonathan Lande, Oxford University Press. © Oxford University Press 2024.
DOI: 10.1093/oso/9780197531754.003.0002

FIGURE 1.1 After the Confederates surrendered Charleston, South Carolina, Black soldiers of the Twenty-First United States Colored Infantry and the Fifty-Fifth Massachusetts Infantry paraded through the city singing "John Brown's Body," a battle hymn that emboldened formerly enslaved men within the US Army to continue their fight for freedom as they served in the ranks. "'Marching On!': The Fifty-Fifth Massachusetts Colored Regiment Singing John Brown's March in the Streets of Charleston, February 21, 1865," *Harper's Weekly*, March 18, 1865. Library of Congress, LC-USZ62-105560.

their escape from slavery nor their enlistment meant their war for freedom had ended.

When US government officials incorporated Black men into the US Army to help save the Union, many envisioned the military as a school for teaching enslaved men free labor and restraining their alleged barbarity. This treatment complicated formerly enslaved men's exodus from slavery within the US Army. Black men volunteered eager to participate in the war and, as a consequence, not only defeat Rebels but also fight for their liberation. But as US government officials embraced the men's enthusiasm for victory, they approached Black military service cautiously. Officials knew that all soldiers, whether white or Black, needed discipline. Yet they conceived of discipline within Black regiments as a school in free labor too. Many Republicans and US Army commanders leading the war were convinced that, unlike white men, enslaved men entering the ranks were ill-suited to live or work as freed people. As a result, they treated military service as a means of supporting the Union war and guiding the enslaved out of bondage. They envisioned military service as a chance to diminish the threat of vengeful Black violence and prepare formerly enslaved men for employment as free laborers. To ensure the soldiers were ready for both war and work, the War Department carefully selected those who would lead the regiments. In so doing, wartime leaders turned the US Army into an institution fighting for the Union as well as an institution that shaped emancipation. The US Army became a space in which many white officers hoped to manage how emancipation unfolded, putting them at odds with formerly enslaved men who treated military service as a route toward liberation.

"De United States Is Fightin' for Me and for My People": Enlisting in the US Army

As tramping troopers and rolling artillery remade the national landscape in 1861 and 1862, Black men and women rebelled against their Confederate enslavers. They disrupted workflow, planned insurrections, and fled to Union lines. With such actions, these freedom seekers undermined the Rebel project and helped US government officials see that a war on slavery was a way to support the Union cause. Republicans managing the war finally embraced emancipation as a strategy and armed Black men as a means of suppressing the Confederate insurrection. Hoping service in the US Army would mean slavery's downfall and racial equality, nearly 180,000 Black men north and south of the Mason-Dixon Line enlisted.

During the war's opening months and throughout the conflict, freedom seekers absconded, believing that the jubilee had arrived, but they navigated perilous terrain on the road to liberation. Confederates posed the most danger. They whipped and hanged those who ran. But enslaved men and women also met mysterious Yankees. Black southerners heard stories from enslavers that the northern soldiers' caps concealed horns. Rebels explained that those Yankee devils meant to enslave or kill them.[7] Some Federals gave credence to certain lies. Although the presence of US forces directly or indirectly undermined enslavers' power and the everyday practices of slavery across the Confederacy, US Army soldiers abused Black refugees throughout the conflict.[8] As one Yankee lamented, his heartless comrades "seemed to take pleasure in insulting" Black men, women, and children. Perpetuating aspects of vassalage, US Army officers demeaned refugees in wartime photography and consigned them to camp chores.[9] After centuries of deception, however, Black southerners were not easily misled by enslavers nor deterred from their journey to freedom. Most recognized in northern civilians and US Army soldiers allies, not enemies. As an enslaved Carolinian confessed, "Somehow we hear de Yankees was our friends, an' dat we'd be free when dey com."[10] As a result, they ran toward the invaders from the North in pursuit of freedom.

Northern reformers near Union lines were among the first to help secure resources for the enslaved men, women, and children who fled, but disagreements over what freedom might look like quickly emerged. The northern philanthropists, who characterized the enslaved as childlike, wished to guide the transition of the formerly enslaved from bondage to free labor. In the most famous instance, reformers set up schools in the Sea Islands of South Carolina after Union forces drove out the Rebels. Although free labor itself was a contested concept, reformers hoped to imbue freedpeople with habits and skills most deemed crucial to freedom, including industry and self-reliance.[11] But Black southerners pushed back against reformers' limited interpretation of freedom. They strove to secure land and control the rhythm of work. The most discontented rejected labor conditions under free-labor advocates altogether. They quit. The experiment in free labor marked the first of many contests between Black southerners and white northerners over freedom's meaning.[12]

By mid-1862, President Abraham Lincoln and fellow Republicans heading the US government appreciated that a more exacting war would be necessary to vanquish Rebels and, to those ends, began supporting enslaved southerners eager to weaken the Confederacy.[13] Republicans not only sought a winning strategy but also saw a chance to deliver poor white yeomen and the enslaved from the albatross of the backward slave-labor economy.[14] Pursuing these goals, Republican legislators backed the erosion of slavery, passing the First and Second Confiscation Acts on August 5, 1861, and July 17, 1862.[15] Then, in September 1862, after the Union victory at the Battle of Antietam, Lincoln threatened to "recognize and maintain the freedom" of enslaved southerners unless Confederates surrendered. The Rebels kept fighting. So, Lincoln "order[ed] and declare[d] that all persons held as slaves . . . shall be free" in areas under rebellion on January 1, 1863. He also announced that Black men "will be received into the armed service." Thus, whatever its limitations, Lincoln's proclamation combined the Union war with a war to end slavery.[16]

Indeed, many Black northerners heralded the Emancipation Proclamation and the chance to enlist. To persuade Black northerners to volunteer, famed Black leaders assumed recruiting roles and responded to Black critics who balked at military service. These opponents of immediate enlistment contended that previous Black soldiers had faded from memory. As such, they called for guarantees that military service would mean full inclusion.[17]

But poems and histories over the previous three decades showed how important military service and the violent assertion of manhood was to inclusion in the body politic, leading some of the most well-known leaders to advocate for service regardless of any guarantees offered and any shortcomings of service to uplift.[18] Although he had his doubts at certain moments before the Emancipation Proclamation, once Lincoln issued the call and the US Army was opened to Black men Frederick Douglass insisted his followers volunteer. "I am one of those Colored men who say officer or no officer, equal or unequal pay, bounty or no bounty, the place for Colored men is in the army of the United States," he wrote.[19] At rallies, he beseeched men to join, pointing to the opportunities service presented. "To fight for the government in this tremendous war," he proclaimed, "is to fight for nationality and for a place with all other classes of our fellow citizens."[20] Although the US Army offered such opportunities, military service would be confined to men, narrowing women's path to citizenship and freedom.[21] Nevertheless, women like Sojourner Truth recruited Black soldiers because they saw enlistment as an expedience to liberation. She asked men to "join the sable army of African descent" and located food and resources to buoy men's spirits.[22]

Douglass's son Lewis was among the first to embrace the cause, volunteering for the Fifty-Fourth Massachusetts Infantry. The freeborn Lewis became a sergeant major, and during his time at Camp Meigs outside Boston, he wrote of the regiment's training. He said that he and his comrades learned "very fast" and became "quite proficient in the manual of arms." Crowds from the city arrived, he penned with pride, and gathered to watch their "evening dress parades."[23] During the preparation for war, the elder Douglass visited his son, and the soldier had his patriotism reinvigorated following such trips.[24] Writing to his sweetheart, Helen Amelia Loguen, the enlisted Douglass echoed his father, offering reassurances about his mission. "Remember that if I fall that it is in the cause of humanity," he wrote, and "that I am striking a blow for the welfare of the most abused and despised race on the face of the earth." He further reminded Loguen "that in [the] solution of this strife rests the question of our elevation or our degradation, our happiness or our misery." Like his father, the young Douglass believed that wartime sacrifices were necessary to end slavery and carve out space for free Black men and women in the body politic.[25]

James Henry Gooding numbered among those who could not resist the patriot's siren song either. Gooding was born enslaved on August 28, 1838, in North Carolina, but he spent most of his life as free man in the North. At eight years old, Gooding was freed by his father and abandoned at New York's Colored Orphans' Asylum. Gooding spent three years at the orphanage and, in 1856, moved to New Bedford. There, he embarked on a seafaring life. He earned a living and, invigorated by the briny air, wrote verse.[26] In February 1863, however, the troubles afflicting Black men and women in the North and South pulled Gooding back to the whaling mecca. The young man attended a recruiting meeting and heard William Wells Brown. Electrifying a crowd, the formerly enslaved Brown told the Black residents that they must "fight until freedom was established in every slave state." After the speeches ended and the recruiting station opened, Gooding was the first in line to sign up. Many fell in with Gooding. An officer of the Fifty-Fourth said the whalers' town proved to be a "fertile field" for enlistment.[27] Like Douglass and Gooding, Black men across the North arrived in camp animated by the possibilities, looking to the advantages service would yield Black men and women. Eventually, approximately thirty-five thousand of the military-age Black men in the North enlisted, pursuing citizenship, equality, and manhood.[28]

Although also eager to end slavery and racism, enslaved southerners' calculations differed. They enlisted to seize freedom itself and carefully deliberated whether service would provide the opportunities they sought as freed men. Before Lincoln issued the Emancipation Proclamation, enlistment began in South Carolina. But any initial excitement shortly waned. Many of the enslaved thought that in joining the US Army they would support a fighting force indifferent to their struggle against slavery and declined to volunteer. James Miller M'Kim, an abolitionist visiting the occupied Confederacy in 1862, learned as much after a conversation with Prince Rivers, a member of a disbanded regiment of liberated South Carolinians. M'Kim told Rivers that he was surprised when enslaved men did not "rise against their masters" in large numbers and asked why. Rivers expressed frustration. He responded, "What would be de use [in rebelling]? Dey has no chance. What could dey do? No gun, no sword, no knowledge, no chance—no nuthin." M'Kim followed up. "But suppose they had a chance, would they fight then?" Rivers replied resoundingly. "*Yes, sah* . . . Only let 'em know for sure—*for sure,* mine you—dat de white people means right; let 'em know for sure dat dey's fightin' for themselves, and I *know* dey will fight." "Well, Prince," M'Kim retorted, "wouldn't you call this a good chance?" "Yes, sah, I do call this a good chance, and I tell my people maybe it's de *last* chance. Dat's de reason I jine de soldier," Rivers clarified. In fact, he added, "I was gettin' big wages in Beaufort, but I'd rather take less, and fight for de United States; for I believe de United States is fightin' for me and for my people." M'Kim sought further illumination: "Do your people feel as you do?" "No, sah," Rivers said, "but dey would if dey knowed de same as I do."[29] With this, Rivers made the view toward enlistment by enslaved men plain: not all trusted the US government and were reticent to volunteer. Rivers thought that if the government established faith in the cause, enlistment would pick up. His prediction proved true.

When officials initiated policies to encourage enslaved men to trust the government, enslaved southerners looked more fondly on the Union cause, and more joined the ranks of the US Army. In 1862 and 1863, Washington shed support for white southerners and swung it to enslaved southerners who sought refuge from their oppressors behind Union lines. With modifications made to policies, Black southerners increasingly trusted Yankee invaders and developed a new social contract with the US government. Men and women both flocked to the US Army seeking freedom. Many entered refugee camps. Scouring those camps for men who might help the Union cause, the government and army procured indispensable laborers—and eventually soldiers.[30]

When recruiters approached potential soldiers around the South and in refugee camps, they communicated to enslaved men the opportunities of service. These recruiters did not always need to stress the value of service, though. For example, recruiters dispatched to Virginia visited Chesapeake farms "to literally strip a plantation of its field hands," but the task of swaying men to leave the grueling labor of bondage for the US Army was not too difficult.[31] Indeed, some seized the opportunity, as a Kentucky enslaver recalled. "The boy 'Sam' lived with me in Davis County, but became dissatisfied on the account of his wife being in Louisville and wished me to hire him in the city," he wrote. Perhaps realizing Sam might run off regardless, the enslaver permitted the move. But, to the Kentuckian's chagrin, Sam "was not there very long until he enlisted in the army."[32] These recruits likely did not demand much in the way of the rhetorical art. Their options were to keep tilling under an oppressor or volunteer, making the choice obvious for many. But not all enslaved men saw the decision in such a stark contrast. Some wished to remain independent and evaded recruiters. When learning recruiters began combing farms, for example, suspicious men wishing to avoid service would "sleep out nights and hide from them in the daytime."[33] As a result, the US Army needed to encourage enlistment by further communicating the government's support for liberation.

To persuade enslaved men to join the army, the US government had to prove it backed Black southerners' cause. Recruiters shared the new policy of emancipation to buttress enlistment. For example, a colonel recruiting in New Orleans appealed to Black southerners by doling out business cards that affirmed the new social contract being forged. "We invite all colored men to join our Regiment," the card read, if such men "desire to serve the government that has protected them, and that is now pledged to secure their freedom." To urge enlistment more subtly, commanders solicited the aid of formerly enslaved men. In South Carolina, Rivers helped recruit, and he was joined by Robert Smalls, an enslaved boatman who stole a Rebel ship and piloted it

Table 1.1: Entire Number of Commissioned and Enlisted Troops in USCT during the Civil War by State

Free State		Enslaving State	
Connecticut	1,764	Alabama	4,969
Illinois	1,811	Arkansas	5,526
Indiana	1,537	Delaware	954
Iowa	440	District of Columbia	3,269
Kansas	2,080	Florida	1,044
Maine	104	Georgia	3,486
Massachusetts	3,966	Kentucky	23,703
Michigan	1,387	Louisiana	24,052
Minnesota	104	Maryland	8,718
New Hampshire	125	Mississippi	17,869
New Jersey	1,185	Missouri	8,344
New York	4,125	North Carolina	5,035
Ohio	5,092	South Carolina	5,462
Pennsylvania	8,612	Tennessee	20,133
Rhode Island	1,837	Texas	47
Vermont	120	Virginia	5,723
Wisconsin	165	West Virginia	196
Colorado Territory	95		
Total Enlisted Men from Free States	34,549	Total Enlisted Men from Enslaving States	138,530
Percent of Enlisted Men from Free States	20	Percent of Enlisted Men from Enslaving States	80
Unknown Origins		5,896	
Total Enlisted Men		178,975	
Total Officers		7,122	
Aggregate Enlisted Men and Officers		186,097	

Source: US Department of War, *The War of the Rebellion: A Compilation of the Official Records of the Union and Confederate Armies* (Washington, DC: Government Printing Office, 1880–1901), ser. 3, vol. 5, 138.

to the Union naval blockade. Smalls achieved fame for his daring and lent his voice to the cause. After Smalls enlisted in the army in early 1863, he returned home and explained the significance of the war and why enslaved men should fight for the Union. But even Rivers and Smalls did not, at first, find a warm reception. Many of the enslaved showed little interest. Yet Rivers, Smalls, and their Union-favoring ilk persisted and finally won ample recruits.[34]

However, while such appeals spoke to enslaved southerners' interests, not all were contented simply establishing a new, more fruitful relationship with the state. Black southerners defined freedom in response to their prior subjugation and looked for concrete support for specific opportunities to pursue freedom. Enslaved men keen on forging and fortifying their bonds with the US government no doubt labored in military encampments and later enlisted, anticipating that military service would improve their relationship with the state.[35] But many Black southerners sought opportunities denied during bondage and hoped to live beyond the reach of violence—even as they served the broader political goal of strengthening their connection with the US government. Many also volunteered anticipating an escape from coercion and the chance to earn wages, support themselves, and maintain families.[36] These men were, therefore, US Army soldiers as well as freedom seekers. But, complicating their march out of slavery, the nearly 140,000 Black southerners would serve almost exclusively under white northerners who believed Black men needed guidance before they could be truly free.[37]

"Employed without Endangering Civil Society": Arming Black Men amid Racial Fears

Republican politicians excitedly anticipated the surge of support Black warriors would provide, yet the decision remained controversial. As one beleaguered general facing difficulties enlisting enslaved southerners said, arming Black men remained a "delicate question."[38] During the transition in strategy, concerns emerged regarding emancipation. As white northerners pondered the consequences of Lincoln's Emancipation Proclamation, racial fears rooted in past emancipation projects surfaced as critical points of contention. White northerners' anxieties about free labor and the eventualities of arming enslaved men played a central role in how Black soldiers were incorporated into the US Army. Officials in the War Department who hoped to manage those who had escaped bondage and entered the US Army determined that the leaders of Black men were critical to the new regiments' success as well as the unfolding of emancipation within the ranks.

White southerners had long voiced concerns about another Haitian Revolution and continued expressing their fears after Lincoln issued the Emancipation Proclamation, condemning the act as the first salvo in a race war.[39] A Kentucky essayist called the preliminary proclamation "a direct incentive . . . of slave insurrection" that would lead to the "indiscriminate massacre of the helpless whites." When Lincoln issued the final version, the essayist feared an army composed of an "alien foreign race" who would usurp white southerners' liberty.[40] White northerners, like their southern counterparts, remained troubled by visions of a postabolition apocalypse as well. Democrats, who had long exploited racial prejudices for political gain, doubled down on the racist appeals following the 1860 election. Frothing in 1863, they rebuked the admittance of Black men into the army in bigoted appeals. Typifying the hatred they peddled, the *Cincinnati Daily Enquirer* crowed that Lincoln was "using servile insurrection as an instrument" of war. In such appeals, Democrats exploited white citizens' fear of a war between

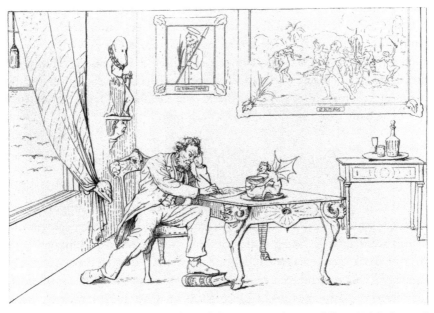

FIGURE 1.2 Baltimore dentist and Confederate sympathizer Adalbert Volck depicted the fear that many white southerners and northerners entertained after President Abraham Lincoln issued the Emancipation Proclamation. The artist illustrated a demonic president scratching out the proclamation with two paintings hanging behind him: one of a holy John Brown and other of Haitian revolutionaries impaling babies. Adalbert Volck, "Writing the Emancipation Proclamation," 1864. Library of Congress, LC-USZ62-100066.

peaceable white citizens and Black renegades while suggesting that swarms of freed southern laborers would crowd northern cities.[41]

To assuage fears related to abolition, reformers offered comfort. Northern trepidations were rooted in conceptions of race, which were constructed to legitimize the enslavement of Africans, and then strengthened by biased histories of emancipation.[42] To parry the historical propaganda, reformer Lydia Maria Child published *The Right Way, The Safe Way, Proved by Emancipation in the British West Indies and Elsewhere* in 1863. In it, she contradicted the "erroneous impressions" and directly addressed misinformed accounts. Child went on to refute such claims, writing that the difficulties "between the white and black races in St. Domingo were the result of oppressive and unlawful treatment of the free colored population [and] . . . an attempt to *restore slavery*." She concluded "that emancipation has *always* been safe," adding that "not one white person has ever been killed, or wounded, or had life or property endangered by any violence attendant upon immediate emancipation."[43]

As the nation came to terms with the dramatic transformation initiated by the Emancipation Proclamation, Congress debated not just whether to enlist Black men but also who should lead them. Although the Second Confiscation Act allowed the US Army to recruit Black men, War Secretary Edwin Stanton authored a bill to gain explicit Congressional approval. Pennsylvania's Republican congressman Thaddeus Stevens introduced the bill to the House of Representatives on January 27, 1863, sparking a heated exchange that revealed entrenched racial thinking continued to shape how emancipation unfolded.

When Stevens proposed the bill, he provoked a strenuous response first from Democrats, including Charles Wickliffe of Kentucky. On January 29, the Kentuckian echoed criticisms he voiced the previous year against arming formerly enslaved men. Yet, in a speech riddled with contradictions, he now also emphasized that Black men as soldiers could not be managed. He repeated suspicions stretching back to the Revolutionary War that arming men of African descent reflected the actions of an uncivilized army prepared to unchain savage warriors who would murder their enemies. He added that Black men "will not stand the firing of a gun. They will fall upon the ground and run away." The Kentuckian avowed that the soldiers would inevitably become officers and said that under "Colonel Sambo" US soldiers would become agents of anarchy. Linking his claims of cowardice and unbridled destruction irrationally, Wickliffe declared, "These negro regiments, I fear, will be instruments in . . . the hands of bad men."[44] His points, in sum, alluded to the inability of making descendants of Africa into civilized soldiers; the absurdity of his claims, including the connection between cowardice and an uncontrollable lust for violence, meant such ideas were impervious to logic, giving them durability and purchase.

Indeed, fellow Kentuckian John Crittenden hammered similar points and highlighted the violence that would result from a lack of control by officers. Arming Black men, he vented, was "a crime against the civilization of the age." He argued that "one white man to command a thousand negroes" would be unable to "restrain them," making the war "a servile war led by white men." He concluded by stating that the bill to arm Black men would "give license to turn this civil war into a servile war."[45] Even as the nation struggled to survive, such speeches demonstrate that racist anxieties remained central to political calculations. But not only proslavery Democrats made such calculations.

In response, Republicans underscored the strategic value of the policy and defended the enlistment of Black men. In their responses, they contended that military service would moderate violent inclinations and thus manage slavery's downfall. William Kelley (Pennsylvania) implored Crittenden to appreciate that Republicans did not aim to "turn loose this terrible fighting population to make insurrection . . . [as] the French undertook to do in St. Domingo."[46] Alexander Diven (New York) reassured Democrats that unrestricted violence was not the goal. "Who, in heaven's name," he asked, "but a mad fanatic, reckless of human life and of all the endearments of society, would employ the black man without organizing and controlling him and subjecting him to discipline?" To the bill's detractors, he said, "The black man may be employed without endangering civil society" and "violating the rules of civilized warfare." Turning the Democrats' claims on their head, Diven reasoned that the army made an ideal place for formerly enslaved men because in the ranks their emancipation would be under the surveillance of white men who "adopted a system of discipline to control them." To Diven, control was central to the enlistment of Black men.[47]

On February 2, Stevens offered the final word on the bill for Republicans, reinforcing Diven's point and revealing the direction Republicans took on enlistment in response to lingering racial fears. Stevens explained that "disciplined troops under the Articles of War do not engage in insurrection."[48] In this statement, he stressed that arming Black men would not violate important customs of civilized warfare. Instead, like white regiments, Black regiments would be governed by the Articles of War.[49] In all, Republicans insisted that service would succeed under proper leadership. The bill passed, yet it had no substantive effect on policy because Senate Republicans tabled the bill, determining that the Second Confiscation Act and the Militia Act provided sufficient executive authority.[50] However, the debate demonstrates that after

Lincoln's Emancipation Proclamation, racial fears endured, and perhaps even intensified among Democrats dreading a second Haitian Revolution. Republicans, meanwhile, translated ideas about managing emancipation and supposedly barbarous enslaved southerners into wartime policies. For Republicans, the US Army was not only a means of winning the war. They also saw it as a tool for shaping emancipation. After the debates, as Stanton assembled Black regiments, these racial ideas influenced policy.

In mid-1863, the US government implemented emancipation. In need of soldiers, the War Department incorporated Black men into the US Army. Stanton was not one to act hastily, though. The pervasive reservations regarding abolition led to debates among white northerners who continued to question the significance and application of Lincoln's proclamation, especially the enlistment of enslaved men. These debates led many white politicians, soldiers, and civilians to stress that emancipation—though a righteous act and a pragmatically sound war strategy—must be controlled. To accomplish these ends, white northerners looked to the US Army, identifying it as an ideal space for lessons in freedom and free labor.

"A Peculiar Class of Officers": Vetting Leaders for Black Regiments

The responses to War Secretary Stanton's bill bolstering Black military service in Congress showed him that white northerners remained divided about arming enslaved men. Fears that abolition and enlistment would degrade a civilized war into a barbarous insurrection persisted after January. White northerners continued discussing the potential hazards into the spring of 1863. These enduring anxieties led to Stanton's careful consideration of emancipation, including who would lead enslaved men in the US Army. Ultimately, Stanton centralized the formation of Black regiments. Jettisoning the popular practices that allowed the rank-and-file to elect its leaders or place men from the soldiers' communities in leadership roles, the war secretary supported the systematic assessment of white men to lead Black soldiers. The decision to formally vet potential leaders for the regiments thus marked a significant departure from typical enlistment practices. This alteration was not a bureaucratic modification intended to streamline the command structure or improve the quality of battlefield performance, however. Instead, Stanton responded to advice regarding leadership within Black regiments. Reformers were hired to examine the collapse of slavery around the South and deemed strict control of the formerly enslaved soldiers necessary. In light of their recommendations, Stanton created regiments led by white northerners. He intended for these officers to guide emancipation and inculcate formerly enslaved men with free-labor habits.

In February 1863, Republicans kept watch over the project of arming enslaved men and touted combat successes to boost public support. Major General Rufus Saxton, an abolitionist leading the Department of the South, helped design an expedition into Florida to probe the Confederate interior. Saxton tasked Colonel Thomas Wentworth Higginson of the First South Carolina (Colored) Infantry (later the Thirty-Third United States Colored Infantry) with leading the campaign.[51] Higginson, a minister who had championed radical abolitionist measures, saw military service for enslaved men as "a vast experiment of indirect philanthropy, and one on which the result of the war and the destiny of the negro race might rest." The expedition into Florida fit this mission. He dreamed the foray would demonstrate that formerly enslaved Carolinians could fight well.[52] For three weeks, he and his men harassed the enemy. As news of the adventure reached northern newspapers, it offered proof that enslaved men could soldier without devolving into uncivilized marauders. The editor for the *Washington Evening Star* reflected on the triumph, calling it a "complete success." He added that the men "conducted themselves in the rebel country as to prove that . . . the apprehensions entertained by many that wherever they penetrated, indiscriminate rapine, arson, and murder of defenceless non-combatants would attend their footsteps, were entirely groundless." Lincoln took note, too. On March 10, he received reports that the men fought courageously and never resorted to vengeful killing. Just as government officials reflected on whether to ramp up enlistment, Higginson's soldiers affirmed the value of arming enslaved men.[53]

As news of the exploits spread, northern intellectuals sympathetic to the Republican strategy calmed nerves in print. Like Republicans in the Congressional debate, supporters of emancipation and arming enslaved men did not couch their advocacy for the policies in moral objectives; they instead reacted pragmatically to racist arguments, showing the apparent need to engage racial views by advocates of Lincoln's policy. In a *New Bedford Mercury* article reprinted as a broadside titled *Will the Blacks Fight?* an abolitionist pastor offered historical guidance to the question following the raid by the First South Carolina. "The history of Hayti shows," he declared, "that Blacks will go with enthusiasm wherever they are led . . . provided their steps never point again in the direction of slavery."[54] In the *Atlantic Monthly*, a reviewer spoke of the recent translation of Augustin Cochin's *The Results of Emancipation*, substantiating the pastor's conclusions. The reviewer identified "practical lessons" in the study, which showed that bad policy, not innately inferior people, led to the disasters. Both the pastor and the reviewer assured readers that liberation would not transform the war into barbarism.⁵⁵

The highly influential *Harper's Weekly* reinforced that message with images. Printed woodcuts of southern wartime scenes revealed that emancipation was unfolding without nightmarish savagery. On February 21, 1863, the magazine portrayed three white soldiers controlling a throng of Black refugees. A witness of the sprawling procession learned from the enslaved southerners that "it was known far and wide that the President has declared the slaves free." However, to communicate the soldiers' authority over the masses, the image rendered one soldier atop his horse, surveying the crowd. To respond directly to anxieties about arming men, the next issue of *Harper's Weekly* showed Black Louisianans disembarking from a transport steamer. The accompanying article assured readers that the soldiers, "as far as the privates were concerned, [were] a more decent, orderly, obedient, and soldierly set of men."⁵⁶ Such discussions of organized manumission and Black men's submissiveness were not idle chatter. These conversations came to directly influence the organization of regiments.

FIGURE 1.3 In this sketch of emancipation, a US Army officer commanded enslaved southerners exiting bondage. Such images assuaged white northern fears that emancipation would unfold violently. Instead of chaos, the soldier led the southerners' peaceable departure from slavery and enforced the US government's control. "The Effects of the Proclamation: Freed Negroes Coming into Our Lines at Newbern, North Carolina," *Harper's Weekly*, February 21, 1863. Library of Congress, LC-USZ62-112158.

In March 1863, Stanton formed the American Freedmen's Inquiry Commission (AFIC) and tasked reformers with gathering information regarding emancipation, including enslaved southerners' work ethic and determining their suitability for military service. He wanted to gauge whether enslaved southerners could become self-sufficient and requested that the AFIC "report what measures will best contribute to their protection and improvement, so that they may defend and support themselves."[57] In late June, the reformers of the AFIC, Samuel Gridley Howe, James McKaye, and Robert Dale Owen, delivered a preliminary report. They notified Stanton that "the two labor systems, namely, that of enforced slave labor and that of free compensated labor, are ... so thoroughly at variance that the change from the one to the other ... cannot safely be left undirected." To ease the transition, the AFIC advocated that enslaved southerners "learn ... that emancipation means neither idleness or gratuitous work, but fair labor for fair wages" under the direction of and paid out by "those who ... sympathize with the African nature" of the liberated.[58] With this, the report affirmed the views of Sea Island reformers hoping to remake the southern slave-labor Sodom into a free-labor Eden.

The AFIC extended their gaze from freed agriculturalists to war workers. Investigating emancipation within the army, the commission interviewed those who had seen formerly enslaved soldiers in action, including Higginson. The AFIC asked the colonel, "Do you think that, as a preparation for the life of a citizen, the organization of negroes in military bodies is important?" Higginson understood (and agreed with) the racial assumptions informing the question. He thought that bondage had stunted the development of the enslaved and left them as the "world's perpetual children." Like civilian reformers, he saw guidance as pivotal in preparing these "children" for freedom. His leadership was intentionally strict for this reason, he explained. He said, "It was clear that good discipline must come first." The soldiers, he added, "must be helped and elevated in all ways as much as possible." Echoing these views, he told the AFIC that military service was "of unspeakable value" to the formerly enslaved. Another reformer reiterated the educational value of military discipline, stating plainly that the army made for "the best school in the world" for enslaved men.[59]

The AFIC's verdict regarding enslaved men and military service drew on these interviews and reflected their broader conclusions on emancipation. The AFIC reported that military service was not dangerous, as Democrats believed. In fact, the commission claimed the army was the most effective place for enslaved men to transition from slavery. The AFIC noted that Black people had "a strong sense of the obligation of law" and, within the army, the "law in the shape of military rule takes for him the place of his master, with this difference, that he submits to it heartily and cheerfully without any sense of degradation." Building on this, the AFIC averred that "of all present agencies for elevating the character of the colored race, for cultivating in them self-respect and self-reliance, military training, under judicious officers, who will treat them firmly and kindly, is at once the most prompt and the more efficacious." If their references to "judicious officers" was not clear enough, the AFIC repeated the importance of leadership. They advised Stanton that "with these people, rather than with a more independent race, success depends upon . . . their leaders." The AFIC explained that "more depends upon [leaders] . . . of colored regiments than in that of white troops" because "colored regiments badly officered would be more liable to give way than badly officered regiments of the more self-reliant white race."[60] In all, the AFIC concluded that enslaved men could be soldiers and that the army was an ideal space for transforming them as laborers. To accomplish either, however, Black men needed discipline administered by well-appointed officers.

Whether Stanton acted directly on the AFIC's conclusions or not, the War Department proceeded in accordance with its prescriptions. Although the earliest regiments of Black soldiers in Kansas and Louisiana appointed Black officers to leadership roles, Black men would, in large part, only receive commissions as chaplains and surgeons for the remainder of the war. Powerful white northerners ranging from legislators like Samuel Cox (Ohio, Democrat) and Horace Maynard (Tennessee, Unionist) to commanders including Major Generals Nathaniel P. Banks and William T. Sherman agreed that Black men should not lead. Even those supportive of Black military service expressed such views. As the New York Union League put it when raising a regiment, Black soldiers needed "a peculiar class of officers." Accordingly, the War Department selected white northerners in hopes of guiding emancipation and pacifying racist anxieties.[61]

On May 22, 1863, Stanton asserted control of Black soldiers and made enlisting specific officers a priority. General Order No. 143 established the Bureau of Colored Troops, and as a result, the regiments were organized by the War Department, not states, and to be designated part of the United States Colored Troops (USCT).[62] The bureau, under the leadership of Major Charles Foster, formalized the enlistment of USCT officers by establishing "Boards . . . to examine applicants for commissions to command colored troops." The War Department stipulated when they would meet and mandated that all those examined "shall be subjected to a fair but rigorous examination."[63] The exams were not only rigorous; they were wide ranging. They inspired one soldier to quip that Napoleon would have had difficulty with their tests. Lincoln, meanwhile, insisted an Illinois doctor "be appointed a Colonel for a colored regiment—and this regardless of whether he can tell the exact shade of Julius Caesar's hair."[64] Nonetheless, the vetting by officials and boards did not always keep soldiers unfit for duty from the regiments. Staffing problems left certain USCT regiments under the command of poor officers or too few officers. But by October 1863, Foster bragged to Stanton that "the examinations have without doubt been conducted impartially, and have resulted in giving to this branch of service a class of efficient and well-instructed officers."[65] As Foster's boast clarifies, the boards served as an important tool for assessing leaders for the USCT.

While drawing on men from varied political backgrounds, USCT regiments were stocked almost exclusively with white northerners. Officers, especially those appointed or selected shortly after the Emancipation Proclamation, included men who had been part of reform movements or the Republican Party. Gravitating toward an antislavery agenda, they yearned to lead Black men against enslavers. For example, the brother of slain abolitionist printer Elijah Lovejoy, US representative Owen Lovejoy (Illinois, Republican), recommended Pennsylvania Reverend William Adain to Stanton. Adain, Lovejoy explained, "will fight if he has the opportunity as he loves liberty and believes in God." In a request for an appointment written to US senator Charles Sumner (Massachusetts, Republican), William Jackaberry announced that he aspired to "take an active part in raising and drilling colored troops... carrying out the wise and beneficent Proclamation of Freedom to the oppressed and down-trodden blacks." Another soldier remarked that he wanted to lead Black men over white men because "I want to [see] the rebels not only whipped but humiliated, and ... a defeat at the hands of colored soldiers would ... crush their pride."[66] These applicants considered themselves reformers in uniform, believing Black military service was progress and a chance to punish enslavers.

Less ardent applicants also joined, and though they were not as paternalistic as some reformers, they held racial views that shaped their outlook on emancipation. The officers included Sam Evans, an Ohio Democrat who broke with his father on the enlistment of Black soldiers after serving in the army, and Calvin Simms Mixter, a Massachusetts soldier who read "the Phrenological Journal for fun" and debated with his comrades in camp whether the government should "employ negroes as soldiers." Facing the War Department's vetting process, these men had to articulate permissible opinions to earn their stripes. They and many others succeeded, and as a result, the USCT was largely led by white men conversant in the discussions over race circulating throughout the wartime North.[67]

Officials within the War Department believed the USCT was an opportunity to strengthen Union forces, yet the racist views debated throughout northern society shaped the approach toward enlistment. The USCT regiments became spaces to implement social policy as well as a military tool for neutralizing the rebellion. As War Department solicitor William Whiting said, "The military organization of Colored Troops, removing all danger of insurrectionary movements, will regulate, control, and utilize the physical force" of Black men.[68] Whiting saw real value in the "experimental" effort to enlist enslaved men, though regulation and control were necessary. In screening white northerners, government officials created a group of officers who were often committed to the project of the USCT (if not abolition) yet entertained popular views regarding race. When they entered the USCT, they drew on these ideas to lead their regiments and discipline the soldiers as they made enslaved men freed men.[69]

By 1863, many white northerners wished to see enslaved people manumitted and the injustices caused by racism eradicated. Yet they harbored a less vitriolic, more paternalistic racism, which nonetheless had power. Perceived consequences of emancipation and entrenched views about African-descended peoples among white northerners shaped the US government's new strategy, including the creation of the USCT. Most importantly for the ongoing process of emancipation, War Department officials selected white northerners to lead Black soldiers. Although the US Army was a space for Black men to fight for freedom, prove their manhood, and nurture citizenship, enduring concerns led to the regulation of emancipation within the army.

The regulation of emancipation resulted in a distinct experience for freeborn and formerly enslaved Black soldiers. Like white soldiers, they braved battle, making sacrifices for cause, comrade, and country. Yet Black soldiers endured discipline meted out by officers who believed them inferior or, at least, distinct and thus in need of guidance. These men had eagerly enlisted seeking freedom but were now bound to follow military discipline and under the auspices of white authorities who reified prewar racial hierarchies. As a result, when they arrived in camp and were preparing for war, some Black men came to wonder whether the freedom they longed for could truly be realized in the ranks.

2

"Parts of the Gigantic Machine of Death": Adapting and Reacting to US Army Discipline

"OUR HOPES WERE not fulfilled," Sergeant Alexander Newton of the Twenty-Ninth Connecticut Infantry mourned. Capturing the tension between service and soldiers' aspirations, Newton, a Black southerner who trekked to Connecticut before the war, reflected on his crestfallen comrades. The "men were bitter in their disappointment," the sergeant wrote, "but such is the experience of war. Men are not free." Instead, "they are the parts of the gigantic machine of death."[1] Newton's resignation captured how the daily grind of rigorous regulations and enforcement of orders troubled soldiers' expectations. They found being gears in a machine especially onerous. Soldiers of the Twenty-Ninth were not alone in this sentiment. White and Black civilians new to soldiering were taken aback by the discipline to which they were subjected. Before the pandemonium of battle, the green men stomached camp tribulations. Transitioning from civilian life to a soldiers' spartan existence required initiates to wake early, forgo meals, and drill until their feet blistered. One white citizen-soldier possibly raised on Homeric epics or, at least, stories of the nation's own Myrmidons of Lexington grumbled about having "a dozen masters, who order me about like a negro." Black recruits hungry for rights and freedom were incensed, writing, "[We] are as much slaves as any." The soldiers' reflections portray how white and Black men alike suffered discipline and labor imposed by officers, who were compared to hard-driving bosses—if not outright "masters."[2] Despite the similar responses, enslaved men joined after having experienced violent discipline meted out

Freedom Soldiers. Jonathan Lande, Oxford University Press. © Oxford University Press 2024.
DOI: 10.1093/oso/9780197531754.003.0003

by white authorities, facts that reminded some of their lives in slavery. Such factors contributed to distinct experiences in the service.

Throughout the war, white and Black soldiers both compared military discipline—from the bone-breaking labor and the relentless daily control to the corporal reprimands and capital punishment—to tyranny. However, as they had not been enslaved, white soldiers spoke hypothetically. By 1864, many traded a recruit's hyperbole for a veteran's recognition that arduous discipline improved a regiment's chances when under fire. Perhaps contributing to their maturation was the realization that, even if they were treated as slaves, they remained in law and essence free men. When the war was over, they knew they would resume their roles as peaceable citizens. Most Black soldiers arrived having been enslaved. For them, the possibilities of abolition and political equality remained unsettled. They coped with an additional element of service, moreover, as many white officers believed Black men were childlike men who needed to be taught how to be free laborers. So, while most undoubtedly expected hardship upon enlistment, many interpreted the discipline as unjust.

Black soldiers compared their treatment to the tribulations they knew before the war. Hoping service would erode prejudice, Black northerners voiced fears that rife disparagement and wartime inequalities might be harbingers of postwar marginalization. Enlisting to escape slavery, Black southerners claimed that excessive violence and demeaning fatigue duties fostered conditions that resembled aspects of slavery. The men contended that the racial hierarchy prominent within prewar society existed within regiments and was now compounded by the harsh disciplinary measures common throughout Civil War armies. While most endured the difficulties silently, aggrieved Black soldiers spoke up. They described military discipline, if not the army itself, as an impediment to, rather than a means of securing, the goals of enlistment from 1863 to the final days of the war. This did not necessarily damper their fighting spirit or determination to help save the Union. But their criticisms reveal that certain freedom fighters thought conditions in the ranks undermined what they viewed as the war's broader objectives: ending slavery and racism.

"Unquestioning Obedience": Disciplining Civilians for War

Just as white soldiers did, Black recruits entering the ranks needed lessons in how to conduct themselves on the battlefield. They required instructions for firing a weapon, marching in formation, and following commands. To prepare their regiments, officers resorted to discipline. George Walcott, an officer who led both white and Black men, encapsulated the aim of Civil War officers, declaring, "Discipline is the thing of the army!" Although Walcott's decree would have suited most, if not all, armies across time and space, his explosive prose reflected its particular significance in the nation's volunteer armies. Unlike countries with professional armies, Americans extolled their citizen-soldier tradition. After independence, believing standing armies would lead to oppression, citizens of the nascent nation recommitted themselves to a small peacetime army that would, if necessary, be supplemented by civilian volunteers. These citizen-soldiers would march to war to protect their communities and the state. This model invigorated Civil War armies, with soldiers galvanized to protect kith and country. Yet the tradition left officers with the difficult task of turning farmers and clerks, carpenters and teachers, and eventually enslaved laborers into soldiers. To meet the challenge, officers leading white and Black men relied on the same discipline—which was doled out violently when needed—to inculcate fighting skills and assert total control.[3]

Discipline was exacting, Ulysses S. Grant explained to volunteers in 1861. A clerk in Galena, Illinois, when the war erupted, Grant had graduated from the military academy at West Point, saw action in the Mexican War, and served in the Regular Army before rejoining civilian life in 1854. Looking to the city's premier expert on the military as the nation was thrown into a war frenzy, Galena recruits were rapt as Grant regaled them with the soldier's ordeals. "Before calling upon you to become volunteers," he said, "I wish to state just what will be required of you. First of all, unquestioning obedience to your superior officers. The army is not a picnicking party." After dispelling the fantasies of those who hoped service would be an adventure, he explained, "You will have hard fare. You may be obliged to sleep on the ground after long marches in rain and snow." To close, Grant clarified to the men used to life as independent citizens that service required total submission. "Many of the orders of your superiors will seem to you unjust," he told the recruits, "and yet they must be borne." Military service demanded absolute subservience, not a boy's naïve exuberance.[4]

The burdens of war were especially difficult because mostly civilians entered Civil War armies. Relinquishing their peacetime vestments for military uniforms, they surrendered their self-determination. Officers exhorted men to abide by the Articles of War, which were read aloud in camp. Officers subjugated men's daily routines, making their days clockwork. Soldiers drudged from reveille around five in the morning to roll call to meals and ended their day with taps, a tune telling them to return to their quarters and turn out their lights.[5] When Black soldiers entered the ranks, they received fresh uniforms, which made them "feel as big as all creation," in one officer's words.[6] Yet camp discipline ensured that these neophytes remembered their place within the ranks. Basic discipline looked similar in regiments of the United States Colored Troops (USCT). They, too, learned that the army demanded unquestioning obedience. This severity drew a comment from one Black northerner serving in South Carolina who said the officers "are very Strick in Camp" and deemed his colonel "the meanest man this Side of hell."[7] But, as constraining as camp discipline could be, it was but one element of army life.

"Armies are disciplined and drilled for the purpose of acquiring the greatest possible amount of destructive power," a Black chaplain wrote, and to ensure men knew how to properly apply their destructive powers, officers made the rudimentary skills necessary for combat second nature with ceaseless drilling.[8] They coached soldiers in the critical transition from marching in columns into a line of battle quickly and remade civilian bodies for war. The officers of an Illinois regiment, for instance, subjected their men to drills on "a range of hills almost [like] mountains" because "they thought it was a good way to strengthen our wind and muskle," a Prairie State private wrote.[9] Lessons in how to handle weapons and execute maneuvers on command filled the lengthy days as well.[10] Although the army briefly entertained teaching Black soldiers simplified tactics on account of supposed mental inferiority, officers ultimately drilled Black infantrymen according to the common practices for hours and, at times, in inclement conditions.[11] Eventually, white and Black troops adopted soldiers' habits. As one Black soldier recalled, he and his peers became habituated to "rigid" commands. Conditions were not always equal. Issued inferior weapons in many cases, Black soldiers learned to handle smooth-bore muskets and ammunition "of the most worthless description," a colonel griped. Yet, as a result of the drills, Black recruits, like their white counterparts, soon knew what to do almost instinctually when a commander yelled, "Double-Time!" "Right Face!" "Left Face!" and "Fire!"[12]

To the disbelief of many, freeborn and formerly enslaved Black men absorbed war's curriculum quickly. *Harper's Weekly* presented the reading public with images and articles intent on correcting the "ignorant prejudice still entertained in parts of the North" regarding Black men's military service. Believing "that the capacity of the negro to drill and fight can not be too strongly insisted upon," the paper portrayed a confident officer directing his men and described the training of soldiers in the Department of the

South. The paper promised readers that "the negroes... evince great aptitude at learning the manual of arms" because, in part, they "are more docile than white recruits," a sentiment that often emerged in letters from white officers and commanders.[13] To persisting racial concerns about emancipation among white northerners, the paper's boasts may have indeed proved to be a salve. Yet, regardless of their results, the reports of the soldiers' acumen showed the nation that Black men could serve and contribute to the cause.[14]

FIGURE 2.1 In this *Harper's Weekly* image, a white officer led numerous Black soldiers during drill. The orderly queue and officer's cool manner suggested to northern readers that white leaders maintained control over emancipation and armed Black soldiers of the US Army. "Teaching the Negro Recruits the Use of the Minie Rifle," *Harper's Weekly*, March 14, 1863. Library of Congress, LC-USZ62-118150.

USCT officers confirmed that newspaper reports were no exaggeration. Second Lieutenant Lawrence Van Alstyne wrote in his diary in October 1863 that he and fellow officers of the Ninetieth United States Colored Infantry (USCI) "commenced teaching our recruits the rudiments of soldiering" and found the men "awkward, but very anxious to learn." The eager soldiers eventually thrived. "They soon got the idea of marching in time," Van Alstyne said, "and on the whole did as well or better than we [white soldiers] . . . when we took our first lesson." Confirming Van Alstyne's conclusion, a colonel declared that "the average colored soldier adapts himself more readily to discipline of a camp, and acquires what is called the drill, in much less time than the average white soldier."[15] As these officers attested, Black men swiftly learned the ways of war.

But not all aspects of discipline came easy, leading officers to employ more heavy-handed management strategies. In addition to creating armies of democrats more apt to use a pitchfork or a pen than a musket, the citizen-soldier ideal filled the ranks with men accustomed to questioning authority. A life spent voting for leaders and debating policies had convinced them that they were (and should remain) their own masters. Military discipline disturbed ingrained notions of independence, fraternity, and deference to authority, as veteran of the Ninth Indiana Infantry Ambrose Bierce observed in a fictional story decades later. Unlike Bierce's narratives that re-created battlefield drama to impress upon readers war's abject, unfeeling gore, Bierce remarked on the "new industry" of soldiering in a tale of a man's bungling adaptation to army discipline. The private struck a schoolyard friend who was now an officer and, to the private's horror, was executed for it. Reflecting on the story's message, Bierce wrote that, for those "imbued from infancy with the fascinating fallacy that all men are born equal," the "submission to authority is not easily mastered."[16] Throughout the war, officers faced the unenviable task of disciplining such greenhorns to defer to rank and used violence to guarantee that the men succeeded on chaotic battlefields.[17] Many USCT officers had been trained by these methods. Like those leading white soldiers, USCT officers also shepherded either Black northerners raised on democratic skepticism or Black southerners who had braved death to escape slavery. USCT officers brandished the harshest methods of army discipline.

Adding to the supposed need for violence, the lack of clear regulations on punishments left many rank-and-file soldiers at the mercy of their commanders. Bereft of guidelines, officers relied on ad hoc penalties and on corporal punishment to demonstrate dominance or enforce their commands. Not all officers managed regiments with beatings and harangues.[18] Yet, as a white veteran reflected, some officers "felt that every violation of camp rule should be visited with the infliction of bodily pain."[19] In one instance, an officer brutalized a white private when he failed to turn out his light, causing what doctors later diagnosed as "derangement of the mind."[20] USCT soldiers experienced similarly harsh treatment. Colonel Robert Gould Shaw of the Fifty-Fourth Massachusetts Infantry wrote with surprise that Colonel James Montgomery of the Second South Carolina (Colored) Infantry (later the Thirty-Fourth USCI) "shoots his men with perfect looseness, for a slight disobedience of orders." Yet, while he was critical of Montgomery's severity, Shaw himself was known for his use of what one of his lieutenant colonels called a "method of coercion."[21] These officers, including leaders like Montgomery and Shaw, believed force was necessary to control soldiers.

Officers also believed the galling brutality had to be openly displayed to teach rulebreakers as well as their peers. The methods had a calculated objective, as a former professor at West Point explained in 1863. "One great end of punishment is the prevention of crime by example," he wrote, so "it should be rendered, in this respect, as extensively useful as possible, by the publicity which attends its execution." In accordance with this view of discipline, officers used humiliation to demonstrate to all men the seriousness of following rules.[22]

Officers invented numerous ways of causing soldiers social, psychological, and physical discomfort. Defiant troopers stood on barrels, carried logs through camp, or suffered being bucked and gagged, a punishment that left a man immobilized, muted, and much pitied. "Well I saw a man bucked & gag[g]ed to day for the first time in my life," a Hoosier sergeant wrote, and "I would not be in that fix for 50 dollars."[23] Thieves and insubordinate men sported placards telegraphing offenses. Some had to march through camp with their heads shaved carrying such boards. This made for "a melancholy sight," an Illinoisian recorded.[24] Men sentenced to endure the wooden horse sat atop a plank above their comrades, burning in shame as well as under the summer sun for all to see. In these punishments—which were often conducted for long stretches to exacerbate physical and social pain—the army demonstrated a central logic of military discipline. An Ohio soldier succinctly described the rationale, commenting that "every thing was done to make as much impression as possible on the troops present."[25] As harsh as these punishments could be, though, the most unfortunate faced ritualistic executions.

The macabre carnival was choreographed to demonstrate the army's unadulterated sovereignty over each soldier. Outlined in the regulations, the "great ceremony," as an officer called it, began with soldiers assembling and forming three sides of a square. (If the soldier were to be hanged, the men would complete the square.) Under the watchful eye of a provost marshal, the soldiers loaded the execution party's guns with ball cartridges. (To appease the executioners' consciences, one gun received a blank cartridge.) As the soldiers stood to study the procession, the provost marshal would lead the band from the condemned man's regiment playing a dirge. In their wake, the firing squad charted the way for the men carrying a coffin, a chaplain, the condemned man, and his armed escort. Once the coffin stopped, the provost marshal leading the execution read the charge, the court-martial finding, and the sentence. The chaplain prayed with the soldier and withdrew to safety. The execution party formed at six or eight paces from the prisoner. The provost marshal motioned and, as an onlooker recalled, "launched [the doomed man] into eternity." The lifeless soldier fell back into his coffin. If he was not dead, a reserve firing party assembled nearby or the provost marshal with a trusted pistol finished the job. Wishing to impress upon the men its power in the last, the army ordered the assembled comrades to file by the grave slowly and, as a soldier wrote, get "a good view of him."[26]

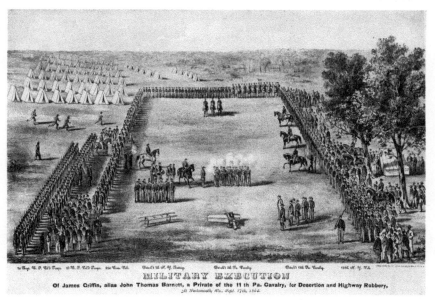

FIGURE 2.2 As a means of demonstrating the absolute subjugation of rank-and-file soldiers, the US Army executed deserters in front of their comrades. During executions by firing squad, the army compelled soldiers to form a horseshoe around their convicted comrade, watch him succumb to the firing party, and finally march by the lifeless corpse. "Military Execution of James Griffin, alias John Thomas Barnett, a Private of the 11th Pa. Cavalry, for Desertion and Highway Robbery, at Portsmouth, Va., Sept. 17th, 1863." Library of Congress, LC-DIG-pga-06288.

Such lessons impressed men—as well as a nation—unused to war. A soldier told his mother that he had to watch an execution, which he and his comrades "dislike[d] to witness but we are oblijed to se."[27] Another soldier recalled the deaths of five deserters. Officers were not immune. "Learned all about the execution," a lieutenant leading the Sixty-Eighth USCI recorded in his journal, and "did not have a wink of sleep last night."[28] New to war, the men grappled with the killings. *Harper's Weekly* portrayed the execution of three soldiers from the Army of the Potomac to ensure that the civilians were familiar with the violence.[29] Even Lincoln's sons appreciated the consequences of disobedience. Willie and Tad Lincoln subjected their Zouave doll to courts-martial trials for sleeping on the post or desertion. They, then, forced the fabric convict to face a barrage (from Tad's toy cannon) and buried the cloth corpse beneath the nation's rosebush.[30] The images in newspapers and stories of erring soldiers clearly commanded the attention of civilians more accustomed to dissenting than reprimand. These moving, violent performances were deemed necessary, however, because officers thought the control necessary. White and Black soldiers faced these deadly lessons throughout the conflict, leading some to condemn their officers and even the army.

"A School of Skilled Labor": Disciplining Freedom in the USCT

Civil War officers leading white and Black men saw themselves as tasked with molding men's character. Officers leading white soldiers confined such instruction to moral crusades designed to curb habits, such tippling or gambling, that could eviscerate their virtues. Seeking to elevate enslaved men considered in need of virtue, USCT officers sought to introduce then cultivate habits. Due to the widespread views regarding emancipation, white northerners thought enslaved southerners were childlike. Either inherent racial characteristics or years as enslaved laborers left them poorly equipped for independence. Aspiring to inculcate behaviors useful to them as free laborers, they taught literacy and proper forms of labor activism. Although they may have believed such lessons altruistic, in holding rank-and-file soldiers to specific free-labor practices, officers effectively turned regiments into spaces that limited the scope of emancipation.

White officers in regiments composed of white men treated subordinates as younger family members. In the absence of an authoritative culture built on a professional military tradition, officers and soldiers of the Civil War's volunteer forces adapted relationships to social structures they and their men were acquainted with as civilians. White soldiers organized the regimental hierarchy and relationships within the ranks based on tiered familial bonds. Higher ranks indicated more senior family members, so privates looked up to and followed fatherlike colonels or brotherlike captains (at least in the minds of officers).[31] As parental figures, officers hoped to refine characteristics considered essential to citizenship and manhood. They enforced, for instance, spirituality, temperance, and cleanliness.[32] Such kin relationships used in the white regiments did not translate to the USCT.

USCT officers looked to prewar relations, too, but views regarding interracial interactions precluded the enactment of familial hierarchies between white officers and Black subordinates. Perhaps most significantly, most white northerners had spent little time with Black people before the war. White northerners also did not think of Black men or women as social or political equals. Those showing concern for Black people often acted as detached benefactors. Rather than soften during the war, such ideas intensified. The Democratic ilk, who expressed dread of servile insurrection, regurgitated time-tested criticisms of interracial contact. Meanwhile, white northerners sympathetic to antislavery rejected full equality. Reformers and Republicans alike articulated paternalistic views. They hoped to help Black men and women from slavery to freedom, revealing their concern for the enslaved. However, these northerners did not trust that the freed people could navigate the transition after spending life under the lash.[33] While Democrats' racial perspectives remained distinct from those of Republicans and abolitionists, racial thinking regardless of political outlook configured how most white northerners organized their relationships with Black people.

Like their peers leading white men, USCT officers drew on prevalent prewar views. On the most fundamental level, many officers saw Black men, especially southerners, as benighted by slavery. For instance, when leading the Fifty-Ninth USCI, Major Robert Cowden described the condition of the enslaved men upon entering camp and the task USCT officers undertook. He wrote that the recruit's "look, dress, manner, and opinion of himself were all the result of generations in slavery." Cowden believed he was a sculptor needing to remove impurities left by bondage and polish the soldiers for freedom. "The average plantation negro was a hard-looking specimen," the major penned, "with about as little of the soldier to be seen in him as there was of the angel in Michael Angelo's block of marble before he had applied his chisel." To dispel enslaved men's "plantation manners," Cowden wrote, white officers addressed the men's character. But the leaders did not think of Black men as grown. Rather, officers considered them children transitioning from slavery. This view of Black adults as childlike was prevalent throughout northern reform literature and shaped many white officers' approach to leadership. Such efforts were evident in the white officers' discipline, as they used military service to remake the childlike men into self-reliant laborers.[34]

Officers based their leadership on the residual influence of bondage on Black men. Perhaps most attentive to questions related to prior enslavement, abolitionist officers shied away from "harsher forms of punishment" to ensure "that every suggestion of slavery might be avoided," as Colonel Norwood Hallowell of the Fifty-Fifth Massachusetts Infantry wrote. Colonel Thomas Wentworth Higginson's leadership in the First South Carolina (Colored) Infantry (later the Thirty-Third USCI) was a prominent example of this. The Massachusetts colonel thought southerners had been brutalized so badly that an officer could not surpass slavery's violence to train them. Higginson deemed his men "docile, gay, and lovable" and cared for the men as children. "Philoprogenitiveness [or love toward one's children] is an important organ for an officer of colored troops," he wrote. A lieutenant in the Sixty-Eighth USCI also believed the men should be treated gingerly, stating that "most of them are easily handled by a kind master." Considering the soldiers' lives in slavery, these officers thought the men needed gentle guidance.[35]

Fellow officers lacking abolitionist credentials took a punitive line, but like their more tender counterparts, coarser commanders couched their harshness in the soldiers' prewar experiences. These men insisted that racial inferiority or enslavement necessitated such discipline. For instance, Second Lieutenant Henry Harrison Brown of the Twenty-Ninth Connecticut applauded an officer for violently subduing a "negro full blooded" who possessed "less reason than a child of five years." Brown called the army "a school" and said that "some [men] must have obdence [sic] whipped into them." Once shown "officers . . . [must] be obeyed," Brown explained, the Black soldiers were as "easy to govern . . . [as] a school of 50 boys."[36] Albeit different, the "education" Brown touted resembled the attitude toward discipline that Hallowell and Higginson exercised. Reflecting the variegated views on race and emancipation prevalent around the North, officers understood their men as "school boys" needing lessons.

Such racial ideas led officers to concentrate on how the army and, more precisely, military discipline coincided with education. While they prioritized battle readiness, officers hoped to mold enslaved men into competent free men (though the officers did not typically distinguish between freeborn northerners and enslaved southerners). Men like Lieutenant Colonel Charles Fox of the Fifty-Fifth Massachusetts Infantry summed this view up in a letter to his father. Fox argued that, ideally, a leader in the USCT was a combination of a soldier and a reformer. To explain, he identified three types of officers and compared them. The first type instructed men "believing in colored troops as an element in this war of vast importance, disposed to educate and use them as such, and thereby fit them to be freemen." The second sort deployed regiments "as a political machine for the benefit of himself and others." The last sort, deemed "radicals," directed a regiment "as an engine of retaliation and destruction." Like critics of enlisting enslaved men, Fox remarked on the hazards of the third sort of leadership, explaining that mismanaged Black men would become a "body of wild, undisciplined, lawless marauders, uncontrollable by their officers." Fox concluded the first sort would be best for the joint causes of Union and emancipation. This sort of officer would make "a body of soldiers disciplined and subject to control, respecting themselves and respected by others." At the heart of his comparison was the belief that Black men could not lead themselves as either soldiers or laborers. Fox, in other words, was implicitly skeptical of enslaved men's ability to self-govern. Yet, like Republicans in Congress and the reformers of the American Freedmen's Inquiry Commission, Fox thought suitable leadership could "fit them to be freemen."[37] In short, officers could be schoolmasters educating Black men in the habits of freedom. Many agreed and followed through.

This approach was most explicitly on display during lessons in literacy. Black soldiers, and especially the formerly enslaved, appreciated the classes in reading and writing. They prized their abilities because southern laws barred enslaved men and women from an education. Liberated southerners vigorously pursued the written word, especially when northern reformers offered lessons in schools established in refugee camps. To the delight of many refugees who enlisted, white officers followed suit, even turning army tents into schoolrooms. As a member of the Eighth USCI recalled, "the Co. went to school" when there was a schoolhouse nearby, and later, after the regiment had moved on, their captain "worked a good deal putting up tents for a schoolhouse." In Louisiana, four schools "fitted with well made seats, desks and blackboards" were created, a chaplain wrote in a letter to Major General Ullman. In amazement, the chaplain added that the men showed an "eagerness for study" to such an extent that the "cartridge box and spelling book are attached to the same belt."[38] But, as much as the men appreciated the lessons, officers thought the lessons served another purpose.

Officers viewed literacy as a means of preparing formerly enslaved men for freedom. Rufus Kinsley had traveled south first as a civilian reformer believing "education of the blacks is... the redemption of the race," and when he became an officer in the USCT, he translated his convictions into military leadership by teaching his subordinates. When appointed first lieutenant of Company G, Second Corps d'Afrique (later the Seventy-Fourth USCI), he began teaching his men as he had refugees. In a letter to his father, Kinsley wrote, "It is wonderful, the earnestness with which they seek after knowledge." By May 1864, the movement to educate the formerly enslaved had spread throughout the area. "All over the state," Kinsley penned, "almost every Yankee soldier has a class of Contrabands or colored soldiers."[39] In Dickson, Tennessee, schools eventually eclipsed soldiering when an assistant adjutant general mandated curricula supersede drill. Speaking to the underlying intentions of his regiment-turned-university, the assistant adjutant general announced, "The surest and only step to a respectable life as Freemen ... is for every man to acquire the best Education he can."[40] Observers thought the efforts in elevating men's intelligence—and character—were quite successful. "Carefully prepared lists show that 380 have learned the alphabet," a white chaplain wrote approvingly. This, he thought, was "very encouraging progress." Taking stock, he added, "A most remarkable transformation of the habits, thinking and character of the men is also going on and all for the better."[41] Another chaplain remarked that the lessons "fit and prepare the freedmen for the duties of a new and higher life." He then celebrated the resultant "progress of freedom."[42] The chaplains' letters made clear that to USCT leaders the lessons in army schoolhouses ably prepared enslaved men for self-governance as camp drilling had equipped soldiers for combat.

Not all schooling for free men centered on literacy. When the War Department decided to pay Black soldiers less than white soldiers, USCT officers took the opportunity to educate soldiers about life in a free-labor society. The soldiers did not need officers' prompting, choosing to respond defiantly to the injustice with letters to newspapers and politicians. But white officers saw an opportunity to support their men and endorse the proper conduct of wage laborers fighting to defend the value of their labor within a republic. Officers believed that the War Department's policy would convey that contract agreements within a free-labor economy were no better than slave-labor conditions, thus undermining their efforts to teach troops the merits of the northern labor system. As a result, officers publicly called out the US government. In letters to the *New York Tribune*, Higginson admonished the "breach of contract." He wrote that the men, although soldiers under military discipline, "were certainly free enough to claim its fulfillment."[43] Colonel Robert Gould Shaw of the Fifty-Fourth Massachusetts Infantry articulated a similar point, writing that if his men did not earn the promised salary that the "regt ought . . . to be mustered out of service, as they were enlisted on the understanding that they were to be on the same footing as other Mass. Vols." When soldiers protested unequal pay, despite the possibility that protests could be construed as mutiny, Higginson and fellow officers within the First South Carolina cheered the activists. Higginson gushed in a diary entry of men refusing to accept unequal pay, and a captain in the regiment trumpeted support. "Boys," he declared, "stand up for your full pay! I am with you, and so are all the officers."[44] By backing the protesters, officers validated the peaceful dissent and reinforced the labor activism.

Officers selectively lauded forms of protest, however. Instructing soldiers in the proper modes of engagement, officers elected to condemn certain acts while honoring others. For instance, after men of the Third South Carolina (Colored) Infantry (later the Twenty-First USCI) refused to do duty and stacked their guns in protest, the most outspoken of the strikers, Sergeant William Walker, was convicted of mutiny by white officers. To demonstrate the seriousness of his actions and prevent further outbreaks, the army executed Walker before his peers.[45] Juxtaposed against the swift rebuke Walker faced, officers of the Fifty-Fifth Massachusetts Infantry allowed the men to celebrate when Congress equalized pay and to mark the success of their peaceful protests with a parade.[46] In October 1864, in stark contrast to Walker's march to his final resting place the previous spring, members of the Bay State regiment strutted in their Union blue through camp. The parade—a potent nineteenth-century civic event that gave voting citizens and marginalized political groups alike the chance to express their views—signaled the prominence afforded the peaceful protesters. The soldiers feted their victorious campaign for equal pay as well as implicitly nodding to free-labor ideals. Fittingly, white officers silently praised their civil engagement. They watched the celebration of pay "won through long suffering and patient endurance," the regimental colonel reported.[47] The encouragement of parading protesters clarified what types of activism were acceptable. The soldiers learned that the freedom to contest power must take the form of nonviolent free-labor protest.

Commanders also saw the work of war as a chance to educate formerly enslaved men in freedom by turning them into military laborers, rather than armed fighters. Charles Francis Adams Jr. pushed the idea of the army as a school to its logical conclusion. The Massachusetts scion had initially hesitated on abolition, believing enslaved men lacked "mental vigor and energy." But he warmed to the idea, became lieutenant colonel in a Black cavalry regiment, and thought military service could be vocational training. He advocated for long-term military service, calling the US Army "the proper school for the race." Articulating what he deemed "my philanthropic plan for the race" while leading in the Fifth Massachusetts Cavalry, he noted that the men "learn to take care of themselves" and "become, from necessity, conversant with every branch of industry." Adams envisioned officers instructing the men in trades, including those of a blacksmith, carpenter, shoemaker, tailor, and clerk. All the efforts convinced him that "the Army [should] become for the black race, a school of skilled labor and of self reliance, as well as an engine of war."[48] As Adams's views attest, some officers saw the army as a space to educate men who could not yet bear the responsibilities of freedom and to monitor emancipation. In doing so, these officers parroted the mission set by government officials who had debated and studied how best to arm enslaved men.

"Driven around Like a Dog": Reacting to Army Discipline

Combat may have been the most dramatic test of a man's mettle, but discipline added to the challenges soldiers faced and often drew the greatest ire from the rank-and-file. At times, officers imposed discipline on Black soldiers with greater gusto, fearing that a servile insurrection might erupt.[49] But white and Black soldiers generally received the same strict, violent discipline. Many white soldiers, largely unused to corporal punishments and excessive violence as civilians, couched the discipline within the broader carnage of war and acclimated to it for the sake of victory. By contrast, many Black soldiers thought that the camp violence revealed the persistence of prejudice among officers and the institutionalization of racism within the army. To be sure, most Black soldiers never criticized the army and quietly served within their regiments. Yet those who spoke on the problems of discipline astutely argued that elements of it, and especially the ritual violence used to enforce it, manifested the brutality of white supremacy and slavery. Black northerners concluded that the army propagated the prewar racial hierarchy, undermining their efforts to secure citizenship and equality. For their part, Black southerners interpreted the violence through the lens of their enslavement. They associated vicious officers with those who used force to police slavery. Whether accurate in their perception of bigotry or not, Black northerners and southerners who offered their opinions on army discipline articulated that, if military service offered a chance to join the body politic or end slavery, the violence of it in effect nullified certain redemptive or emancipatory opportunities.

During service, white soldiers conducted lugubrious hard labor, or fatigue duties, leading to complaints. When the Civil War engulfed the country, white men ranging from stevedores and sailors to students and scholars anxious to embody the citizen-soldier ideal volunteered to defend the nation. Such soldiers largely anticipated their soldiering to be brief. They expected daily action dedicated to fighting an enemy, not building earthworks.[50] But war often resembled work, and men griped about the grueling war chores and compared service to civilian jobs. As a Connecticut trooper reflected, for instance, "Soldiering does well for a few months," but "it dont ware like farming."[51] Others concluded that military duties were so onerous they worked like "slaves."[52] Yet, as distasteful as fatigue duties were, white men saved much of their criticism for the harsh discipline, especially early in the war.

White soldiers initially reacted vigorously to punitive regulations while in the ranks. As they coped with deadly fighting and fatal illnesses as well as new rules, army novices witnessed the war's violence—ranging from battlefield carnage to dreadful diseases to tough discipline—with awe, anger, and abhorrence.[53] Although popular activities like boxing showcased violence and dueling remained a possible means of resolving disputes in the North, white soldiers in the US Army found the use of violence to enforce regulations as angering at first. Sergeant Isaac Little of the Eighty-Fourth Indiana Infantry recalled that soldiers reacted vehemently when a rumor spread that a general planned to flog one hundred men caught "catch[ing] hogs." Nearly "a thousand boys went up there & the Excitement got pretty high & all the boys in camp was mad," the Hoosier penned. Ominously, he closed, "If he had whip[p]ed the boys gosh what a time."[54] Unaccustomed to violent discipline, even gossip of a possible whipping sufficed to ignite the men's tempers. Soldiers also found the gruesome spectacle of executions repulsive initially. Upon arriving in camp, white soldiers had little experience with community-enforced violence, most notably public executions. Northern towns and cities had largely banned the state-enforced killing from view by 1860. As a result, many soldiers disliked watching executions.[55] "It was a painful sight to see them following their coffins, the band playing their dirge, and then to see them executed," one soldier grimaced after beholding the ritual.[56] But, as they became acquainted with the possibility of death (if not inured to the bloodshed), such responses increasingly faded.

By 1864, some white soldiers embraced the brutality, and others largely stomached the discipline because they trusted it would bring victory. While executions remained a rarity, they became palatable, one soldier conceded, because "military discipline must have its course."[57] Another soldier made a point to watch the execution of two deserters: "I went down to see them shot, and although it was not a pleasant sight," he admitted, "I think I should not hesitate to see more shot for the same thing. Because if we are [to be] successful we must have some discipline." Although such responses were not categorical, many white soldiers thought that victory demanded a firm hand—if not an executioner. These battle-hardened, war-weary soldiers greeted punitive enforcement as necessary.[58]

Black soldiers, by contrast, never voiced their assent to camp violence even as they continued serving and bravely faced death in combat. Black men from the North and South instead equated officers' severity with prewar anti-Black violence and chided their abuse. In letters, Black northerners described ill-treatment as a sign of persisting prejudice. Black men around the North had witnessed anti-Black racism before the war. Aside from day-to-day discrimination, white vigilantes had trampled aspiring Black men and women to prevent social, political, and economic elevation.[59] Black northerners expected such treatment to end when they enlisted to serve. Making sacrifices for the nation, the soldiers hoped and fought for such ideals. Alas, they faced the same disgraceful practices during service.

Black soldiers complained of onerous labor, not unlike white soldiers, yet those of the USCT sometimes saw the labor as a sign of inequality. Before entering the US Army, many enslaved men found themselves impressed to serve the whims of Confederate soldiers or to build Rebel defenses. This perhaps led to some soldiers' distaste for such work. When Lincoln opened the army to Black men with the Emancipation Proclamation, he ordered Black soldiers be kept to noncombat roles. Eventually, the demands of war necessitated Black men fight, but most USCT regiments worked throughout the war.[60] Such duties sparked ire. From "one of the most horable swamps" north of New Orleans, an anonymous New Yorker from the Twentieth USCI explained in a letter to the commander in chief his regiment's blighted condition. "Instead of the musket It is the spad and the Whelbarrow and the Axe" for work, the soldier complained. The labor and meager rations led to "ignominious Death" or a "state of misery," the soldier added.[61] To some, though, the reason they worked was the real problem. Serving in South Carolina, a Philadelphian in the Thirty-Second USCI concluded that the army deemed them "not fit for anything but . . . picket duty and drudgery." He added in disgust that "the rations . . . condemned by the white troops are sent to our regiment." The "hard tack that we have to eat," he moaned, is "mouldy and musty and full of worms, and not fit for a dog to eat." To the Pennsylvania penman, the work they had been ordered to complete demonstrated the low view commanders held of Black soldiers. The food his regiments received only underscored the disrespect.

White officers meted out violent discipline and "put . . . irons" on Black soldiers, leading Black northerners to scorn their treatment.[62] For instance, a member of the Forty-Third USCI wrote from Virginia that the officers "strike the men with their swords, and jog and punch them in their side to show them how to drill." One soldier warned, "Our officers must stop beating their men across the head and back with their swords" because "men in this regiment . . . born free . . . will not stand being punched with swords and driven around like a dog." To these men, army discipline undermined their status as free men, treating them no better than animals.[63]

More than censuring the army for degrading work, wormy hardtack, and generally inhumane treatment, Black northerners criticized the army's use of violence. In a marked contrast to the white soldiers who sanctioned executions for victory's sake, a Black soldier under the penname "Picket" wrote to the *Weekly Anglo-African* about his refusal to re-create an execution's violent subjugation. As he told readers, "Such scenes are of too frequent occurrence and have been depicted too often to need any description here." Perhaps he believed that narrating the event would reconstruct the inhuman subjugation. His words might conjure the unjust power wielded during the ceremonial killing, so he chose to instead concentrate on the executed soldier.[64] "We will be contended with saying that the prisoner . . . displayed the most unflinching courage and met his death with stoical indifference." Before closing, "Picket" made a wish: "I sincerely hope it will be the last [execution]."[65] Rather than identify the importance of such punishments to the cause, "Picket" interpreted the violence as unreasonable and, determined to forestall further injustice, chose not to describe the gory performance.

Although "Picket" might represent an extreme, his view was not countered by others. Indeed, after reviewing Black soldiers' letters to newspapers and family and the relatively few diaries of Black soldiers that have survived, not a single endorsement, or even an accommodation, of the army's disciplinary violence has been located. Of course, a quiet or illiterate soldier may have agreed that the force used to keep soldiers in line was necessary to win the war, and he may have uttered his agreement under his breath or in a late-night debate with a comrade in a tent or over a campfire. But any such remarks have been lost to posterity. Without evidence of such reflections, it can therefore be plausibly concluded that USCT soldiers did not react to executions or beatings like those white soldiers who consented to it after 1864.

To some, the disciplinary hierarchy of the USCT re-created the white supremacist elements of prewar life. Signing his letter to the *Weekly Anglo-African* "Bay State," a soldier from the Fifty-Fifth Massachusetts Infantry presented a litany of complaints, centering on the "old and troublesome subject of pay." From regimental headquarters in Palatka, Florida, he described unequal pay as a "great injustice" that left families "to suffer" and even drove one "stout-hearted" soldier to tears that "rolled in floods from his ... eyes." "Bay State" charged that there were "no chances for promotion, no money for our families, and we [are] little better than an armed band of laborers with rusty muskets and bright spades." He noted that service held gallant men to lower ranks and plenty of menial laboring. But he ultimately connected Black men's success with that of the Union, showing that patriotism and hope for the future kept his spirits buoyed.[66] Yet soldiers' animosity was not always confided to newspaper columns.

At times, Black northerners' anger spilled over into open confrontations between the men and their officers. For instance, when hounded by Captain Sherman Conant for allegedly feigning illness, Pennsylvania barber Charles Merritt cursed all the officers of the Third USCI as "a damn set of tyrants ... trying to abuse him as much as they could" before locating an axe to presumably defend his liberty.[67] Merritt's actions suggest that the private saw officers as oppressors enforcing stringent labor practices on men deemed untrustworthy shirkers. Whether the racism the men articulated was real or perceived and whether it was widespread or isolated, many nonetheless saw the violence enforced by white officers as tyrannical.

At times, Black southerners responded aggressively when army life resembled slavery. Fewer accounts of the formerly enslaved appeared in Black newspapers, likely the result of higher levels of illiteracy and the absence of a Black southern newspaper. However, in scattered accounts of soldiers' reactions to discipline, Black southerners expressed their disillusionment. In a letter found in the streets of New Orleans, for example, a soldier bluntly accused officers of disciplining the men as enslavers, stating that soldiers of the USCT had "two masters." He concluded, "Our white officers may be union men but [they are] Slave holders at heart."[68] The officers' zeal for control went well beyond military necessity and was seen as an extension of the violent, systematic, and patronizing discipline inflicted on generations of enslaved southerners.[69] Not all soldiers believed that officers acted as "masters," to be sure. But men from various parts of the South suggested that military service perpetuated the daily manipulation to which they had been subjected during slavery.

As a result, these southern-born Black soldiers condemned officers vehemently when the leaders used punishments reminiscent of slavery. When Lieutenant Colonel Augustus Benedict lashed two drummers in the Fourth Corps d'Afrique (later the Seventy-Sixth USCI) in 1863, for example, the regiment exploded in mutiny. They demanded an end to the abuse, shouting during their revolt, "Give us Colonel Benedict; we did not come here to be whipped by him." Similarly, freedom seekers from North Carolina to Florida to Mississippi reacted to officers who hung them by their thumbs, a punishment that used torturous pain to strengthen discipline. Such reactions persisted throughout the war. These soldiers expressed their animosity toward violence and abusive treatment generally.[70]

Sometimes individuals retaliated against invidious officers, as in the case of Private Wallace Baker of the Fifty-Fifth Massachusetts Infantry. In May 1864, Second Lieutenant Thomas Ellsworth reprimanded Baker for arriving to drill late without his gun or cap, ordering the Kentucky-born soldier to his quarters. Baker retorted, "I shan't do it; I'll be damned if I'll go; I'll go to the guard's house first." Ellsworth hit the private for his insubordination. "You damn white officer," Baker barked, "do you think that you can strike me, and I not strike you back again? I will do it, I'm damned if I don't." A fight ensued. Only with the help of another officer could Ellsworth wrangle the surly soldier. Baker's reaction was not unlike that of truculent white soldiers, yet he specifically called attention to officer's whiteness and chafed under his command.[71]

Baker ultimately condemned the entire US Army for its use of violence. For his insubordination, a court-martial convicted the Kentuckian for mutiny and sentenced him to be executed.[72] On the day of his death, Baker denounced the punishment as an egregious use of public violence. After marching to the portion of Folly Island beach where a grave had been dug, Baker declared, "They make a heap of ado to kill one man." He then added, "If it was Jeff. Davis they could do no more."[73] Baker resented that his punishment was equal to what would be inflicted on the chief traitor if caught. Baker also pointed to the "ado to kill one man," a reference to the ritualistic violence that resembled enslavers' reprimands. As a nineteenth-century southern legal expert observed, violence against Black bodies had been the primary means of enforcing slavery because the enslaved "can be reached only through his body." Of course, enslavers resorted to alternative forms of coercion, including threats of sale and threats toward loved ones, yet bodily harm remained a fundamental component of slavery. To ensure all received the message, enslavers forced family, friends, and fellow enslaved folk to watch the executions, especially of Black resisters.[74] Baker suggested that the premeditated ritual emulated the "ado" enslavers used to demonstrate their power and excoriated the army for similarly deploying violence to maintain order.[75]

Black southerners, victims of years of unremitting toil, proved particularly sensitive to the disproportionate menial labor assigned to them in the army. Members of the USCT spent more time on average laboring than their white comrades. Members of the rank-and-file who hoped service meant securing liberty found the daily routine quite the opposite. Sergeant William J. Brown of the Third United States Colored Heavy Artillery (USCHA) complained in a letter to War Secretary Edwin Stanton that he and the Black southerners "have had to toil day and night." The sergeant closed by touching on the problem of pay and excessive labor, stating, "We Shall be Satisfied" with "as much [pay] as White Soldiers" and soldiering "on the field of Battle."[76] In South Carolina, a captain concerned that his men had to complete too much hard labor explained similarly that "perform[ing] the work of menials" might injure "the self-respect and discipline of the negroes."[77] As this officer noted, Black soldiers found the laboring undignified and would prefer to be on the battlefield.

Private Aleck Williams proved them correct. An enslaved North Carolinian who enlisted in the First North Carolina (Colored) Infantry (later the Thirty-Fifth USCI), Williams had served in the army faithfully for nearly nine months. But, after weeks of digging earth, he fumed when a white lieutenant ordered him to keep working. The private shouted back, "I will not go another God damned inch." He then raised a stick and seized the lieutenant by the throat. Williams was ready to strike, but fellow soldiers restrained him before he could land a blow. Although he had served without incident for nearly a year, his actions signaled his growing anger during onerous labor under a white officer.[78]

For soldiers like Medal of Honor recipient Sergeant Major Christian Fleetwood of the Fourth USCI, such treatment undermined the important contributions military service provided. In June 1865, the freeborn Baltimorean candidly wrote of contempt for the army after being denied an officer's commission. "I see no good that will result to our people by continuing to serve," he penned. He went on to acknowledge the army's role in ending slavery and protecting the nation, yet experiences convinced him that other means of elevation were necessary. "It strikes me," he added, "that more could be done for our welfare in the pursuits of civil life." Like white soldiers tired of the war, he may have been looking forward to antebellum pursuits even as he sought a commission. Yet, even if his thoughts reflected an interest in resuming civilian routines, Fleetwood specifically believed that racial prejudice limited the liberation and uplift opportunities for Black men in the US Army. "No matter how well and faithfully they may perform their duties," he wrote, Black soldiers "will shortly be considered as 'lazy n—— sojers'—as drones in the great hive." This battle-hardened soldier concluded that Black men had—and would remain—disparaged and consigned to menial chores.[79] Initially, he had anticipated that the army would support his hopes. Whether he should have had such aspirations or not, he was disappointed after suffering indignities similar to those he endured before the war.

Violent discipline and the inglorious work of war did not offset the successes of the USCT or the significance of military service to Black men's liberation. Looking to the future and grasping that the Confederates posed the gravest danger, Black men from North and South fought and succeeded on the battlefield. In 1863 alone, they had, in the words of Major General Ulysses S. Grant, "behaved well" in combat.[80] The same could be said for Black soldiers' service overall. They mostly abided by army regulations, followed officers' commands, and, in so doing, established a war record that attested to their valor. During and after the war, many recognized the magnitude of their service, touted it, and with their accolades and sacrifices in hand, gained rights previously denied.[81]

But war heroes like Fleetwood also criticized the US Army and exposed the tension roiling the USCT throughout the war. They observed the challenges faced within the ranks and questioned the ultimate value of military service to uplift. Yet, while some spoke up, others acted. Black northerners protested democratically, condemning treatment in papers or on the public pulpit. For their part, Black southerners turned to tactics developed to ameliorate lives in bondage and widely used in the decade preceding the war. Rather than lift their voices, they raised their feet.

3

"No Intention of Deserting": Escaping Camp and Taking Leaves of Freedom

"MY INTENTIONS WERE to go up town and See my relations," Private Napoleon Bonaparte explained after leaving camp without permission. Escaping bondage in Jefferson County, Mississippi, the twenty-two-year-old carpenter chose to pursue a more suitable career for a man with such a name. On August 1, 1863, he enlisted in the Ninth Louisiana Infantry (African Descent) (and later served in the Fifth United States Colored Heavy Artillery or USCHA). But just ten days later, he decamped at Vicksburg. He did not mean to leave the regiment altogether, he clarified to his superiors. He departed with the plan to "come back." Corroborating his explanation, he said, "I left all my things in camp."[1] Bonaparte had traveled home because he wished to preserve a relationship with his family even after enlisting. Although military service was a job that traditionally subsumed autonomy in favor of order and discipline, he treated soldiering as empowering. He saw no issue with exercising his independence and visiting kin before returning to duty.[2]

Enlisted freedom seekers who decamped acted much like Bonaparte throughout their service in the US Army. By war's end, the US government calculated that 12,440 of the 178,975 Black men in the United States Colored Troops (USCT) had deserted. The rate of desertion within the USCT was, therefore, 7 percent. This was lower than the rate of desertion among white soldiers in either the US Army or Confederate Army, which was between 10 and 15 percent.[3] Those formerly enslaved soldiers who left offered many of the same reasons as freeborn soldiers in Union and Rebel forces: they returned home to help family, recuperate from injuries and ailments, and escape unjust officers. Not unlike fellow Civil War soldiers, Black southerners justified decisions to leave based upon their understanding of service, views on

Freedom Soldiers. Jonathan Lande, Oxford University Press. © Oxford University Press 2024.
DOI: 10.1093/oso/9780197531754.003.0004

government policies, and personal independence. For them, though, mobility had an additional meaning. During slavery, flight was a political tool. They had ameliorated conditions, softened unremitting labor demands, and evaded cruel overseers by absconding. Although their flight was deemed criminal by the US Army, Black soldiers from the South did not see such actions as unsoldierly. Accustomed to negotiating labor conditions with their feet, men like Bonaparte expressed their views regarding jobs as soldiers and continued their march out of slavery by taking these self-granted breaks—or leaves of freedom. Their flight from service reflected their ongoing effort to negotiate the terms of military service and move further from their prewar lives in southern bondage.

"The Right to Quit": Decamping the US Army

Flight by disgruntled soldiers was hardly new during the Civil War. From the beginning of the republic, colonists liberated from the British yoke and newly minted US citizens had chafed under military discipline and run. Rank-and-file soldiers of the Regular Army had left camp when they grew tired of drill or fatigue duty. In 1825, after the nation settled its last war with the British, War Secretary James Barbour declared that "desertion" was "a serious evil." From 1815 to 1860, the working-class northerners and immigrants who predominantly filled the Regular Army left for a host of reasons related to labor conditions. They ran when rations were meager, shelter inferior, or pay paltry. War Department officials determined that desertion rates from 1820 to 1860 hovered around 15 percent.[4]

When the Civil War broke out, each side created volunteer forces, attracting men from a range of backgrounds. Entering the ranks were elites of Boston and Charleston, students of Providence, Cambridge, and New Haven, and mechanics, stevedores, and butchers from Richmond, Baltimore, and Chicago. Despite their choice to fight, the soldiers left in sizable numbers. By war's end, up to 120,000 Rebels decamped, and about 300,000 Federals did the same. Since there were approximately one million Rebels, about 10-12 percent deserted, and as there were approximately two million Federals, about 14-15 percent did. (These numbers do not account for those who took leaves without permission but were not recorded as deserters.)[5] As it had for the peacetime force, then, desertion posed a problem for the Civil War armies.

Most freeborn deserters left because they saw themselves as self-governing citizen-soldiers. As civilians making sacrifices for the state, white volunteers believed they could leave when the government failed to uphold its side of the social contract. Noting the consequences of democracy on the military character of Americans, the perceptive French visitor Alexis de Tocqueville observed in 1835 that "soldiers of a democratic army... do not consider themselves as seriously engaged in the military profession and are always thinking of quitting it." While they may "adapt to military duties," he added, "their minds are still attached to the interests and duties that engaged them in civil life." As de Tocqueville understood, soldiers in a democratic army—even after volunteering and being conditioned in the duties of service—sustained a spirit of self-governance. They continuously weighed when it was appropriate (if not necessary) to end their service. In their calculations, such volunteers factored in the direction of the war, the policies guiding their governments, and their responsibilities at home.[6]

In 1861, although the ardor for war and obligation to protect the state swelled in men's breasts North and South, soldiers retained their democratic sensibilities. When the war opened, Americans accustomed to civilian life lacked an understanding of the military as a profession, which contributed to their inclination to desert. The men felt free to come and go as they pleased. As the war progressed, men adjusted to military life, but their mentality did not change. They continued deserting. The ideological grounding of desertion does not mean that all men of a specific circumstance deserted, all left for the same reasons, or all meditated over political theory before decamping. Rather, the soldiers' desertions were triggered by policy changes, difficulties at home, and conditions in camp. Believing in their bones that the war must not deviate from the cause for which they had enlisted, soldiers remained resolute and served as long as the war stayed on course. If there was a change in policy, some thought it appropriate to desert. Others thought the state had a duty to provide supplies for families. When the state failed to do so, soldiers returned home to help plow the fields and feed the children. Likewise, as food, clothing, or bullets became scarce or men felt unjustly treated, they packed up. Regardless of their reasons, the conviction that they could leave at will emerged from a democrat's skepticism.[7]

Black northerners decamped for similar reasons, though their unique motives for enlistment influenced their decisions. Although Black northern men and women had been denied key aspects of citizenship or were barred from participating fully within the body politic, they had incorporated the prevailing democratic traditions into their daily lives and political activism since at least the 1820s. Editors of *Freedom's Journal* Samuel Cornish and John Russwurm had used newspapers to protest segregation, and leaders such as Martin Delany had denounced inequalities publicly. During the war, free

Black northerners likewise demanded equality and pressed for first-class citizenship.[8] Those who volunteered for the US Army carried the tradition into the ranks.

Black soldiers from the North challenged injustices democratically. They wrote letters describing the ways they were wronged to newspapers like the *Weekly Anglo-African* and *Christian Recorder*. They refused segregated accommodations on public transit. When the government failed to pay them the same as white soldiers, they wrote letters to officials and railed against inequality and broken promises.[9] For instance, James Henry Gooding, the New Bedford mariner serving in the Fifty-Fourth Massachusetts Infantry, penned a letter to President Abraham Lincoln, stating that men from the North had stepped up and "dyed the ground with blood, in defense of the Union, and Democracy" before asking the president to pay them as promised.[10] When appeals went unanswered, Black northerners rallied together and demanded to be paid justly, leading to open dissent in camp. Black protesters showed the same views as white citizen-soldiers regarding expectations of service and a willingness to act on those convictions.[11]

When letters and protests failed to remedy injustices, Black northerners demanded their release from service. In a joint letter to Lincoln, for example, seventy-four members of the Fifty-Fifth Massachusetts Infantry stressed that "money is no object," as they had enlisted and "Left our Homes our Famileys Friends & Relatives" to "fight For Liberty justice & Equality," but after months of being offered pay "not acording to [the terms of] our enlistment," they deserved release. "[W]e Deem these sufficient Reasons for," they said, "our imediate Discharge Having Been enlisted under False Prentence." Although the men had not decamped, they insisted they should be legally permitted to leave. Since the civic and legal bond between them and the government had been broken, they thought that they should no longer be held in the ranks.[12]

Going a step further, Ohioan William Joseph Nelson acted on these beliefs by decamping. He articulated his reasons by drawing on conceptions of individual rights. During his incarceration for desertion, Nelson wrote to Lincoln explaining his reasons for deserting and why he should be pardoned. A charlatan, Nelson wrote, persuaded him to join by offering a two-hundred-dollar bounty, but then "made me drunk and sold me to another man for a substitute." Nelson then told Lincoln that he had not received "any money atall." The Ohioan told the president that he had refused when the army "tried to make me be mustered in as a substitute." Ultimately, Nelson said he had "bin ronged out of my Writes," unjustly enlisted, and should be permitted to leave. He was not alone in this thinking either. When he described the circumstances of his enlistment to his comrades, they agreed that he could return home. The "soldiers told me that I Was right and they could not hold me," Nelson wrote. Showing their support, he added, "the guards let me out of the camp." Nelson's explanation and his peers' encouragement show that, when conjoined with Black northerners' democratic political methods, Black soldiers raised in the North felt that decamping was an appropriate response when they were "ronged out of... Writes."[13]

Black southerners decamped as well, but unlike their counterparts from the North, they considered flight a tool for ameliorating unacceptable working conditions. Many Black southerners volunteered to demonstrate their allegiance to the US government, and they withdrew their loyalty in protest or to express fealty to family over country by leaving.[14] Yet service was about more than their political relationship to the state. Military service was employment that helped them attain liberation, as the enslaved Virginian Tom clarified to a *New York Tribune* reporter. "We mean to sell ourselves for freedom—we hope to you Northern men," but "if your politicians and Generals kick us away," Tom explained, "we will try to make our market with rebels."[15] Although no elected spokesperson for Black southerners, Tom stated in no uncertain terms that the objective impelling men to join was the pursuit of freedom. Their drive to be free made them arguably the most motivated soldiers of the war. But this was a double-edged sword. If freedom was jeopardized within the US Army, such fighters' ambition could lead these freed laborers to boldly agitate. To push back against objectionable restraints or treatment, they turned to various tactics of resistance, such as strikes, rebellions, and most commonly, flight.[16]

Lincoln appreciated the soldiers' motivations and why they might run. Noting that the primary incentive for Black southerners to enlist was freedom, he refused to renege on emancipation because, he believed, they would quit the army if they thought their liberty imperiled. "Negroes, like other people, act upon motives," he announced. "If they stake their lives for us they must be prompted by the strongest motive—even the promise of freedom." He added that "to join in re-enslaving those who shall have served us in consideration of our promise... would ruin the Union cause itself. All recruiting of colored men would instantly cease, and all colored men now in our service would instantly desert us."[17] As his position made clear, Lincoln understood that Black southerners would decamp to secure freedom.

White soldiers in the field witnessed firsthand how the enslaved saw military service. They recognized that some enlisted freedom seekers treated military service as an opportunity to exercise freedom. Arriving in Milliken's

Bend, Captain James Harvey Greene of the Eighth Wisconsin Infantry encountered nine regiments of Black soldiers raised in Louisiana, Mississippi, and Arkansas, and he acknowledged how their prior enslavement influenced their views on service. "It is difficult to get them to forget old habits of servility," he said, and noted that the men habitually "say Marse, instead of Colonel or Captain." Their difficulties adjusting to military life could be more serious, though. "Desertion is a too common evil amongst them," Greene remarked. They "do not seem to realize the enormity of the crime." But, as Greene soon discovered, they did not see desertion as a crime at all. "Many of their families are living in camps of contrabands, or on plantations in the neighborhood of their own camp," Greene wrote, "and they imagine that as they are free men they have the right to quit their duties and visit them whenever they please." Upon reflection, Greene construed that they placed their actions squarely within the emancipatory state of military service: "Their ideas of freedom are exag[g]erated, and some of them no doubt think that a soldier is the freest of all free men." Greene realized that military service itself gave rise to the soldiers' views on flight from the army. By contrast to white soldiers, who likely anticipated military service as constraining, Black southerners treated enlistment as empowering and thought they could quit in protest to unjust constraints.[18]

The men's leaves were not sanctioned, making them distinct from furloughs, yet to the soldiers, their leaves were also not criminal. The formerly enslaved men took such leaves to assert power over their lives and labor, making their unauthorized leaves "leaves of freedom." Although the term was not used at the time, it underscores three critical facets of soldiers' overlapping exodus from slavery in the service. First, rejecting the concept of desertion, which denoted wrongdoing and depended on a civic bargain between soldiers and the US government that remained for enslaved men ambiguous at best, these leaves emphasized the soldiers' commitment to the ongoing process of emancipation. Second, the phrase accounts for the military aspect of the soldiers' departures. Like "leaves of absence" that exempted men from military duties, leaves of freedom excused them from soldiering temporarily. But whereas furloughs or leaves of absence were sanctioned, formerly enslaved soldiers issued leaves of freedom themselves. Third, much like leaves of absence, leaves of freedom entailed traveling. Like enslaved southerners before and during the war, formerly enslaved men approached mobility as a means of controlling their bodies, resisting spatial restrictions, and seeking out liberation.[19]

In addition to the utility of the term, the term "leaves of freedom" also recognizes how emancipation remained unsettled within the army. The men's

FIGURE 3.1 This set of images created during the war reveals the transition of an enslaved man from labor in the fields to labor in the US Army. The images begin with work, continue with the enslaved man resisting his oppressor, and then fleeing to join the ranks. Many enslaved southerners took a similar path into the ranks. For them, flight from bondage remained an integral part of the enslaved men's journey. It would not have been easily forgotten—even as they served in regiments of the United States Colored Troops. James Fuller Queen, "Journey of a Slave from the Plantation to the Battlefield," 1863. Library of Congress, LC-USZC4-6677.

actions were part of a broader process of liberation that did not conform to a single linear trajectory of slavery-to-freedom. By leaving, soldiers attempted to shape military service—which was for nearly all their first job as free men. To ensure they pursued liberation even as they served within the US Army, they took leaves of freedom.

"Come and Go as They Pleased": Taking Leaves of Freedom in 1863

Freedoms attained through mobility fundamentally conflicted with the discipline necessary for being a dutiful soldier, making for a unique process of emancipation for formerly enslaved soldiers. To be sure, freedom seekers in Union blue learned how to participate in combat and follow orders. But they sought to achieve their bondage-born dreams of freedom, too, and fled the army for breaks in 1863. Not unlike white soldiers in late 1861, they anticipated returning after short visits home. Yet they ran to escape restraints common within bondage and to secure opportunities not afforded during slavery while white men left to reclaim freedoms they had grown accustomed to as civilians before the war. Many Black southerners who chose to decamp navigated strict discipline and officers determined to repress individualism. They fought off rampant diseases that hounded Black refugees throughout the conflict. They strengthened familial ties after decades of forced migration. In taking their leaves, they demonstrated a commitment to freedoms such as the power to care for their health, work without the threat of violence, exercise choice over their employers, and provide for kin.

One of the earliest efforts to arm enslaved men foundered because the US Army failed, in part, to respect the men's pursuit of freedom. On April 3, 1862, Major General David Hunter asked the Lincoln administration if he could arm the enslaved men of South Carolina's Sea Islands. The administration never responded, but the general proceeded to form the "First Contraband Regiment" anyhow. He began gathering men in May.[20] Whether the men wanted to or not, Hunter forced them to join the army because, he thought, "the discipline of military life will be the safest and quickest school... [for] these enfranchised bondsmen." The general also believed that the "enrollment [of enslaved men] in regular military organization" would give "a legitimate vent to their natural desire to prove themselves worthy of freedom" while making them "less likely [to engage in] ... servile insurrection."[21] Hunter's reformist approach did not endear him to Sea Islanders, many of whom did not want to abandon their families. One woman reformer reported her fruitless effort "to inspire a desire to fight," stating that "none will volunteer to leave their homes."[22] Making matters worse, when too few men volunteered, Hunter ordered a round-up of men ages eighteen to fifty from Beaufort to Hilton Head.[23] The Sea Islanders despised the draft, creating lingering problems for Hunter and future commanders. One such commander reflected on the problems Hunter created. "Squads of soldiers were sent to seize all the able-bodied men on certain plantations, and bring them to camp,"

Thomas Wentworth Higginson wrote. The "immediate consequence was a renewal of the old suspicion . . . that they were to be sent to Cuba, as their masters had predicted. The ultimate result," Higginson added, "was a habit of distrust, discontent, and desertion."[24] This disposition, Higginson observed, led impressed soldiers to flee camp constantly and generally deepened their wariness of the US Army. When Lincoln disbanded Hunter's unauthorized regiment and the soldiers returned home without pay, they had not forgotten their time in the First Contraband Regiment.[25]

In late 1862, Brigadier General Rufus Saxton revived the project to arm Sea Islanders, but to his frustration, the formerly enslaved men kept leaving. The general promised not to impress men and hired Black southerners to recruit volunteers.[26] Formerly enslaved southerners remained disenchanted, however. A reformer from the North helping to facilitate cotton production noted, "I think it will be difficult to induce men to enlist." He pointed to Hunter's abortive scheme as the cause. "Their treatment in the spring and summer was such as to prejudice them against military duty under any circumstances. They were forcibly impressed, were ill-treated by at least one officer, . . . [and] have never been paid a cent; they suffered from the change of diet, and quite as much from homesickness." These factors led soldiers to decamp.[27] After becoming colonel of the First South Carolina (Colored) Infantry (later the Thirty-Third United States Colored Infantry or USCI), Higginson suggested that the problems had subsided in January 1863. "I found a good deal of anxiety among officers as to the increase of desertions, that being the rock on which the 'Hunter Regiment' split," the colonel reflected in his diary. "Now this evil is very nearly stopped, and we are every day recovering the older absentees."[28] His diary entry proved too upbeat.

Men left as the year wore on. For instance, Private Robert Simmons, an enslaved laborer from Beaufort, joined Higginson's regiment on November 2, 1862. He left Camp Saxton in Port Royal, South Carolina, in March 1863, remaining on the lam until April 1864. After his conviction by a court-martial, he was sent to a military prison in Georgia. In April 1865, he returned to duty until he was mustered out in January 1866.[29] Meanwhile, Simmons's comrade, Private James Brown, exited the regiment not once but twice before the end of his first year of service. The eighteen-year-old field hand enlisted on April 23, 1863, and decamped on August 2. Arrested on October 1, he returned to duty shortly after. On November 1, he left again, not returning until March the following year and remained in the army until he was mustered out in January 1866.[30]

Although Higginson declined to acknowledge the ongoing issue in his diary, he and his fellow commanders took actions to recover absentees who had returned home to farm and care for their families.[31] During a trip to South Carolina in May 1863, Lincoln's personal secretary John Hay followed Saxton to farms under military control and listened to formerly enslaved "women begging for their relations to be discharged from the army." Black southern women frequently found themselves lacking resources during their own difficult journeys to freedom. They also often had to care for children without support after their male kinfolk had enlisted. When wartime conditions grew especially taxing, women like those Hay overheard demanded the state provide means of subsistence or release their husbands, fathers, sons, or brothers from their military duties. As Hay learned, other women directly called on the soldiers to furnish aid—even if it meant leaving without permission.[32] The secretary reported soldiers "were out looking for deserters" who had already returned home, suggesting that the men did not wait for their commanders to release them from army responsibilities.[33] Colonel James Montgomery of the Second South Carolina (Colored) Infantry (later the Thirty-Fourth USCI) faced similar problems when his regiment returned from a mission in June. Formed in May 1863 from men of the Sea Islands, the Second South Carolina resembled Higginson's regiment. Like Higginson, Montgomery, a veteran of the war over slavery in Kansas, dealt with soldiers who took leaves of freedom. His soldiers, a fellow officer wrote, "being near their homes have deserted rapidly." In two days, the officer remarked, Montgomery "lost seventy men by desertion." To stymie their flight, Montgomery "sent word by their wives & others to the deserters that those who returned of their own free will should be pardoned—[and] that those, whom he caught, he would shoot."[34] Higginson, meanwhile, formed search parties, which ventured to farms cultivating the famous Sea Island produce to root out absentees. The raiders secured three men on one occasion, and another raiding party returned for more. Pursuits became quite intrusive, a reformer operating a farm said, and eventually the search for deserters interrupted the cotton ginning. "The holidays and the hunt for deserters have so broken up the labor that nothing of any consequence can be done now till after New Year's, when I hope the work will move on more smoothly," the reformer lamented.[35] These Carolina absentees reveal that, rather than only serve in the army to defend their freedom, some Black southerners were eager to also quietly work the earth closer to home.[36]

Officers in the Eastern Theater were not alone in coping with soldiers returning home. USCT officers in the Western Theater quickly learned that the once-enslaved hoped to retain many of the liberties they recently won—even as they served. On March 25, 1863, War Secretary Edwin Stanton sent Adjutant General Lorenzo Thomas to the Union-occupied territory along the Mississippi River to enlist formerly enslaved men and reestablish agricultural production. Thomas recruited refugees from Mississippi, Tennessee, Louisiana, Alabama, and Arkansas. Thomas looked for officers among the regiments of white midwesterners, and he avoided any "whose hearts were not fully in the work." On May 5, 1863, following Thomas's crusade, the US Army created the Eighth Louisiana Infantry (African Descent) (later the Forty-Seventh USCI) and promoted Captain William Parkinson to help lead the regiment. Parkinson and the regiment's other officers quickly discovered that the enlisted men thought it perfectly acceptable to wander in and out of camp. Remarking on their view of service in Lake Providence, Louisiana, Parkinson reported that the men were "very ignorant, and they expected too much." He explained that the soldiers "thought they would be perfectly free when they became soldiers." They even believed they "could almost quit soldiering whenever they got tired of it, & could come and go as they pleased." Parkinson and fellow officers found it "hard to make them understand that they are bound to stay and soldier until discharged." Just as Higginson had in South Carolina, Parkinson was pleased with the officers' progress in "gradually letting them know" the meaning of duty, but his boasts proved premature too.[37]

When a formerly enslaved soldier fell ill, for example, he thought himself free to leave the army to recover. Sergeant Henry Hall joined the Eighth Louisiana regiment at its formation at Lake Providence on May 5, 1863, and was moved with his regiment to Milliken's Bend where he became ill. "I was very sick and unable to do duty," he later explained. An army physician provided him an excuse from duty, but his health did not improve. "I went to the Doctor pretty much every day while I was there sick," Hall said. "I saw," he continued,

> that I was getting worse and I asked the Doctor if I couldn't get a furlough home till I got well and could come back to my comp again. He then asked me what I wanted to go home for—if I had not as soon die in the Regiment as to die at home.

Although likely unamused by the physician's grim remark, Hall remained in camp. He took a turn for the worse, however.

> On the fourth [of July] I was out on picket about a mile or so from camp. I stayed until I was relieved at my post. The next day was Sunday. In the morning I was taken very sick and remained very sick until Monday night, when I started for home. I didn't leave when I was on duty, because I thought it wasn't right that I should. Monday night I started for home. I thought I should not live, and I would try to get home before I died.

Despite his bleak self-prognosis, Hall hoped that he might recuperate at home. He insisted that he "intended to come back" if he regained his strength. When he did, he explained to army authorities, he was as "anxious to get back to my regiment as I was to leave." Rather than being rewarded for this, he faced a court-martial for desertion and was imprisoned for a year after his conviction. But, to Hall, the act was not criminal. It also did not reflect waning faith in the army.[38]

Hall's experience with illness had already become a common experience among Civil War soldiers and continued to plague those within the USCT. As new recruits amassed in the close quarters of camps, they were subjected to new diseases. In the early months of service, white men, especially those coming from rural areas where they had not been exposed to large populations, fell ill to diseases that frequently take root in towns and cities. Companies decreased in size even before meeting the enemy.[39] Black southerners experienced many of the same health difficulties as their white peers, though they faced added challenges. Observing the results of slavery, the War Department concluded that "the negro, in condition in which the war found him, was less able than the white to endure the exposures and annoyances of military service." For this reason, US government officials concluded, they were "constantly upon the sick-list." Black soldiers who fell ill could remain in camp to receive medical attention from the US Army, but they were unfamiliar with military medicine.[40] As one relief agent treating Black soldiers wrote, "It is a difficult task to take care of them as they are so childish" and "seldom use the word 'pain,'" choosing "misery" instead.[41] Rather than visit hospitals, some Black southerners decided to leave.

The departure of sick soldiers reflected prewar medical practices. Most were accustomed to being tended to by family members, not professional doctors in hospitals. White soldiers decamped briefly, often practicing self-care or regaining their strength under more trusted care and, once recuperated, returned to camp.[42] Black soldiers, especially the formerly enslaved, often made the same choices, including Private Hall. After he was convicted for desertion, he served his six-month sentence without pay in the regimental guardhouse and then resumed duty. He rose again to the rank of sergeant, and on March 5, 1864, participated in a skirmish at Yazoo City. His service record reveals that he spoke honestly when he detailed his early bout with disease. He never meant to quit the army and, once he regained his health, willingly fulfilled his duties.[43]

To formerly enslaved men, medicinal care was part and parcel of their freedom seeking. They considered power over their own care as a means of claiming autonomy because, during bondage, they had distrusted the white doctors that their enslavers hired. Flaunting the Hippocratic oath, these white physicians had prioritized enslavers' demands, not patients' health, and often treated Black men, women, and children as laboring chattel, not humans. As a result, some sick Black southerners opted to be cared for by Black women at home. Enslaved southerners also resisted excessive discipline during bondage and temporarily avoided the burden of unceasing toil by faking a stomachache or other illnesses. Upon entering the Union ranks, freedom seekers continued these practices.[44]

Appointed an assistant surgeon for the Fifty-Fifth Massachusetts Infantry on May 22, 1863, Burt Wilder learned all too well of Black southerners' tactics to secure greater autonomy. Wilder earnestly attended to the health of the regiment, but he grew cynical when Black soldiers feigned illness. Within months of enlistment, Wilder obsessed over whether the soldiers faked symptoms. To ensure the men put in an honest day's work, Wilder interrogated those claiming to be ill. He noted in his diary, for instance, that "200 reported themselves sick" until he "cut down the excused to 140." Afterward, he lectured them about lying. "It was a good occasion," he remarked in his diary, "for a short but severe address to them on the folly and wickedness of such deception, wronging their comrades and me and their country." Wilder framed their actions as a betrayal, and he thought they received the message, adding that "the good effect of my words was apparent in the demeanor and language of those who came to me afterward for advice and medicine." But the lecture did not stop the phenomenon. "One would like to begin the day pleasantly," he moaned, "but among the 150 to 175 men who report for treatment or excuse from duty are always a few whom I have reason to suspect of malingering; the effort to detect frauds irritates me and sometimes, probably, renders me unjust to the really ill." To detect deceit, Wilder grilled the soldiers individually. In one case, men from Companies F and H declared themselves unfit for nearly a week "by reason of swollen abdomens." Wilder "chloroformed one of them as if preparatory to opening his abdomen to let out water," but, the physician wrote in disbelief, when his bluffing failed, the soldier "still he did not yield." A week later, the surgeon exclaimed in exasperation, "An army doctor should have a lawyer by his elbow" to deal with soldiers' fraudulence. Wilder's suspicions may have signaled his racist beliefs that Black men were duplicitous, but his experiences demonstrate the extent to which soldiers went to either report their ailments truthfully or to feign illnesses to evade excessive labor.[45] In either case, the men communicated that they should not be forced to work against their will.

In addition to retreating home for their own care, Black southerners like Sergeant Richard Johnson took leaves of freedom within the first year of service because they needed to help ill family members. Born in Mississippi, Johnson was a cotton sampler in Baton Rouge before enlisting on October 27, 1863. He was mustered into the Eighteenth Corps d'Afrique Infantry (later the Ninetieth USCI) and served faithfully through December. Like white soldiers, he requested a furlough in hopes of seeing his family.[46] Perhaps eager to spend Christmas with his mother, Johnson traveled home on a seven-day furlough. But for "ten days after reaching Baton Rouge he was confined to the house and his bed" battling for his health. Just as he recuperated, he said his "mother was very sick," and rather than desert her—and despite his furlough expiring New Year's Eve Day—he later said, "I waited." He remained home until mid-month, likely tending to his mother. On January 15, when he "was about to return to my Regiment," he said, "I was arrested as a deserter." Johnson did not perceive his decision to remain home to care for himself and then nurse his mother as unacceptable or transgressions of army regulations. His officers disagreed. They placed him on trial for desertion, and a court-martial convicted him. The officers of the court-martial sentenced him to be shot, but his luck slightly improved. The army held him in the New Orleans city jail until his transfer to the military prison at Fort Jefferson on September 22, 1864. Neither prison records nor his service record mention his fate after his admission to the prison, but it seems he was saved from the executioner.[47]

As Black soldiers experienced their first year of service, they defined for themselves what an acceptable act by free men looked like. If aspects of the freedom they envisioned were not supported by their military superiors, some thought they could just as easily leave for short or open-ended breaks as stay. The officers labeled these men deserters, but the freedom seekers saw their actions as efforts to assert control over themselves within the military.

"Absent from Camp Regardless of Regulations": Taking Leaves of Freedom in 1864 and 1865

By mid-1864, Black southerners who joined shortly after Lincoln issued the Emancipation Proclamation had had a year or more to grasp army regulations and camp customs. Many had experienced grueling, often dispiriting aspects of military service, such as combat and fatigue duty. Yet, even after enduring these tests of service, Black southerners continued decamping. Unlike white soldiers who deserted for a host of reasons in 1864 and 1865, including disagreement with government policies, waning morale, and battlefield setbacks, formerly enslaved soldiers remained consistent, choosing to leave for many of the same reasons they left in 1863. Flight among Black southerners in the USCT therefore remained a means of continuing their march out of slavery. Taking leaves of freedom, they claimed opportunities that had been denied to them before enlistment, such as helping family, and evaded coercion and disrespect.

In 1864, even after they had learned the rules and battled Rebels, many enlisted freedom seekers still approached military service as if it permitted them to leave camp as they wished. Thomas Knox, the *New York Herald* correspondent reporting on USCT regiments along the Mississippi River, incorrectly concluded that the soldiers left because they were ignorant of the rules. "It was difficult to make them understand they were doing wrong," Knox believed. "Army regulations and the intricacies of military law were unknown to them," he wrote. "None of them know what 'desertion' meant, nor the duties of a soldier to adhere to his flag at all times." Offering a solution, Knox argued that the army needed to teach formerly enslaved men "the wickedness of desertion, or absence without leave." Ignoring the men's efforts to negotiate the terms of service, Knox thought the soldiers acted out of ignorance. But enlisted freedom seekers understood. As Private Spencer Watson, a formerly enslaved Georgian who enlisted in the Fifth USCHA at Vicksburg, admitted, "I know I was doing wrong in going away without leave but had no intention, whatever, of deserting." The soldiers had clearly articulated their view that they could leave and did not necessarily think of it as desertion. After the first year of service, they still thought—even after having participated in combat—they could leave.[48]

Certain soldiers of the First Corps d'Afrique Infantry (later the Seventy-Third USCI) put a point on Black southerners' sentiments regarding flight in 1864, both by continuing to take leaves of freedom and decrying the army's efforts to track down freedom seekers. On May 27, 1863, the First Corps d'Afrique had performed well at the Battle of Port Hudson, a strategic position on the Mississippi River that would aid efforts to take Vicksburg. Although their attack ended in retreat, the soldiers demonstrated bravery. But men of the First Corps d'Afrique did not translate battlefield feats into a blind commitment to regulations. By the end of 1863, the regiment was losing soldiers. The men decamped for the same reasons they had before. Summing up the motivations, a commanding officer concluded that they left because they had been ordered to labor on fortifications, had not received pay and equipment as promised, and "are not able to maintain their families."[49] In addition to these reasons, soldiers including Privates Joseph Norbert and Anthony Primbow decamped when illness laid them low. In September 1863, Norbert left due to rheumatism. Several months later, Primbow escaped the army hospital in New Orleans and returned home to the care of his mother. The problem of desertion in the regiment became so grave by the summer of 1864 that officers assigned soldiers to hunt down the wayward men, leading to a confrontation over the legitimacy of desertion.[50]

On July 4, 1864, a Black sergeant called Lionel Macarty condemned the efforts to capture those who left, making plain that he thought the men had the right to leave. Having enrolled the previous August in New Orleans, Macarty had spent over a year serving faithfully. He did not, however, hesitate to articulate concerns with the army's policy toward fleeing soldiers. During a visit to the laundress on Independence Day, Macarty raged against their persecution when he encountered Sergeant Major John Cage, a Black Mississippian who joined in September 1862. Cage was gathering his clothes before traveling to New Orleans to root out suspected USCT deserters on orders from Lieutenant Colonel Henry Merriam. Macarty cursed and threatened Cage for accepting the mission. Sergeant Armand Leblanc witnessed Macarty's outrage and recounted the incident. "I wouldn't go if I was in your place," Macarty reportedly admonished Cage, "because you know the men suffer and never had furloughs to go home. They get bad treatment. You ought not to do it." Cage defended his actions, revealing disagreement among USCT soldiers. He told Macarty he would follow orders and capture the men. Incensed, Macarty browbeat Cage. "You ought to protect your own color," Macarty retorted, "and not see them punished." His indignation reveals that Macarty, even after a year of military service, still thought it fine for his comrades to return home.[51]

For his outburst, Macarty was charged with mutiny, but even after facing reprimand within the military justice system, he would not relinquish his beliefs about the so-called crimes of desertion and absence without leave.

During his court-martial, he reiterated that he thought it unjust that the men be arrested for leaving. He explained the circumstances of the men's departures. He flatly stated that "after months of hard laboring through the swamps and woods," the army "took away the rations" that the soldiers "had [to] give to our families," a move that left kin "in a complete state of starvation without support." The men's families were "driven away from their houses they had rent[ed] on account [that] they couldn pay their rent." Many families lacked "shoes" and "bread," he added with details gesturing to the travails Black women and children endured across the South. Macarty believed the men were justified in leaving to help kin living under such conditions. The court-martial convicted Macarty and sent him to the military prison at Fort Jefferson on November 26, 1864. Despite his incarceration for his outspokenness (and not even for taking such a leave himself), Macarty neither recanted nor felt remorse. Instead, in a letter from prison, Macarty reiterated his position yet again. After a month of incarceration, he asked for release. "I am not guilty of any offense," he wrote to Brigadier General Daniel Ullman. Macarty's letter demonstrates that he still believed his condemnation of Cage correct and his comrades' leaves of freedom appropriate. The December letter went unanswered, and Macarty remained imprisoned until May 1, 1865.[52]

In the East, Black southerners tutored in military discipline and practiced in war flouted spatial restrictions as well. After Colonel Montgomery of the Second South Carolina had issued a warning that he would shoot deserters and carried out his threat once, a fellow white officer reported that Montgomery had disabused his men of their wanderlust. "Since the execution not one has gone," Colonel Robert Gould Shaw of the Fifty-Fourth Massachusetts Infantry wrote. Moreover, he added, "thirty or forty have secretly returned in the night." Some authorities questioned such severe methods, but others thought Montgomery's leadership contributed to the regiment's success. The overall "result [of Montgomery's discipline] is extremely beneficial," Shaw concluded.[53] The son of a washerwoman who had joined the Third USCI agreed. Upon meeting Montgomery's men when his regiment arrived in South Carolina, the Black soldier from the North wrote that the Carolina regiment was thriving. The "contrabands" were part of an "exceedingly well drilled regiment and their discipline is almost perfect," he explained in mid-1864. The correspondent thought that their "habit...of deserting...to their families" had ended. But the assessment of Montgomery's discipline by Shaw and the correspondent proved wrong. A month after the soldier's letter went into print, Private Hardtime White decamped, and in late 1864 and 1865, Privates Charles Adams, Hector Fields, Robert Humbert, and Joseph Smith

"No Intention of Deserting" 73

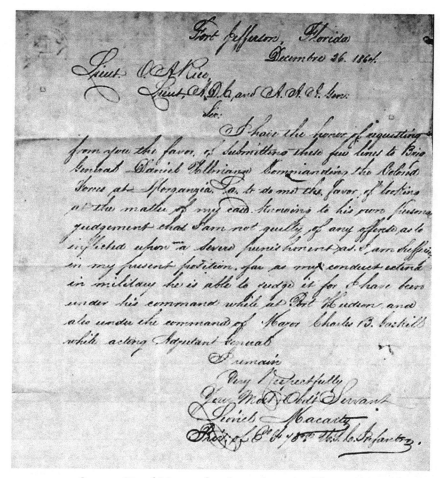

FIGURE 3.2 Sergeant Lionel Macarty fiercely condemned a fellow USCT soldier for hunting for enlisted Black southerners who decamped. Although convicted by a court-martial for berating the soldier, Macarty penned a letter from prison refuting that he had committed any crime. In the letter, he also affirmed his comrades' right to depart and take leaves of freedom. (Spelling of the soldier's name reflects how Macarty signed his name, which is distinct from how the US Army recorded it in his military record.) Leonel McCarty, Compiled Military Service Record, National Archives, Washington, DC.

followed White out of camp. The continued flight of men in the Second shows that leaving was not the result of lax discipline or untutored men. Some formerly enslaved men were ardent freedom fighters yet also fervent freedom seekers willing to risk their lives to return home as well as kill Confederates.[54]

Black southerners not only left to see family. They also continued decamping when impressed by the US Army. Around the Confederacy, US Army recruiters forced an untold number of formerly enslaved men into the

USCT, much as Hunter had done in 1862. One USCT officer recalled that recruiters "brought into camp hundreds of animals and negroes as spoils" and pressured these "spoils" into the ranks.[55] Crawford Wilcox, a formerly enslaved man born in North Carolina, numbered among them. On an April 1864 day, along a road outside Memphis, Tennessee, two recruiters stopped Wilcox. The Carolinian showed the recruiters a pass, presumably a pass from a US government official permitting the formerly enslaved farmer to labor in some fashion rather than serve. Wilcox then conveyed that he did not want to join. The recruiters snatched the pass, as Wilcox later reported, and "they tore it up and pressed me in. I refused to be mustered and they made me hold up my hand." Ordering Wilcox to raise his right hand to take the oath of service, these recruiters used a technique of impressment that formerly enslaved men around the Confederacy recounted. With the oath recited, Wilcox became a private in the Seventh USCHA against his will.[56] His fight to maintain his freedom had not ended, though.

Wilcox evidently vowed not to allow the recruiters to obstruct his journey toward liberation. He already had braved death to flee bondage, as many Black men and women in the region knew enslavers who captured those who ran might hang freedom seekers.[57] He was now determined to escape the army, despite the risks. In June, while he was on garrison duty at the barracks at Fort Pickering outside Memphis, the chance came. "I left as soon as I could," he later said. Making his convictions plain, he added, "I would just as soon be Shot right away as stay there." He then denied any fear about serving, perhaps anticipating charges of cowardice: "if I can go into a Regiment which I want to," he said, "I will make as a good a Soldier as any one." He swore that he would make a "good" soldier and left, not out of cowardice, but rather because he wanted to self-govern. "If I go into a Regiment I want to choose," he said, mincing no words. If he was denied that right, he said he would accept the consequences—even execution. He eluded authorities for a few months. In July, the army captured him and placed him on trial. The court-martial officers convicted Wilcox as a deserter and sent him to Memphis's Irving Block Prison, a dilapidated penitentiary that housed captured Rebels and convicted Federals.[58] He grew ill and languished for six months. He survived a Rebel raid on the prison, but in December 1864, he succumbed to pneumonia.[59]

Men in the East were also driven into the ranks, and to keep them in camp, commanders sent Black northerners to recapture their formerly enslaved comrades. Private John Lovejoy Murray, a freeborn Michigander serving in the 102nd USCI, recalled the persistent need to chase freedom seekers when they fled the army. In September 1864, he explained in a letter that "we have an

FIGURE 3.3 Following his court-martial trial for desertion, Private Crawford Wilcox entered Irving Block Prison in Memphis, Tennessee. During his trial, he had explained that army recruiters forced him to take the oath of service and thus seized his newly won freedom. Although he testified that he had been impressed, the court-martial officers convicted him and sent him to the dilapidated Irving Block Prison. There, he survived a raid by Rebels yet ultimately died of pneumonia. "Forrest's Raid into Memphis: Rebel Attack on the Irving Prison," *Harper's Weekly*, September 10, 1864. The Miriam and Ira D. Wallach Division of Art, Prints and Photographs: Picture Collection, The New York Public Library Digital Collections.

order to go and cetch Contreba[nd]" because "those who are Drafted ... Run away Into the Swamp to hide from Us." The desperate Black southerners did not have much luck, however, for Murray added, "they cant get away from US" since the cavalry and the Twenty-Seventh USCI "are on the scout for them." The combined forces demonstrate how widespread the problem became and that the army went to significant lengths to ensnare the soldiers. Such missions to capture the men proved effective as well, Murray explained. An October undertaking, for example, succeeded in apprehending seventeen "Deserters and Contreband," many of whom had been "Press[ed] Into the Army." Murray spoke with those caught, and "they Say," the private wrote, that "the Government have no Business with them."[60] Such pronunciations left much to the imagination; however, these Black southerners made clear that they saw their impressment as overreach by the state and ran to regain autonomy.

But even for those who volunteered, military service remained employment with regulations subject to negotiation, as Captain Henry Harrison Brown of the Twenty-Ninth Connecticut (Colored) Infantry learned. Stationed in Virginia in May 1865, Brown reported the difficulties he faced with one delinquent soldier. "He will be obedient till the Devil gets into him again," Brown concluded of the decamping man. This unnamed soldier refused to abide by rules restricting him to camp, exasperating his captain. He "will not learn what an order means till punished for disobeying it," Brown groused. Despite being among the "best appearing and most active men, . . . [who] always keeps his gun and accouterments in good order," Brown added, the soldier "will absent himself from camp and is entirely regardless of time or regulations." He "wanted to go a courting last night and instead of coming to me for a pass," Brown wrote, "he went out on a church-pass" and did not return. Feeling compelled to teach the man and his peers a lesson Brown "reprimanded him before" the company by "put[ting him] on a barrel till Tattoo." The captain figured the lesson might work—but only temporarily. He acknowledged that it would last only "till the Devil gets into him again."[61] Brown recognized the soldier's insistence on being permitted to forge relationships despite regulations and being a good soldier.

As in the Eastern Theater, soldiers fighting farther west took leaves of freedom due to unacceptable conditions in the war's last year. Private Rollin Burgess had been born in Richmond, Virginia, in 1843, but by the time of the war, he lived in Mississippi. Unlike so many of his enslaved compatriots forced to pick cotton in the region, Burgess worked as a carpenter before enlisting in Vicksburg in December 1863. He became a member of the Fourth Mississippi Infantry (African Descent) (later the Sixty-Sixth USCI) and saw over two years of war in the regiment. Serving post duty, the regiment remained in the riverfront city, and Burgess earned a promotion, graduating from private to sergeant on December 15. He served nearly a year as a noncommissioned officer in Company A, but on March 1, 1864, just over a year after volunteering, he was reduced to a private for defying orders. He served without incident until August 1865. On a summer day, he arrived at inspection with a dirty gun. Looking over the men, a lieutenant spotted the state of Burgess's weapon and ordered him to report to the first sergeant to be bucked. Bucking was a common army penalty that used well-placed ropes to immobilize soldiers.[62] Burgess left inspection and, according to a comrade, stormed into company quarters: "He came and pulled off his accouterment and threw them down." Burgess then "told the 1st Sergt. not to put his hands on him" and exclaimed that the officer "talked very disrespectful to me." Rather than submit to the punishment, Burgess walked out of the camp. A few months later, guards captured Burgess wearing, the guard reported, "a full suit of rebel grey." Weary of the treatment in the USCT, Burgess had apparently chosen to live among Confederates as a camp servant. Although the optics of a Black soldier in a

Rebel uniform and the political culture surrounding desertion might suggest it, Burgess neither expressed that he had given up on the Union, nor did he convey a conversion to Confederate views. Rather, he switched to the other side because an officer had disrespected him. After being convicted for desertion, Burgess spent the remainder of the war imprisoned in Natchez.[63]

White and Black soldiers alike grew disgruntled or disheartened by harsh discipline, the ravages of war, and distance from kin, leading some to decamp without permission. The democratic ethos of citizen-soldiers convinced some freeborn men that leaving was a permissible response to violated expectations or wartime challenges. Whether government policies perverted the cause the men joined to support, conditions within camp became impoverished, or civilian obligations demanded their attention, white soldiers and Black soldiers raised in the North left the ranks. Formerly enslaved men decamped as well, but their lives in bondage and the ongoing challenges they and their families faced as a result of slavery and wartime emancipation made their actions distinct. When Black southerners entered the US Army, they felt empowered and determined to push back against restraints that smacked of slavery. By taking leaves of freedom, they not only attempted to shape military service, but they also continued marching toward freedom.

The enlisted freedom seekers posed a serious problem to the US Army. The men sapped the army's fighting strength and its capacity to effectively occupy conquered portions of the South. US Army commanders could neither permit the men's flagrant disregard of regulations nor treat camp borders as porous. To rectify the issue, USCT officers looked to the military justice system. Trying soldiers' leaves of freedom as criminal acts in the courts-martial and sending convicted soldiers to army prisons, officers looked to the law to support their mission to discipline soldiers and end the men's unsanctioned leaves.

PART II

Freedom in the Military Justice System

4

"Unworthy of Freedom": Policing War Workers and Emancipation in the Courts-Martial

"NOT GUILTY," PRIVATE James Brown pleaded when arraigned for desertion during his court-martial. An enslaved laborer before the war, Brown had escaped bondage and enlisted in the Second Mississippi Infantry (African Descent) (later the Fifty-Second United States Colored Infantry or USCI) three days before Major General Ulysses S. Grant received the surrender of Vicksburg. Brown may have spent the memorable July 4, 1863, overjoyed to be serving in the liberating army. Just over a month later, though, he left Camp Hope near the riverfront bastion and returned home. Arrested two days hence, he was held in the guardhouse and tried in December. To prove Brown had been part of the regiment and left by his own free will, the judge advocate probed a lieutenant about Brown's enlistment. The witness said he watched Brown's mustering in and explained that the Mississippian "absented himself without leave and without . . . authority." Satisfied with the evidence after additional witnesses confirmed Brown's service, the judge advocate closed. Brown offered his defense to the seven white officers sitting in judgment. "*I went* away Saturday night to see my father and went to come back and the guards took me and wanted me to cook for them." He then stated, "I told them I would rather come back to my company again, but they wouldn't let me." When he finished his statement, the jurors deliberated. They found him guilty of the lesser charge, absence without leave, and sentenced him to forfeit a month's pay.[1]

Brown's trial reflected the dramatic wartime transformation of enslaved men's lives. In contrast to the interrogation and hostility he would have

Freedom Soldiers. Jonathan Lande, Oxford University Press. © Oxford University Press 2024.
DOI: 10.1093/oso/9780197531754.003.0005

faced as an enslaved rulebreaker in southern courts, he had been tried in the same legal space as white men. Instead of answering to his enslavers, Brown explained himself to white men who examined his case and determined to treat him fairly. Yet the trial reflected elements of his prewar life, too. Brown responded to laws that he, at best, partially understood. He also faced a panel of white authorities. Despite promises of freedom accompanying military service, these white jurors did not concern themselves with his aspirations. Brown was indicted for visiting family, which many Black southerners hoped to do after leaving slavery. If he expected service to yield such liberties, the prosecution of his travel would have been shocking. Brown's experiences in slavery also meant that the rulings in his case, even if fair, could be seen as prohibiting his efforts to be free. Indeed, white judge advocates and jurors enforced employment contracts during the desertion cases of Black soldiers, making the military justice system an accidental site in the broader transformation of the slave-labor system. White northerners of the courts-martial brought the army's disciplinary apparatus to bear on convicted Black deserters and demonstrated to fellow soldiers the consequences of desertion. In trying and convicting Brown and fellow formerly enslaved men for taking leaves of freedom, therefore, white officers enforced soldiers' enlistment on contractual grounds and, consequently, policed Black southerners who thought it permissible to leave the army as they wished.

"Blackstone Has Been Superseded": Delivering Justice amid War

If seized, an alleged US Army deserter entered the courts-martial, a legal realm alien to white and Black soldiers alike. In philosophy and composition, the courts-martial stressed discipline, not justice. White and Black men received equitable treatment in these legal venues. Due to those who sat in judgment and the soldiers' differing backgrounds, however, accused white and Black soldiers had distinct experiences. While white men from the North anticipated justice as many would have in civilian courtrooms, Black soldiers interpreted the courts-martial through the prism of the racism and enslavement they knew before enlisting. As a result, Black soldiers would have feared that white officers of the courts-martial would not understand them and, consequently, would deliver unjust decisions.

Although commanders coped with minor disciplinary problems within camp, they sent graver offenses to the courts-martial. Under the authority of the military law, the president, the war secretary, and the courts-martial ruled over soldiers, from privates to generals, and those living in camp or receiving wages from the army.[2] Military common law (known as *lex non scripta*) afforded the courts-martial the power to interpret regulations, and circumstances yielded ambiguous guidelines.[3] The Articles of War, which became famous for regulating warfare between enemy combatants, also offered guidance on governing trials. Among other elements, it addressed the rules of fairness and the oaths to be administered.[4] Regulations outlined the different courts and their specific roles. For minor crimes, like petty theft, an officer called the garrison or regimental court-martial. Capital crimes, including desertion, called for a general court-martial. Generals commanding armies convened and assigned officers to staff these courts, which consisted of five to thirteen jurors. To try a capital offense, the court-martial required two-thirds to sentence a soldier to death.[5]

A soldier standing trial in the military entered a peculiar legal space shaped by war. The accused, often having been housed in a guardhouse as he awaited trial, was to be arraigned within "eight days, or until such time as a court-martial can be assembled." On the day of his trial, he was escorted to the makeshift courtroom. These courtrooms were set up in camp, sometimes during campaigns, in the open air, or on troop transport ships.[6] The cacophony of cannon wheels rolling by and the chatter of fretful men anticipating a skirmish added to the atmosphere of these wartime courtrooms. The court the prisoner entered was modeled on a civilian criminal court but had significant differences in structure and terminology. There was no single judge but rather a panel of officers known as "commissioners" who served in a role analogous to that of a civilian jury. The "president" of the commission was the officer of the court closest to a civilian judge. He was responsible for ensuring that proper procedures were followed: he opened and closed the proceedings, suspended them if necessary, and oversaw commissioners' deliberations. Meanwhile, every court had a "judge-advocate," who was less analogous to a civilian judge than was the president of the commission. The judge-advocate, who, like the members of the commission, was a US Army officer, was analogous to a prosecutor in a civilian criminal trial. He presented the charges and the case against the defendant, who was as likely to be identified as a "prisoner" as a "defendant." The judge-advocate chose and examined witnesses against the prisoner and cross-examined witnesses who supported the prisoner. None of the officers of a court-martial had to be trained lawyers, but many of the jurors were. Indeed, courts-martial manuals of the era spoke of the jurors' responsibilities as being similar to jurists. The prisoner was allowed legal representation, and lawyers for the defense, unlike other officials in the court, did not have to be members of the armed forces. Although there was no appeal process for a court martial akin to the appeals process of a civilian criminal court, every decision by a court-martial was supposed to be reviewed by the US Judge Advocate or his staff. The officer who reviewed the case either approved or disapproved the findings. Yet the formality of such courtrooms unfolded amid the often-chaotic and frequently changing context of a military camp.[7]

Wartime circumstances placed unique burdens on those participating in cases and led to specific practices that reflected the military hierarchy. Before he began prosecuting the accused, for instance, the judge advocate had to prepare by reading about the courts-martial and scavenging for space as well as materials needed to conduct court business. One soldier appointed to serve as a judge advocate explained in a letter that he had "found benches and tables, pen, ink and papers" before a trial.[8] Another remarked that he had "see[n] that the fire is built" to keep the jury warm.[9] As members of the court took their places, they sat at the table according to rank. Jurors sat on the right and left of the president, who sat at the head. The prisoner was seated on the

FIGURE 4.1 Unlike the civilian courtrooms often gilded by suggestions of power and images intimating justice, the courts-martial courtrooms were spartan in décor as well as manner. Officers, who acted as judge advocates and served as jurors, sat around a plain table during trials. They then made decisions based upon the maintenance of discipline, not justice. "Court-Martial on Major General Fitz-John Porter, Held December 1862 at Washington, D.C.," *Harper's Weekly*, January 3, 1863. Library of Congress, LC-USZ62-2219.

right of the judge advocate. Any witnesses usually sat to the left of the judge advocate.[10]

The legal reasoning was also unique to war. Captain Channing Richards of the Twenty-Second Ohio Infantry noted the difference between his law practice back in the Buckeye State and his role as a judge advocate. "I might almost imagine my self a lawyer once more," he wrote, but not all was the same. "The 'code' has given way to 'regulation,' and Blackstone has been superseded by De Hart," he added.[11] With this, Richards referenced the replacement of *Blackstone's Commentaries on the Laws of England* (1765 to 1796) with William Chetwood De Hart's *Observations of Military Law and the Constitution and Practice of Courts-Martial*. Richards thus observed the dramatic difference between civilian courts, which had been deeply influenced by *Blackstone's Commentaries*, and the courts-martial, where a soldier, not a jurist, had defined the legal practices. Published initially in 1846 following DeHart's service as aide-de-camp to Winfield Scott, DeHart's guide on martial jurisprudence saw new editions published during the Civil War and gave soldiers like Richards a handbook for constructing cases, interrogating witnesses, and persuading military jurors of the courts-martial.[12]

With the fire warmed, the necessary parties assembled, and the pen dipped and readied to record, the court-martial president called the trial to order and began the proceedings. Regulations mandated that the judge advocate keep a complete and accurate record of each case. The president preserved order, maintained the tempo, read the special orders calling the court together, and listed the members of the court. He then informed the prisoner of the charges, detailing the specifications of the charges. The prisoner entered his plea, and arguments commenced. The judge advocate, who frequently lacked any legal expertise, called witnesses and produced evidence. The prisoner articulated his case, questioning witnesses and presenting evidence. In a final act before the court, the prisoner could offer a statement.[13] When both sides finished their arguments, the president cleared the court, and the officers deliberated.

Unlike civil courts, the courts-martial mollified Mars before they served Justitia. As jurors, officers weighed the facts and acknowledged, as one Kentucky soldier wrote, that "important evidence [was] adduced" during deliberation.[14] Yet officers of the court did not evaluate the evidence or testimony as civilian jurists might. The courts-martial modus operandi was the maintenance of order and adjustment of civilians to military authority. So, although the jurors were technically constrained by earlier findings (*stare decisis*), they had not scoured tomes for precedents before adjudicating.[15] Officers sitting in judgment, in fact, gained knowledge during cases, as Captain George Bliss discovered. A member of the First Rhode Island Cavalry, he left Albany Law School during the war. A commander appointed Bliss to the court, but he was hardly a learned jurist. He conceded that he gained "valuable knowledge of military law" while sitting as a juror. A few months later, he wrote dryly that he was "eminently qualified" to judge or, as he put it, "sit in an easy chair and look wise."[16] A USCT officer revealed the entire panel's ignorance, writing that after "many serious objections [were] raised," the trial paused, so the jurors could "study up the law and make ourselves acquainted with the authorities on the mooted points."[17] The officers generally did not determine cases based on esoteric knowledge but based on what kept good military order. Discipline was their watchword. It was held that equitable justice meted out by officers sufficed because these jurors understood how to lead soldiers, not because they understood the law.[18]

As part of this jurisprudence, officers of the courts-martial were supposed to arbitrate soldiers' character. Writing on the officer's role, former professor of ethics and law at West Point Captain Stephen V. Benet noted that the courts descended from the "ancient court of chivalry" and that "the purpose" of the jurors was to regulate "the citizen in his character of soldier."[19] This played out during the war with officers compelling the rank-and-file to appreciate the proper conduct of soldiers as fighters, as white men, and as citizens according to officers' partisan views.[20] White men standing trial experienced these military courts as another space for enforcing severe discipline. This likely left many prisoners anxious when facing officers presiding over their fates. But formerly enslaved soldiers, whose experiences with interrogation and judgment during slavery would have given them little reason for optimism, likely entered the court with even greater trepidation.

If accused Black soldiers knew the true nature of the courts and the outcome of many of the trials, they might have been less worried. The legal process within courts-martial was largely fair. From the opening days of the conflict, white soldiers enjoyed opportunities for justice, much as they had prior to service. With safeguards against abuse, such as a statute of limitations and a prohibition on double jeopardy, soldiers often received fair trials. Any errors along the way could lead to overturned convictions or commuted sentences.[21] Although state and federal legal systems marginalized Black men and women, the courts-martial treated Black soldiers the same as their white comrades. The US Army allowed Black men to testify against white men, a right denied to enslaved southerners as well as some Black northerners. Like their white peers, Black soldiers could engage in the appeal process, ensuring that those who suffered procedural violations had a chance at justice.[22] These prospects not only gave them unmatched access to the law but also enabled Black men to practice skills useful to citizenship.[23]

Nonetheless, judicial impartiality is distinct from individuals' experiences within courtrooms. The lives of those sitting in judgment can influence jurisprudence regardless of procedural protections. Prejudice is not always explicit. Defendants also interpret judicial systems, including those sitting at the helm, based upon their backgrounds.[24] So, even when soldiers were treated impartially, men interpreted their trials not solely on procedural grounds but inflected by their experiences. Accused white northerners entered the courts with expectations distinct from either Black northerners or southerners, especially because of the men who presided over the cases.

Rather than a jury of peers or professional jurists, commissioned officers assigned to the courts-martial determined the fates of soldiers who allegedly violated the code of conduct.[25] Not all officers were considered "competent to sit as members of the courts-martial," West Point graduate and Mexican War veteran Henry Coppée wrote in a field guide for the courts-martial. The US Army excluded chaplains, surgeons, assistant surgeons, and paymasters because, Coppée continued, "they have not such a knowledge of command, discipline, tactics, etc., as to make them the most intelligent judges of military offences."[26] The army only allowed those familiar with imposing discipline to judge soldiers. This rule ensured that the central goal of the courts-martial—maintaining discipline—was kept at the fore. There was no expectation that officers arrive with legal knowledge, as Colonel Thomas Wentworth Higginson affirmed. The leader of the First South Carolina (Colored) Infantry (later the Thirty-Third USCI) wrote, "It is the characteristic of army life, that one adapts one's self, as coolly as in a dream, to the most novel responsibilities. One sits on court-martial, for instance," he mused, "and decides on the life of a fellow-creature, without being asked any inconvenient questions as to previous knowledge of Blackstone."[27] By making only commissioned officers the jurors, the army dramatically influenced Black soldiers' trials. Because the army largely barred Black men from becoming officers (and many commissioned Black men were chaplains and surgeons), when rank-and-file USCT soldiers entered the courts-martial, they faced white officers. While officers like Higginson had spent the war with formerly enslaved men, many officers trying Black soldiers were white men who had only led regiments of white men, not members of the USCT, and thus had scarcely any contact with Black men, including the formerly enslaved, and knew little of their struggles, such as those during wartime emancipation. Since only white officers were appointed as jurors of the courts-martial, therefore, white and Black soldiers had profoundly different experiences in the military courts.

As citizens, most rank-and-file white soldiers would have grown up expecting justice within courtrooms. They would have anticipated fair trials decided by an unbiased jury, thanks to the US Constitution. The Fifth and Sixth Amendments, with their safeguards for citizens against arbitrary prosecution, due process guarantees, and promises of an impartial jury, would have contributed to white soldiers' optimistic outlook. The details of these juridical protections may have been too academic for uneducated young men in the ranks. Many soldiers hailing from the working class may have, moreover, carried a skepticism of the law and loathing of attorneys into the courts-martial and thus not warmed to military law. But the precepts of justice and protection from tyranny surrounded—and inspired—soldiers throughout the ranks. Such principles were embedded in the idea of Union, which many white northerners had enlisted to save.[28]

US Army soldiers expected justice in the courts-martial, even as they acknowledged the importance of discipline. As a clerk explaining service to fresh recruits in 1861, for instance, Ulysses S. Grant promised the volunteers that they would be treated fairly thanks to the courts-martial. The future general noted that all orders must be obeyed, including those that "seem . . . unjust," but he added that "if an injustice is really done you . . . there are courts-martial where your wrongs can be investigated and offenders punished."[29] Higginson spoke even more glowingly. While he had deemed civilian law a "fossilized system of injustice" in his youth, the abolitionist colonel embraced the courts-martial. He claimed that the courts-martial were an "accurate & admirable, though most tedious, method for sifting out the truth." The painstaking search made them "much more formal and careful than those civil courts," resulting in a more scrupulous process in determining guilt or innocence.[30] Those reflecting on the system at large admired it, but they were not alone.

Those engaged in the military justice system had a similar outlook. A soldier sitting as a clerk for a session of trials agreed, writing, "I am quite sure the members of the Court discharged their duties faithfully and impartially."[31] Men awaiting trial also looked forward to a fair hearing, as Colonel Nathan Daniels of the Second Louisiana Native Guards (later the Seventy-Fourth USCI) communicated. With growing anxiety over his impending trial for unbecoming behavior as an officer, Daniels trusted the courts-martial. He desperately wanted his trial to commence because he believed he would be vindicated in court. Indeed, although thoroughly committed to emancipation and leading formerly enslaved men, he threatened to quit if he was not tried by the courts-martial shortly. "Shall send in my resignation if I do not get Justice very soon," he wrote, expecting the court to clear his name.[32] Soldiers expressed relief following their trials as well. "They took seven months pay from me for going home," a Yankee private in the Seventh Ohio Cavalry exclaimed, "but did not punish me any other way." After his conviction for absence without leave, he added, "I am glad they let me off that easy."[33] At heart, each of the white soldiers spoke to the white citizens' outlook on the rule of law. Whether participating in deliberations, waiting for a trial, or paying the penance, white soldiers sustained a hope that justice would be or had been done.

Black soldiers saw the white officers of the courts-martial in a different light, as a soldier calling himself "Sergeant" wrote in an October 1864 missive to *The Liberator*. "We want black commissioned officers," the member of Fifty-Fourth Massachusetts Infantry began, "and only because we want men we can understand and who can understand us. We want men whose hearts are truly loyal to the rights of man. We want to be represented in courts martial, where so many of us are liable to be tried and sentenced." Speaking for his comrades, he concluded, "In short, we want simple justice." Connecting the absence of Black officers to outcomes in the military justice system, he reasoned that white officers lacked an understanding of Black soldiers on trial and were thus responsible for justice denied.[34]

Another freeborn Black man went further, contending that the courts-martial were as unjust as slavery. Philadelphia cabinetmaker Private George Stephens of the Fifty-Fourth Massachusetts Infantry reflected on the system of military justice after witnessing the execution of a Black soldier. "I know in the South the negro is hung sometimes for mere pastime to his bloody executioners," he wrote, "and it may be that we are so far South that its Southern atmosphere has so far tainted our moral sensibility—our regard for the man's life and our respect for the rights of even the basest criminal." He then called the trial and execution unjust. "If men are to be shot or hung without a legitimate trial," he said, "the life of no man is protected or safe, and we are living under a tyranny inexorable as slavery itself."[35] The Philadelphian thus construed military justice not only as a farce but also as a venue that re-created southern oligarchs' despotism. Wherever else Stephens gained his impression of slavery, he likely learned about slavery's evils from William Wells Brown's *The Black Man, His Antecedents, His Genius, and His Achievements* (1863), a collection of biographies of Nat Turner, Denmark Vesey, and other Black men and women he praised as an "aid in the great and good work of dispelling the sin-begotten, infatuated notion—negro inferiority."[36] From

Brown's work, Stephens reached an understanding of slavery's contours. Although a bias within the courts-martial cases was not apparent, Stephens perceived the courts-martial as unjust and tyrannical because the use of violence within the military justice system resembled the naked brutality of enslavers he read about in accounts of bondage.[37]

Formerly enslaved men entering the courts probably reached similar conclusions. The law deemed enslaved people property, technically placing them beyond the reach of rights. White southerners codified racial categories, establishing a link between Blackness and enslavement by the mid-nineteenth century. Enslaved people sometimes entered the courts, but they associated white authority with oppression and doubted that they would receive a fair hearing in the southern legal system. Alleged Black criminals may have expected white jurors to be harsher, especially if the charges were related to resistance to white authority. Although some Black men and women successfully argued for their manumission, the law remained largely a space that pushed Black men and women to the periphery, buttressed their enslavement, and underwrote their enslavers' authority.[38] When formerly enslaved men faced white jurors of the courts-martial, they undoubtedly recalled decades under the lash and perhaps their marginal legal status.

Enslaved men's experiences suggest that they too looked at white courts-martial jurors with suspicion because they distrusted white men in leadership roles. Many referred to their enslavement and their enslavers while giving testimony. Although the presence of so many white northerners at the vanguard of USCT regiments may have renewed Black southerners' faith in justice, lives in slavery undeniably left residual skepticism about white authority. The men standing trial were also often those who had been disobedient under slavery, as they had escaped, and in the army, since they stood trial. This was even more true in alleged deserters' cases. They had already confronted the limitations of service and decided to decamp. A history of such experiences likely resulted in worries that white authorities would not honor justice.

Formerly enslaved men probably expected white officers within the military justice system to exercise discipline as they had in camp and thus undermine their freedom. Camp violence had been part of the daily regimen. When white officers deliberated in courts-martial cases, Black soldiers might have wondered whether more of the same oppression awaited them and whether white jurors would impose punishments that inhibited their liberation. Black soldiers in Tennessee almost surely expected such treatment if convicted after the trial of Moses Smith, a formerly enslaved undercook serving in the 111th Illinois Infantry. After fighting a white farmer who attacked him as he ransacked a smokehouse, Smith was convicted of assault with intent to kill. White officers sentenced him to be "paraded before the colored troops in this command" in a black-and-white suit emblazoned with the scarlet inscription, "Unworthy of Freedom." The officers chose a corrective slogan prevalent among wartime reformers to specifically target the status of Smith's emancipation.[39] For formerly enslaved soldiers who had watched Smith trudge through camp and awaited the verdicts of their cases, the possibility that white officers would treat them similarly seemed a probable outcome.

"Keep Us In": Enforcing Contracts in the Courts-Martial

When a formerly enslaved soldier accused of desertion entered his court-martial, he might have been eager to disavow any assumption that he was a coward or disloyal. But judge advocates did not prosecute soldiers' courage. Officers sitting in judgment did not decide whether the accused was guilty based upon his fidelity to comrade, cause, or country either. Officers approached desertion as a labor contract violation and deserters as errant war workers. Military service was employment established by a contract, so judge advocates and officers of the courts-martial prosecuted and determined cases accordingly. In particular, the military applied a narrow interpretation of a labor contract in an era when contracts were increasingly becoming more rigid yet remained in flux. In these military courts, prosecutors and jurists of the courts-martial, because their preoccupation within the military justice system was the reinforcement of discipline, imposed contracts as inflexible labor agreements and pacts that favored the employer—the US Army—over the employee.

Many soldiers doubtlessly treated military service as an honorable act when the republic was in jeopardy. From the founding of the colonies to the formation of the new republic through the Mexican War and into the Civil War, men under the Union Jack and later Old Glory considered military service part of the social contract. If their community or government was under threat, they thought they should fulfill their civic duty by fighting.[40] Answering the call in 1861, these citizen-soldiers demonstrated their loyalty, upheld the moral imperative, and defended the inviolable Union or embryonic Confederacy.[41] But the jurisprudence of desertion belies this widespread view of military service. The American military tradition drew on less ideological foundations for the actual formation of armies. This does not mean military service was an occupation in the same sense that men were physicians or attorneys, clerks or shipwrights. Yet Americans blurred the line between ideological motivations for military service, the work of war, and the legal basis of employment within the army. This was especially true when it was time to determine obligations when a young Zouave's zeal wore thin, a citizen-soldier's resolve to defend the nation waned, or a uniformed father's family called him home.

Military employment was established by a legal, not sociopolitical, contractual obligation. Although armies had enlisted soldiers and sustained armies in a variety of ways, such as kings demanding that knights ride to battle or enslavers driving captives into combat with promises of freedom or violent threats, the US Army contracted volunteers (and eventually conscripts) to serve for specific periods. Undoubtedly, volunteerism rooted in ideological motivations played a meaningful role. It inspired men to join in the aftermath of the First Battle of Bull Run or reinvigorated morale following the slaughters at Shiloh and Antietam. But the US Army was an employer, not merely the embodiment of the nation. When passion faded or duty faltered, contractual obligations kept soldiers in camp. As Justice James Thompson of the Pennsylvania Supreme Court affirmed in 1863, "Voluntary enlistment, as by contract, was the general method of raising armies."[42] Not only educated jurists drew on such ideas.

This approach to soldiering as labor was in keeping with popular views on employment. Although the contours of contract employment remained unsettled during the nineteenth century, capitalists and laborers alike gradually thought that free individuals owned their labor. Contracts signaled a financial agreement fairly reached between an employee and employer. The employee exercised his or her free will signing a contract. An employee's breach of said agreement became seen increasingly as criminal while violations by employers were perceived as a plutocrat's treading on a worker's liberty.[43] Freeborn soldiers on either side of the war hailed from communities where such thinking was fundamental to daily life. These views became enmeshed with the political basis of military service and shaped the popular mentality toward soldiering. For instance, President Abraham Lincoln's initial call for ninety-day enlistees yielded recruits who returned home when enlistments expired. They did not necessarily leave the ranks because they were tired of war. They did so because the contracts ended, and many rejoined under three-year contracts.[44] Others who became convinced that the army failed to uphold certain responsibilities—such as providing food and clothing—left because the contracts had been voided.[45] Citizen-soldiers approached service as a mixture of republicanism, Lockean social contract theory, and a labor agreement sanctioned by law. Judge advocates applied this thinking, prosecuting alleged deserters as contract-violating employees.

To reach a conviction, judge advocates marshalled evidence to validate that a contract was freely reached and clearly violated. As in civilian employment contracts, desertion cases relied on questions of volition. Judge advocates were encouraged to use "every thing tending to show the intention of the accused."[46] To do so, they needed to establish that the soldier in question had agreed to an enlistment contract and then demonstrate that the accused signed the contract willingly. The state ensured that recruits were legally incorporated into the army as a result. "Volunteer Enlistment" forms became crucial to these ends. Initiates attached their signature (or mark, if illiterate) to the forms and declared that they "volunteered," indicating their free will. They recited the "Declaration of the Recruit," an oath printed on the form. Spoken before witnesses, the recruit proclaimed that he would serve "honestly and faithfully."[47] The language of the forms—or enlistment contracts—made clear to each enlistee that he committed not only to serving as a citizen but also as a (free) laborer who had provided his consent. To guarantee the forms survived (and could be employed to prosecute deserters), regulations directed recruiters to produce three (later two) copies of the contracts and then send the forms with each soldier to his regiment.[48] This paperwork improved judge advocates' ability to enforce contracts.

The US Army codified rules to prevent challenges to contracts related to coercion. As in civilian courts, enlisted men could cast doubt on the legitimacy of contracts by demonstrating that at the moment of signing them they had been under duress. To avoid such claims, regulations stipulated procedures that recruiters had to follow when enlisting. No volunteer was to be "deceived or inveigled into the service by false representations," the rules stated. The US Army required recruiters to "explain the nature of the service … to every man before he signs the enlistment." Once informed, soldiers "desiring to enlist in the Army" had to attach their signatures to oaths as witnesses watched.[49] Similar practices continued in the South, as the US Army enlisted formerly enslaved men. Recruiters had those who had escaped slavery take the oath of service and, since most could not sign their names, make their marks on enlistment forms. For instance, when enslaved Kentuckian Daniel Burton reached Camp Nelson in September 1864, he made his mark after a surgeon assessed his mental abilities and a recruiter determined he was sober and of lawful age to volunteer. A witness then confirmed Burton took the oath of enlistment, permitting the forty-year-old to join the Fifth United States Colored Cavalry.[50] In the North and South, although questionable practices might

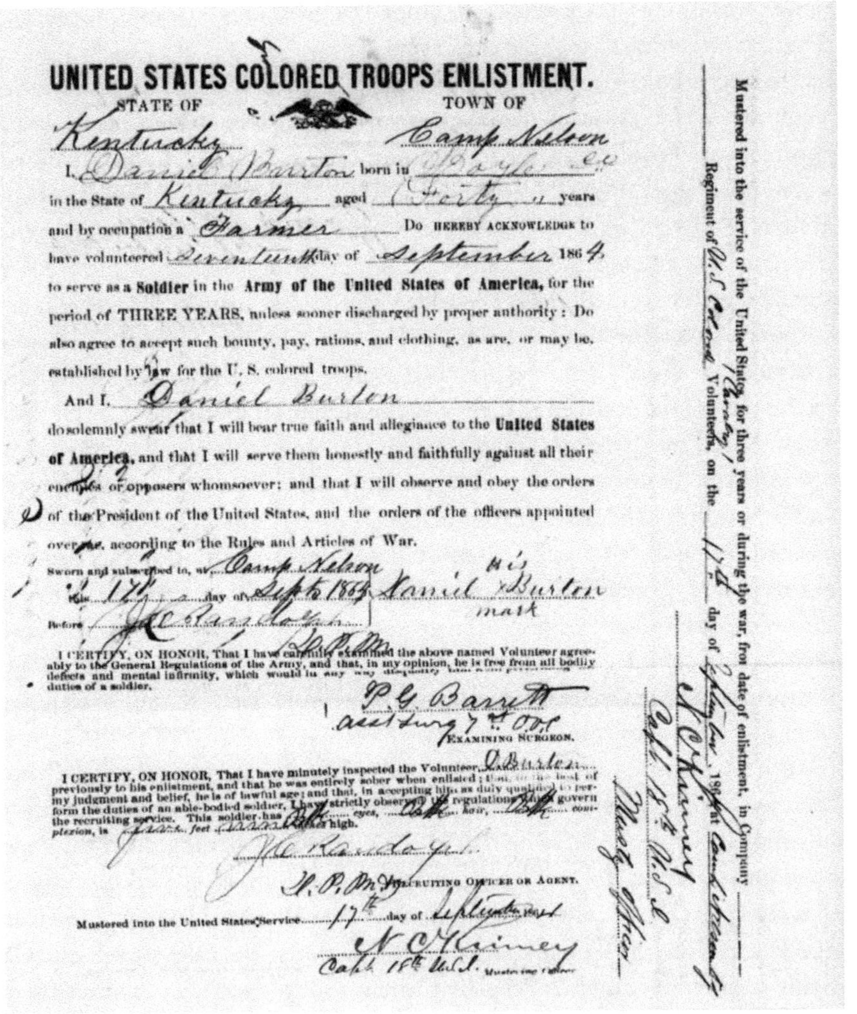

UNITED STATES COLORED TROOPS ENLISTMENT.

STATE OF Kentucky TOWN OF Camp Nelson

I, Daniel Burton born in Boyle Co in the State of Kentucky aged Forty years and by occupation a Farmer Do HEREBY ACKNOWLEDGE to have volunteered Seventeenth day of September 1864, to serve as a Soldier in the Army of the United States of America, for the period of THREE YEARS, unless sooner discharged by proper authority: Do also agree to accept such bounty, pay, rations, and clothing, as are, or may be, established by law for the U. S. colored troops.

And I, Daniel Burton do solemnly swear that I will bear true faith and allegiance to the United States of America, and that I will serve them honestly and faithfully against all their enemies or opposers whomsoever; and that I will observe and obey the orders of the President of the United States, and the orders of the officers appointed over me, according to the Rules and Articles of War.

Sworn and subscribed to, at Camp Nelson this 17th day of Sept 1864 Daniel his mark Burton

Before J C Randolph

I CERTIFY, ON HONOR, That I have carefully examined the above named Volunteer agreeably to the General Regulations of the Army, and that, in my opinion, he is free from all bodily defects and mental infirmity, which would in any way disqualify him from performing the duties of a soldier.

P. G. Barrett
asst surg 7th USC
EXAMINING SURGEON.

I CERTIFY, ON HONOR, That I have minutely inspected the Volunteer, D Burton previously to his enlistment, and that he was entirely sober when enlisted; that, to the best of my judgment and belief, he is of lawful age; and that, in accepting him as duly qualified to perform the duties of an able-bodied soldier, I have strictly observed the regulations which govern the recruiting service. This soldier has Blk eyes, Blk hair, Blk complexion, is five feet seven inches high.

J C Randolph
RECRUITING OFFICER OR AGENT.

Mustered into the United States Service 17th day of September 1864

N C Kinney
Capt 18th U.S.C. Mustering Officer

Mustered into the service of the United States for three years or during the war, from date of enlistment, in Company — Regiment of U.S. Colored Cavalry Volunteers, on the 17th day of September 1864 at Camp Nelson Ky

N C Kinney
Capt 18th U.S.C.
Musterg Officer

FIGURE 4.2 Daniel Burton, an enslaved Kentuckian, travelled from the farm of his enslaver John Burton to Camp Nelson outside Lexington. There, on September 17, 1864, Daniel enlisted. But before he was officially admitted, a surgeon examined his mental and physical state, and a recruiter verified his sobriety and age. Of sound mind and age, Burton took the oath and made his mark, joining the US Army. His enlistment record captured this information and stored it for potential use in a court-martial. These records became useful to a judge advocate after Burton decamped in December. After his arrest, Burton was tried for desertion, and the judge advocate employed the record to show Burton had willingly enlisted. Daniel Burton [aka Benton], Compiled Military Service Record, National Archives, Washington, DC.

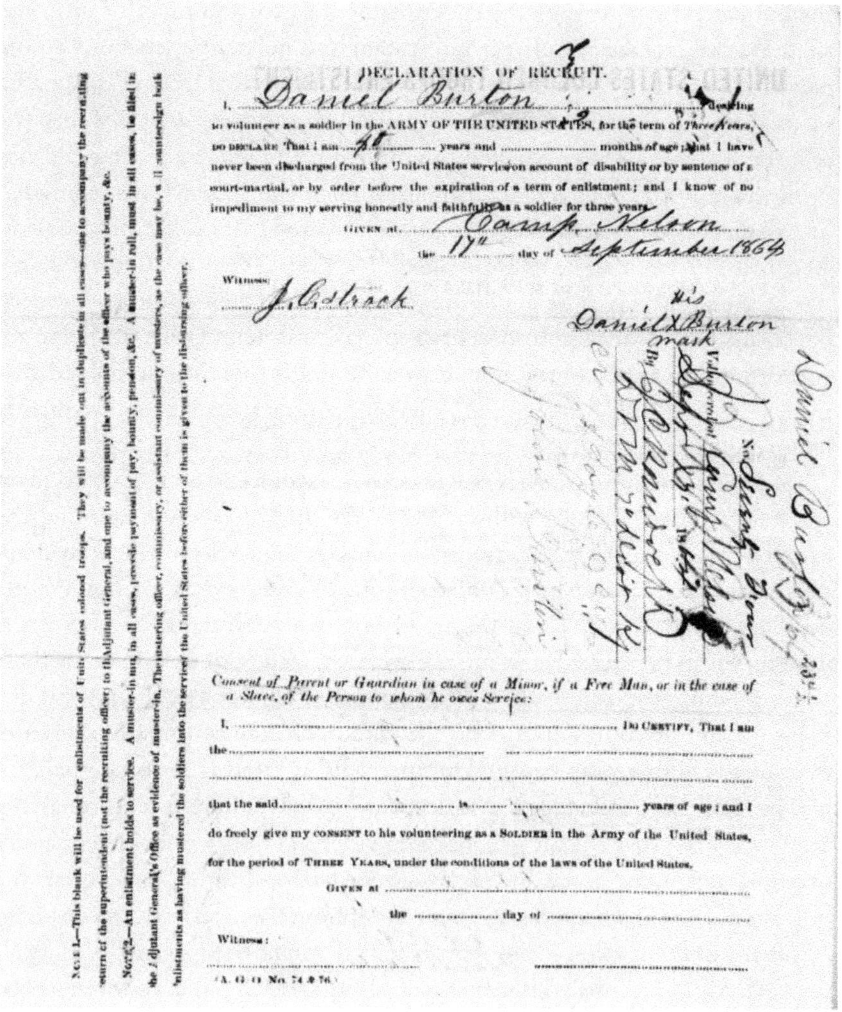

FIGURE 4.2 Continued

raise suspicions, the explicit guidelines and oath-taking practices reduced the chances of clerical error.

Once the trials of alleged deserters commenced, a judge advocate validated whether a soldier furnished consent by framing the case and calling witnesses to attest to the alleged deserter's volition. A judge advocate began by reading the charge, including the soldier's name, and establishing, in this consistent phrasing to announce the recruit's commitment, that the alleged deserter had "been duly enlisted." The prosecutor frequently resorted to the bureaucratic reports created at enlistment to corroborate this information. He produced not only the enlistment and muster papers but also the payrolls for alleged deserters to demonstrate the accused freely participated in the army. He might additionally call on a recruiter to testify that the accused had not been compelled to enlist. But the judge advocate did not need the contract or a verbal affirmation from the accused, his comrades, or an officer to prove the alleged deserter accepted his role within the army. According to the *Digest of Opinions of the Judge Advocate General of the Army*, the judge advocate could demonstrate that when a soldier accepted pay, clothing, or rations he consented to his enlistment. Once the judge advocate validated the contract or showed voluntary service, he proved that the accused willfully broke the employment contract. Such proof frequently led to convictions.[51]

Extenuating circumstances might lead to acquittals or a conviction of the lesser charge, absence without leave. Yet the reasons undergirding the exceptions accentuate the centrality of contract logic within the army's employment practices and its legal disciplining of deserters. Similar guidelines outlined the prosecution and rulings of boys who enlisted in the US Army with or without parental consent and were charged with desertion. In these cases, the importance of soldiers' state of mind emerged as the critical element within the courts-martial (as they did in civilian courts). During cases of enlisted children who deserted or those who enlisted against their parents' wishes, attorneys debated the legitimacy of the children's enlistment by attempting to prove the alleged deserter either did or did not agree or could or could not agree based on his age. Specifically, attorneys addressed the bottom of the enlistment form, where an optional section with the heading, "Consent in the Case of Minor," provided guardians the space to "freely give my CONSENT to his volunteering as a SOLDIER." Since children lacked the legal authority to indenture their labor, the courts debated the legality of these contracts.[52] As in the general approach to desertion cases, the jurors identified consent as vital. Cases were won and lost on the determination of whether a soldier understood what he was doing by enlisting and if he was of a reasoning state of mind (or age) to accede. As in cases involving minors, during the courts-martial trials of deserters over age eighteen, the appreciation of service as contractual remained fundamental.

Officers of courts-martial listened to concerns regarding the validity of contracts, but the US Army enforced the labor agreement in a way that favored the employer, the US Army.[53] Soldiers might think it was acceptable to decamp if the government did not uphold its end of the deal. But desertion was considered too serious a crime and, if left unchecked, could spell doom for an army. As Lincoln acknowledged in June 1863, "Long experience has shown that armies can not be maintained unless desertion shall be punished by the severe penalty of death."[54] As such, jurors reinforced that agreements to serve were not soldiers' prerogative to break. Even if he disagreed with his commanders or the cause or if he merely wanted to return home, a rank-and-file soldier lost the right to quit when he enlisted. The courts-martial tried over twenty-seven thousand US Army soldiers for desertion, thirteen thousand more than conduct prejudicial to military order, the second most common offense. Overall, the US Army courts-martial convicted 87 percent charged and sentenced many to be shot. While many condemned soldiers received clemency, the rate of conviction and possibility of execution were sobering signs that showed how important stopping desertion was to the US Army.[55]

The court's strict enforcement of contracts aggravated freeborn soldiers expecting justice. Private Robert Winn articulated his understanding of service as a contract while serving in the Third Kentucky Cavalry. He had signed up for a three-year term in December 1861, yet he began entertaining ideas about reenlisting in December 1863. But his musings gave way to indignation when he learned he would be held in the service after his contract expired. He knew the US Army policed desertion with great severity and expected he would fail if he tested his luck by leaving without permission. A few months later, in pronounced agitation, he wrote that they "keep us in after our enlistment expires," and such an act violated the soldier's "inherent right to freedom." It amounted to the "re-enslaving [of] the old army of volunteers." The cavalryman remained in the ranks, fearing that if he left he might be tried and shot for desertion. As he served in Georgia under Major General William T. Sherman, he griped about his "involuntary servitude" and "that gross injustice [that] has been dealt out to me." When he was mustered out in May 1865 after marching through the Carolinas, he exclaimed, "Once more free and equal to anybody else in rights." Winn's vexed service reveals that soldiers carried the logic undergirding civilian labor conditions into the US Army. To them, enlistment was contractual. They also saw intrusions as trampling on their freedom.[56] Yet the courts' enforcement of contracts, as Winn's hesitation to leave demonstrates, kept men in.

The asymmetrical contractual system took on new significance when the US government began drafting soldiers and enrolling Black men in early 1863. With the northern population fatigued by the war, the War Department recruited Black men and, after Congress passed the Enrollment Act (March 3, 1863), drafted male citizens ages twenty to forty-five.[57] Although the draft shifted enlistment from volunteerism to conscription, the enforcement of contracts went unabated. The US Army still prosecuted men as if they had signed a classic labor contract. It even prosecuted those who failed to enlist after being drafted. In other words, the army applied the paper instruments of the free-labor system on a population that had not volunteered and on a population that had been enslaved.

Within the courts-martial, judge advocates approached drafted men as if they had signed a contract, much to the chagrin of Joseph Edwards and John Phillips of Danbury, Connecticut. Despite entreaties to join the army, Edwards and Phillips chose not to serve. But they had no choice when the army drafted them. To their relief, Danbury supplied substitutes for any drafted man averse to service. Edwards, a farmer, and Phillips, a laborer, approached the town for substitutes and were told not to worry. However, substitutes could not be found, critical information the town failed to share with Edwards and Phillips. After the deadline to report for service passed, the army issued warrants for their arrest. Empowered by the Enrollment Act to seize civilians who evaded the draft, provost marshals arrested the men in November 1863. Although neither man had signed a contract, the US Army tried them for desertion. The accused tried reasoning with the officers, explaining the town's substitute policy and why they did not enlist. Edwards stated "that it was not because I was afraid to go to war that I wished to furnish a substitute. I was in good steady employ, [and] had a family who hated to have me go away." In his testimony ten days later, Phillips gave the same explanation. Both declared that they had no intention of evading the draft. As Edwards plainly said, "I have no objection to going for a soldier but do not wish to go as a deserter for that thought never entered my mind." The jurors nevertheless convicted both men. As punishment, the officers placed Edwards and Phillips in the Thirty-First USCI.[58] With the ruling, the men learned that the contractual basis of service applied to drafted men who never signed paperwork.

Although deserters might be maligned as disloyal in the political sphere, the military justice system treated them as wayward laborers. It also would not permit men to leave the ranks regardless of contract expiration. The men had lost the right to abandon their employer—even if the contract expired. When the US Army began incorporating formerly enslaved men into the ranks, it tried alleged deserters according to this logic without considering that many, if not most, men accused of deserting had never before signed a labor contract or worked as free men.

"Just Punishment Due a Deserter": Prosecuting Leaves of Freedom

When the soldiers faced judge advocates who prosecuted them as deserters and stood before jurors who convicted them as deserters, the freedom seekers endured a judicial process that criminalized acts of self-liberation. The judge advocates used typical judicial techniques and state documents to verify contracts, ignoring motivations and stressing contractual obligations with which formerly enslaved men had limited experience. Officers who condemned and punished the soldiers endorsed such efforts. As a result, although no court-martial ever sentenced a guilty deserter to march before his comrades with the words "Unworthy of Freedom" painted in red across his back as they had the freed army undercook, formerly enslaved soldiers tried for desertion may have experienced the trials as if the officers had treated them this way. In their view, the all-white panel convicted them for pursuing freedom.

The US Army treated desertion by Black soldiers as a serious offense. The courts-martial convicted Black soldiers more often than white soldiers. Overall, the US Army convicted 87 percent of those soldiers tried for desertion, and of the Black men charged with desertion, 96 percent were convicted of either desertion or absence without leave.[59] Among the USCT soldiers tried for desertion, more Black southerners stood trial than Black northerners numerically and statistically. According to the War Department's figures, 138,530 (or 80 percent) of the men enlisted in the USCT hailed from a state where slavery was legal and widespread, and 34,549 (or 20 percent) came from a state where slavery was either not legal or not widespread. Of the 482 men tried for desertion whose service records include the soldiers' birthplace, 410 (or 85 percent) were born in an enslaving state, 65 (or 13 percent) were born in a free state, and 7 (or 1 percent) were born in Canada. Of the 591 men tried for desertion whose service records include the state of the soldiers' enlistment, 485 (or 82 percent) enlisted in the enslaving states while 106 (or 18 percent) enlisted in the free states. Of the 637 men tried for desertion whose service records include the soldiers' location at the moment of their departure, 584 (or 92 percent) decamped their regiments while serving in the enslaving states, and 53 (or 8 percent) absconded while in a free state. These numbers show that officers took desertion among USCT soldiers at least as seriously as they did desertion among white soldiers. They also reveal that more men from an enslaving state faced desertion charges than those born in the North, suggesting that officers thought it particularly important to discipline those raised in the South within the courts-martial.[60] To do so, they drew on the same techniques used to prosecute white men.[61]

The courts-martial became a space where Black southerners like Private Mose Germain faced rebuke for their decisions to leave. Born in Madison County, Mississippi, in 1842, the Black laborer escaped bondage and enlisted in the Second Mississippi Infantry (African Descent) (later the Fifty-Second USCI) on July 1, 1863. At the end of August, the private left his post at Camp Hope near Vicksburg for home. He was arrested and brought back to camp. On December 2, he was tried for desertion. During his trial, the judge advocate concentrated on proving volition. He asked a captain about Germain's service. "How do you know that he is such Private, and how long has he been such to your knowledge[?]" "He has been such from the first day of July, 1863," the captain replied. "He has done duty—he has drawn clothing and allowances as such in my Company. He has never drawn pay." With this, the judge advocate had sufficient evidence to prove that Germain had joined and willfully participated in the regiment. Germain had acted in accordance with his contract.[62]

Yet after a life in slavery, Germain may not have been exposed to the logic undergirding labor contracts or at least the legal culture surrounding contract negotiations. To make a legal labor contract, a person had to own himself and his own labor. According to the laws establishing chattel, however, enslavers owned the bodies and labor of enslaved men and women, giving the enslaved few chances to interact with contracts. Some attained knowledge of contracts if they participated in commerce, were rented to other enslavers for a period, negotiated wages with potential employers, or devised plans to work for enslavers with the promise of future manumission.[63] Not all engaged in such exchanges, however, and when Germain offered a defense, it became apparent that he had no experience with self-ownership or contracts. He failed to address the questions officers of the court sought to answer when determining guilt, namely questions of contract. "I went away to see my family," he said, and "I stayed away about three weeks." In his statement, he defended his leave, implying that he could visit his family. Although furnishing an articulate defense by clarifying his reasons for decamping, Germain did not refute evidence establishing his participation in the regiment. Without such engagement, his defense lacked the fundamental elements of contractual logic. With the judge advocate's prosecution verifying a contract, jurors convicted and sentenced the Mississippian to forfeit pay, be imprisoned, and do hard labor for six months.[64]

Table 4.1: States Where Black Soldiers Tried for Desertion during the Civil War Were Born

Free State		Enslaving State	
Connecticut	1	Alabama	22
Illinois	1	Arkansas	6
Indiana	1	Delaware	2
Iowa	0	District of Columbia	8
Kansas	0	Florida	1
Maine	0	Georgia	16
Massachusetts	1	Kentucky	46
Michigan	2	Louisiana	28
Minnesota	0	Maryland	13
New Hampshire	1	Mississippi	85
New Jersey	12	Missouri	8
New York	15	North Carolina	33
Ohio	5	South Carolina	24
Pennsylvania	26	Tennessee	67
Rhode Island	0	Texas	0
Vermont	0	Virginia	51
Wisconsin	0	West Virginia	0
Total from Free States	65	Total from Enslaving States	410
Percent from Free States	13	Percent from Enslaving States	85
Canada		7 Total	1 Percent
Total			482

See Appendix for details and sources

With this conviction, the tribunal did more than condemn him for desertion. They denied him the freedom to take a leave to see his family. White soldiers left to see their family and likewise saw it as masculine duty to kin. Yet formerly enslaved men like Germain associated such travel with their ongoing emancipation. The officers ignored the importance of familial bonds to those accustomed to forced separation. So, in effect, he and fellow southerners who had been born into bondage observed white officers demarcating the boundaries of emancipation during desertion trials. From Germain's perspective, white officers implemented a narrow definition of contracts. They regulated his mobility and condemned him for exercising it. Like Kentuckian

Table 4.2: States Where Black Soldiers Tried for Desertion during the Civil War Enlisted

Free State		Enslaving State	
Connecticut	6	Alabama	6
Illinois	4	Arkansas	29
Indiana	0	Delaware	1
Iowa	0	District of Columbia	15
Kansas	1	Florida	0
Maine	0	Georgia	4
Massachusetts	11	Kentucky	33
Michigan	7	Louisiana	100
Minnesota	0	Maryland	11
New Hampshire	0	Mississippi	99
New Jersey	6	Missouri	8
New York	17	North Carolina	6
Ohio	7	South Carolina	14
Pennsylvania	41	Tennessee	146
Rhode Island	6	Texas	0
Vermont	0	Virginia	12
Wisconsin	0	West Virginia	1
Total from Free States	106	Total from Enslaving States	485
Percent from Free States	18	Percent from Enslaving States	82
Total		591	

See Appendix for details and sources

Robert Winn, he probably interpreted his sentence as a reversion to captivity. If there was any question, the jurors ensured Germain remained an immobile captive. They ordered that a twelve-pound ball be tethered to the freedom seeker's leg with a four-foot chain.[65]

Fellow Mississippian John Mitchell learned a similar lesson when tried for evading a violent officer. Born near Jackson in 1843, Mitchell escaped bondage in 1863 and, on October 28, volunteered for the Third Mississippi Infantry (African Descent) (later the Fifty-Second USCI). If he entered with heroic dreams of liberation serving in Union blue, they were soon dashed. Mitchell suffered physical torment inflicted by an officer. Longing for an end to the violence—especially as he likely experienced similar abuse on the notoriously brutal cotton fields of western Mississippi—he requested a transfer.

No reprieve came. By November 22, 1863, he abandoned his post and traveled to the Mississippi River. There, he worked on the steamboat *Shenango*, following the lead of other enslaved men who sought solace in work and achieved greater independence on waterways.[66] But Mitchell did not get to enjoy his freedom long.

On April 15, 1864, Mitchell was taken into custody and tried as a deserter. He faced a court-martial on June 15, 1864. He articulated his struggles within the regiment. He explained that a captain "kicked and cuffed" him. He further stated that he had petitioned for transfer to "any other company in the Regiment." The officers disregarded his testimony and convicted him for his unauthorized leave. They ordered Mitchell to forfeit his pay and to work at hard labor with a twelve-pound ball chained to his leg.[67]

After Germain, Mitchell, and fellow formerly enslaved men took leaves of freedom, Brigadier General John Hawkins found that Black southerners within the Department of the Gulf required an education in the meaning of desertion. When Hawkins reviewed Mitchell's case, the general considered the hard-labor sentence too mild. In his review of the case, he noted that Mitchell "by his own statement . . . shows his desertion was premeditated" and added that the Black soldiers did not understand that remaining "faithful to their oath of service" was of critical importance. "Desertions have been too common in this command," the general declared, "and they will become more frequent unless Soldiers are made to understand the severe punishment they must suffer for not being faithful to their oath of service to the Government." Hawkins ominously wrote, "They know very well they should not desert. It is time they learned as well the just punishment due a deserter." After receiving the general's acerbic review, the jurors in Mitchell's case reconsidered and "after a mature deliberation do sentence Private John Mitchell . . . to be shot to death with musketry." The sentence was approved. On September 15, 1864, Mitchell faced a firing squad. At three that afternoon, he fell in a hail of Union gunfire.[68]

Mitchell's case is a brutal, unique example of enforcement. Yet his trial reflects the same central goal as Germain's and how US Army commanders trusted such enforcement would quash Black southerners' mobility. Neither the tribunal nor Hawkins treated Mitchell unfairly by comparison to white soldiers. The execution of deserters was also not uncommon in the first half of the war. But Mitchell explained that he left to escape abuse. As in Germain's case, the officers did not listen to Mitchell's reasoning. The judge advocate, the jurors, and Hawkins had not factored in how a life of physical abuse in the cotton kingdom may have made harsh army discipline sting as the lash once had. When convicted, Mitchell learned that his specific view of being liberated—avoiding violence—was unacceptable because it defied his obligation to the army. By teaching Black soldiers of the department "the just punishment due a deserter" with a public execution, the army set an example for other soldiers, likely quelling any nascent plans to exercise freedom. Mitchell was the only convicted USCT deserter to be executed, but the procedural steps used in his case and conviction fit the broader pattern of prosecution.

If his death did have any effect, the threat of execution did not last long in the Department of the Gulf. Black soldiers in the area did not stop taking leaves of freedom. After presumably witnessing the execution, five members of Mitchell's regiment decamped, revealing that some soldiers decided taking the unauthorized leaves was worth the risk.[69] Formerly enslaved men elsewhere continued absconding as well.

USCT soldiers decamped throughout the conflict and faced the courts-martial for their flight. Those who left enlisted throughout the conflict, and overall, of those tried for desertion during the war, most left after Mitchell had been judged for his leave. Of the 580 men tried for desertion whose service record includes the date of their departure, 21 percent left in 1863 while 51 percent left in 1864, 26 percent left in 1865, and 2 percent left in 1866.[70] Although some of these men may have decamped before Mitchell was executed, many left after he met his fate. These men apparently would not stop fighting for freedom with their feet. Hoping to prevent further flight, the army continued prosecuting USCT deserters. Those freedom seekers ensnared and tried soon experienced the power of the courts-martial to police their mobility.

Private Gustav Glover of the Third United States Colored Heavy Artillery (USCHA) was among them. Glover, a twenty-four-year-old Nashville farmer, enlisted on November 13, 1863, during the US Army's occupation of the city. His service was marred by illness, and on January 16, 1864, he decamped from Fort Pickering. The army finally caught up with him in May. Later that month, he was tried. After entering his plea, he explained to the officers of the court-martial his motive: "I was sick in camp and they did not pay any attention to me. I called for medicine and they did not give me any. So I came over. I had just got well again when they caught me." The jurors nevertheless convicted and sent Glover back to the fortifications at Fort Pickering to work at hard labor for six months.[71]

The same fate awaited Glover's comrade, Private Allen Guy. Born in Marshall County, Mississippi, Guy made his way north to Tennessee and, on

Table 4.3: States Where Black Soldiers Tried for Desertion during the Civil War Decamped

Free State		Enslaving State	
Connecticut	3	Alabama	14
Illinois	0	Arkansas	34
Indiana	0	Delaware	0
Iowa	0	District of Columbia	8
Kansas	2	Florida	5
Maine	0	Georgia	9
Massachusetts	2	Kentucky	28
Michigan	5	Louisiana	119
Minnesota	0	Maryland	11
New Hampshire	0	Mississippi	100
New Jersey	0	Missouri	2
New York	2	North Carolina	6
Ohio	2	South Carolina	28
Pennsylvania	35	Tennessee	157
Rhode Island	2	Texas	5
Vermont	0	Virginia	58
Wisconsin	0	West Virginia	0
Total from Free States	53	Total from Enslaving States	584
Percent from Free States	8	Percent from Enslaving States	92
Total		637	

See Appendix for details and sources

March 9, became a member of the same artillery unit as Glover. In June, he decamped. He was apprehended in December and faced a court-martial five days later. Apparently seeing no prospect of persuading the jury of his innocence, he pleaded guilty. His guilty plea meant the judge advocate offered no evidence. In an endeavor to earn the sympathy of the jurors, the prisoner offered a statement. "When I went away I did not know the rules and regulations, and did not think any-thing about being punished. I was pressed in some time in March and was only in about two months when I went away. I never heard the Articles of War read." In this statement, Guy articulated an awareness of his ignorance of the rules, a point that could be meaningful to the officers of the court. He further argued that he had been improperly

Table 4.4: Month and Year Black Soldiers Tried for Desertion during the Civil War Enlisted

	1862	1863	1864	1865	Total
January	*	1	34	17	52
February	*	4	20	11	35
March	*	3	44	11	58
April	*	4	13	15	32
May	*	18	15	*	33
June	*	31	15	*	46
July	*	26	13	*	39
August	5	35	14	*	54
September	23	17	26	*	66
October	1	24	13	*	38
November	4	36	8	1	49
December	2	77	12	1	92
Totals	35	276	227	56	594
Percents	6	46	38	9	100

See Appendix for details and sources

*No data

forced into the regiment. The jurors discounted both contentions, perhaps deeming his participation in the regiment for four months evidence of consent. They convicted him and sent him to join Glover to work at hard labor on the fortifications at Fort Pickering for six months.[72] These men asserted their guilt and detailed their reasoning for taking leaves of freedom yet discovered that even such appeals would not earn them exoneration. Upon enlistment, they had lost control over their labor. When convicted and sent to prison, they returned to captivity.

Commanders considered desertion among the most dangerous crimes because fleeing soldiers dwindled ranks and eroded an army's fighting strength. Although many soldiers or civilians saw desertion as the result of a soldier's waning patriotism, weak constitution, or enfeebled courage, judge advocates dealt with deserters as disobedient employees. Establishing

Table 4.5: Month and Year of Departure by Black Soldiers Tried for Desertion during the Civil War

	1862	1863	1864	1865	1866	Total
January	*	1	16	16	2	35
February	*	2	33	10	6	51
March	*	3	33	13	4	53
April	*	2	48	13	*	63
May	*	1	24	11	1	37
June	*	4	33	21	*	58
July	*	7	18	19	*	44
August	*	18	31	14	*	63
September	*	23	9	13	*	45
October	1	18	19	14	*	52
November	*	13	11	2	*	26
December	*	31	16	2	*	49
No Month Recorded	*	*	3	1	*	4
Totals	1	123	294	149	13	580
Percents	.2	21	51	26	2	100

See Appendix for details and sources

*No data

volition with testimony and paperwork, judge advocates proved that men willingly enlisted and convicted them. When formerly enslaved men entered the courts-martial, they enjoyed unprecedented opportunities for equal justice. But the administration of jurisprudence equally in desertion cases meant that white officers prevented freedom seekers from controlling mobility and compelled them to abide by labor conditions the soldiers had rejected.

White jurors' equitable enforcement of desertion led to the violation of Black southerners' freedom. As white officers considered the fates of once-enslaved soldiers who took leaves of freedom, they applied the logic of contracts, asking questions regarding volition and drawing on state documents to verify enlistment. By arraigning cases according to these legal rules, they marginalized factors that formerly enslaved men considered fundamental to freedom and thus sound reasons for departing. These reasons included a family member in danger or violence inflicted by an officer. The white jurors decided cases without taking into account the men's experiences during bondage. Ultimately—and by design—they restricted soldiers' actions. For the freedom seekers, this meant limiting the scope of emancipation and denying certain freedoms. The officers sitting in judgment enforced contracts on formerly enslaved men who had affirmed aspects of their lives they thought fundamental to their liberation by decamping. Many such freedom seekers ended up pleading guilty and were incarcerated as convicted deserters. But not all Black southerners gave up the fight for freedom. Some charged with desertion argued against the strict enforcement of their enlistment, demanding freedom and justice within the courts-martial.

5

"Establish My Innocence": Defending Flight and Freedom in the Courts-Martial

"I HOPE THE Court wont be hard on me," Private Abraham Coombs implored. The Kentuckian had escaped slavery in Fayette County and, arriving at Camp Nelson, enlisted on September 23, 1864. Mustered in as part of the Sixth United States Colored Cavalry (USCC), he was stationed at Camp Nelson, a camp where refugees from bondage found sanctuary, including perhaps Coombs's family. Indeed, they were not far away, and longing to see them as winter approached, he decamped in November. He was arrested in March 1865 and tried for desertion. After the judge advocate closed the prosecution, Coombs presented his defense to the court-martial. "I went home to see my mother. While I was there I took sick and could not get back. I was sick when they arrested me. They took me out of bed and brought me back in a buggy." He then stated that he was being held accountable for rules he did not know. "I never had the Articles of War read to me," he explained. "I dont know the punishment of a deserter is," he added, and "I never was told by any one what the punishment would be. I asked my Lt. for a pass before I went away and he said I could not get any then." Making one last appeal, this time to the humanity of the white officers on the tribunal, he remarked, "I went away three weeks before Christmas." In this adroit defense, he offered a sympathetic anecdote, noted his inability to return due to illness, and keenly reasoned that he should not be held responsible because he neither heard the rules nor knew what would happen if he left. Despite his effort, the officers impaneling his court-martial found him guilty. They sentenced him to three months in a Lexington prison with a ball chained to his leg.[1]

Like Coombs, other enlisted freedom seekers accused of desertion sought to remake trials into opportunities to shape the conditions of military service, secure liberty, and express their views on justice. From their enlistment onward, formerly enslaved men accused of desertion disputed stringent discipline and requested that officers of the courts-martial account for mitigating conditions and show leniency. They offered stories that stressed their commitment to family, hoping that introducing the plight of overburdened kin would encourage sympathy. In doing so, they articulated relationships that were distinct from the occupational relationships with the US Army, which were affirmed through legal documents. They insisted upon the recognition of their humanity in dimensions other than those communicated in such documents. Their statements later in the war shifted to direct engagement with desertion jurisprudence. They responded to the legalistic, inflexible contract enforcement central to prosecution. Throughout their trials, they not only presented arguments to win cases. They also and simultaneously critiqued labor conditions. They contested strict contract administration, and they defended their leaves of freedom. They claimed that they were committed to employers who permitted laborers to air grievances, abstained from violent reprimands, and accommodated workers' desires to look after their health and family. In making such defenses, the accused did not present cases that altered the legal order. But they called on officers of the courts-martial to see that they fled in the pursuit of freedom and, rather than rigorously enforce labor obligations, to grant them greater latitude to secure opportunities they had longed for during bondage.

"Didn't Know Anything": Shifting Culpability to Enslavers' Despotism

When a rank-and-file soldier entered a court-martial, the US Army expected the accused military criminal to present a defense without legal training. This burden was not necessarily a disadvantage, though. Unlike decisions in civilian legal systems, decisions in the military justice system were based upon equitable justice. This meant that soldiers, including the formerly enslaved, could argue their cases and potentially win them because they needed no specialized knowledge to participate. The soldiers were not always without support. Those accused of a crime could receive aid from counsel (or amicus curiae) to conduct their defenses. Former West Point professor Captain Stephen V. Benet wrote that the counsel could furnish advice and questions "on separate slips of paper," or a counsel could write "any legal objections that may be rendered necessary by the course of the proceedings." However, the army prevented the counsel from addressing the court or interfering in the proceedings. Benet summed up the counsel's role: "his presence is only tolerated as a friend of the prisoner." As a result, even if assisted by counsel, the prisoner had to craft his own defense and could do so without needing scholarly knowledge of common law or precedent.[2]

In its courts-martial system, the US Army offered Black soldiers an opportunity to articulate their reasoning in court.[3] Black soldiers, like white soldiers, could defend their innocence and explain why they violated regulations. In cases of mutiny, Black soldiers sometimes succeeded in constructing defenses and, by participating in the system, gained lessons useful for securing rights.[4] The jurisprudence of desertion differed from that of mutiny, leading to distinct defense strategies and tactics. In response to the prosecution of desertion, formerly enslaved men engaged in the prevailing legal reasoning, yet they also augmented this with their own emancipatory visions of labor and self.

The freeborn rank-and-file of the US Army, whether white or Black, voiced defenses that cut to the heart of labor contract law. As their arguments in the courts-martial make clear, soldiers, like those of the Nineteenth New York Infantry, expected that the US Army would enforce the terms of enlistment similar to employment contracts. In 1861, men of Cayuga County who felt the urge to enlist signed ninety-day contracts and became part of the Nineteenth New York. When those three months expired, though the war had not ended, several men left without the army's permission. They were arrested and tried as deserters. Defending themselves in the courts-martial, accused soldiers, including Privates George Brown and Joseph Rundall, argued that their contracts had elapsed, which released them from service. "I thought I had been mustered in for three months," Brown said, "and at the end of the time could go away just as if I was working for a man."[5] Rundall echoed Brown's belief, yet he added, "I was illegally held."[6] As Brown and Rundall made plain, they acted on the belief that they fulfilled their labor contracts and to be kept in camp was a violation of their right as free laborers.[7] Their reasoning reveals the underlying logic shaping white soldiers' perspective on service. They may have been inspired by loyalty, but they were bound to serve by contract obligations. When that agreed-upon time of service expired, they could return home. Since the courts-martial focused on discipline and sided with the men's employer, the US Army, and not the employees, the soldiers, Brown, Rundall, and seven fellow members of the Nineteenth New York lost their cases and were convicted.[8]

In addition to pointing to the expiration of contracts, prisoners on trial for desertion also argued that there had been a breach of their employment contracts. They offered a range of reasons, including that they were mistreated, that they had been placed in the wrong regiment, and that the army had not fulfilled some substantive element of the agreement such as providing pay, clothing, or food. For example, Private John Murphy, a member of the Fifth United States Artillery, told the court, "I wished to desert because I was abused. I had no place to sleep." During his trial for desertion, Private George Bagwell, a free Black barber from New York City serving in the Third United States Colored Infantry (USCI), pumped witnesses regarding his oath of service. In an effort to show he had not offered legal consent to serve, Bagwell asked one witness: "Was the accused sworn in at the muster into the U.S. military service at the time that you was?" Although Bagwell was convicted, he steadfastly maintained that he had not been properly enlisted months later. "On the trial I reported that I had never been sworn in to the service," he wrote.[9] The accused disputed volition as well, detailing some circumstances that prevented them from returning to the army or a lack of understanding. When Black Philadelphia Corporal Charles Wilson of the Thirty-Second USCI missed a transport meant to carry him back to his regiment, for instance, he blamed a sergeant who "was in liquor" for giving him the wrong departure time. Wilson claimed he was innocent. In such defenses, the soldiers communicated that the US government failed to uphold its part of the bargain, releasing them from theirs or distancing themselves from responsibility.

Guided by similar logic, accused deserters disputed the legitimacy of their enlistment. Like soldiers under age eighteen, men claiming ignorance due to incapacity or insanity at enlistment contended that they did not comprehend the obligations of contracts or understand the rules of desertion outlined in the Articles of War. Facing charges for desertion after leaving Maryland's Public Guard and joining the Twenty-First Indiana Infantry without proper discharge, Private Henry Bennett had the captain from his Midwest regiment offer evidence regarding his fitness to serve. "I thought," the captain admitted to the court, "he was a man of very unsound mind [and] that we might as well let him go." Bennett held fast on this point, noting in his statement to the court, "I was anxious to serve my country" and joined two different regiments not "know[ing] that I was committing a crime." In his defense, Private Thomas Stanley of the Eleventh New York Infantry explained that "I did not mean to desert." Medical officers affirmed Stanley's underlying assertion, "find[ing] that altho' possessing no marked aberration of intellect, he is still deficient in ordinary intelligence." Such defenses allowed men to show that, although they had left, they were not blameworthy.[10]

Still others rooted their defenses in a different element of the logic of contracts: they argued that they had upheld the contract even though they had left their regiment. For example, Private Jerome Ray, a New Jersey laborer in the Twenty-Ninth Connecticut (Colored) Infantry, stated that after leaving his regiment near Hatchers Run, Virginia, he continued working for the US Army yet performed a different job. "I left it to visit a friend," he testified, yet upon returning, "I could not find my Regiment." He had not quit the army, though. He explained that he "was employed . . . in the Quarter Master's Department of the time during my absence." He concluded, "I admit that I am guilty of absence from my Regiment, but I . . . was in the employ of the government all the time." Alas, the jurors did not find that his work for the quartermaster qualified. The court adopted a different, more rigid logic of labor law: the contract was for the performance of a specific job rather than generic service. The court sentenced the convicted soldier to hard labor without pay for the remainder of his enlistment term.[11] Albeit a failure, Ray's argument reveals that he, like his fellow rank-and-file northerners charged with desertion who claimed their contracts were broken or illegitimate, defended his actions according to his understanding of labor contracts.

When tried for desertion, Black southerners deployed legal arguments and offered evidence to mitigate their obligation or demonstrate that extenuating circumstances led to their flight as well. As early as 1863, formerly enslaved soldiers succeeded in defending their leaves of freedom through a demonstration of the basic tenets of contracts, despite their unfamiliarity with and marginalized place within the southern legal system before the war. Although limited in how they could articulate cases, enslaved southerners had previously fought for security, rights, and freedom and managed to disrupt enslavers' power.[12] When once-enslaved southerners charged with desertion faced the courts-martial, they offered claims that repeated such arguments. Their ability may have signified that they were conversant in the legal reasoning from freedom suits, which engaged questions of contract at times.[13] However, given the number of defendants facing the courts-martial, it is more likely that the soldiers used the same incisive reading of military jurisprudence during their service as they had when they needed to decipher the law during enslavement. Regardless of how they came to the ideas, enlisted formerly enslaved men devised legal tactics to fit their wartime quest for liberation.

Freedom seekers charged with desertion transformed the courts into a space to challenge the constrictions imposed by military regulations. This may have been their first time appearing before a court, which made their experiences unique, as enslaved men and women had largely dealt with the courts through lawyers and on paper. As they defended themselves before white authorities in person, some delivered statements detailing their decisions to leave camp or not return while deploying a range of rhetorical techniques that encouraged officers sitting in judgment to consider their prior enslavement. Similar to their freeborn peers, these formerly enslaved men pushed back against the army's rigid enforcement of labor agreements. Yet they specifically pressed the courts to consider circumstances stemming from wartime emancipation and requested leniency on the grounds of their prior enslavement.

Private Paris White, for example, gestured to ongoing illness to win exoneration in 1863. Born in Charleston, South Carolina, White ran to the invading US Army and enlisted at Hilton Head on April 25, 1863. He apparently told the recruiter he was thirty-four years old, but a doctor later surmised that the South Carolinian was at least fifty. Although twice the age of the average soldier, the formerly enslaved man performed exceptionally in the Twenty-First USCI. Sergeant Sussex Brown praised White for executing his duties dependably, later calling him a "faithful man." As he soldiered, though, an unknown disease took its toll. Small sores covered his legs. The wounds worsened. Festering continued to plague him. After a few months of service, his condition deteriorated to the point he thought could no longer serve, and he left. The army caught and tried him for desertion. During his trial, he never denied that he had decamped. Instead, he explained his affliction, intimated that he had honored his contract, and asserted that lesions prohibited him from performing his duties any longer. To corroborate his story, he called on fellow soldiers. When asked if he knew of the sickness, one witness assented. White probed for details. The witness affirmed having seen the lesions. The judge advocate, evidently recognizing White's questioning might impede conviction, prodded the witness. Inquiring whether the prisoner left because he was sick, the witness expressed uncertainty. Seeking clarification, the court asked, "Did he return on his own free will?" The witness did not know. White perceived the suspicion created by this cross-examination. Striving to verify his commitment to duty, he brought forward "several certificates of good character from persons under whose employ he had been since connected with the Government." Another document stated that White "had never been well or sufficiently so as to bare exposure," and it asserted "that he was afflicted before he was conscripted with [the] unknown disease." To strengthen his case, he offered a final piece of evidence. He reached down and peeled back his pantleg to expose a collection of fresh sores layered on top of lingering scars. White's argumentation reflected a skilled engagement with the logic of the court, and he succeeded. The court-martial deemed him not guilty of desertion but convicted him of the lesser charge, absence without leave. The court also made a statement about his punishment, explaining that the evidence of good character and White's "sickly appearance" meant that the time he had served from his capture through his trial "is sufficient for the offense." Speaking to his litigation skills, White walked free that day.[14]

Like White, the sickly Private William Owens argued in court that bodily limitations prevented him from fulfilling his duties. In addition to his inability to perform, Owens claimed evidence of ignorance. Owens had taken his freedom on August 26, 1863, enlisting in the army in Columbus, Kentucky, and was mustered into the Fourth United States Colored Heavy Artillery (USCHA). He fled shortly after but was soon caught. During his trial, when the court asked why he left, Owens responded, "I was a green hand." He added, to be clear, "I didn't know anything. I don't know one letter from another." When the court pressed him to explain, Owens persisted in this defense. "My mind got stirred up. I got scared," he said, "and I didn't know what on earth to do." The court moved to questions regarding Owens's whereabouts. He said he traveled home before reenlisting in a different regiment. To defend his innocence, he changed tactics to head off a new line of interrogation. He said that he was discharged from the other regiment due to his inabilities. "I wasn't able," he remarked. "I had the rheumatism in my leg [and] . . . can hardly move." Unable to explain his absence, he contended that illness prevented him from meeting his responsibilities. As White had during his defense, Owens trusted that the officers would appreciate the mitigating circumstances resulting from disease. Owens also implied that he had become ill during service, perhaps hoping the officers might appreciate that the rampant disease afflicting soldiers had claimed another victim. Finally, Owens gestured to his ignorance, casting doubt on his culpability after communicating his feebleness. His hopes that the jurors would forgive his absence were dashed, however. The court convicted Owens and mandated the deserter forfeit the wages due. In an effort to demonstrate to fellow soldiers that they should not desert, the court further stipulated that Owens trudge around camp with a ball chained to his leg for one month.[15]

Freedom seekers also pointed to their prior enslavement to suggest that bondage left them poorly equipped to fulfill their duties. On December 6, 1863, Henry Tinder enlisted in Columbus, Kentucky, but he later ran back to the plantation where he had been enslaved. Once arrested and tried, Private

Tinder offered a defense that no freeborn soldier could make. The Kentuckian explained to the court that a former enslaver swayed him to leave the army. Tinder may have been less than honest. Many enslaved southerners had used ruses to avoid punishment before the war or to gain freedom during it. During the war, for example, an Alabamian called Sam convinced a US Army recruiter who forced him to serve to allow him to return home and collect a forgotten coat, only to go into hiding to avoid impressment.[16] Although Tinder may have been fleeced, he also plausibly fabricated the story to shift the blame for his desertion from himself to his oppressor. Regardless of whether he lied or not, the private clarified for the court that it was the beguiling despot who coerced him to leave the army and return to bondage. The appeal worked. The tribunal decided that the enslaver was someone who "had long possessed great influence" over Tinder and that Tinder suffered from "extreme ignorance." As a result, the court was lenient, only sentencing him to yield his pay.[17]

As the cases of White, Owens, and Tinder show, formerly enslaved men explained to officers of the courts-martial that circumstances led them to break their commitment to the US Army. By rendering themselves unable to fulfill their duties, the soldiers undercut their culpability by pointing to the consequences of having been enslaved. In making such appeals, the men tacitly admonished the army for preventing them from recuperating their health and disciplining them when they lacked a clear understanding of the regulations. In these cases, they articulated arguments that forces beyond their control undermined their ability to meet their contractual obligations to their employer. In doing so, they used the injustices of slavery to underscore the injustice of conviction.

"To See My Folks": Telling Stories of Family

Formerly enslaved soldiers on trial also looked to a time-tested tool that afforded them the chance to simultaneously offer justifications to win their cases and affirm their humanity: they told detailed stories about commitments to family. Such accounts were undoubtedly strategic. Stories from men like Kentuckian Wesley Ball, who served as a musician in the 119th USCI, were obvious attempts to elicit sympathy. When Ball noted that he left to see his mother, he added, "I hope the Court will be as easy as they can with me I am very sorry I went and wont do so any more."[18] Officers, like the rank-and-file, endured the loneliness of war, as distance and duty kept them from their children, sweethearts, and dear friends. Presenting the suffering of family, the soldiers would have stirred the officers' yearning for home as a means of winning cases. But, likely many, if not most, Black southerners would have assumed that white officers serving as jurors would not show them compassion. The US Army dealt harshly with men charged with desertion. Of all the men tried for desertion, 87 percent were convicted, and 56 percent of the 256 soldiers executed by the US Army were deserters. Of course, the men did not know the percentage of men convicted or how many men were executed, yet they would have probably seen the signs. Many likely saw their peers being captured, tried, and convicted. Since commanders pointedly made examples of deserters, it is probable that Black southerners knew that courts-martial cases resulted in punishment, including death. These men likely witnessed the execution of a deserter in camp, read of an execution in a newspaper, or at least heard from a fellow soldier of a man being shot. So, while defendants may have offered details of their circumstances in the faint prospect of securing kindness, they likely did not expect officers' benevolence and resorted to storytelling for other reasons.[19] Aside from arousing an emotional response, this tactic afforded freedom seekers a chance to articulate relationships they valued and could now cultivate as liberated men. It enabled them to express a vision of personal emancipation far different from the emancipation communicated through legal abstractions.

Enlisted Black southerners valued stories during the war, and they were not alone.[20] Aside from the stories told around campfires, white and freeborn Black soldiers offered their officers accounts of sick wives and starving children to get permission for furloughs or to induce compassion.[21] For instance, Private William Gillum, a Black Canadian serving in the Twenty-Seventh USCI, explained that he left to care for his younger sister who "was not expected to live."[22] But formerly enslaved men in the US Army, like freedom seekers across the South, looked to stories during the process of emancipation to adjust to life after abolition. During the war, stories permitted those fresh to liberty the means to manage the dramatic process of becoming free and regulate the contours of their individual emancipation.[23] Men on the road of emancipation carried the power of stories with them into the US Army, including the courts-martial, where they deployed narratives not only to win cases but also to claim their status as free men.

As they undermined their obligations or presented the extenuating circumstances leading to their departure from the army, USCT soldiers on trial told stories that linked them to important relationships. Freeborn men might take the chance to sustain kin relationships for granted, but for those who escaped slavery, the chance to maintain a family was a sign of the jubilee. During their defenses, USCT soldiers told stories that tied them to their families as a means of navigating emancipation. The stories connected them to their kin because Black southerners placed great, possibly unparalleled, importance on such bonds. Americans generally valued families, yet to many leaving slavery, kin connections, which enslavers had systematically denied to them, marked the advent of freedom itself. Soldiers regaled jurors with stories of kin to affirm these relationships. In doing so, the accused asked officers to see beyond the scope of military service and to recognize them as more than soldiers. They claimed an identity higher than that of war workers. Foregrounding their humanity, the accused attached themselves to those they cared for rather than abide by the articulation of self as communicated in legal documents.

During his case for desertion, for instance, Private Anderson Phillips responded to the judge advocate with a story. Phillips enlisted in the 111th USCI on January 10, 1864, in Lynnville, Tennessee, and was placed on garrison duty at the fortifications in northern Alabama. He and his comrades protected the Sulphur Creek Trestle, which served the Tennessee and Alabama Railroad. Later that spring, on March 20, he left his post, and on July 20, the army arrested him. Shortly after, he faced a court-martial for desertion. As in other desertion cases, the judge advocate needed to prove, first, that Phillips was a soldier by choice and, second, that he fled. To do so, he used government documents that validated Phillips's service and identity, like enlistment forms and descriptive lists. The documents established events and defined the accused deserter based on his enlistment and individual features, including hair and skin color or height and age. The documents spoke of Phillips's personhood only to verify facts for prosecution in the court-martial.[24] They completely overlooked certain aspects of his personhood, leaving out circumstances surrounding his choices and categorizing him based upon isolated fragments.

This was not unlike other versions of the bureaucratic erasure of humanity that Phillips would have experienced as enslaved property. A freedom seeker who managed to secure liberty in his youth, James Pennington wrote of the administrative evisceration of humanity in bondage: "it is the chattel relation that robs him of his manhood, and transfers his ownership in himself to another." It is chattelhood that "leaves him without a single record to which he may appeal in vindication of his character, or honour."[25] The state played a critical role in this enterprise, as fellow freedom seeker Frederick Douglass observed. "The institutions of this country do not know me, do not recognize me as a man." Instead, "the political institutions of this country . . . pronounce me a slave and a chattel."[26] Such legal documents establishing bondage explicitly purged individuals of their humanity. Other documents expunged individuals of their personhood, too, and they were not unlike those used to define Phillips's employment in the US Army. While the cataloging of captive Africans on slaving vessels initiated the dehumanizing process in previous centuries, the reducing of enslaved generations to a person's gender, age, and childbearing abilities supplied enslavers the means of transmuting men, women, and children into fungible items for pricing.[27] Enslavers utilized the power of the state to further the commodification, turning bodies into legal tender and verifying the exchange of the people as property.[28] Enslavers searching for enslaved men or women who ran provided rich descriptions in newspaper advertisements, noting scars, languages spoken, manacles carried away, and other characteristics that might identify those who escaped.[29] Pioneering enslavers, meanwhile, adopted innovative managerial paperwork to boost productivity.[30] Each of the enslavers' papers separated Black men, women, and children from people in society. This paperwork deprived the enslaved of meaningful relationships like family, which defined a person and were critical to individuals' resistance to commodification. Offering an example of the liminal position of the enslaved, Pennington reviewed the futile path an enslaved man might proceed down to locate himself in society. The man, Pennington lamented, only "find[s] his name written down among the beasts of the field."[31] In short, these forms erased individuality, making the enslaved nothing more than chattel. Enslaved southerners like Phillips would have known well this bureaucratic elimination of personhood.

The US Army's use of contractual documents during the prosecution of deserters relied on similar practices and likewise drew power from the state. As critics of contract wage-labor contended, the obligation of an individual's labor marked the sale of the person as a whole.[32] The documentation proving desertion operated by reversing that logic: documents affirming the labor one owed demarcated the whole laborer while elements that might be attributed to one's personhood had no bearing in the law. As a result, the process of proving desertion reduced men to nothing more than laborers. The process of prosecution isolated men from relationships with people and institutions aside from the US Army.[33] The documents did not account for aspects of a man's life beyond the paperwork, casting a soldier's personhood as an identity solely rooted in his capacity to labor yet again. Phillips disrupted the process of alienation.

To stop the legal process from making him simply a laborer once more, Phillips explained what happened. "When I was relieved," he testified, "I went . . . to see my wife," and "I did not make any effort to avoid the Military

Authorities nor did I know I was violating any obligation." With this, Phillips suggested that when he was "relieved," which likely meant furloughed, he thought he did not need to return. But rather than concentrate on his ignorance or dispute his contract, he alluded to his relationship with his wife. He avoided discussing his unfamiliarity with regulations or his labor obligations. He instead asserted his humanity by ensuring that he was not defined by his labor or confined to a name on a form or descriptor on a list. By situating himself in relation to his spouse, he undermined the law's attempt to isolate his personhood from relationships outside the army. Although the court-martial convicted him, the tribunal's comments show Phillips succeeded in establishing his humanity. The jurors remarked that "it appears in evidence that he had not the ordinary and prescribed instruction respecting the nature and punishment of desertion." The jurors went further, noting "his general character [which] is proved to be very commendable." They nevertheless sentenced him to hard labor for six months. Phillips would not finish his sentence, though. In September, when Rebel forces attacked the Union fortifications in Alabama, Phillips was taken as a prisoner of war and reenslaved by his attackers.[34]

In constructing their stories, freedom seekers also referenced relationships with their parents, claiming equality with free people who valued caring for elders. For these formerly enslaved men more used to losing connections with parents when sold off, the maintenance of such relationships proved a bedrock of liberation. Private Nelson Wright, for example, spoke of his ailing parents during his trial in hopes of winning exoneration while also affirming the meaningful relationship with his parents. On December 9, 1863, at age eighteen, Wright left his parents in Mississippi and enlisted in Memphis. He entered the Third USCHA stationed at Fort Pickering. Like many soldiers at the fort, Wright maintained close ties with his family. In the spring of 1864, he learned that his parents had become ill. Feeling responsible for them, he traveled home on April 15, but during their recuperation, he became sick and chose not to return. Eventually arrested for desertion, he explained to the jurors, "I went out into town to see my folks," but "when I started back I was taken sick and went to the Hospital with Small Pox." Although he admitted to becoming ill, he intimated that it was appropriate to leave and visit his family. In doing so, he upheld a bond to his parents, a relationship that was so important that his absence for helping them warranted leniency. Officers on the court-martial disagreed, convicting him and forcing him to do hard labor for one month.[35] Although convicted, Wright had used the chance to articulate his case and situated himself as a free man in a familial relationship that was more meaningful than the relationship established by his labor contract with the US Army.

Sergeant Stephen Jones suggested that he should be permitted to care for his family, too, yet during his defense, he also implied that he could not return to the regiment after helping them. A laborer from Giles County, Tennessee, Jones enlisted on December 7, 1863, leaving his wife behind. Five days after his enlistment, the army mustered him into the 110th USCI in Pulaski, Tennessee. After six months in the service, he decided to see his wife when he discovered she was ill. On June 25, 1864, he left his regiment at Big Shanty, Georgia. When the army captured him, he pled guilty but appealed to the officers of the court-martial, stating that he journeyed home to tend to his sick wife. He clarified that he alone could help: "she had no one to take care of her," he explained. While away, he added, he heard of a Confederate bivouac nearby, learned that the Rebels had seized members of the 110th USCI, and questioned whether he could make a safe return to his regiment. "I concluded that there was no use of me trying to hunt it up" and decided to stay home. Like Wright, Jones contended that he should be permitted to care for his family. The court disagreed with Jones's conclusions, convicted him, reduced him to the ranks, and sent him to prison in Huntsville, Alabama, for two years.[36]

As disappointed as Jones and others may have been when their stories failed to sway officers on the courts-martial, the stories themselves were significant. For the men transitioning from slavery in both the law and society, storytelling afforded them an opportunity to upend the depersonalizing legal processes and place themselves within relationships aside from those validated in legal documents. Underscoring their dedication to family, men like Phillips, Wright, and Jones refused to be bound to society only by their contracts of enlistment. Through the articulation of their associations with people, experiences, and institutions outside the US Army, they turned the courts into spaces to reckon with the familial dimensions of emancipation. They confirmed their roles as dutiful husbands and sons. As the war proceeded, men continued offering stories, yet they also presented more calculated arguments meant not to skirt contractual logic but to counter it with arguments directly addressing it.

"Pressed In": Disputing Contracts

By mid-1864, lessons in free labor gleaned during emancipation and military service partially reshaped the defenses that accused deserters made in the courts-martial. As the US government and US Army implemented policies to transform the southern economy in conquered portions of the Confederacy, enlisted Black southerners were exposed to rudimentary aspects of free labor. In South Carolina, for instance, reformers set up farms or provided employment on coal vessels or as mechanics that offered wages and rations to the formerly enslaved.[37] Meanwhile, commanders obligated Black southern laborers to work in Louisiana for compensation and enforced labor agreements reached between planters and freedpeople.[38] These reformers and commanders, often under Republican orders, thus applied a version of freedom defined by free-labor practices and individual obligations. Northerners empowered by the government and army urged Black men and women to make contracts with employers.[39] Those hailing from the Union-occupied regions who had family living under government protection learned of these free-labor philosophies.

The soldiers received free-labor lessons within USCT regiments, too. After the government welched on its promise of equal pay, officers and soldiers from the North familiarized southern comrades with the notion of contract violations. White and Black northerners alike penned letters calling for USCT soldiers to be "paid their just dues," as thirteen officers of the Third South Carolina (Colored) Infantry (later the Twenty-First USCI) wrote in November 1863. Because the government continued refusing the men equal pay, seventy-four members of the Fifty-Fifth Massachusetts Infantry sent a letter to President Abraham Lincoln in July 1864, "Demanding our Pay from the Date of our inlistment & our imediate Discharge Having Been enlisted under False Pretence."[40] Although USCT soldiers conceived of the pay issue as part of the larger struggle for equality, the letters reveal that they litigated it as a labor dispute, framing the injustice as a contract breach. Following the increased exposure to the implementation of free-labor policies, accused deserters from the South disputed charges, not only using the logic of contracts to win cases but also overtly engaging this logic during their defenses.

Since enlistment contracts played such a central role in desertion cases, accused deserters from the South constructed defenses that more forcefully and expressly addressed volition and contract legitimacy. Offering more precise challenges to the enforcement of contracts, they argued that they never truly deserted or intended to or that their contracts were invalid. Some, meanwhile, accepted the validity of their contracts yet called for a more capacious understanding of their responsibilities to the army. In making these arguments, they pushed back against the strict execution of contract obligations. They called for work conditions that allowed for their momentary departures from camp or their release from service. Although they did not always win their cases, freedom-seeking litigants thereby articulated a view of free labor that expanded on the predominant, legalistic approach central to employment in the US Army. Such an approach may not have altered the legal landscape or officers' jurisprudence, but it reflected Black southerners' efforts in the courts-martial to articulate their views on freedom and further shape military service in accordance with their views.

Accused deserters like Private Eli Graham directly addressed the enlistment contracts, arguing that the army had violated rules of enlistment by impressing them. Born enslaved in Warren County, Mississippi, in 1843, Graham traveled to Memphis during the war and, on December 9, 1863, entered the army, becoming a member of the Third USCHA. On May 20, 1864, he decamped. When captured and tried for desertion on July 8, Graham offered a statement to the court. "I was on duty that morning and when I went off duty," he began,

> I fired my gun for which I was arrested. They put me at work all day and said they were going to put me in the stockade so I ran away and joined the cavalry and was with them when I was arrested. I belong to the 11th LA. Infty. And was captured at Milliken's Bend. I never enlisted in this Regiment but was pressed in.

In his explanation, Graham noted that he left for fear of being imprisoned. He did not stop at that, however. By joining another regiment, he was perhaps strategically demonstrating that he was willing to fight. He then ended by noting his conscription, a point that threw the entire premise of the charge into question. He intimated that the recruiters violated his right to choose an employer and challenged the legitimacy of his enlistment contract. While showing that he was not a shirker, Graham maintained that the first contract was illegitimate, thus undermining the judge advocate's case. Although the court-martial convicted him and sentenced him to military prison for one month without pay, the case exemplifies soldiers' efforts to contest contracts outright.[41]

Unlike Graham, Private Alexander Gardner accepted responsibility for deserting, but he, too, challenged the contract. During his trial, he undermined his ability to fulfill his contract, offering a defense that stressed his gullibility while pinning the blame on fraudsters. Born in Garrett County, Kentucky, Gardner traveled to Meadville, Pennsylvania, by May 1864. There, he enlisted in the Forty-Third USCI.[42] On July 11, Gardner left camp on a pass but did not return. The army arrested him shortly after. When Gardner faced charges of desertion, the judge advocate followed the necessary steps to convict, proving the army lawfully enlisted and employed the prisoner. First, the judge advocate called a captain from the Forty-Third USCI and asked, "Was he properly enlisted into the U.S. service?" The captain said he "appears as such on the muster rolls." Next, the judge advocate produced the descriptive list detailing Gardner's name and age, where and when he was enlisted, and the company he joined. The prosecution thus verified Gardner's employment in the Forty-Third USCI.

Finally, to establish volition, the judge advocate recalled the captain and interrogated him about Gardner's state at enlistment. The judge advocate questioned whether the prisoner had full control of himself to be considered a deserter, which opened up an opportunity for Gardner to dispute the contract. The judge advocate asked, "Were there not substitute brokers there who made a business of reenlisting ignorant men when they caught them away from Camp by getting them intoxicated[?]" The captain confirmed such exploits: "There were." Gardner picked up on this point, offering his version of events.

"I went to the City on Sunday on pass," he commenced in a story to prove he never intended to leave the army. Then,

> on Monday about 1 o'clock I started back to Camp Wm. Penn. Pa. and got lost and met two men who asked me where I going, I told them I going to Camp William Penn, they said I was on the wrong road, they said I should let them look at my pass, they looked at my pass and tore it up and said it was no account. They brought me to town again, it was night when we got back, they said they would take me back to camp, they could make something by taking me to camp. They put me into the Car. I went to sleep and when I waked up I found myself changing cars and when they stopped I was in Boston, where they reenlisted me and gave me sixty ($60) dollars bounty. I wouldn't enlist unless they gave me something.[43]

In his explanation, Gardner shifted the blame from his shoulders to others' by presenting two popular tropes. First, he pointed to bounty brokers, nefarious men who were known to profit off the government's policy and attract volunteers with signing bonuses. These shady dealers were the subject of government inquiry as well as cartoons in *Harper's Weekly*.[44] Second, Gardner introduced a familiar theme from antislavery tracts: white tricksters duping Black men and women and dragging them into slavery. Works such as

Solomon Northup's *Twelve Years a Slave*, which went through six reprintings in the 1850s, popularized knowledge about such despicable enslaving practices. Throughout the 1850s, the seizure of freeborn or formerly enslaved men, women, and children and the publicity of such cases led many northerners to revise their mild acceptance of slavery in neighboring states.[45] In his statement, Gardner evoked animosity toward the internal human traffic across the North. To draw attention away from his faults, he may have also been encouraging the officers judging his actions to question his aptitude. If intentional, his technique risked requiring white authorities to make assumptions about the intelligence of people of African descent Gardner knew to be false, yet he strategically used such prejudices. He utilized the supposedly inherent inferiorities of Black people to win a case. In all, while admitting guilt, Gardner intimated his virtue and indicated that the deplorable predators taking advantage of him were ultimately responsible. He had crafted a story that demonstrated that he was another casualty of bounty brokers (if not man stealers) and persuaded the tribunal that the swindlers fooled him. Legally speaking, he undermined volition by representing himself as dimwitted. Strategically, though, he maintained his reputation, a quality more valuable than shrewdness when litigating blameworthiness.[46] By touching on these themes, he invited officers to consider a political problem while ignoring desertion jurisprudence. Gardner succeeded. The tribunal acquitted him of desertion.[47]

Gardner was not alone in suggesting that circumstances released him from his labor obligation, yet instead of pointing to charlatans, accused deserter Private Andrew Thompson of the First USCI attributed his absence to a geographic encumbrance. During his trial, Thompson pleaded guilty to being absent (which was articulated in the specification) but not guilty to the charge of desertion. In a statement to the court, he explained, "I received a thirty day furlough" on January 10, 1864, but when returning

> to join my regt. at Chattanooga, Tenn. at the expiration of my furlough I found [the bridge] burned crossing the Cumberland river. Then reported myself to Prov. Mar. at Louisville, Ky, and was by him sent to City Point Va. from thence I was sent to Camp Distribution Va. near Alexa. Va. where I remained until Aug. 21/64 when I left camp without permission and remained absent until arrested by a detective on 12th Sept. 1864 [and] taken to Prov. Mar. at Alex. Va. and by him sent to Prince St. Military Prison [in] Alexandria Va.

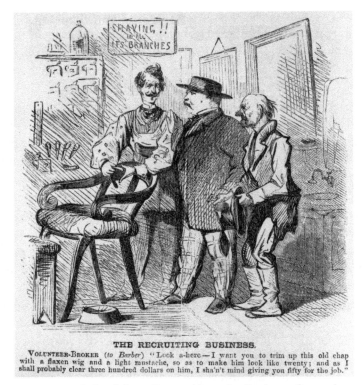

FIGURE 5.1 In his defense, Private Alexander Gardner referenced nefarious bounty brokers who located men and took portions of recruits' bounties. This cartoon depicted such charlatans. It showed a broker, presumably rich from government money, arriving at a barbershop with a gaunt, elderly man. The broker insisted the barber mask age and infirmity to dupe the US Army, so he could "clear three hundred dollars." "The Recruiting Business," *Harper's Weekly*, January 23, 1864. Library of Congress, LC-USZ62-132935.

With this meandering explanation, he contended he should not be held accountable because he was unable to return to his regiment and had made a significant effort to do so. The argument persuaded the court in part: the officers determined him guilty of the specification while only convicting him of absence without leave, not desertion. They sentenced him to be returned to his regiment under guard, forfeit ten dollars of his pay for two months, and make up the time he was absent.[48]

As the war entered its final year, soldiers continued challenging the legitimacy of their contracts. In his court-martial, accused deserter Private Solomon Fuquay of the 111th USCI threw doubt on the lawfulness of his enlistment and stressed his poor health. When the trial commenced, the judge advocate pulled the enlistment records and payroll of Company H and asked the enlisting officer, Captain Robert Hamilton, to confirm that Fuquay, a formerly enslaved Alabamian from Lauderdale County, volunteered willingly. On the stand, Hamilton verified Fuquay enlisted for three years. With the paperwork and testimony, the judge advocate was confident that he confirmed Fuquay's enlistment as well as the defendant's knowledge of the regulations and closed the prosecution.[49] During his defense, Fuquay contested the contract. But first he communicated to the court why he chose not to enlist. The prisoner began by asking a fellow soldier called as a witness whether he knew him and for how long. The witness told the court he became acquainted with the prisoner about two years earlier. The prisoner then asked the witness, "Has his health been good for the last three or four years?" to which the witness answered, "No sir, he has been complaining more or less of pains." The prisoner followed this by asking, "Did he enlist willingly?" "No sir," the witness answered, "he didn't want to hold up his hand to be sworn." "Was he forced to hold up his hand?" the prisoner pressed. "Yes sir," the witness exclaimed. Recruiters for the regiment had impressed enslaved men in the region before, perhaps leading to concern by the judge advocate that the line of questioning would doom the prosecution. So he stepped in, asking the witness whether the recruiter "threatened the prisoner if he should not raise his hand." Maybe feeling cowed by the prosecution's interrogation, the witness became uncertain, replying, "I disremember any thing about that now." Despite the prosecution's cross-examination, the court, whose curiosity had been piqued, asked the witness how many men Hamilton swore in when "he forced the prisoner to hold up his hand." "Right smart of them. Don't know how many," the witness stated. "Did Lieut. Hamilton do any thing more than tell them all to hold up their hands?" the court asked. "No sir," the witness muttered. The witness's testimony ended, and Fuquay closed his case, hopeful that the witness's account of the prisoner's persistent illness and the coercion by Hamilton would delegitimize the contract upon which the prosecutor based his case. But without unequivocal proof of coercion, the officers of the court-martial apparently did not consider the contract voided and convicted Fuquay of desertion. The court sentenced the prisoner to be dishonorably discharged and to have half of his head shaved before being drummed out of camp.[50]

Like Fuquay, Private Edmond Johnson challenged the army when it deemed him a deserter, but when tried in November 1865, Johnson argued that wartime conditions prevented him from fulfilling his contract. Born enslaved in Germantown, Tennessee, Johnson traveled to Corinth, Mississippi, during the war and volunteered on May 1, 1863, becoming a member of the 110th USCI. But his freedom was taken in September 1864, when his regiment surrendered to General Nathan Bedford Forrest at Athens, Alabama. He and many of his comrades became prisoners of war and were virtually reenslaved by Rebels who forced to do menial labor around Mobile until General Richard Taylor surrendered the city to Major General Edward Canby on May 4, 1865.[51] When released from Confederate captivity, Johnson reentered the service. He soon learned that he was categorized as a deserter. Upset, he penned a letter to an officer on November 2. "I have the honor to call your attention," he wrote, "that I have been reported a deserter and am restored to the Rolls without trial upon condition that I forfeit all pay and allowance due me for the time I may have been reported a deserter." But, he said, "I cannot accept as it would be virtually confessing a crime of which I am not guilty." For "the preservation of my character as a soldier," he continued, "I most respectfully request . . . that I be ordered before the military court to establish my innocence of the charge or if found guilty to be punished according to law." Trusting in his ability to tell his story and contest the charges, he had asked for a trial.[52]

The trial began on November 3, 1865, and during it, Johnson sought to undermine the designation of deserter by denying volition. During cross-examination of Sergeant William Barton, Johnson tried to prove he had been captured. He asked, "State if you ever heard the accused say that he had been a prisoner of war?" Barton replied, "I have." The court had questions of their own. "Did you ever hear the prisoner expressing an intention to desert the Army?" "I did not," said Barton. The court asked, "Do you know of him having been prevented by unavoidable circumstances on his part to join his company at an earlier time?" "I don't know," Barton answered. He then submitted, "He has said he was taken prisoner and taken to Mobile Ala with the Regiment." When the prosecution closed, the trial was paused. When it resumed on November 22, Johnson called Jack Wilson, a former captain of the 110th USCI. Johnson asked Wilson to explain his position and their relationship. Wilson said he had "command of 10 odd men, stragglers, +c." and was in charge from July to "the 24th day of September at which time we were surrendered to General Forrest." Johnson then prompted, "State if the accused became a prisoner of war by that surrender?" "He did," Wilson replied. Johnson asked about the "manner in which the accused performed his duty while with your Company." Wilson said, "He performed his duty well. I considered him a good soldier." With this testimony, Johnson demonstrated

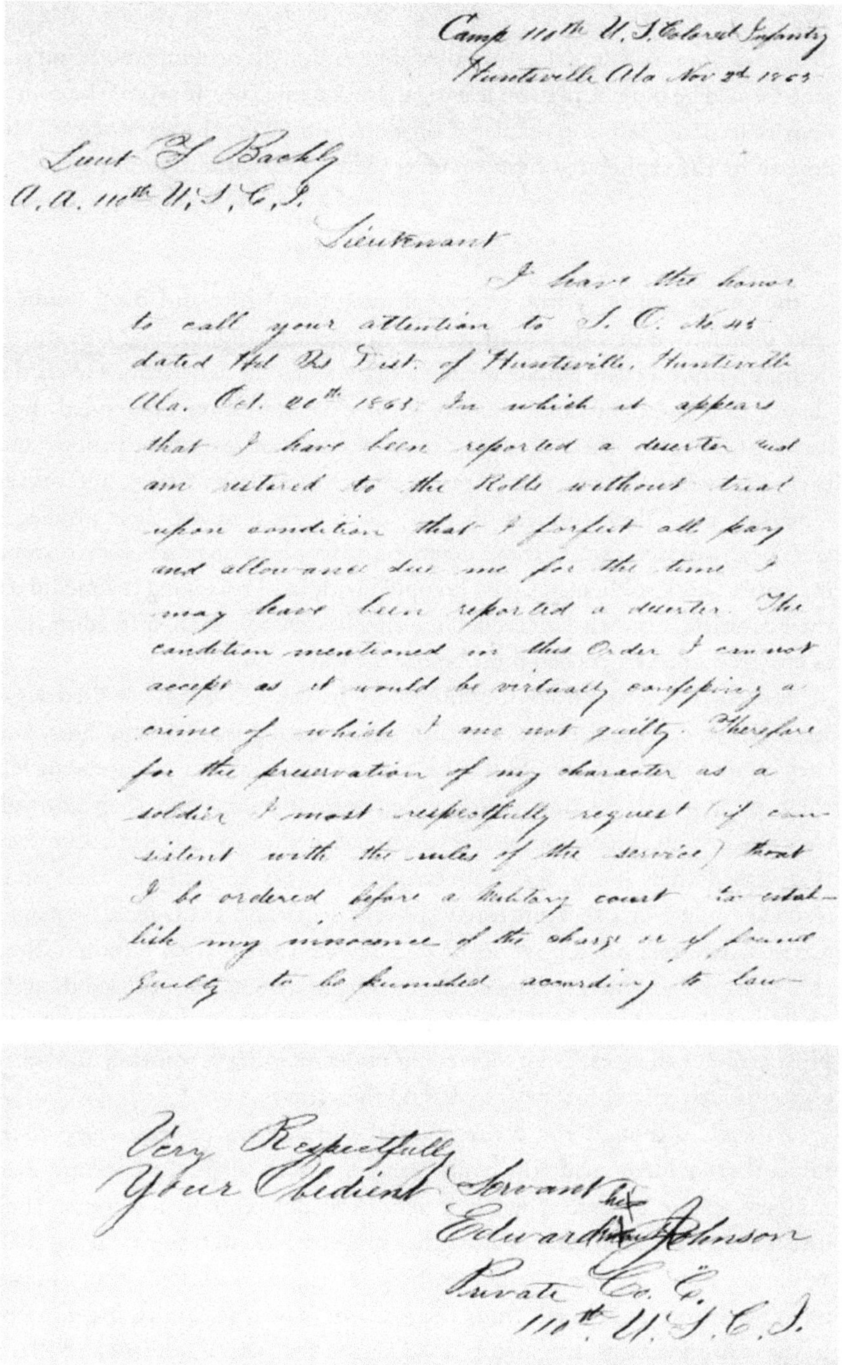

FIGURE 5.2 Captured while stationed in Alabama and held as a prisoner of war, Private Edmond Johnson was deemed a deserter during his time in Confederate captivity. When he returned to duty in the summer of 1865, he requested a trial to prove he was no deserter. Like many Black southerners, he trusted his ability to defend himself in the court-martial. Edmond Johnson, Compiled Military Service Record, National Archives, Washington, DC.

that he conducted himself as a soldier ably. Although he admitted being absent, he said he did not plan on leaving his regiment. The officers of the court-martial accepted Johnson's explanation, determining that he was not guilty of desertion. The exonerated Johnson returned to duty with his honor intact.[53]

In the courts-martial, white officers ensured that white and Black soldiers alike understood that they must remain in the ranks, honor their enlistment oaths, and fulfill their employment obligations to the US Army. Given the chance to argue their cases, though, formerly enslaved men defended their leaves of freedom. These accused deserters were not trained attorneys, and their arguments did not always prove effective. As late as 1865, one officer remarked that Black soldiers on trial "do not understand their privileges and means of defense."[54] These desertion cases show that, at least in some instances, Black soldiers not only grappled with legal reasoning to ameliorate their conditions but also succeeded in using the law to win their freedom, just as enslaved southerners had done before the war.

Indeed, formerly enslaved southerners in the US Army devised legal strategies to carve out liberties within a dominating legal system. Early on, they argued that they should not be blamed because their enslavement left them unprepared. As they addressed circumstances beyond their control, they also avoided being completely subsumed by the bureaucratic documents that erased their humanity. Countering a process of verifying their contractual obligations that mirrored slavery's legal and managerial violence, accused deserters offered stories that connected them with families. They thus affirmed a humanity outside the law. By mid-1864, the accused directly addressed the logic undergirding desertion jurisprudence, offering more sophisticated challenges. They showed an understanding of volition and what elements legitimized contracts to defend their leaves.

As such, although the courts-martial were arenas for enforcing discipline, these soldiers made the courtrooms spaces to shape the conditions of military service by defending their actions against certain restraints. They insisted that, if circumstances arose that prevented them from working, such as illness, responsibilities to family, or poor labor conditions, they should be allowed to take a break from the army or leave the service indefinitely. In these justifications, the men echoed claims that white soldiers and Black northerners offered during their trials for desertion. But formerly enslaved men were also fighting to define the scope of emancipation, making their arguments defenses of freedom. They had survived the violent conditions of slavery and strove to attain liberation on their own terms in the army. They critiqued the strict enforcement of labor obligations and argued for greater liberty of travel or the right to quit. They insisted on labor conditions that allowed them to absent themselves when they suffered as a result of uncontrollable circumstances, personal failings, or enfeebled bodies. These freedom seekers considered themselves liberated from having to abide by the overly strict workplace discipline of the US Army. Such claims did not influence how the army operated, but the men nevertheless transformed oppressive courtrooms into spaces where they could challenge the constraints imposed by officers. Since not many won their cases, a majority ended up in military prisons. Even there, though, the men remained determined to shape their lives—and freedom—within the ranks.

6

"Ought Not to Be in Prison": Petitioning State Officials for Freedom during Incarceration

"I TAKE THE pen to let you know by this letter my position," Private Charles Baltimore began his prison missive to Major General Edward Canby. A French-speaking Louisianan, Baltimore had joined the US Army in March 1863. The army placed him in the First Louisiana Native Guards (later the Seventh United States Colored Heavy Artillery or USCHA), a job demanding mental acuity and muscular dexterity.[1] Once mustered in, he headed to Fort Livingston, a stronghold on the Gulf of Mexico abandoned by Confederates when New Orleans fell to Union forces. He remained in service for over a year. Then, on August 4, 1864, he decamped. Six days later, his sojourn was cut short. The army apprehended him and, in October, tried him in New Orleans. He pleaded not guilty to desertion, but the officers of the court-martial convicted and sentenced him to two years of hard labor. On November 26, his sentence commenced at Fort Jefferson, an island fort that served as a US Army prison for thieves, mutineers, and deserters.[2] After a month of imprisonment, Baltimore yearned to return home and decided to write Canby. A West Point graduate, Canby was a professional general well regarded for his studiousness.[3] Perhaps knowing something of the general, Baltimore did not attempt to explain away his flight or challenge the court-martial ruling. He instead noted family suffering. "My mother and my wife are sick," he told the general, and "I'd like to go see them." Avoiding questions of duty, Baltimore closed the letter invoking the Almighty. "I beg you to send an order to my officers to give me this permission [to head home] because . . . it would be a great service for me and God will bless you for that." Baltimore's

Freedom Soldiers. Jonathan Lande, Oxford University Press. © Oxford University Press 2024.
DOI: 10.1093/oso/9780197531754.003.0007

prayers were answered. Canby forwarded an endorsement for release to the War Department, and Baltimore exited Fort Jefferson in March 1865.[4]

Baltimore's letter was one of many sent by convicted freedom seekers. These documents reveal how formerly enslaved prisoners made compassionate appeals, yet they also expose the soldiers' struggles during incarceration. In letters to US government officials and military commanders, incarcerated Black southerners often referenced the sacrifices made on the state's behalf to persuade officials they should be released, thus drawing on their relationship to the state to ensure their arguments registered. They requested that officials recognize that they had helped—and could still help—win the war. When leaders turned from the war on the battlefield to the war to reassert the US government's authority around the occupied South, prisoners shifted their arguments. They contended that they could return home as veritable Reconstruction soldiers. They would assist their families and, in doing so, support the project of remaking the South into a free-labor society built on male-headed households. In seeking exoneration, the inmates rarely offered contrition. They instead pointed to the relationship created at enlistment and

FIGURE 6.1 Private Charles Baltimore and many Black southerners convicted of desertion or absence without leave entered Fort Jefferson, a wartime prison in Florida. "Fort Jefferson, Garden Key, Key West, Monroe County, FL." Library of Congress, HABS FLA, 44-____, 1—22.

urged state officials to respect the exchange of service for freedom. Engaging the state, these formerly enslaved prisoners insisted that officials salute their sacrifices. They asked wartime leaders to recognize that their leaves of freedom were legitimate responses to conditions and sought release. The officials may have ignored such appeals (and often did), but the prisoners nevertheless demanded that the state justly adjudicate their leaves from the army. In their appeals, then, the prisoners voiced their views on the nature of military service and the relationship between themselves and the state to insist emancipation reflect their contributions to victory and aspirations following slavery's destruction.

"Appeal to You": Petitioning from US Army Prisons

Those convicted in the courts-martial often were incarcerated in prisons operated by the US Army. Hoping for an early release, freeborn and formerly enslaved men sent requests to officials. Although unaccustomed to and unschooled in petition writing, formerly enslaved inmates learned quickly and constructed unique petitions. Rather than criticize contract enforcement by the courts-martial as freeborn men had, once-enslaved soldiers stressed the social contract created at enlistment and pressed officials to see their value to the Union cause. Some freeborn soldiers used this tactic as well, but by their very nature, the letters from Black southerners were distinct. These incarcerated southerners endeavored to define freedom by asking officials to legitimize their reasons for decamping.

Courts-martial sentences ranged from fines and dishonorable discharge to death by a firing squad, but most commonly, tribunals ordered convicts to be remanded to hard labor in prisons.[5] The US Army did not have an obvious place to house convicted soldiers, however. Before the war, states, rather than the US Army or US government, largely operated prisons. (Not until after the war did the US government establish a facility at Fort Leavenworth in Kansas to imprison soldiers.)[6] As the number of prisoners convicted by the courts-martial mounted, it was unclear where soldiers could be placed.

In June 1862, Interior Secretary Caleb Smith wrote to Attorney General Edward Bates about the legality of sending courts-martial convicts to state penitentiaries. The US Supreme Court had settled the question in *Dynes vs. Hoover* (1857), which decided that US Navy sailor Frank Dynes, who had been convicted for attempting to desert, could be imprisoned in a penitentiary with common criminals.[7] Apparently unaware of the case, Smith asked Bates about the lawfulness of moving the increasing number of US Army prisoners to civilian prisons. Smith was also curious because he did not think army convicts and civilian criminals were analogous. He expressed the view that the goals of the military justice system and the judicial system for civilians were incongruous. "The fact is that the discipline of the Army and the penitentiary are wholly unlike except in so far as they respectively inflict personal suffering," Smith contended. He reasoned that imprisonment for military crimes was "not intended to crush the spirit, to humiliate and degrade" as was incarceration for civilian crimes.[8] Whether that truly was the intent of civilian incarceration depended on the reformer or penal philosopher one asked. But such thinking nonetheless reflected the widespread association civilians made between criminals and humiliation.[9] Smith's view of the punitive aims ended up mattering less than the Supreme Court's ruling, and the US government began sending those convicted after standing trial for desertion to a variety of penitentiaries that housed criminals convicted by civilian courts.

Without definitive guidelines, commanders generally sent white soldiers convicted in the courts-martial where it was most convenient or best suited circumstances dictated by the war. Early on, white deserters ended up in guardhouses near their regiments, as a Hoosier discovered. After numerous courts-martial, he explained, "the guard house is full of boys that ran of[f] home & come back." But inmates also lived in converted barracks and forts; they served their time in prisons with captive Rebels; and they were behind bars in state penitentiaries with local criminals.[10] In short, the US Army sent soldiers where it could house them, as President Abraham Lincoln affirmed late in the war. He stated that "prisons . . . the Secretary of War may designate for the confinement of prisoners under sentence of Courts Martial shall be deemed and taken to be military prisons."[11] As a result, convicted soldiers found themselves scattered around the Union and Confederacy.

Once the US Army admitted Black men to the ranks, convicted freeborn and formerly enslaved deserters of the United States Colored Troops (USCT) joined white deserters. Of the USCT soldiers convicted for desertion or absence without leave, a majority were imprisoned in a US Army prison located in a border state or an occupied portion of the Confederacy.[12] In Vicksburg, Mississippi, prisoners occupied a guardhouse adjacent to their regiments.[13] Convicted Black deserters spent time in Forts Norfolk and Yorktown in Virginia, which had allotted space for military prisoners. Others were confined in Forts Jefferson, Clinch, and Marion in Florida, or Fort Pickering near Memphis, Tennessee. Fort Delaware in Delaware City and Fort Macon in North Carolina provided further space.[14] The army incarcerated Black men in other occupied parts of the Confederacy, such as Morris Island and Hilton

Table 6.1: States Where Black Soldiers Convicted of Desertion or Absence without Leave during the Civil War Were Incarcerated

Free State		Enslaving State	
Connecticut	0	Alabama	6
Illinois	10	Arkansas	7
Indiana	0	Delaware	6
Iowa	0	District of Columbia	1
Kansas	0	Florida	54*
Maine	0	Georgia	4
Massachusetts	1	Kentucky	17
Michigan	0	Louisiana	16
Minnesota	0	Maryland	0
New Hampshire	0	Mississippi	33
New Jersey	0	Missouri	3
New York	6	North Carolina	3
Ohio	6	South Carolina	10
Pennsylvania	2	Tennessee	77
Rhode Island	0	Texas	1
Vermont	0	Virginia	16
Wisconsin	0	West Virginia	0
Total Imprisoned in Free States	25	Total Imprisoned in Enslaving States	254
Percent Imprisoned in Free States	9	Percent Imprisoned in Enslaving States	91
Total Imprisoned		279	

See Appendix for details and sources

*Before they were finally moved to a military prison in Florida, two soldiers were incarcerated in Mississippi and one soldier was incarcerated in Louisiana. Since they were ultimately imprisoned in Florida, they are included in the total number of convicted soldiers incarcerated in Florida.

Head, South Carolina; Ship Island, Mississippi; and Pulaski, Nashville, and Memphis, Tennessee.[15] Inmates completed their sentences in the Washington Street and the Prince Street prisons of Alexandria, Virginia, or the military prisons in Little Rock, Arkansas, and Chattanooga, Tennessee.[16] The county jail of Wilmington, North Carolina, and the jail at Camp Nelson in Kentucky furnished additional space.[17] Jails in St. Louis, Missouri; New

Orleans, Louisiana; and Charleston, South Carolina, gave the army space during Union occupation, too.[18] The fortifications around Washington housed convicted deserters. Black deserters also ended up in northern cells, like the former state prison in Alton, Illinois.[19] The army sequestered soldiers in state institutions, including penitentiaries in Auburn, Sing Sing, Clinton County, and Albany, New York, and the prison in Columbus, Ohio.[20] The variety of spaces reflected the haphazard incarceration of military convicts common during the war.

The overcrowded military prisons often lacked proper supplies and shelter for the men, and those convicted by the courts-martial yearned to escape these conditions and rampant disease.[21] But while Rebel prisoners of war could be exchanged when the Dix-Hill Cartel remained in force (July 22, 1862, to July 30, 1863), US Army soldiers convicted of crimes needed exoneration from US government authorities.[22] The surest means of release was an appeal. The men did not necessarily need to write a petition, as military officials examined courts-martial cases to ensure military justice was served. If officials discovered inconsistencies, oversights, or evidence of prejudice, they could overturn cases and set soldiers free. Yet thousands of soldiers also sent petitions, or letters from individuals or groups, seeking a pardon. From November 1863 to March 1865, Judge Advocate General Joseph Holt personally reviewed thirty-four thousand cases.[23] While Holt was the most industrious in conducting reviews, the most famous pardoner was Lincoln. The charitable commander in chief used the power to pardon repeatedly. Holt chalked Lincoln's enthusiasm to magnanimity, stating that he was "on the side of mercy" and "constant[ly] desire[d] . . . to save life."[24] Yankees hoped for such clemency from Holt, Lincoln, or other officials.

In these cases, freeborn soldiers, whether white or Black, petitioned based upon a belief that they could engage the state to obtain justice. Presidents commonly received pardon requests from citizens, who often felt a special connection to the executive during the nineteenth century. Lincoln's reputation as a common man meant many identified with him. Citizens thought the frontier attorney–turned–chief executive was truly their representative and would appreciate their plight. Letters arrived on his desk almost immediately after he took office. Although Lincoln may have inspired particularly strong connections, citizens' decisions to petition reflected a broader relationship they had with the state.[25]

Many thought it not only acceptable to write local, state, and federal officials with their concerns, but they also believed it was their representatives' responsibility to listen. White northerners and southerners frequently penned letters to leaders on an array of topics. Even those lacking suffrage, like women looking to end slavery, voiced their opinions in petitions. Abolitionist Angelina Grimké Weld, for instance, "urge[d]" women to petition legislators because, with "no such right" to the ballot box, "[i]t is peculiarly your duty to petition."[26] Black northerners also wrote to local, state, and federal officials to demand an end to racial discrimination and argue for policies, though they largely lacked voting rights. They flooded Congress with demands for an end to slavery despite these limitations.[27] Such beliefs in the state provided freeborn soldiers, whether white or Black, the knowledge and tools to engage the state. Throughout the war, freeborn soldiers petitioning for release deployed these skills.

In letters to officials for pardons, some freeborn soldiers convicted of desertion stressed the injustice of the courts-martial enforcing expired labor contracts. In a petition to Lincoln by way of Massachusetts senator Charles Sumner (Republican), attorney Alfred Bloor wrote on Private Philip Margraff's behalf. Margraff had enlisted in the Fifth New York Infantry, a regiment raised in April 1861. When the army transferred him to the 146th New York Infantry and extended his enlistment to three years, he thought it an illegal action and decamped. A court-martial tried and convicted him for desertion. Awaiting his execution, Margraff issued a criticism, which Bloor detailed for Lincoln: "He thought it an oppression that, enlisted, as he supposed, for 6 or 8 months, he should be required to serve for 3 years." Bloor added that the private thought that "it is the doctrine in which all citizens of the United States have been reared—that it is right to resist oppression." Margraff contended that the court-martial sustained an illegitimate contract that amounted to an oppression worthy of resistance. With the petition for clemency, he implied his trial was an injustice and called for Lincoln to overturn the ruling. Lincoln did not explicitly state whether he agreed with the prisoner's criticism, but he did stay the execution.[28]

Other soldiers disputed the legitimacy of contracts. A Marylander and two Hoosiers sentenced to be executed for desertion and thought to be "insane" or "ignorant and illiterate" sought reprieve. The cases were objected to because, it was implied, the enlistment contracts were invalid since the men had not volunteered with clear heads. In these cases, Lincoln released the Yankees from service. In another case, Lincoln requested "brief facts" about a convicted deserter in the Fourth Maryland Volunteers after an "appeal" was "made on the ground of unsoundness of mind," but the commander in chief never received follow-up information as there was no soldier of the name in the regiment. As in Margraff's case, Lincoln was silent on why he made his decisions or why he sought further information.[29] He might have shown sympathy rather than any concern for the legality of their contracts. In a letter to US House Representative Erastus Corning (Democrat, New York) after having dealt with a Copperhead dissenter, Lincoln asked, "Must I shoot a simple-minded soldier boy who deserts, while I must not touch a hair of a wiley agitator who induces him to desert?" Such reasoning may have guided the president.[30] But, whatever the cause of Lincoln's pardons, these soldiers (or those writing on their behalf) concluded that unsound contracts voided the sentences.

Not all argued on the basis of contracts. Men also simply sought compassion.[31] As they did so, they promised to staunchly serve the Union. To win a pardon, freeborn men like Black Cincinnatian Isaiah Price impressed upon officials his illness and his family's suffering. Price volunteered on November 30, 1863, and joined the Fifty-Fifth Massachusetts Infantry. The private received a pass after a month to return home. He overstayed his furlough and was later arrested as a member of the Fifth Massachusetts Cavalry. He was tried for desertion. He pleaded guilty to the specification of prolonging his furlough but not guilty to the charge. In other words, he disputed that he intentionally deserted. The court-martial convicted and ordered him taken to Castle Williams, a penitentiary in the New York harbor. In a "humble petition" written in October 1864, Price explained to a general that "your petitioner has been closely confined . . . which is daily causing a severe injury to his health."[32] Not granted a reprieve, the prisoner petitioned Lincoln less than three months later. Rather than stress his own health, Price pointed to his family. He began by summarizing his travails. He told Lincoln that he "received a pass" and "whent home and failed to return at the specified time." Feeling "asshamed to go back" and wanting "to keep from punishment," he enlisted in another regiment. His trial and conviction led to a sentence that "is pretty hard," he wrote. "I would not care so much for myself," he admitted to Lincoln, "but I have a wife and two little children" without "no way to get along." Under these circumstances, "I threfore appeal to you to do something for me and [my] family and I will be thankfull and prove my gratitude by being faithfull to you and contry herafter." He then asked Lincoln to "show some mercy to me and my family." Making the thrust of his letter his family's struggles, Price asked the president to consider their welfare and promised to be a dependable husband, father, and soldier upon his release. Lincoln's secretary passed the letter to Holt but, thinking Price was a bounty-jumper, he refused to release him. Price was sent to Fort Jefferson in February where he remained until his release a year later.[33]

Formerly enslaved soldiers imprisoned for desertion or absence without leave sent petitions as well. The soldiers likely learned how to construct these appeals from white officers and freeborn prisoners during their time in prison.[34] Yet the formerly enslaved prisoners did not adhere to the same reasoning as their freeborn peers. In their description of events leading to their cases, the soldiers obliquely engaged the notion of contracts. They undermined volition and shifted blame from themselves to violent officers. Unlike Margraff or the "insane" soldiers, though, they did not speak of contracts narrowly defined as labor contracts. They did not suggest that the officers unfairly held them to an expired agreement or that they were incapable of making a contract due to a mental disability. Instead, like Price, they pressed officials to see them as potential soldiers who could still contribute to the war. They additionally called on officials to honor the social contract they made at enlistment. They engaged the state and insisted officials read their petitions.[35] They argued that they had exchanged their service and labor for freedoms and urged officials to hear their pleas. In addition to gesturing to the agreement and labor already furnished, the formerly enslaved prisoners referenced the wartime goals of Republican officials and US Army commanders. They promised that, if freed from captivity, they would help defeat the Confederacy and rebuild the South as a free-labor society. The inmates strategically appealed to US government officials' interests by emphasizing that they had been—and remained— unfaltering patriots.

The letters reveal the ways in which prisoners developed their relationship with the state and learned to employ new tools for securing their freedom. By calling on officials, the prisoners demonstrated the view that they could—despite being convicted by courts-martial—make demands on the state. They pressed officials and commanders to comprehend the difficulties of maintaining their pledges to serve. They asked them to appreciate the extenuating circumstances caused by war or emancipation. With these documents, the petitioners pushed back against an unforgiving, unfeeling authority. The men pressured officials to recognize their overall value, not only their lapses in judgment, and respect obligations aside from those owed to the US Army. The inmates also challenged courts-martial sentences that deemed their desertions to see kin or their reactions to violent treatment as insubordination and, as such, punishable violations of the wartime social contract and enlistment contracts. Black soldiers averred that protecting family and living beyond the reach of violent authority were integral to freedom. In making these claims, inmates impugned the legitimacy of incarceration, arguing that it caused innocent people to suffer and eroded the broader goals of emancipation by undermining their power within the household. These consequences made incarceration an unjustifiable punishment and use of state power. In seeking release, then, they requested officials overturn rulings because they had been justified in leaving. Since the departures had been efforts to secure certain liberties, the prisoners insisted that officials come around to their versions of freedom. In other words, release was validation of their leaves of freedom, and validation of their leaves of freedom, and thus their views regarding emancipation, was just given their contributions to the Union cause.

"Wil Be a Good Soldier": Petitioning as Patriots

By the summer of 1864, formerly enslaved men imprisoned for deserting crafted letters requesting clemency that rested upon their relationship to the state. Although echoing courtroom defenses that undermined volition, these once-enslaved inmates did not directly attack the abusive or unjust enforcement of labor contracts. They instead stressed their service and ability to contribute to the war if given a pardon. Impressing upon authorities their military contributions, the prisoners touted their role in the war, intimating that the terms of the agreement held regardless of their conviction and incarceration. The framing allowed prisoners to shift the officials' attention away from disciplinary infractions. The soldiers called on authorities to respect their role in helping suppress the rebellion and insisted that they acknowledge that leaving when they did not understand the law, became ill, or were attacked were acceptable actions. By reclaiming their status as dutiful soldiers, therefore, the inmates hoped to redeem their reputations. They further recast themselves as capable contributors who could still subdue the Rebels, making their release not only just but also beneficial to the Union. In addition to the rhetorical value of highlighting their service, the emphasis on sacrifices affirmed their burgeoning relationship with the state and, in turn, empowered them to critique military justice.[36]

Prisoner Private John Handy, for example, spoke of his reputation and military service when he called on Major General Nathaniel P. Banks to value his past sacrifices and possible future contributions to the Union cause. Enlisting in Carrollton, Louisiana, on May 22, 1863, Handy joined the First Louisiana Engineers (later the Ninety-Fifth USCI). He served only briefly. On June 29, he decamped from Port Hudson and made his way to Texas. A provost marshal arrested Handy in May 1864, took him back to Louisiana, and locked him up in a New Orleans cell. A court-martial convicted him of desertion, sentencing him to work at hard labor for the remainder of his enlistment at Fort Jefferson. While awaiting transfer to Florida, Handy penned a letter to Banks that detailed his life as an enslaved man. Had Handy hoped for compassion to persuade Banks to release him, the incarcerated soldier would have misjudged the officer. Banks had exhibited little warmth toward Black soldiers, vetoing a bill that would have eliminated racial restrictions on the Massachusetts militia as governor and purging the Louisiana Corps d'Afrique regiments of Black officers upon assuming control of the Department of the Gulf.[37] Likely appreciating that mere sympathy would not be effective, Handy never appealed to Banks's good nature or claimed that the court wrongfully convicted him.

Handy detailed the circumstances surrounding his absence from this regiment in his July 1864 letter. He explained the crime and his suffering as a formerly enslaved man, an effort that contextualized his actions and attested to his character. "Sir," Handy began, "I have ben in prison 3 months and am tired of it and would like to get out and go to my regt again." He then gestured to his crime and his prior enslavement. "I was arested for desertion but I did [not] knows that I was doing anything wrong," he said. "I left my master 2 years ago and went and cooked for" Company I of Ninety-First Illinois Infantry after decamping. Here Handy did not deny that he undermined discipline by leaving. He instead requested an exception for his insubordination and mentioned an ignorance born of bondage. He continued, describing how a white soldier he trusted misinformed (or, possibly, lied to) him: "I had enlisted in the first la engineers [and served until] Capt Jones one of the men belonging to the 91 ill told me to come along with thee regt and it would be all right and I would be a soldier all the same and so I went with him and cooked for his company til we got to Brownsville." After leaving with the Illinoisians, Handy said he was arrested, convicted, and "I have ben here [in prison] ever since." Before closing his letter, he stressed his conduct as a soldier and affirmed his commitment to the war.

In his final pitch to Banks, Handy spoke to his behavior as a soldier. "I am a por corld man," he explained, and "I have ben a slave al my life." Such a life, he added, meant that "I never had the rules [or] regulations of the army read to me and I therefore knew nothing about the army I thought that it was just as good to be in the 91 ill as to be in my own regt." With this statement, he pointed to his inexperience and argued that this was not a punishable offense. His credulity stemmed from a life spent in bondage, a claim that squared (perhaps strategically) with many northerners' perceptions of slavery's evils.

Handy did not stop at that, however. "I hope that you will be so kind as ta forgive me this time and let me go to my regt," he said. "I promise you that I wil be a good soldier and know beter next time." Here, Handy spoke of his overall character while demonstrating that he had upheld his obligation to the US Army. He reported that he had intended the entire time—including the months spent with Ninety-First Illinois—to do his duty as a soldier. To accentuate his indefatigable commitment to duty, he promised he would "be a good soldier." With this, he ensured that Banks understood the stakes of the case—as it pertained to the war rather than Handy's life alone. If nothing else, Handy suggested, he could still support the cause. His entreaty succeeded. A reviewing officer assessing the case recommended the prisoner be returned to his regiment, "as it appears that his crime was committed entirely through ignorance, and with no intention on his part to do wrong." The officer revoked the prison sentence in September 1864.[38]

Corporal John Johnson penned a letter from Fort Jefferson to Lincoln, referencing his illness rather than ignorance, yet he also touched on his patriotism. Born enslaved in Baltimore, Johnson had been removed from his Maryland birthplace to Louisiana. On August 20, 1863, he enlisted in New Orleans and was placed in the Fifteenth Corps d'Afrique Engineers (later the Ninety-Ninth USCI). Johnson left his regiment while in Brashear City, Louisiana, decamping on October 5. He returned to the farm where he had been enslaved, apparently to see his wife and recover from a lingering illness. Arrested in January 1864, Johnson was tried as a deserter. During the February trial, an officer testified that Johnson had mentioned being sick before asking "to return home to be cured." The officer was unconvinced by Johnson, though. Casting doubt on his story, the officer added that Johnson also griped when he had not received a promised promotion. Johnson presented no defense, and the court convicted him, reducing the corporal to the ranks and sentencing him to hard labor without pay for ten years, which was later reduced to five years. On March 1, he was sent to Ship Island to begin his sentence. Three weeks later, he was transferred to Fort Jefferson.[39]

Arriving March 30, Johnson probably spent the summer like so many Fort Jefferson inmates, coping with the hot sun and scorpions, and on August 13, he decided to appeal to the president, citing disease.[40] Like Handy, Johnson submitted a pardon request that explained the broader circumstances of his crime and stressed that he was an ally against Rebel foes. Adding to these appeals, he mentioned his bout with microbial enemies. He first pled ignorance, stating that he "knowd nothing about" desertion. He then delved into his reasoning. "I went away from the righment," he said, "because I was sick

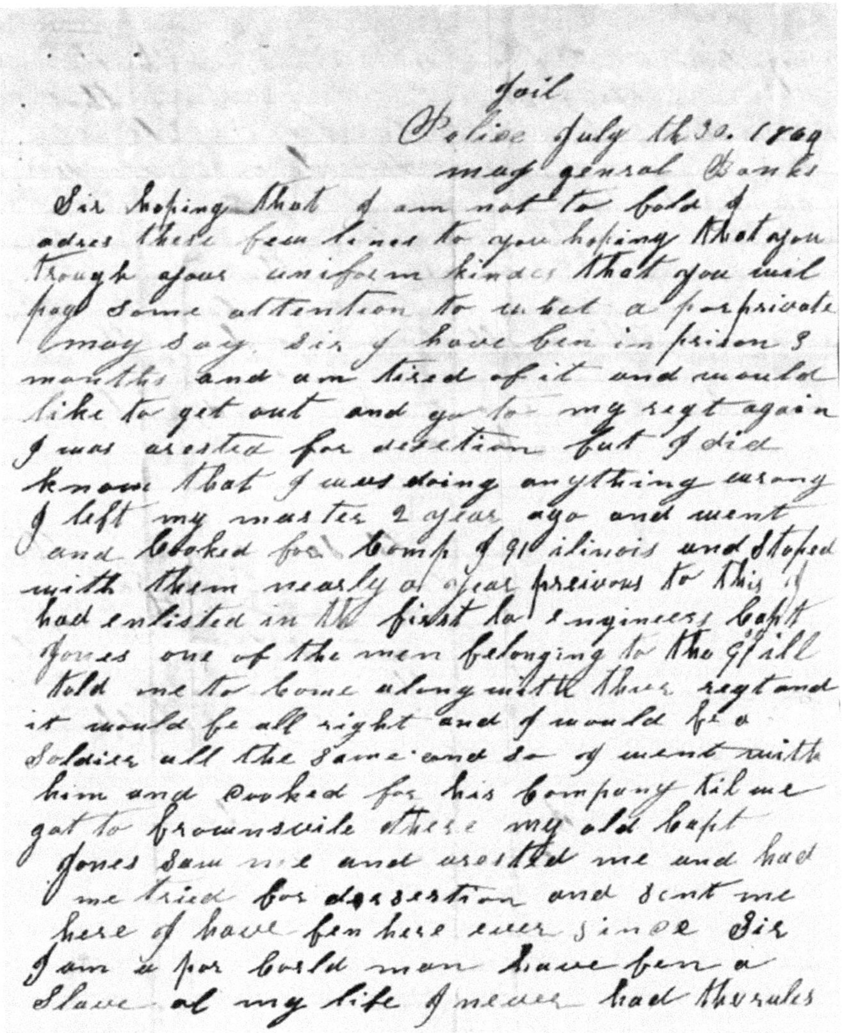
Jail
Police July th 30. 1864
maj general Banks
Sir hoping that I am not to bold I
adres these few lines to you hoping that you
trough your uniform kindes that you wil
pay some attention to what a por private
may say. Sir I have ben in prison 8
months and am tired of it and would
like to get out and go to my regt again
I was arested for desertion but I did
know that I was doing anything wrong
I left my master 2 year ago and went
and cooked for Comp I 91 ilinois and stoped
with them nearly a year preivous to this I
had enlisted in the first la engineers Capt
Jones one of the men belonging to the 91 ill
told me to come along with there regt and
it would be all right and I would be a
soldier all the same and so I went with
him and cooked for his company til we
got to brownsvile there my old Capt
Jones saw me and arested me and had
me tried for desertion and sent me
here I have ben here ever since Sir
I am a por colord man have ben a
Slave al my life I never had the rules

FIGURE 6.2 In a letter to Major General Nathaniel P. Banks, Private John Handy requested release from the Fort Jefferson military prison following his conviction for desertion. In addition to his plight, Handy mentioned the widespread problem of incarcerated Black soldiers in a postscript to his letter. John Handy, Compiled Military Service Record, National Archives, Washington, DC.

[and] stade untell I got well and I went and give myself up to them for the sake of giting Back to the rigment a gaine." Framing his desertion as such, he demanded that Lincoln consider issues other than discipline. He asked Lincoln to account for his intention of returning to do his duty before he fell ill. After offering his reasons, he reiterated his unfamiliarity with the

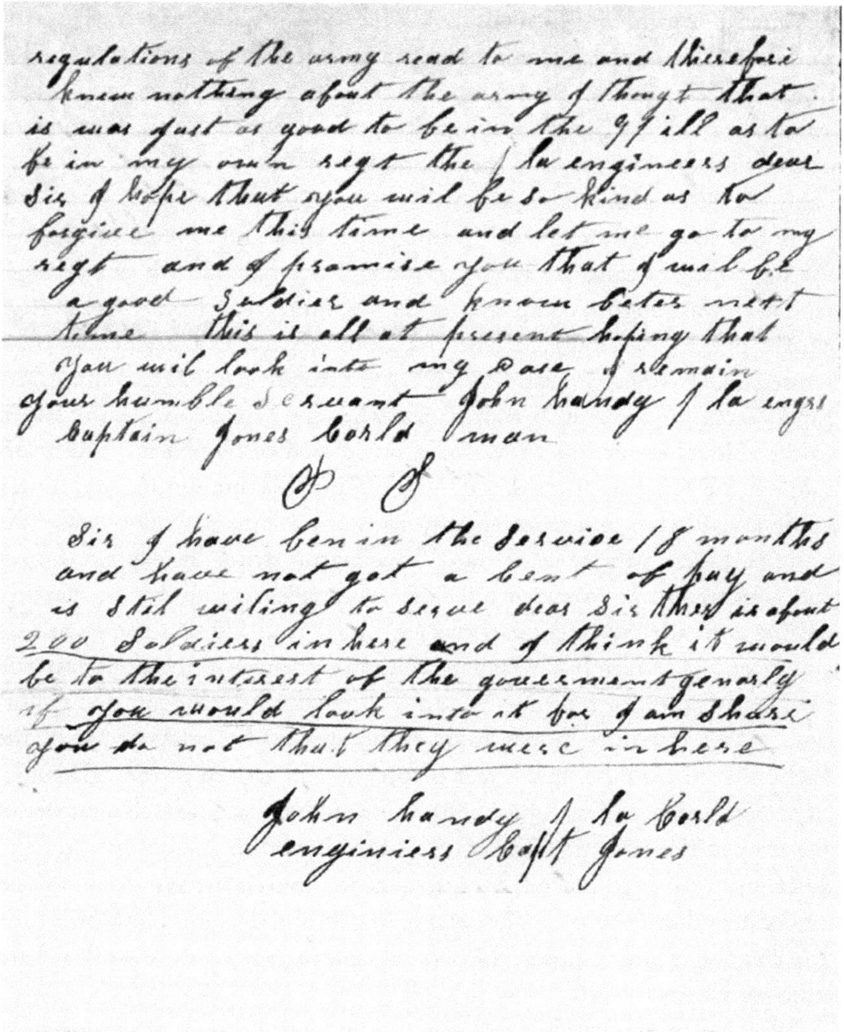

[handwritten letter reproduction]

FIGURE 6.2 Continued

Articles of War. To this, however, he contributed a statement regarding his inexperience with army protocol as it related to disease. "I never knowd," he petitioned, "that It was any harme for aman to leave the army to get well when he wase sick." Finally, he expressed his commitment to the nation and continued desire to support it, declaring, "I listed for to trie to be a servist to the united states and I wish to go back againe to the righment againe as I com out for a souldere." The letter, overall, issued a veiled critique of punishing sick men pursuing health (a criticism white soldiers also made early in the war) while requesting absolution based upon a determination to be a soldier. Lincoln's secretary read the letter and referred it to Holt. Whether Lincoln eventually read it, records do not say. Apparently, no reason to overturn the case could be found. Johnson spent another summer at Fort Jefferson before being released on September 6, 1865.[41]

In late 1864, Private David Washington appealed to Lincoln to consider the mitigating circumstances due to the violence he endured. On October 13, 1863, Washington completed a sixty-six-mile trek from Washington, Mississippi, to Vicksburg. At the riverfront city, he enlisted in the Third United States Colored Cavalry (USCC). On August 9, 1864, Captain Andre Emery attempted to punish Washington when the Mississippian complained to the colonel about Emery. Washington refused to be tied up. Like many soldiers, the Mississippian decried being hung by his thumbs. He told Emery he deserved better and threatened to leave the company. Unmoved by the protests, Emery persisted. Unheard, Washington struck his captain. Emery and another officer wrangled him. Left alone and tied up, he (or maybe a passing comrade) severed the manacles. Likely realizing that the assault on an officer would earn him a stay in a military prison—if not a one-way trip to an early grave for mutiny—he ran. He remained on the lam for a short time before the army caught him. As he awaited his trial, he sat in the Vicksburg guardhouse. Just a year before, he had arrived in the Mississippi city, volunteered, and won his liberty, but now, he found himself a captive of the army in the same city. The army charged him with insubordination and desertion. Washington needed to persuade the court-martial to look beyond his conduct during his trial. The defense fizzled, and the jurors convicted him. The court sent him to prison for one year and required him to work at hard labor for no pay.[42]

Washington thought himself unjustly imprisoned and sought exoneration on account of Emery's treatment. The prisoner directed a letter to Lincoln on November 26, 1864. Perhaps he appealed to the commander in chief, knowing of his reputation as being kindhearted. But Washington did not rely solely on Lincoln's goodwill. He asked Lincoln to overlook his defiance and reflect on why he reacted to Emery as he did. He pointed to Emery's flawed, cruel leadership. Likely hoping that by sharing knowledge of violence he could shift Lincoln's frame of reference from insubordination to injustice, Washington described the mistreatment he suffered. He started the letter explaining the situation. "Dear Sir," he said, "My Capt fell out with me [and] fer what I dont know he struck me [and] I came up to the courthouse and reported him." The prisoner said he sat in the courthouse until his captain, who was summoned, arrived and added, "the capt he then came up frome campt and reported me feradeserter." Washington told the president a court sent him to jail for twelve months without pay before proceeding to make his appeal. "I am agood solger all ways has done what is right[, but] my cap[tain] drew apistole on me," suggesting that he had been compelled to act. "I drop these fewlines asking fer Jested [justice]." He explained to Lincoln that he had been wrongly imprisoned. "I ought not to be in prson if I had Jested done me [for] I am a colerd man [and] I have no edication[.] I dont know nothing at all abought law [and] I am willing to do all I can for you as a solger or a man[.] if you please doe all you can fer me[.] please let me hear from you."[43] Like Handy, Washington set the facts within a broader context and offered the full story to call attention to the violence he suffered. Washington challenged the army's jurisprudential inclination toward discipline. He unburdened himself of blame for striking Emery by focusing Lincoln on the captain's behavior.[44] He appealed to Lincoln to recognize that the crime was a singular error, not part of a pattern of downright insolence, and perhaps justified self-defense. Washington affirmed his character and insisted that the infractions did not spoil it—especially because his actions were provoked by an abusive officer. In closing, he promised Lincoln he could still be of service to the Union in the final phases of the war, a point perhaps meant to coincide with Republicans' attempts to continue the fight in 1864.[45] Whether Lincoln personally read the letter or not, Washington's attempt misfired. Holt recommended against clemency, and War Secretary Edwin Stanton concurred. The court's decision stood, and Washington ended up in St. Louis's Gratiot Street prison. Although this prison was less horrific than more notorious Civil War prisons, Washington likely suffered until the War Department ordered his release in September 1865.[46]

The letters from these prisoners reveal how formerly enslaved soldiers emphasized their commitment to soldiering to persuade officials of their character. The men did not dwell on the misery or gild letters with flowery or sentimental prose. They jettisoned mere appeals to sympathy, even when they could have spoken of serious travails. They instead attested to their patriotism. They argued that they had been capable soldiers who broke the rules because they knew no better, they succumbed to disease, and were subjected to violence by officers. In doing so, the inmates asked authorities to overlook, if not condone, their actions and release them so they could continue serving patriotically. The men sought clemency, but they went beyond asking for forgiveness.

FIGURE 6.3 Black soldiers convicted by the courts-martial spent part of their war in military prisons. Some formerly enslaved men convicted of desertion served out their sentences in the guardhouse in Vicksburg, Mississippi, pictured here behind the soldiers forced to "ride the wooden horse." "Provost Marshal's Guard House, Vicksburg, Miss." Library of Congress LC-DIG-ppmsca-35292.

By situating themselves as soldiers unjustly imprisoned for reacting to harsh treatment, prisoners affirmed their continued commitment to the Union.[47] As patriots, they called for a revision of the military justice system and for authorities to respect their wishes for a more understanding, less violent workplace. Instead of strictly interpreting their actions according to military regulations, inmates argued that authorities should consider the abuse they were subjected to by officers and recognize insubordination as a slip of judgment or the result of a reasonable reaction to the situation.

"My Poor Famely Is Suffering": Petitioning on the Behalf of Kin and Country

Formerly enslaved men carried their "good soldier" strategy into the later stages of the war, but they went beyond noting their future military contributions. Thinking of the postwar regime, they contended that they could be of service to the Republican project of rebuilding the South. In this, they were unique from northern comrades because, as southerners, they planned to return to the former Confederacy and to care for their families as providers, an important goal of Republicans. This fact gave formerly enslaved army prisoners the distinct opportunity to argue that their return home would put them at the vanguard of Reconstruction. The emphasis on kin reflected the transition of inmates' patriotic appeals to civilian objectives. They suggested that by freeing them to return to their wives, children, and parents they would assist the broader goal of remaking the South as devoted free-labor husbands, fathers, and sons. They would support turning the razed Confederacy into a collection of independent, self-reliant households, a view that mirrored Republicans' postwar aspirations.

By 1865, Republican leaders, as well as many US Army soldiers, saw the war as a mission not only to suppress secession but also to eradicate backward thinking in the South and deliver white and Black southerners from the world enslavers built. Many Republicans questioned how well a free-labor system would succeed in the former Confederacy, especially as most laborers had been trained to respond to force rather than incentives.[48] Republicans had encouraged economic advancement through reform in response to proslavery ideologues who believed that people of African descent could only be coerced to work. Accordingly, Republican authorities implemented policies to support the transition of Black southerners, especially in 1864 and 1865. The formation of the Bureau of Refugees, Freedmen, and Abandoned Lands (or Freedmen's Bureau) by Congress on March 3, 1865, marked Republicans' dedication to this project in the waning days of the war. But the Freedmen's Bureau was not the sole means of reconstructing the South. The US Army had been (and would remain) the enforcement arm of the Republicans' postwar project. While the US Army rooted out Rebels, northern reformers descended on the South to alter the economy. Abolitionist crusaders, free-labor prophets, and government agents imposed northern reforms that ranged from new foundations for employer-employee relations, like wage labor and contracts, to education in socioeconomic behaviors. One of the more critical goals for reformers was showing Black families how they should function.[49]

Following stories of separation in prewar narratives by Black abolitionists and in abolitionist literature, such as in Harriet Beecher Stowe's *Uncle Tom's Cabin* (1851), northern reformers thought that they needed to remake Black families torn asunder by enslavers and ill-equipped for freedom. Often ignoring the familial practices enslaved people made to accommodate the horrors of human trafficking, many northerners assumed that slavery destroyed Black families. Fearing that without a Black family that looked and functioned like a white middle-class family emancipation would falter, they encouraged monogamy and familial structures with Black men adopting patriarchal roles. Commanders supported this outlook, encouraging soldiers to take wives and remain committed to one woman. Government policy tacitly endorsed such views, making Black southern women, their freedom, and their rights visible to the state only through male kin. Black southern men, including soldiers, learned of the government's objectives and, in many cases, bought into them. They hoped to start families and assume responsibilities over their wives and children, so the men took the opportunity during the war to do so. Indeed, some married in camp and provided for kin to the extent they could while serving.[50] When imprisoned for desertion, some formerly enslaved inmates tapped into this strain of reform, asking authorities to release them to care for their families and, in doing so, contribute to the postwar reconstruction of the South. They implied that their absence due to incarceration meant that their families were a burden on the state, a problem Republicans strove to avoid. As such, the men invoked their paternal obligations to persuade authorities to respect their potential contributions toward remaking the South.

In the early part of 1865, Private Jack Morris, with the help of fellow inmate Private Samuel Roosa, presented his release as both a boon to his family in need and to the country. Before the war, Morris and Roosa lived in dramatically different worlds. Morris, a formerly enslaved Louisianan who joined the First Corps d'Afrique (later the Seventy-Third USCI) in September 1862, met Roosa, a New York painter drafted into the army and mustered into the Twentieth USCI, at Fort Jefferson. A court-martial convicted Morris for theft and desertion, sentencing him to two years of hard labor without pay. A different court-martial convicted Roosa of aiding a recruit in deserting and sentenced him to six months at hard labor with a twelve-pound ball chained to his right leg. At the fort, the men became acquainted. During their conversations, Roosa learned of Morris's court-martial case and found the facts distressing. Likely familiar with the appeals made by Black leaders to gain rights in the North, Roosa assisted Morris in petitioning for release. Roosa wrote to Lincoln on January 24, 1865, asking him to appreciate the contributions Morris had made to the military and could still make to his family. Morris, Roosa wrote, "dont mind the punishment that he is receiving here but he would like to be where his serviseses may be of some use to the contry and the proceeds of which may be used for the support of his famely which is in great need of it." Here, Roosa noted Morris's devotion to the cause. Unfortunately, the attempt failed. Holt forwarded the letter to Lincoln and advised the merciful executive against clemency, explaining that Morris had admitted guilt and the court proceedings confirmed that he committed the crime.[51] Although he was not released, Morris had learned skills he swiftly applied on his own.

On February 26, 1865, Morris fired off a letter to Brigadier General Daniel Ullman that stressed the importance of family and his role as a soldier equally. Perhaps Morris strategically selected Ullman. Ullman had demonstrated compassion toward Black southerners when advising officers to lead USCT regiments with "kindness . . . [as] your guide" and had pushed for Black soldiers to be given greater autonomy, advancing the controversial idea of allowing freeborn Black men to elect their officers. Such actions might have suggested to Morris that Ullman would be sympathetic to his pleas.[52] The Louisianan offered appeals emulating Roosa's. Given that Morris misspelled similar words as Roosa, Roosa likely contributed to or even wrote the letter. Nonetheless, Morris signed it with his name, meaning the letter reflected, at the very least, more of a joint effort than the letter to Lincoln. Morris began with an apology. "I am sory" for the "military offance," he wrote, and "if I should remain here five years I would be no less sory." After expressing his regret, the prisoner said he wanted to be released but "not on the account of the work we have to perform." He instead wanted to be released "because my poor famely is suffering for a daily support." He then said he would do the work necessary to provide for them. "I am willing to return to my regimetn and do my duty as a true and patriocic soldier," he explained to Lincoln. Unlike Roosa, who wrote at length about his devotion to the fight, Morris also stressed his importance to his family's well-being.

Morris's rhetorical strategy drew the general's attention away from his wrongdoing and concentrated on the consequences of his imprisonment on his family. While he surely anticipated gaining sympathy by mentioning his kin, he did not detail their misery, suggesting that he did not invoke their pain to inspire an emotional response. He gestured to his family to shift the frame of consideration from discipline to the casualties of incarceration. In the appeal, he also spoke to prominent conceptions of an intact family and his masculine duty. Morris echoed reformers who wished to regulate Black families and articulated white northerners' views about proper gender roles within a free-labor society. He implied that incarceration denied him the ability to uphold the responsibilities many white northerners considered critical to the success of emancipation. It seems Ullman remained unmoved by the adroit appeal, however, for Morris labored in prison until December 3, 1865.[53]

As the war entered the last few months, the US Army continued enlisting formerly enslaved men, including a thirty-three-year-old carpenter and father of six from Nashville, Tennessee. Isham Barr, who had enlisted as a substitute for a drafted man, was mustered into the Eighty-Eighth USCI in January 1865. Yet miliary duties were not always top of mind. During the first few months of service, he often traveled home to see his wife and children without explicit permission. Following a trip home in March, the army arrested Barr. Needing to maintain disciplinary integrity, a court-martial convicted him as a deserter. Likely hoping the stint in prison would curb his wandering ways in the future, the court-martial had him incarcerated at Fort Pickering from June to September 1865. As Rebel armies crumbled, the soldier sat imprisoned. A few months after his release, the US Army transferred Barr to the Third United States Colored Heavy Artillery (USCHA). But neither his imprisonment nor a new regiment served to alter Barr's behavior.[54]

In late 1865, the US Army occupied cities within the former Confederacy, and with most white northerners heading home, Black soldiers manned forts around the South. Stationed in Memphis, Barr continued doing his duty for the army—and to his kin. Even as he helped enforce abolition and the transformation of southern society, he made unapproved journeys. On December 19, he traveled to spend a month with his family. On January 22, 1866, he returned to camp. Apparently seeing nothing amiss in his extended trip, he notified his captain of his return. The captain had Barr promptly arrested and tried for desertion. The court-martial convicted him, this time for absence without leave. The court then sent him back to Fort Pickering for four months without pay. To keep him from absconding, he was put to hard labor with a ball chained to his leg.[55]

In a plea for release to Major General George Stoneman on March 12, 1866, Barr deemed his incarceration unjust. He showed no penitence for his flight. He defended his visits home. He explained that the army unfairly imprisoned him. Persuading the inscrutable Stoneman was no easy task, though. Stonemen had aligned with Democrats before the war and, in 1866, still lacked much concern for formerly enslaved men, women, and children. While not condoning anti-Black violence, he strictly enforced regulations on USCT soldiers as commander of the Department of Tennessee in Memphis and had a difficult time imagining Black men as citizens, even as the US Army became a pivotal player in protecting the emancipated. Barr noted the injustice of his imprisonment, yet he concentrated on his wish to uphold his responsibility to his family to coax the Democratic general. "Sir, I take the liberty of addressing . . . you in hopes of obtaining . . . justice," Barr began. Providing context, he said, "I went out side the fort to see my wife and family and remained about 3 hours away and came back and reported to my captain. He as soon as I reported to him put me in the stockade." Then, Barr offered an explanation for his flight, "I was always accustomed . . . to go between roll calls to see my family and thought of course I could do [the] same here but I was most disagreeably mistaken." With these remarks, Barr conveyed his interpretation of service. By stressing that he reported to his captain, he implied that he had faithfully served, for his trip home was within the terms of duty. As such, the disciplinary actions amounted to a violation of the agreement to serve and take a leave of freedom when he wished. But Barr did not stop at this.

Speaking to broader issues throughout the South, he stressed his family's dire needs. "I have a large and helpless family without a provider and if I am kept here much longer they will starve." Barr observed the importance of helping care for his family, and in referring to himself as an absent "provider," he highlighted men's patriarchal role at the center of Black homes during Reconstruction.[56] Like fellow incarcerated freedom seekers, Barr asserted that he wanted to support kin—as he was expected to under the auspices of free-labor manhood—and could do so if released. If he remained imprisoned, the government would need to take up his responsibility, leading to government welfare. He implied that his incarceration hindered progress toward a new South. In short, Barr framed imprisonment as the reason Reconstruction might fail. In referencing his family, Barr spoke to his contribution to the Union cause while also downplaying his role as a soldier, a significant point given the ongoing problems in Memphis.

By not defining himself as a fighting patriot, Barr responded to tribulations that he may have realized Stoneman faced in Memphis. Stoneman confronted white southerners' unrelenting efforts to reassert power and reimpose the prewar racial code. Black civilians had pushed back, making plain their determination to choose when and where they worked and to take control of their

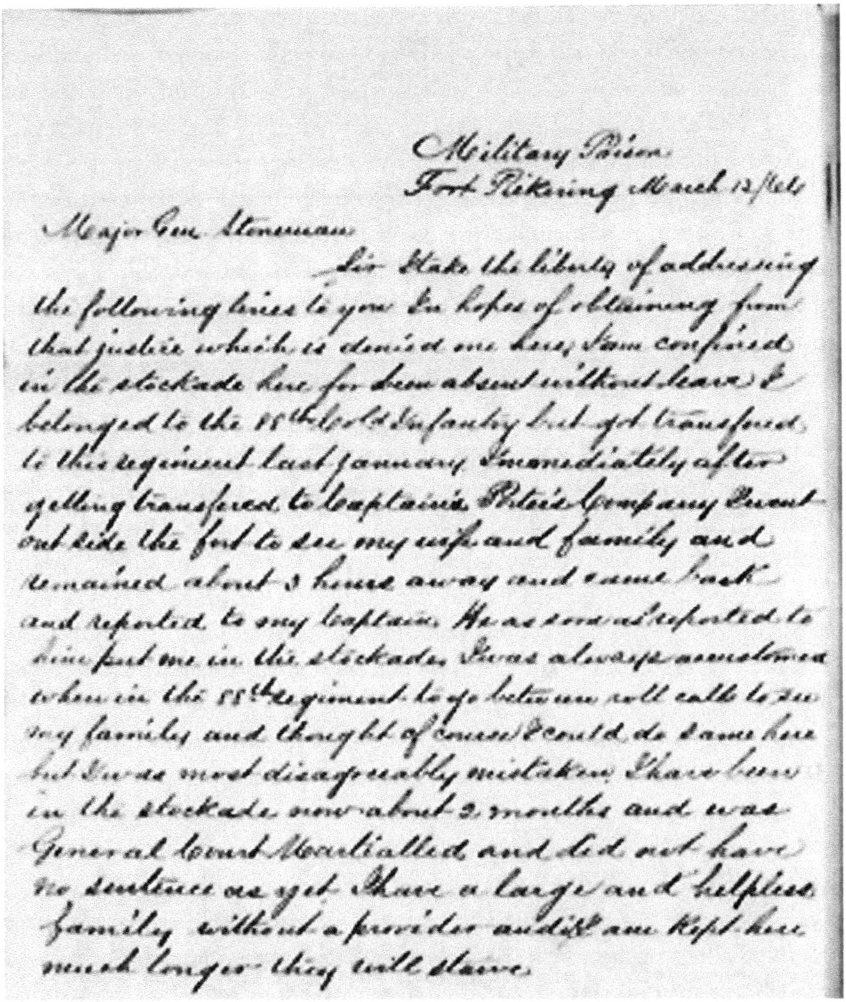

FIGURE 6.4 In a letter from the military prison at Fort Pickering, Private Isham Barr appealed to Major General George Stoneman for freedom and justice. Barr said his family in Memphis needed his help and suffered in his absence. Isham Barr, Compiled Military Service Record, National Archives, Washington, DC.

bodies. Black soldiers generally realized that effusive violence and vengeful acts could result in a backlash and distract from their goals of gaining citizenship and equality.[57] However, these objectives did not deter Black soldiers in Memphis from furnishing armed support to their civilian friends and family. Stoneman recognized the soldiers' part. To placate white supremacists, he shockingly disarmed the US Army soldiers of the USCT despite civilian

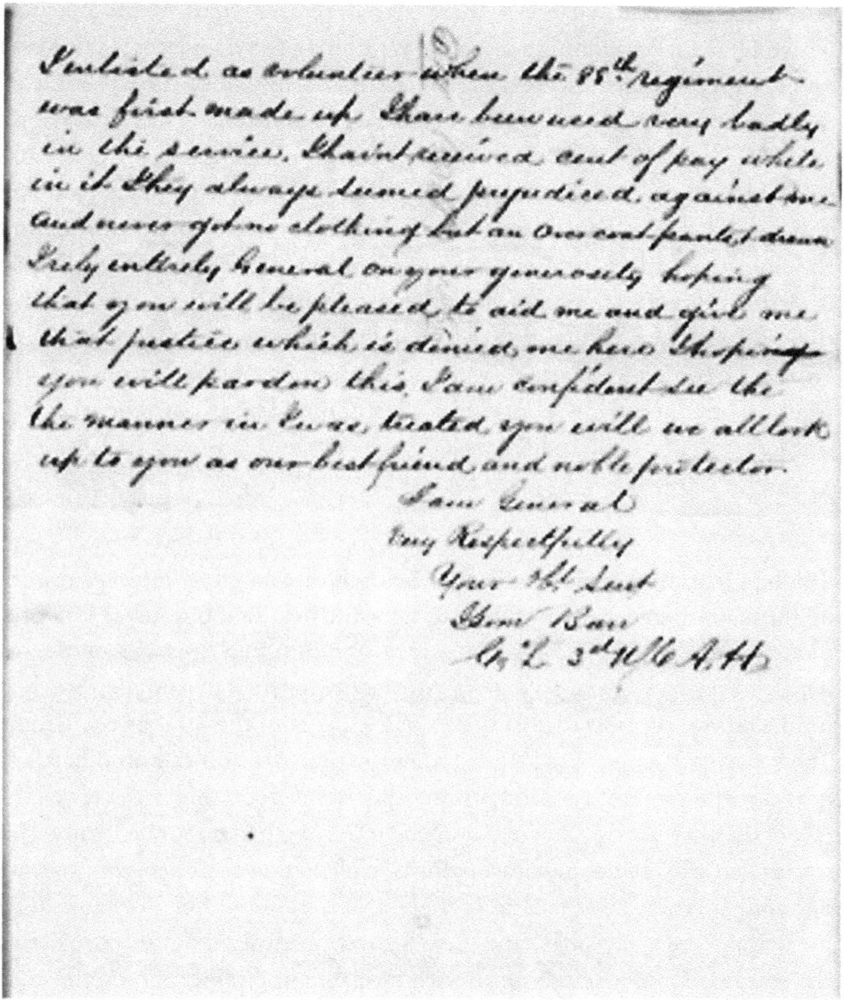
I enlisted as volunteer when the 88th regiment
was first made up. I have been used very badly
in the service. I haint received cent of pay while
in it. They always seemed prejudiced against me
and never got me clothing but an Over coat pants & drawers.
I rely entirely General on your generosity hoping
that you will be pleased to aid me and give me
that justice which is denied me here. I hoping
you will pardon this. I am confident see the
the manner in I was treated you will we all look
up to you as our best friend and noble protector.
I am General
Very Respectfully
Your Obt Servt
Geo Barr
Co L 3rd U.S.C.A.H.

FIGURE 6.4 Continued

threats and outbursts of violence committed by white supremacists. Perhaps anticipating that an appeal that stressed his wartime contributions might fail to persuade the beleaguered Democrat managing the reconstruction of Memphis, Barr instead identified his duty as a husband and father. Unlike other alleged deserters, therefore, he did not focus on his potential as a "good soldier." Barr's rhetorical strokes failed to move Stoneman, but a month and a half after he wrote, the US Army mustered him out. Barr headed home on April 30, 1866, probably anticipating a joyous permanent reunion with his wife and six children.[58]

But, as he returned home, Barr may have seen signs of the mayhem white Tennesseans would unleash on Memphis a few days later.[59] On May 1 and 2, white supremacists seeking to overthrow the gains formerly enslaved men and women made during the war attacked Black neighbors and soldiers across the city. White rioters killed forty-six Black residents and caused nearly one hundred thousand dollars of damage to Black churches and homes.[60] This brutal attack would be but one of many throughout the South. As Black soldiers stationed around the South or languishing in prisons received the news that they would be returning to civilian life, they encountered recalcitrant white southerners who attacked formerly enslaved people to reclaim power and erode their coveted freedoms. The trials of emancipation continued after Confederates surrendered and soldiers resumed civilian life.

The humiliation and discomforts of being incarcerated in military prisons might have sapped soldiers' desire to fight for freedom, but instead, imprisonment inspired new forms of resistance. The prisoners operated on the belief that they had agreed to a social contract with the state and, despite their incarceration, considered themselves participants in the war for the Union. Their sacrifices empowered them to engage the state and call on officials to hear their plight. From behind prison walls, these "good soldiers" stressed the role of their service to the nation and said it outweighed minor incidents. This strategy enabled the imprisoned patriots to claim that their decisions to leave due to ignorance, poor health, or violent officers should be overlooked. As the war entered a new phase and the US government set about reconstructing the defeated Confederacy, imprisoned husbands and fathers noted the need to care for their wives and children, not only shifting the emphasis from insubordination to blameless people's suffering but also to the ongoing effort to transform the South into a free-labor society.

In conveying their claims, the inmates insisted that government authorities listen to their views regarding the burgeoning relationship between the formerly enslaved and the US government. They asked officials and commanders to be sensitive to extenuating circumstances and accommodate them, rather than punish them for conditions resulting from their enslavement. They demanded employment that afforded them the latitude to care for themselves, avoid violence, and provide for their families. Once the war entered its final stages and Republicans looked toward reconstructing the seceded states, prisoners explained that they would support this project, serving as veritable Reconstruction soldiers. With their letters, therefore, these convicts expressed their views on military service and their relationship to the state as early as 1864, making them among of the first of the formerly enslaved to offer their views. They would not be the last, of course. Throughout Reconstruction, freedpeople called on the US government to provide them with numerous rights, contributing to the development of the social contract and shaping postwar ideas of citizenship.[61] But these prisoners engaged the state, urging leaders to honor the exchange of service regardless of their incarceration, and offered their views how the postemancipation state would operate before the war had even ended.

Conclusion: The War for Liberation within the Ranks

"AFTER REACHING HOME the disability continued with such severity as to render me physically unable to return to the command," Joseph Williams wrote about the inglorious end to his Civil War service. The Mississippian's time in the US Army had likely begun with more grandiose martial dreams. Deserting slavery in 1864, he had traveled northwest from his home in Pontotoc County to Memphis as the US Army tightened its grip on the Confederacy. In July, the twenty-five-year-old enlisted. The US Army mustered him into the Fifty-Ninth United States Colored Infantry a couple of weeks later.[1]

He joined a regiment that had recently earned accolades for its engagement with Rebels who served under Major General Nathan Bedford Forrest. The Fifty-Ninth spent much of the war garrisoned around the western edge of Tennessee at Memphis. By June 1864, though, the US Army needed them for combat when Brigadier General Samuel Sturgis defended the rail lines in northern Mississippi. The task was critical, for the rails supplied Major General William T. Sherman's forces during the campaign against Atlanta. Despite widespread views of Black men as cowardly, white officers of the Fifty-Ninth had faith in the "average plantation negro" that they had supplied with a "new suit of army blue" in preparation for just such an occasion.[2] They drilled and equipped the men for battle, giving one officer hope. The white Buckeye hailed from a Democratic family in which the patriarch possessed "no confidence in Negroes." After seeing the men drill, the Ohioan reassured his father: "I am pretty well satisfied that Negros can be made to fight."[3] At the Battle of Brice's Crossroads, the men proved him right. Confederate forces assailed US cavalrymen and infantrymen north of Tupelo, and when Forrest flanked the Yankees, the white soldiers retreated. The Fifty-Ninth covered that retreat and, as the regiment's colonel later reported, repelled the Rebels "with bayonets and clubbed muskets."[4] Their success was modest. Indeed, Forrest's cavalry ultimately proved victorious and spent the evening after the battle killing and reenslaving Black soldiers.[5] But those in the Fifty-Ninth who survived must have been proud to have faced off against attacking Rebels under Forrest after the massacre of Black soldiers at Fort Pillow. Williams might have been bullish about his service after hearing of his comrades' combat feats. Yet, after being mustered in, he learned that not all adversities in Civil War service came during the heat of battle.

Williams joined during a lull in the regiment's combat action but nonetheless served a harrowing, albeit brief twenty days. In camp, the men endured spartan discipline under exacting leaders. Some Black southerners were introduced to the military's force during enlistment. They had been impressed, as a lieutenant recalled. "The plan for '*persuading*' recruits," he wrote, "never failed to get the 'recruit.'" As the Yankees saw it, the "negroes were held as property by their masters," so recruiters "appropriated [them] as such, along with mules and horses . . . as a 'military necessity.'"[6] Men like the enslaved Tennessean Samuel Davis opposed service yet ended up in the ranks anyway.[7] Once in the regiment, the men endured relentless officers. "The strings are drawn very tight," an officer wrote. "I have never Seen a white Regt. Governed by as rigid discipline," he added.[8] If necessary, another officer wrote, discipline was enforced "at the point of the bayonet."[9] Such discipline was common throughout the US Army, but some formerly enslaved men accustomed to working under conditions enforced by the systematic use of violence would not abide. Men like Davis decamped.[10] Whether or not Williams struggled against this stringent discipline and wished to run, he quickly encountered a more pressing issue.

Posted to Waterford, Mississippi, Williams succumbed to disease. Many in the Fifty-Ninth fell prey to the epidemics that swept through the enslaved population during the war.[11] In 1863, an officer of the Fifty-Ninth had reported that "the condition of the health of the regiment was very discouraging," with nearly eighty dying in two months. Contributing to the problem, the formerly enslaved men were frightened of care at US Army hospitals. To them, the officer wrote, "going to the regimental hospital was considered equivalent to death." Superstition kept some away. Others had a longstanding distrust of white physicians.[12] Williams contracted what he later surmised was a combination of diarrhea, dysentery, and leptospirosis. Like many soldiers, he did not visit the hospital for care. In his weakened state, he managed to trek home to recuperate instead. Comrades had decamped and returned shortly after. Williams may have likewise anticipated rejoining the ranks once he recovered. But before Williams could return, the army mustered his regiment out in January 1866. He was labeled a deserter, a brand he wore for forty years.[13]

In 1896, Williams filed to have the label removed. His decision was in part financially motivated. An 1889 law offered soldiers who had been unable to finish their "term of enlistment by reason of ... wound, injuries or disease" a chance to have desertion expunged and to earn a pension.[14] Williams might have also wanted the designation dropped and his short time in the service honored. Whatever the motivation, his petition signaled that he did not accept the label. He testified that he had been sick and upon "reaching home the disability continued with such severity" that he could not "return to the command."[15] In other words, he had left to recover his health and remained absent when he could not shake disease. These actions, he argued, did not make him a deserter. He had taken a leave of freedom.

Williams may have been crafting his story to persuade pension bureau agents who would decide if he should receive compensation. He may have been willing to try countless tactics, even dubious schemes, to navigate the bureaucratic labyrinth and locate the various documents demanded for a pension. Although the system was not intentionally racially discriminatory, Black veterans like Williams often lacked the skills necessary to work through the bureaucracy, the money required to succeed, and the records to prove their identity and other facts.[16] Yet Williams was not attempting to defraud the government in defining his flight as a leave of freedom.

Three comrades testified on Williams's behalf, including Virginian Hillard Johnson. Johnson had served from the regiment's creation to June 30, 1865. He had witnessed discipline, battles, and diseases throughout the conflict, experiencing successes and heartache. He was, in short, an unimpeachable patriot, yet he empathized with the man deemed a deserter. He said in 1896 that Williams had "without any entention of deserting left his company and Regiment at Memphis, Tenn, while very sick with Flux and swomp fever." Johnson had also gathered from people who knew Williams that "after arriving home ... he became ... disabled for military duties by reason of the effects of the disabilities ... and wholley unable to return to his said command." Johnson affirmed Williams's intent, sickness, and inability to serve. He supported his claim to have "desertion" removed from his service record. In his eyes, Williams was not a deserter. Despite his testimony, Williams's application was denied. He died still officially labeled a deserter.[17]

Freedom Soldiers shows that the formerly enslaved Mississippian was more than a deserter. He was an enlisted freedom seeker. The history of once-enslaved soldiers who left the army is not simply an account of sullen, unfaithful, cowardly men who decamped without permission. Historians of white deserters demonstrate that, while their actions were first condemned and then chronicled as evidence of soft patriots, craven men, and bounty-jumpers, their flight exposes truths about the era and its people. Freeborn men abandoned armies because they believed that as citizen-soldiers they remained profoundly independent. The flight of men like Williams chronicled throughout this book exposes deeper meanings as well. The soldiers' stories reveal that formerly enslaved southerners did not truly become freed men upon enlistment. Emancipation was a protracted process contingent upon wartime circumstances, and that process continued even after they suited up in Union blue and killed their onetime captors. During their service, soldiers like Williams marched toward freedom, but they could be thrown back toward slavery. Undoubtedly, for Williams and his comrades, as for so many formerly enslaved soldiers, the US Army offered opportunities. It especially presented them the chance to fight oppressors and earn wages. Yet, when officers brutalized, families cried out for aid, disease spread, or wounds festered, some soldiers decamped. Their flight, as well as their defenses of their departures within the courts-martial and from US Army prisoners, expose the challenges enslaved southerners faced during their wartime exodus from bondage within the ranks.

Enslaved men identified the US Army as a potential ally, a powerful force to counter the will of their enslavers, but military service was a constraining occupation, not a liberating job. Unsurprisingly, the incongruity between the men's expectations about freedom in the army and the necessity of strict discipline to manage a fighting force led to conflict. Indeed, enslaved men enlisted to protect their kin or fill their empty stomachs. They donned uniforms because the rags enslavers outfitted them with hung from their undernourished bodies. They carried rifles, as it was the first time many could hold a gun without deadly retribution. They willingly dug latrines and felled trees, knowing that they excavated for a liberator rather than an oppressor. In short, many formerly enslaved men wholeheartedly embraced their first job as free laborers in the US Army. They thought service liberated them. Yet for many, military service proved to be an exceptionally controlling occupation. Some who were manumitted upon joining the United States Colored Troops (USCT) chafed under the command of white northerners determined to shape the men as soldiers and free laborers. This conflict between the officers and the soldiers caused discord within the ranks.

After the enlistment of tens of thousands of men who had been enslaved, the War Department devised a new system to select leaders. Vetting white northerners, officials chose USCT officers set on controlling the imagined chaos that emancipation might unleash. White officers came to their work convinced that African-descended soldiers were either racially inferior or sullied by slavery. Racial prejudices were exercised not only on an individual basis but were incorporated into institutional frameworks that empowered individual preconceptions. The newly manumitted soldiers experienced firsthand the ways in which racism—even if latent or paternalistic—shaped government policies without conscious effort and how biases regarding the nature and scope of liberation limited the possibilities of institutions charged with managing emancipation. Through military regulations and such practices common within camps and the military justice system, white officials impeded liberation. Not all formerly enslaved men would submit. They turned to time-tested tools of resistance.

Recently enslaved southerners in the ranks used prewar political tools to resist white officers and bureaucratic impediments. They adapted methods crafted to ameliorate the conditions of slavery to suit the challenges within the US Army. They used mobility to evade harsh disciplinaries. They cared for themselves and their families. They acclimated to the courts-martial, learned desertion jurisprudence, and challenged prosecution. When convicted and incarcerated, they learned to incorporate the language of Republican policies and wartime sacrifices into petitions, and they requested release, arguing that the army reproduced injustices common during slavery while ignoring the problems stemming from wartime emancipation. In each of these instances, the men pushed back against institutionalized racism and notions of free labor strictly enforced. They engaged with the state, maneuvering and experimenting with flight, appeals, and petitions to create a productive or, at least, less hostile relationship with the state. In doing so, they trudged on toward freedom, as they wished to labor under conditions without violent enforcement and for an employer who permitted them breaks to pursue self-liberation.

These conflicts show that emancipation was a drawn-out process within the US Army that lasted from the moment the men left slavery through to Reconstruction. Formerly enslaved soldiers faced continuous trials. The very events and institutions that made their freedom possible constrained how they could live. The stories of Civil War freedom seekers who ran from the army and defended their actions in the courts-martial or prisons lay bare these limitations and exposed the practical challenges dogging them. Such stories do not discount the valor they and their comrades demonstrated in their army careers, in and out of combat. Yet the divergent accounts shift the lens to the USCT soldiers who did not find that military service afforded them the chance to be fully free. Their experiences show that enlistment was transformative. But it did not end their struggle. Black southerners in the army strove toward liberation based upon years of captivity because no single moment, event, or government policy could undo the multifaceted oppressions that constituted southern bondage. The road to liberation was protracted, winding, and encumbered, littered with obstacles and antagonists. In pursuit of liberty, Black men in the army kept fighting after they fled enslavers and entered the ranks.

Military service may have been a boon to the men, but all did not end in glory. The men's experiences immediately after emancipation typified the persistence of unfreedoms throughout Reconstruction. Historian W. E. B. Du Bois wrote of Black southerners basking in the warm rays of freedom before bewailing the reemergence of oppression and the dark pall of Jim Crow eclipsing liberation. "The slave went free," Du Bois penned, and "stood a brief moment in the sun; then moved back again toward slavery."[18] But, as the manumitted southern soldiers learned from 1862 to 1865, the violence and racial confines that came to define the new order did not emerge after the war. There was undoubtedly sunlight. There was, however, little solace in its glow. While the war may have marked the dawn of a new day, the process of emancipation did not culminate when Black southerners entered the US Army. Nor were the gains of abolition turned back only when Confederate veterans returned to civilian life, when unreconstructed white southerners overthrew Republican governments, or the Civil War Amendments became dead letter. The struggle against forces determined to waylay freedom seekers began during the war. For Black southern men serving in the US Army, the march out of slavery commenced when they deserted their enslavers and enlisted, but it continued throughout their service and into Reconstruction.

Recognizing the persistence of such unfreedoms complicates the story of Black military service. Without a doubt, Black men bravely fought for liberation on Civil War battlefields and found the experience empowering. In the years following the war, the soldiers and their families used the memory of gallantry and sacrifices as a weapon against discrimination and as leverage to demand rights.[19] Black descendants, including novelist Richard Wright, shared stories of kin who "ran off" and then "resentful of slavery . . . joined the Union Army to kill southern whites."[20] Black artists and activists, from poets Paul Laurence Dunbar and Henrietta Cordelia Ray to educators Booker T. Washington and

Fannie Barrier Williams, recounted and celebrated their heroism in odes.[21] As an activist rather than solely a scholar, Du Bois kept his faith in the significance of Black Civil War service a decade after he grew skeptical of Black military service generally. "Results prove that" fighting for the country "loyally and fully" was "justified only in the Civil War, where Negroes were after all fighting for their own freedom," he claimed.[22] These luminaries' perspective on Black Civil War service reflected the import assigned to the soldiers' courage for the first generation of Black men and women after slavery's demise.

In the late twentieth and early twenty-first centuries, the soldiers still loomed large. They became not just a symbol for Black Americans but for the nation. They embodied downtrodden patriots' triumph over oppression. Their patriotism depicted in movies such as *Glory* (1989), *Lincoln* (2012), and *Emancipation* (2022) yielded touchstones for audiences. In schoolrooms and at National Military Parks, Black Civil War reenactors recovered memories of these fallen heroes to subvert stereotypes and tout positive characteristics of Black masculinity. Such lessons for schoolchildren and battlefield tourists reframed popular Civil War narratives around the War for Emancipation, rather than the War of Northern Aggression or the Brothers' War.[23] Monuments built across the country of Black soldiers, including *The Spirit of Freedom* in the nation's capital, confronted Confederate shrines primarily erected early in the Jim Crow era and in response to civil rights activism after the mid-century defeat of fascism.[24] At the launch of the National Museum of African American History and Culture on the National Mall in 2016, President Barack Obama pointed to the benighted years of bondage when the enslaved "felt the cold weight of shackles and the stinging lash of the field whip," but he then called attention to those who "buttoned up . . . Union Blues to join the fight for . . . freedom" to demonstrate the active contributions of African Americans to the destruction of slavery and the nation's survival.[25] Scholars have continued exposing the heroism of those who fought for freedom. The most recent accounts of the soldiers' experiences, including those that grapple with the enslaved people's dark prewar days in bondage and complicated entrance into the US armed forces, stressed the relationship between the formerly enslaved soldiers and the US Army as they worked together to overturn enslavers' mission to build a monstrous new nation. These works showed the empowering aspects of military service, such as the battlefield heroism of brave individuals and the dramatic raids into enemy territory to liberate enslaved southerners.[26] These histories, like those offered as early as 1867, have further enriched the history of the conflict, detailing the contributions freeborn and enslaved Black men and women made during the country's fratricidal war. Each of these efforts helped supplant reductive or erroneous histories of the war in highly visible public spaces and in the erudite pages of history. Such a triumphant story of uplift served as an important corrective to longstanding prejudices and the interpretations of the past peddled by apologists for slavery. Yet there were those whose wartime experiences included but were not confined to the valorous conduct that has been recorded for over a century.

The story of Black Civil War service has many dimensions. The complications exposed by formerly enslaved men who decamped reveal the many obstacles even the most stouthearted and patriotic individuals faced on the rocky road to freedom. Such struggles show that the fight was waged off the battlefield as well as on it.

FIGURE C.1 Erected in Washington, DC, *The Spirit of Freedom* monument offers a tangible expression of the symbol Black Civil War soldiers have come to embody in the national memory. The men—whom the inscription deems "fighters of freedom"—stand bearing their muskets with Frederick Douglass's call to arms etched in marble behind them: "Who would be free themselves must strike the blow." Library of Congress, LC-DIG-highsm-04880.

When enslavers looked to establish an eternal sanctuary for bondage, enslaved men across the Confederacy acted, first escaping their captors and then joining the Union cause. Like formerly enslaved men and women across the South, they strove toward freedom, hoping to eradicate the many vestiges of slavery in their daily lives, yet they specifically pursued liberation in the US Army. The drive to end slavery steeled formerly enslaved soldiers who defied Rebels, including those who had raised the black flag, in combat. But this drive also led some to respond to impediments to their deliverance within the US Army. These enlisted freedom seekers balked at constraining discipline and abusive officers. They also strove to care for their family and health. Such men left the army, as they had bondage, yet remained committed to the broader war because the pursuit of certain opportunities denied during captivity could not be relinquished. They left the army without authorization, defended their actions in courtrooms, and petitioned from dank jail cells. The enduring fight to seize these chances within camps, courts, and prisons shows that some men kept chasing liberty. On and off the battlefield, they marched toward freedom, fighting a war for liberation against enslavers—and within the ranks.

Acknowledgments

"Children ran about with bundles of blankets or knapsacks for their papas, or begged the privilege of carrying a gun [for their fathers]," the artist observed of the jubilant meeting of Black soldiers and their families. Drawing the heartrending reunions in Little Rock, Arkansas, for the May 19, 1866, issue of *Harper's Weekly*, the artist captured the day's "high good humor" and the "outburst of uncontrollable affection" as the soldiers exited military service and embraced their wives and children. The image of the reunifications (which graces this book's cover) showed the soldiers' delight. It was plain to the artist that family had, at least in part, sustained the warriors as they encountered terrible perils during the Civil War. Researching and writing of such soldiers, I learned the true importance of love and support so vividly on display in Arkansas. I discovered that many enlisted freedom seekers could not have made it through the war or emancipation without others. This lesson is prevalent in our oldest stories and a proverb I have often heard. Yet, in researching the soldiers' tribulations over the last decade and knowing that the stakes were life, death, or reenslavement, I came to more keenly appreciate how crucial kindness and guidance can be, especially on dark days. This lesson has made me a more compassionate man as well as a more grateful person. I am now more thankful for the aid provided by others, including those who furnished encouragement and direction as I researched, wrote, and revised this book. I could not have completed this project without the following teachers, archivists, scholars, and kin.

As a first-generation student who had been urged by his high school guidance counselor to forgo college, I am indebted to undergraduate professors who inspired me when the prospect of finishing college was daunting. Without sufficient finances and unsure whether to pursue a degree or find a job, I began at Harper Community College. There, Tom DePalma turned my nascent interest in Abraham Lincoln and reverence for the film *Glory* into an abiding obsession. In classes on rhetoric, Joshua Sunderbruch dragooned me into thinking, a particularly important contribution given my many years of academic lethargy. When I continued at DePaul University, Margaret Storey nurtured my burgeoning Civil War fascination, coaxing me to research Chicago's Copperheads. In my final year as an undergraduate, she spurred me to spend an enchanted semester of research at the Newberry Library, an experience that convinced me that days in the archives could be long and lonely yet exhilarating. Matthew Abraham, meanwhile, introduced me to thinkers like Frantz Fanon and Edward Said, the study of whom galvanized my curiosity, and recommended that I pursue a doctorate. I thank these professors for opening the door to a gratifying life of thought.

I found graduate school to be a blessing, and it was, in part, because of the many good folk I met during my years in Northern Ireland and New England. I appreciate the camaraderie of Neil Harris, Ronan Hart, Conleth Mullan, Kristin O'Brassill-Kulfan, Tamsin Reilly, and Connor Salters at Queen's University Belfast. They welcomed me to Ulster County and made my first year in graduate school uplifting. Those concurrently pursuing their doctorate at Brown University, including Felicia Bevel, Amanda Boston, Ashley Bowen-Murphy, Samuel Caldis, Charles Carroll, Patrick Chung, Suzanne Enzerink, Javier Fernandez Galeano, Anne Gray Fisher, Talya S. Housman, Henk Isom, Rachel Knecht, Alicia Maggard, Harry C. Merritt, Isadora Mota, Daniel Platt, Les Robinson, Elizabeth Rule, and Luke Smith, furnished some of the best conversations I have had in and out of seminars. Such discussions made my time in Providence a pleasure and contributed to the development of this project.

Several historians offered studied counsel, which proved useful either before entering graduate school or during my education. I am most grateful for the advice or assistance of Faiz Ahmed, Roquinaldo Ferreira, Paul Finkelman, Linford D. Fisher, Eric Foner, Matthew Guterl, Jennifer L. Lambe, Brian Kelly, Heather Ann Thompson, and Seth Rockman. At Queen's, Catherine Clinton provided invaluable guidance, equipping me with the knowledge for success in graduate school.

Without the supervision and patience of the following dissertation committee members, this project would be seriously inadequate and scarcely coherent. I thank Jim Downs, who helped me better understand how enslaved men, women, and children experienced the transition from slavery to freedom during the Civil War era. I thank Françoise Hamlin, who pressed me to challenge myriad assumptions and cheered me on when my confidence faltered. For his careful counsel and unyielding encouragement, I am indebted to Michael Vorenberg. He prodded lazy thinking and sharpened my ideas. I owe these scholars much and offer them each my sincerest gratitude.

Traveling to archives and libraries around the United States to research this project, I received aid tracking down sources at institutions that permitted me to spend years searching for clues in countless dusty boxes and decaying books. I thank the industrious archivists and librarians associated with the New England Regional Fellowship Consortium, including the Rhode Island Historical Society, the Massachusetts Historical Society, the Connecticut Historical Society, the Boston Atheneum, the Rauner Library (Dartmouth College), and the Houghton Library (Harvard University). I appreciate the support of those at stops along the way at the Historical Society of Pennsylvania, the Schomburg Center for Research in Black Culture, the Huntington Library, the New-York Historical Society, the Gilder Lehrman Institute of American History, the William L. Clements Library (University of Michigan), the Beinecke Library (Yale University), the John Hay Library (Brown University), the Newberry Library, the Special Collections and University Archives at Virginia Tech, and the Filson Historical Society. With backing from Brown University, the American Historical Association, the American Society for Legal History, and the Organization of American Historians, I made multiple trips to Washington to research at the National Archives and Library of Congress and thank the archivists, librarians, and especially Craig D'Ooge for the knowledge and assistance supplied during these research excursions.

Becoming a professor as I revised the project meant learning to adapt to various regions of the country and four colleges. The respite provided by colleagues as I acclimated to these areas while revising proved indispensable. Moving from Rhode Island to Mississippi to teach at Tougaloo College, I was afforded the opportunity to serve at an institution pivotal in dismantling segregation. Daphne Chamberlain made this rewarding opportunity possible and offered warmth to my wife and me during our stay. The following year, I was glad that upon trekking north as a fellow at the New-York Historical Society I received support from colleagues at the New School for Social Research. After moving west the next year to Ogden, Utah, I found helpful guidance from Sara Dant, Branden Little, Susan Matt, and Gene A. Sessions at Weber State University. In 2020, I rambled to the Midwest to teach at Purdue University, where colleagues including David Atkinson, Kathryn Cramer Brownell, Cornelius L. Bynum, Frederick Rowe Davis, Deborah L. Fleetham, William G. Gray, Stacy E. Holden, T. Cole Jones, Kathryn Maxson Jones, Rebekah A. Klein-Pejšová, Wendy Kline, John Larson, Robert

E. May, Yvonne M. Pitts, Randy W. Roberts, Margaret Mih Tillman, and Melinda S. Zook softened the transition to West Lafayette amid the pandemic. I thank them all. I also thank Purdue students Taylor Cash, Zachary Logsdon, and Jonathan Soucek for research assistance.

Transforming the dissertation into a book was a hefty undertaking, but the succor and assistance from fellow historians I received during the process sustained my mental vigor and steeled my determination so that I could finish this enterprise. The American Society of Historians conferred the Allan Nevins Dissertation Prize for the best written dissertation in American history on the project, and the American Society of Legal History honored the project with the Cromwell Dissertation Prize. These awards bolstered my confidence as a historian and energized me to keep working.

The academy is filled with bighearted scholars, many of whom supplied productive feedback and their precious time to help me improve this project. I thank members of two writing groups who scrutinized messy chapters and saved me from verbose inclinations. Mary Hicks, Wangui M. Muigai, Kathryn Olivarius, Carolyn Roberts, and Christopher D. E. Willoughby offered expertise in the history of slavery and racism. Meanwhile, Megan Bever, Laura June Davis, Angela Esco Elder, Laura Mammina, Lindsay Rae Privette, and Evan C. Rothera endured dizzyingly long drafts and bettered my understanding of the Civil War era. I also thank the editors and anonymous reviewers of the *Journal of Social History* and *Civil War History*, who provided feedback on the articles "Trials of Freedom: African American Deserters during the U.S. Civil War" (*Journal of Social History* 43, no. 3 (Spring 2016): 693–709) and "'Prisoners with Undaunted Patriotism': Incarcerated Black Soldiers and Battles of Citizenship in Military Prisons during the Civil War" (*Civil War History* 68, no. 3 (September 2022): 229–267). Their recommendations honed certain conclusions and stimulated new ideas. I am grateful for the sources, guidance, and hours spent reading portions of my work provided by Adam Arenson, Amanda Bellows, James J. Broomall, Peter S. Carmichael, Dillon J. Carroll, Frank Cirillo, Abigail Cooper, Deirdre Cooper Owens, Enrico Dal Lago, Andrew Delbanco, Douglas R. Egerton, Lorien Foote, Sarah Gardner, Lesley J. Gordon, Michael P. Gray, Sarah L. E. Gronningsater, Vanessa M. Holden, Pippa Holloway, Ryan W. Keating, Evan Kutzler, Andrew F. Lang, Justin Leroy, Brian Luskey, Sarah Ludin, Stephanie McCurry, Cynthia L. Nicoletti, Emily A. Owens, Jason Phillips, Paul Quigley, John W. Quist, Steven J. Ramold, Marcy Sacks, Aaron Sheehan-Dean, Rachel A. Shelden, Manisha Sinha, Andrew L. Slap, Amy Murrell Taylor, Jonathan D. Wells, and Michael Woods. I also thank the extraordinarily generous Joseph P. Reidy, who read through two entire drafts. I greatly benefited from his knowledge of emancipation and Black military service.

Once I drafted the project, I benefited from the assistance of several who offered notes and ideas on the entire draft during a workshop hosted by Purdue University. Gregory P. Downs, Laura F. Edwards, Caroline Janney, and Chandra Manning supplied useful recommendations on framing and saved me from grievous errors. This book is better because of their sage advice. I thank them for their insights.

I finished re-drafting this manuscript during a fellowship at the Gilder Lehrman Center for the Study of Slavery, Resistance, and Abolition at the MacMillan Center of Yale University. I thank David Blight, Daisha Brabham, Melissa McGrath, Lisa Monroe, Daniel Vieira, and Michelle Zacks at the center for the opportunity to research in New Haven and for accommodating my request to reschedule the fellowship when I learned I was to be a dad for the second time.

At Oxford University Press, I thank three anonymous readers for their incisive reviews and Susan Ferber for her feedback and time. I also thank those at Oxford University Press who prepared this manuscript for publication.

Like so many of the men studied in his book, my spirit was nourished by the support of kin, and I owe them my thanks. Sojourns at my in-laws, John and Patricia Bayer, with the Vertels, Nicole, Jacob, and Gale, were filled with robust meals and roving conversation, which proved rejuvenating. Aunts and uncles kept me occupied during summer stops in southwestern Illinois while my maternal grandparents, Pauline and Vernon Billhartz, served hot meals. My paternal grandparents, Jean Norman and Andrew Theodorou, served ample dolmades, keftedes, and conversation, ensuring I had sufficient energy and clarity of purpose to carry on. I am grateful my sister Erica humored me by feigning interest during Civil War themed vacations, including trips to the homes of Joshua Chamberlain and Mary Lincoln. I have not met a more hard-working man than my dad, Alan. When I was twelve, he adopted me and embraced me as his own. I thank him for his superabundant kindness—and the steady supply of deep-dish pizzas. My mom, Joyce, made sacrifices as a single mother that I try to fathom but remain unable to imagine ever making. Without the right words existing, I can only say that I thank her—and always will.

During the process of writing and revising this project, my family grew. My wife and I welcomed August, our fleet-footed toddler, and Maximillian, our gregarious, grinning newborn, as well as our feline companions, Ulysses and Sullivan Ballou. These rascals provided plenty of distractions that guaranteed

I returned to my project mentally refreshed (if not physically reenergized). My eagerness to be there for each of their cries, giggles, and purrs supplied the final (and perhaps the most compelling) reason to finish this book. For this—and for all the joy they bring—I heartily thank my boys.

Finally, I must thank my wife, Kate. No one else discussed the Civil War more with me, pilgrimaged to battlefields on hard-earned holidays, or moved across the country with me (several times). But she not only listened, curated road-trip playlists, and passed up deli sandwiches during drives to far-flung archival repositories, historic locales, and academic posts. She also sustained me. She pulled me away from documents when work dulled my mind, buoyed my spirits after (many) rough reviews, and joined me in savoring medium-rare T-Bones after I had grown weary from hours spent crafting history. I thank her for her patience and for the love that kept me going.

APPENDIX

Black Soldiers Tried for Desertion during the US Civil War

This appendix of Black soldiers tried for desertion includes the age, birthplace, place of enlistment, date and location of desertion, trial outcome, and the location of convicted soldiers' imprisonment based upon the soldiers' compiled military service records. The data has been collated from the Records of the Adjutant General's Office (Record Group 94) and the Records of the Office of the Judge Advocate General (Record Group 153) at the National Archives. To verify the information within the courts-martial records and cull data about the soldiers tried to construct the following table, courts-martial cases of Black soldiers tried for desertion were cross-referenced with the soldiers' compiled military service records. Additional Black soldiers may have been tried and incarcerated, but because their court or service records were not located during research or were not reliable, the soldiers' information was not included. Therefore, the list of those in the United States Colored Troops (USCT) who were tried for desertion below is not comprehensive, and the following information and percentages are not definitive. However, the table includes information about 653 USCT soldiers drawn from the men's compiled military service records, and such information yields a more detailed portrait of the Black soldiers tried for leaving the US Army without permission. Based upon the information collected by officials in these documents (which was not the same for every soldier), the following table encompasses: (1) the states where 482 men were born; (2) when 594 men enlisted; (3) the state where 591 men enlisted; (4) which states 637 men were in when they left camp; (5) the month and year when 580 soldiers departed; (6) whether the soldier tried for desertion was convicted of desertion, absence without leave (AWOL), or found not guilty; and (7) the states where 279 convicted soldiers were incarcerated. (Note: If the soldier left two or three times, as many did, the table references the first place he decamped from and the first date he left according to his service record. Throughout the table, "nr*" refers to "not recorded" by the US government in the compiled military service record.)

A comparison of the records reveals the following. Black southerners tried for desertion in the courts-martial were represented more numerically and statistically than their northern counterparts within the USCT. According to the War Department's figures, 138,530 (or 80 percent) of the men enlisted in the USCT hailed from an enslaving state, or state where slavery was a central feature of the legal, economic, and/or social foundation, and 34,549 (or 20 percent) from an entirely or primarily free state. Of the 482 men tried for desertion whose service records include the soldiers' birthplace, 410 (or 85 percent) were born in an enslaving state, 65 (or 13 percent) were born in a free state, and 7 (or 1 percent) were born in Canada. Of the 591 men tried for desertion whose service records include the state of the soldiers' enlistment, 485 (or 82 percent) enlisted in an enslaving state while 106 (or 18 percent) enlisted in a free state. Of the 637 men tried for desertion whose service records include the soldiers' location at the moment of their departure, 584 (or 92 percent) fled their regiments while serving in an enslaving state, and 53 (or 8 percent) fled their regiments while serving in a free state. Turning to the date of enlistment for the 594 men tried for desertion whose service records include the month and year of enlistment, the records show that 35 (or 6 percent) enlisted in 1862, 276 (or 46 percent) enlisted in 1863, 227 (or 38 percent) enlisted in 1864, and 56 (or 9 percent) enlisted in 1865. The service records also show that, for the 580 men tried for desertion whose service records include the date of their departure, 1 (or .2 percent) left in 1862, 123 (or 21 percent) left in 1863, 294 (or 51 percent) left in 1864, 149 (or 26 percent) left in 1865, and 13 (or 2 percent) left in 1866. Looking at the convictions of Black soldiers tried for desertion, the records show that 25 of the 653 (or 4 percent) were found not guilty; that 529 of the 653 (or 81 percent) were convicted of desertion; and that 99 of the 653 (or 15 percent) were convicted of AWOL. Ultimately, then, 628 of the 653 (or 96 percent) charged with desertion were convicted by the courts-martial. Finally, of the 279 soldiers convicted of desertion or AWOL whose service records include the place of their imprisonment, 254 (or 91 percent) were incarcerated in an enslaving state while the remaining 25 (or 9 percent) were sent to prisons in a free state.

Regiment	Rank, Name, and Alias(es)	Age	Birth State	Date Enlisted	State Enlisted In	State Left Camp	Date Left Camp	Crime Convicted Of	State of Imprisonment	Court File(s)
1 Cav.	Pvt. Randolph Young	23	MA	8/1864	VA	VA	9/1864	Desertion	VA	NN3341
1 Cav.	Pvt. Theophilus Butler	27	VA	5/1864	VA	VA	8/1864	Desertion	nr*	LL2907
1 Hvy. Art.	Pvt. Baalam Kirks	25	SC	4/1864	TN	TN	8/1864	Desertion	TN	LL3173
1 Hvy. Art.	Pvt. Terry Smart	22	TN	7/1864	TN	TN	10/1864	Desertion	TN	MM2664
1 Hvy. Art.	Pvt. Richard Brewer	21	VA	9/1864	TN	TN	12/1864	Desertion	nr*	MM2664
1 Hvy. Art.	Pvt. Henry Newton	25	TN	9/1864	TN	TN	1/1865	Desertion	TN	MM2664
1 Hvy. Art.	Pvt. Lewis Harden	18	KY	10/1864	TN	TN	12/1864	Desertion	TN	MM2664
1 Hvy. Art.	Pvt. William Henry	19	TN	9/1864	TN	TN	1/1865	Desertion	nr*	MM2664
1 Hvy. Art.	Pvt. George Laine	38	TN	9/1864	TN	TN	1/1865	Desertion	nr*	MM3134 MM2664
1 Hvy. Art.	Pvt. Newton Henry (aka Henry Newton)	25	TN	9/1864	TN	TN	1/1865	Desertion	TN	MM3134
1 Hvy. Art.	Sgt. John Hall	21	TN	3/1864	TN	TN	4/1865	Desertion	nr*	MM2664
1 Hvy. Art.	Pvt. Isaac Varnell	36	TN	8/1864	TN	TN	9/1864	Desertion	nr*	LL3257 MM3514 MM3433
1 Hvy. Art.	Pvt. Henry Evans	20	NC	5/1864	TN	TN	8/1864	Desertion	TN	MM2921 MM3103
1 Hvy. Art.	Pvt. Henry Harrison	21	TN	2/1865	TN	TN	3/1865	Desertion	TN	MM2921 MM3103
1 Hvy. Art.	Pvt. Henry Jackson	23	SC	5/1864	TN	TN	8/1864	Desertion	TN	MM2921 MM3103
1 Hvy. Art.	Pvt. Levi Johnson	18	MS	7/1864	TN	TN	3/1865	Desertion	nr*	MM2921 MM3103
1 Hvy. Art.	Pvt. Hector Talley (aka Tally)	32	TN	5/1864	TN	TN	6/1864	Desertion	TN	MM2921 MM3103
1 Hvy. Art.	Pvt. James Tyler	20	TN	nr*	TN	TN	4/1865	Desertion	nr*	MM3513

(continued)

Regiment	Rank, Name, and Alias(es)	Age	Birth State	Date Enlisted	State Enlisted In	State Left Camp	Date Left Camp	Crime Convicted Of	State of Imprisonment	Court File(s)
1 Hvy. Art.	Pvt. Champ Jack	28	TN	6/1864	TN	TN	7/1864	Desertion	TN	MM3513
1 Hvy. Art.	Pvt. Jerry Blair	27	TN	6/1864	TN	TN	3/1865	Desertion	nr*	MM3513
1 Hvy. Art.	Pvt. Joseph Hayes	20	GA	7/1864	TN	TN	4/1865	Desertion	TN	MM3675
1 Hvy. Art.	Pvt. Tipton Bright	18	TN	9/1864	TN	TN	10/1864	Desertion	TN	MM3675
1 Hvy. Art.	Pvt. William Hines	20	OH	11/1864	TN	TN	6/1865	Desertion	nr*	MM3535
1 Inf.	Pvt. William H. Grant	17	MA	6/1863	DC	VA	nr*	AWOL	nr*	NN585
1 Inf.	Pvt. Thomas J. Harris	21	MD	6/1863	nr*	VA	7/1864	Desertion	nr*	NN643
1 Inf.	Pvt. Henry Williams	26	DC	6/1863	DC	VA	7/1863	Desertion	VA	NN643
1 Inf.	Pvt. John Lomax	32	DC	6/1863	nr*	DC	8/1863	Desertion	VA	NN643
1 Inf.	Pvt. Lewis Beeler	44	KY	1/1864	MI	MI	1/1864	Desertion	nr*	NN1502
1 Inf.	Pvt. Thomas Seymour	19	nr*	11/1863	MI	MI	2/1864	Desertion	nr*	NN1502
1 Inf.	Pvt. William P. Harris	20	AL	12/1863	MI	nr*	2/1864	AWOL	nr*	NN1839
1 Inf.	Pvt. Thaddeus Robinson	18	NY	12/1863	MI	MI	2/1864	Desertion	nr*	NN2260
1 Inf.	Pvt. William Harris	20	AL	12/1863	MI	MI	2/1864	AWOL	nr*	NN2413
1 Inf.	Pvt. Andrew Thompson	37	VA	6/1863	VA	VA	8/1864	AWOL	nr*	LL2900
1 Inf.	Pvt. Robert Wilson	nr*	nr*	nr*	nr*	VA	nr*	AWOL	nr*	LL3037
1 Inf.	Pvt. William (aka Babe) Lomax (aka Lomacks or Gustus)	24	nr*	6/1863	VA	MD	9/1863	Desertion	DE	MM2609 OO1248
1 Lgt. Art.	Pvt. Philisan Dupuy (aka Depney)	25	LA	4/1864	MS	MS	6/1864	Desertion	IL	LL2851

10 Hvy. Art.	Pvt. Emile Calice	37	LA	5/1864	LA	8/1864	Desertion	FL	NN3186 LL2892
10 Hvy. Art.	Pvt. William Vickers	20	LA	9/1864	LA	nr*	Desertion	FL	NN3186 LL2892
10 Hvy. Art.	Pvt. Esau Joseph	20	LA	11/1864	LA	11/1864	Desertion	FL	NN3359
10 Hvy. Art.	Pvt. Charles Wadsworth	22	nr*	12/1862	LA	7/1865	AWOL	nr*	MM2792 MM2808
10 Hvy. Art.	Pvt. Henry Johnson	18	LA	2/1864	LA	8/1864	Desertion	nr*	MM3347
10 Hvy. Art.	Pvt. John Scott	nr*	nr*	nr*	LA	8/1865	Desertion	nr*	MM3734
10 Hvy. Art.	Pvt. Alexander Walton	18	MS	9/1864	LA	3/1866	Desertion	MS	MM3734
10 Hvy. Art.	Pvt. Richard (aka Dick Henderson)	19	nr*	nr*	LA	3/1866	Desertion	MS	MM3734
10 Hvy. Art.	Pvt. Silas Ellis	30	MS	9/1864	LA	3/1866	Desertion	MS	MM3917
10 Hvy. Art.	Pvt. Edmund Sam	nr*	nr*	2/1865	LA	3/1866	Desertion	MS	MM3917
100 Inf.	Pvt. Richard Hatfield	21	VA	5/1864	KY	nr*	Desertion	TN	LL3101 LL3055
100 Inf.	Pvt. Jefferson Sharp	25	KY	5/1864	KY	1/1865	Desertion	nr*	MM2870 MM2891
100 Inf.	Pvt. James James	24	KY	6/1864	KY	10/1864	Desertion	TN	MM3882
101 Inf.	Pvt. Charles Thompson	23	SC	7/1864	TN	nr*	Desertion	TN	LL3224
101 Inf.	Pvt. Andy Wilcox 1	49	TN	11/1864	TN	12/1864	Desertion	nr*	MM5523
101 Inf.	Pvt. Andy Wilcox 2	49	TN	11/1864	TN	12/1864	Desertion	TN	MM3835 MM3881
102 Inf.	Pvt. Noah Pardue (aka Perdue)	23	nr*	10/1863	MI	10/1864	Desertion	nr*	NN1915
102 Inf.	Pvt. Lewis Morgan	37	VA	9/1863	MS	3/1864	Desertion	nr*	LL2139
102 Inf.	Pvt. John Anderson	21	OH	12/1865	MI	8/1864	Desertion	nr*	LL2988
103 Inf.	Pvt. Lucius Ursury	19	GA	1/1865	GA	5/1865	Desertion	GA	MM2813
103 Inf.	Pvt. William Roberts	20	GA	2/1865	GA	6/1865	Desertion	nr*	MM2813

(continued)

Regiment	Rank, Name, and Alias(es)	Age	Birth State	Date Enlisted	State Enlisted In	State Left Camp	Date Left Camp	Crime Convicted Of	State of Imprisonment	Court File(s)
103 Inf.	Pvt. Lunnon Hale	19	GA	2/1865	GA	GA	6/1865	Desertion	GA	MM2813
103 Inf.	Pvt. Jacob Haman	32	GA	2/1865	GA	GA	6/1865	AWOL	nr*	MM2784
103 Inf.	Pvt. Caleb Gough	25	MS	2/1865	SC	GA	nr*	AWOL	nr*	MM3585
106 Inf.	Pvt. Charles Swope	35	AL	3/1864	AL	AL	6/1864	Desertion	nr*	LL3213
108 Inf.	Pvt. Henry Lloyd	19	KY	7/1864	KY	MS	9/1865	Desertion	MS	MM3394
108 Inf.	Pvt. David Lockard (aka Lockhart)	28	KY	7/1864	KY	MS	nr*	Desertion	nr*	MM3414 MM3441
11 Hvy. Art.	Pvt. David Jackson	25	NC	8/1863	RI	LA	11/1863	Desertion	nr*	LL2229 LL2231
11 Hvy. Art.	Pvt. Webster Demann	20	NY	12/1863	RI	LA	6/1864	Desertion	FL	NN2565 LL2524
11 Hvy. Art.	Pvt. Benjamin J. Richardson	18	NC	12/1863	RI	RI	1/1864	Desertion	nr*	NN2565 LL2524
11 Hvy. Art.	Pvt. Henry Thompson	21	NY	12/1863	RI	RI	3/1864	Desertion	FL	NN3359
11 Hvy. Art.	Pvt. Richard Champlin	18	NY	11/1863	RI	LA	7/1865	Desertion	FL	MM3115
11 Hvy. Art.	Pvt. George Bryant	23	NY	10/1863	RI	LA	3/1864	Desertion	nr*	MM3102 MM3115
11 Inf.	Pvt. William Brunson	20	MS	11/1864	MO	TN	1/1865	Desertion	TN	MM2021 OO809
11 Inf.	Pvt. William Colwell	25	TN	11/1863	AR	AR	6/1864	Desertion	OH	MM2026
11 Inf.	Pvt. Boston Ward	21	SC	3/1864	TN	TN	6/1864	Desertion	TN	MM3191
11 Inf.	Pvt. Edmund (aka Edmond) Ward	22	SC	3/1864	TN	TN	6/1864	Desertion	nr*	MM3191
11 Inf.	Pvt. Frank Ward	19	GA	3/1864	TN	TN	6/1864	Desertion	TN	MM3191

11 Inf.	Pvt. James Ward	25	MS	3/1864	TN	TN	6/1864	Desertion	TN	MM3191
11 Inf.	Pvt. Benjamin Young	23	MS	3/1864	TN	TN	6/1864	Desertion	TN	MM3191
11 Inf.	Pvt. Frank Evans	25	GA	3/1864	TN	TN	4/1864	Desertion	nr*	MM3191
11 Inf.	Pvt. Charles Holliday	18	MS	3/1864	TN	TN	4/1864	Desertion	TN	MM3191
11 Inf.	Pvt. Frank Holliday	20	MS	3/1864	TN	TN	6/1864	Desertion	TN	MM3191
11 Inf.	Pvt. Nathan Potter	28	VA	3/1864	TN	TN	11/1864	Innocent	nr*	MM3191
11 Inf.	Pvt. Charles Keye	19	SC	9/1863	TN	TN	9/1865	Desertion	TN	MM3327
11 Inf.	Pvt. Richard (aka Dick) Moore	nr*	nr*	nr*	nr*	TN	9/1865	Desertion	nr*	MM3455
110 Inf.	Pvt. Milton Acklyn	nr*	nr*	nr*	TN	TN	nr*	Desertion	nr*	LL1475
110 Inf.	Cpl. Robert Carr	25	TN	12/1863	TN	TN	1/1864	Desertion	TN	NN2828 NN2785 MM1974 LL2676
110 Inf.	Pvt. Booker Johnson	20	TN	12/1863	TN	TN	12/1863	AWOL	nr*	LL1892 NN1766
110 Inf.	Sgt. Joe Robinson	34	TN	12/1863	TN	AL	5/1864	Desertion	nr*	LL3329
110 Inf.	Pvt. Robert Mason	25	TN	12/1863	TN	AL	7/1864	Desertion	nr*	MM3339
110 Inf.	Pvt. Mat Swoap (aka Swoops)	40	VA	nr*	MS	AL	4/1864	Desertion	nr*	MM3339
110 Inf.	Pvt. Green Malone	23	AL	12/1863	AL	AL	10/1865	Desertion	nr*	MM3339
110 Inf.	Pvt. John Davis	23	TN	12/1863	TN	TN	3/1864	Desertion	AL	MM3339
110 Inf.	Sgt. Stephen Jones	21	TN	12/1863	TN	GA	6/1864	Desertion	AL	MM3339
111 Inf.	Pvt. Jacob Skillen	19	TN	1/1864	TN	TN	4/1864	Desertion	nr*	NN2952
111 Inf.	Pvt. Henry McNary	32	TN	1/1864	TN	AL	5/1864	Desertion	nr*	LL3308
111 Inf.	Pvt. Simon (aka Simeon) Gaston	25	AL	1/1864	TN	TN	2/1864	Desertion	nr*	LL3305

(continued)

Regiment	Rank, Name, and Alias(es)	Age	Birth State	Date Enlisted	State Enlisted In	State Left Camp	Date Left Camp	Crime Convicted Of	State of Imprisonment	Court File(s)
111 Inf.	Pvt. Joseph Smith	22	nr*	1/1864	TN	TN	3/1864	Desertion	nr*	LL3213
111 Inf.	Pvt. Anderson Phillips	nr*	nr*	1/1864	TN	TN	3/1864	Desertion	nr*	LL3213
111 Inf.	Pvt. Lewis Patterson	21	TN	1/1864	TN	TN	12/1864	Desertion	nr*	MM2890
111 Inf.	Pvt. Daniel Fuquay	27	AL	2/1864	TN	TN	8/1865	Desertion	nr*	MM3810
111 Inf.	Pvt. Solomon Fuquay	27	AL	2/1864	TN	TN	8/1865	Desertion	nr*	MM3810
111 Inf.	Pvt. Alfred Thompson	19	AL	3/1864	AL	TN	9/1865	Desertion	TN	MM3810
112 Inf.	Pvt. Peter Lagrand (aka La Grand)	26	NC	3/1864	AR	AR	5/1864	AWOL	nr*	LL2621 LL2616
112 Inf.	Pvt. Clark Thomas	34	GA	3/1864	AR	AR	5/1864	Desertion	AR	LL2621 LL2616
112 Inf.	Pvt. John McHenry	22	AL	3/1864	AR	AR	4/1864	AWOL	nr*	LL2672
112 Inf.	Pvt. Ezekiel Steele (aka Steel)	28	NC	3/1864	AR	AR	3/1864	AWOL	AR	NN2825
113 Inf.	Pvt. Lewis Smith	21	NC	6/1864	AR	AR	6/1864	AWOL	nr*	NN3677
113 Inf.	Pvt. Samuel Roddy	21	AR	4/1864	AR	AR	9/1864	AWOL	nr*	MM3771
113 Inf.	Pvt. Ranch Roddy	30	AR	4/1864	AR	AR	12/1864	AWOL	nr*	MM3771
113 Inf.	Pvt. John Lee	28	MD	3/1864	AR	AR	10/1865	Desertion	AR	MM3796
113 Inf.	Pvt. Frank Merrill	20	TN	3/1864	AR	AR	1/1866	Desertion	nr*	MM3796
113 Inf.	Pvt. Henderson Brown	18	AR	4/1864	AR	AR	6/1864	AWOL	nr*	MM3902
117 Inf.	Pvt. William Hudson	19	MS	10/1864	OH	TX	8/1865	Desertion	TX	MM3609
119 Inf.	Pvt. Lewis Thomas	24	KY	2/1865	KY	KY	6/1865	Desertion	nr*	MM2973

119 Inf.	Mus. Wesley Ball	20	KY	1/1865	KY	6/1865	Desertion	KY	MM3031
119 Inf.	Pvt. Joe Washington	28	KY	1/1865	KY	3/1865	Desertion	nr*	MM3630
119 Inf.	Pvt. William Red	29	VA	4/1865	NC	1866	Desertion	nr*	MM3630
119 Inf.	Pvt. Young Bush	45	KY	2/1865	KY	9/1865	Desertion	KY	MM3650
119 Inf.	Pvt. Thomas Turner	32	KY	2/1865	KY	7/1865	Desertion	nr*	MM3725 MM3572
12 Hvy. Art.	Pvt. Henry Robinson	18	KY	7/1864	KY	nr*	Desertion	KY	MM2915
12 Inf.	Cpl. James Shanklin	20	AL	7/1863	TN	8/1863	AWOL	nr*	NN3105 LL2861
12 Inf.	Pvt. James Morgan	18	AL	8/1863	TN	6/1865	Desertion	TN	MM3874
12 Inf.	Pvt. Milton (aka Amilton Barksley)	19	TN	9/1863	TN	nr*	Desertion	nr*	MM3882
12 Inf.	Pvt. Robert Fisher	nr*	nr*	nr*	TN	nr*	Innocent	nr*	MM3882
122 Inf.	Pvt. Henry Clay	18	KY	10/1864	TX	7/1865	AWOL	nr*	NN3994
127 Inf.	Pvt. John Henson	26	PA	9/1864	PA	9/1864	Desertion	VA	LL3041
128 Inf.	Cpl. Henry Furroby	21	SC	3/1865	SC	6/1865	Desertion	nr*	MM2810
128 Inf.	Pvt. John Martin	21	SC	3/1865	SC	6/1865	Desertion	SC	MM2810
128 Inf.	Pvt. Tero Ashmo	18	SC	4/1865	SC	6/1865	Desertion	NY	MM2810
13 Inf.	Sgt. John Q. Adams	21	KY	10/1863	TN	3/1864	Desertion	nr*	NN3283 NN3282
13 Inf.	Pvt. Joseph E. Williams	29	PA	9/1863	TN	1/1865	AWOL	nr*	MM2054 OO849
137 Inf.	Pvt. Albert Jones	23	GA	4/1865	GA	6/1865	Desertion	GA	MM3507
137 Inf.	Pvt. Johnson Brown	36	GA	4/1865	GA	7/1865	AWOL	nr*	MM3507
137 Inf.	Pvt. Lewis McSpadin	17	AL	4/1865	GA	9/1865	Desertion	nr*	MM3287
14 Inf.	Pvt. Richard Lewis	21	TN	10/1863	TN	11/1864	Desertion	nr*	LL1529

(continued)

Regiment	Rank, Name, and Alias(es)	Age	Birth State	Date Enlisted	State Enlisted In	State Left Camp	Date Left Camp	Crime Convicted Of	State of Imprisonment	Court File(s)
14 Inf.	Pvt. Andrew Thompson	29	KY	12/1863	TN	TN	1/1864	Desertion	FL	NN1187
14 Inf.	Pvt. Bailey Wiley	18	TN	10/1863	TN	nr*	12/1863	Desertion	nr*	NN2352 LL2263 LL2352 LL2351
14 Inf.	Pvt. Anthony Wiley	21	TN	11/1863	TN	AL	12/1863	Desertion	nr*	LL2351 NN2352 LL2263
14 Inf.	Sgt. Henry Ellison	22	TN	11/1863	TN	AL	1/1864	Desertion	TN	NN3007 NN3470
14 Inf.	Pvt. Edward Allen	22	TN	10/1863	TN	TN	2/1864	Desertion	OH	NN3470 NN3007
14 Inf.	Pvt. Edmund Duglass (aka Edward Douglass)	23	TN	10/1863	TN	TN	12/1863	Desertion	nr*	MM2799
14 Inf.	Pvt. Joseph Simpson	19	NC	12/1863	TN	TN	10/1865	Desertion	TN	MM3797
14 Inf.	Pvt. Isham Troupe	23	AL	12/1863	TN	TN	9/1865	AWOL	TN	MM3675
14 Inf.	Pvt. William W. Brown	18	VA	11/1864	nr*	TN	9/1865	Desertion	TN	MM3675
15 Inf.	Pvt. William Clark	23	DC	1/1864	TN	TN	3/1864	AWOL	nr*	LL2489
15 Inf.	Pvt. Squire Edquire (aka Square Ellis)	19	TN	12/1863	TN	TN	9/1865	Desertion	nr*	MM3881
15 Inf.	Pvt. Henry Jackson	17	KY	12/1863	TN	TN	8/1865	Desertion	nr*	MM3881
15 Inf.	Cpl. Andrew Horshaw (aka Horshan)	20	NC	1/1864	TN	TN	8/1865	Desertion	nr*	MM3839
16 Inf.	Pvt. Solomon Parish	20	KY	12/1863	TN	TN	2/1864	AWOL	nr*	MM2008
16 Inf.	Pvt. Munroe (aka Monroe) West	20	KY	12/1863	TN	TN	4/1864	AWOL	nr*	MM2964

16 Inf.	Pvt. Ned Wilson	22	VA	12/1863	TN	TN	12/1863	Desertion	TN	MM2799
16 Inf.	Pvt. Woodson Wheeler	43	VA	1/1864	TN	TN	3/1864	AWOL	nr*	MM2799
16 Inf.	Pvt. William Parish	22	KY	1/1864	TN	TN	2/1864	AWOL	nr*	MM2964
16 Inf.	Pvt. Aaron Medley	21	VA	1/1864	TN	TN	2/1864	Desertion	TN	MM2964
17 Inf.	Pvt. Jesse Hailey (aka Haily)	20	TN	2/1864	TN	TN	2/1864	Desertion	nr*	NN2119
17 Inf.	Pvt. George Tomlinson	nr*	nr*	5/1864	TN	TN	6/1864	Desertion	TN	MM2054 OO849
17 Inf.	Pvt. Lewis Bass	25	TN	11/1863	TN	TN	3/1865	Desertion	TN	MM3889
18 Hvy. Art.	Pvt. James Gardener	nr*	nr*	nr*	nr*	LA	nr*	Desertion	nr*	NN3359
18 Inf.	Pvt. James Howell	nr*	nr*	nr*	nr*	MD	nr*	Desertion	nr*	LL2898
18 Inf.	Pvt. John W. Ferrin	nr*	nr*	nr*	nr*	TN	nr*	AWOL	nr*	MM3031 MM3031
18 Inf.	Pvt. Jacob Drummin	20	MO	6/1864	MO	TN	8/1865	Desertion	AL	MM3339
19 Inf.	Pvt. James Palmer	22	MD	1/1864	MD	VA	7/1864	Desertion	DE	NN2158
19 Inf.	Pvt. Gerrett Brown	30	MD	5/1864	MD	MD	6/1864	Desertion	nr*	LL2947
2 Cav.	Pvt. Jonas Connally (aka Connelly)	19	NC	12/1863	VA	VA	8/1864	AWOL	nr*	MM1682
2 Cav.	Pvt. Jonas Connally (aka Connelly)	19	NC	12/1863	NC	VA	8/1864	Desertion	nr*	MM1669
2 Hvy. Art.	Pvt. William Jones	28	VA	3/1865	MD	TX	8/1865	AWOL	FL	MM3571
2 Hvy. Art.	Pvt. Isaac Randal	22	KY	6/1863	TN	TN	11/1863	AWOL	TN	NN1697
2 Hvy. Art.	Pvt. James Posey	21	KY	11/1863	TN	TN	12/1863	Desertion	TN	LL2051
2 Hvy. Art.	Pvt. James Baker	20	KY	8/1863	TN	TN	2/1864	Desertion	TN	LL2051

(*continued*)

Regiment	Rank, Name, and Alias(es)	Age	Birth State	Date Enlisted	State Enlisted In	State Left Camp	Date Left Camp	Crime Convicted Of	State of Imprisonment	Court File(s)
2 Hvy. Art.	Pvt. Carroll Grizer	24	nr*	11/1864	TN	TN	4/1864	Desertion	nr*	NN2926
2 Hvy. Art.	Pvt. John Nelson	21	NC	8/1864	AR	AR	1/1865	Desertion	OH	MM2720 MM2727
2 Inf.	Pvt. James Heathcock	22	NC	8/1863	nr*	VA	8/1863	Desertion	NY	MM2326 NN939
2 Inf.	Pvt. James F. Bell	31	DC	9/1863	DC	VA	9/1863	AWOL	nr*	LL1413
2 Inf.	Pvt. John W. Butler	22	DC	9/1863	DC	VA	10/1863	AWOL	nr*	LL1406
2 Inf.	Pvt. George Watkins	nr*	nr*	nr*	nr*	TN	nr*	AWOL	nr*	LL1908 NN1795
2 Inf.	Pvt. Peter Watson	nr*	nr*	nr*	nr*	TN	nr*	AWOL	nr*	LL1908 NN1795
2 Inf.	Pvt. Burl Barrett	27	TN	12/1863	TN	TN	4/1864	Desertion	nr*	NN2804 NN2879
2 Inf.	Pvt. Harry Walker	nr*	nr*	nr*	nr*	TN	nr*	Desertion	nr*	NN2804 NN2879
2 Inf.	Pvt. James Bander (aka Beinder)	22	DC	9/1863	DC	VA	10/1863	Desertion	nr*	NN2328
2 Lgt. Art.	Pvt. James Watkins	19	nr*	11/1863	TN	TN	6/1864	Desertion	TN	LL2699 LL2856
2 Lgt. Art.	Pvt. Carroll Grazier (aka Grizer)	24	nr*	11/1863	TN	TN	5/1864	Desertion	TN	LL2739
2 Lgt. Art.	Pvt. James Myer (aka Meyer)	40	LA	4/1864	MS	MS	6/1864	Desertion	MS	LL2851
2 Lgt. Art.	Pvt. Peter Steele	nr*	nr*	nr*	nr*	KS	nr*	Desertion	nr*	LL3131
2 Lgt. Art.	Pvt. Richard (aka Dick Haywood)	23	SC	4/1864	SC	SC	8/1864	Desertion	FL	MM2209
2 Lgt. Art.	Pvt. John Nelson	21	NC	8/1864	AR	AR	1/1865	Desertion	OH	NN3806

2 Lgt. Art.	Pvt. Morris Thomas	27	MS	10/1863	nr*	MS	1/1864	Desertion	MS	MM2869
2 Lgt. Art.	Pvt. Solomon Ray	18	nr*	9/1863	TN	TN	6/1865	Desertion	IL	MM3238 OO1327
20 Inf.	Pvt. Henry Whitfield	29	OH	12/1863	NY	LA	5/1864	Desertion	nr*	NN2365 LL2524
20 Inf.	Pvt. Daniel Walters	23	Canada	11/1863	NY	LA	8/1864	Desertion	nr*	LL2998 NN3471
20 Inf.	Pvt. George Corse (aka Couse)	29	NY	12/1863	NY	nr*	7/1864	Desertion	nr*	NN2858
20 Inf.	Pvt. Samuel Rosa	20	NY	9/1864	NY	LA	6/1864	Desertion	FL	NN3056 LL2816
20 Inf.	Pvt. George Atkins	24	NY	12/1863	NY	LA	6/1864	Desertion	nr*	LL3138
20 Inf.	Pvt. John Benton	23	Canada	11/1865	NY	LA	2/1865	AWOL	nr*	MM2050
20 Inf.	Sgt. Stephen A. Johnson	33	NJ	12/1864	NY	LA	2/1865	Desertion	FL	MM2025
20 Inf.	Pvt. Jacob Henry (aka Henry Jacob)	20	TN	6/1864	NY	LA	7/1865	Desertion	LA	MM2724 OO1316
20 Inf.	Pvt. George V. Johnson (aka Atkins)	20	NY	12/1863	NY	LA	6/1864	Desertion	LA	MM3347
21 Inf.	Cpl. William Lucas	28	VA	9/1863	SC	SC	2/1864	Desertion	FL	NN2457 NN2641 NN2445
21 Inf.	Pvt. King Singleton	25	SC	6/1863	SC	SC	2/1864	Desertion	nr*	MM1839
21 Inf.	Pvt. Samuel Orr	20	SC	3/1865	SC	SC	10/1865	Desertion	nr*	MM3228
21 Inf.	Pvt. Carolina Grant	25	SC	9/1864	SC	SC	11/1865	Desertion	nr*	MM3893
22 Inf.	Pvt. William Johnson	25	AL	12/1863	PA	PA	2/1865	Desertion	nr*	LL3079
22 Inf.	Pvt. John Riley	22	NJ	1/1864	PA	PA	10/1864	AWOL	nr*	LL3090
22 Inf.	Pvt. John Adams (of Co. D)	23	NJ	12/1863	PA	VA	nr*	Desertion	nr*	LL3133

(*continued*)

Regiment	Rank, Name, and Alias(es)	Age	Birth State	Date Enlisted	State Enlisted In	State Left Camp	Date Left Camp	Crime Convicted Of	State of Imprisonment	Court File(s)
22 Inf.	Pvt. John Adams (of Co. E)	23	NJ	12/1863	PA	VA	11/1864	Desertion	nr*	NN3550
23 Inf.	Pvt. William Doyle	22	DC	3/1864	DC	VA	5/1864	Desertion	nr*	NN2207 NN2102
23 Inf.	Pvt. Samuel Carter	23	PA	3/1864	DC	VA	7/1864	AWOL	nr*	NN2858
23 Inf.	Pvt. Charles M. Johnson	nr*	nr*	nr*	nr*	VA	nr*	Desertion	nr*	LL2900
23 Inf.	Pvt. William A. Barship (aka Bashup)	18	VA	5/1864	MA	VA	8/1864	Desertion	nr*	LL2974
23 Inf.	Pvt. William Johnson	nr*	nr*	nr*	nr*	VA	nr*	Desertion	nr*	LL2967
23 Inf.	Pvt. Robert H. Johnson	nr*	nr*	nr*	nr*	VA	nr*	AWOL	nr*	LL2983
23 Inf.	Pvt. John Day	24	NJ	8/1864	DC	VA	8/1864	Desertion	nr*	LL2988
23 Inf.	Pvt. Oliver Williams	27	NC	4/1864	DC	VA	6/1864	Desertion	VA	MM1773
23 Inf.	Pvt. James Johnson	20	VA	1/1864	DC	TX	8/1864	Desertion	nr*	MM2980
25 Inf.	Pvt. Parker Forward	23	PA	1/1864	PA	PA	3/1864	Desertion	PA	LL2675
25 Inf.	Pvt. Benjamin Yellets	21	PA	1/1864	PA	PA	3/1864	Desertion	PA	LL2675
25 Inf.	Pvt. Henry C. Ramsey	30	NJ	2/1864	NJ	FL	5/1864	Innocent	nr*	NN3832
25 Inf.	Pvt. James Buckingham	20	MD	3/1864	DC	VA	8/1864	Desertion	nr*	LL2792
25 Inf.	Pvt. William Johnston (aka Johnson)	42	NJ	2/1864	NJ	PA	3/1864	Desertion	VA	LL2983
25 Inf.	Pvt. Robert Fullman	nr*	nr*	nr*	nr*	nr*	nr*	Desertion	nr*	LL3135

25 Inf.	Mus. Charles E. Stokes	18	MI	1/1864	PA	FL	8/1864	Desertion	FL	MM2164
26 Inf.	Pvt. Jeremiah Johnson	30	Canada	1/1864	NY	SC	5/1864	Desertion	nr*	LL2227
26 Inf.	Pvt. Henderson Jackson	22	MD	1/1864	NY	SC	7/1864	Desertion	FL	NN2812
26 Inf.	Pvt. James Harris	28	PA	3/1864	NY	NY	4/1864	AWOL	VA	NN2604
26 Inf.	Pvt. John H. Johnson	19	NY	1/1864	NY	SC	nr*	Desertion	nr*	MM1833
27 Inf.	Pvt. Franklin Farley	18	nr*	1/1864	OH	OH	4/1864	Desertion	FL	LL2148
27 Inf.	Pvt. William Hannah	18	OH	2/1864	OH	VA	6/1864	AWOL	nr*	LL2394
27 Inf.	Pvt. William Gillum	18	Canada	10/1864	OH	OH	10/1864	AWOL	VA	LL2898
27 Inf.	Pvt. Henry Brown	19	NY	2/1864	OH	NC	nr*	Desertion	DE	MM3226
29 Conn.	Pvt. Amos T. Carpenter	30	CT	12/1863	CT	LA	6/1865	AWOL	VA	LL2708
29 Inf.	Sgt. Eli W. Prime	nr*	nr*	nr*	nr*	SC	nr*	Desertion	nr*	LL2227
29 Inf.	Pvt. Aaron Willett	42	PA	12/1863	CT	nr*	2/1864	AWOL	nr*	LL2708
29 Inf.	Pvt. Miles Shephard	24	MD	12/1863	CT	CT	2/1864	Desertion	nr*	LL2708
29 Inf.	Sgt. Solomon M. Honard (aka Howard)	30	VA	1/1864	CT	CT	3/1864	Desertion	nr*	NN3041
29 Inf.	Pvt. Allen Gunnell	39	VA	12/1863	IL	VA	5/1865	Desertion	nr*	LL2981
29 Inf.	Pvt. John Lewis	nr*	nr*	nr*	nr*	PA	nr*	Desertion	nr*	MM1892
29 Inf.	Pvt. Jerome B. Ray	20	NJ	12/1863	CT	VA	8/1864	Desertion	nr*	MM1916
29 Inf.	Pvt. John Alexander	nr*	nr*	nr*	nr*	LA	nr*	Desertion	nr*	MM2025
29 Inf.	Rec. Charles Longstone	23	VA	8/1864	VA	VA	8/1864	Desertion	DE	MM2609 OO1243
3 Cav.	Pvt. Walton Green	19	VA	12/1863	MS	MS	12/1863	Desertion	nr*	LL2011
3 Cav.	Pvt. Page Woodward	23	MS	11/1863	MS	MS	3/1864	Desertion	nr*	LL2216

(continued)

Regiment	Rank, Name, and Alias(es)	Age	Birth State	Date Enlisted	State Enlisted In	State Left Camp	Date Left Camp	Crime Convicted Of	State of Imprisonment	Court File(s)
3 Cav.	Bglr. David Washington	24	MS	10/1863	MS	MS	8/1864	Desertion	MO	LL2783 NN2705
3 Cav.	Pvt. Samuel Jeffers	23	MS	11/1863	MS	MS	6/1864	Desertion	MO	LL2783 NN2705
3 Cav.	Pvt. James Roach	18	MS	2/1864	MS	MS	5/1864	Desertion	nr*	NN2713 LL2658
3 Cav.	Pvt. Samuel Chapel	25	MO	10/1863	MS	MS	11/1863	Desertion	TN	NN2865 NN2785 MM1974 LL2627
3 Cav.	Pvt. Francis Nesbit	21	MS	12/1864	MS	MS	1/1864	AWOL	nr*	NN3258
3 Cav.	Pvt. Washington Pierce	25	MS	10/1863	MS	MS	11/1863	Desertion	nr*	NN3258
3 Cav.	Pvt. Alfimore Watkins	20	MS	11/1863	MS	MS	1/1864	Desertion	MS	LL3114nr*OO481
3 Cav.	Pvt. Haynes Sharkey	20	MS	10/1863	MS	MS	11/1863	Desertion	TN	MM1866
3 Cav.	Pvt. Robert McCorkerl	23	VA	1/1865	MS	TN	5/1865	Desertion	nr*	MM2986
3 Cav.	Cpl. Richard (aka Dick Harris)	19	MS	11/1863	MS	TN	7/1864	Innocent	nr*	MM3191
3 Cav.	Pvt. Albert Williams	nr*	nr*	nr*	nr*	AR	nr*	Desertion	nr*	MM3887
3 Cav.	Pvt. Henry Damonds	18	MS	10/1863	MS	TN	1/1865	AWOL	nr*	MM3338
3 Hvy. Art.	Pvt. Eustis (aka Gustav) Glover	24	TN	11/1863	nr*	TN	1/1864	Desertion	TN	LL2284
3 Hvy. Art.	Pvt. Henry Wright	18	AR	12/1863	TN	TN	4/1864	Desertion	nr*	NN2174
3 Hvy. Art.	Pvt. Robert Waller	18	TN	12/1863	TN	TN	2/1864	Desertion	nr*	NN2174
3 Hvy. Art.	Pvt. Jackson Kendall	32	NC	12/1863	TN	TN	4/1864	Desertion	TN	NN2174

3 Hvy. Art.	Pvt. Hardin Perkins	19	TN	12/1863	TN	4/1864	Desertion	nr*	NN2174
3 Hvy. Art.	Pvt. Samuel Pierce	18	TN	12/1863	TN	1/1864	Desertion	TN	NN2174
3 Hvy. Art.	Pvt. Samuel Hope	27	NC	12/1863	TN	4/1864	Desertion	TN	NN2174
3 Hvy. Art.	Pvt. Nelson Wright	18	MS	12/1863	TN	4/1864	Desertion	TN	NN2174
3 Hvy. Art.	Pvt. Eli Graham	20	MS	12/1863	TN	9/1864	Desertion	TN	NN2174
3 Hvy. Art.	Pvt. Joseph Oliver	18	TN	11/1863	TN	2/1864	Desertion	TN	NN2241
3 Hvy. Art.	Pvt. Church Stanley (aka Sauley)	37	TN	11/1863	TN	4/1864	Desertion	TN	NN2182
3 Hvy. Art.	Pvt. Harris Waller	21	TN	11/1863	TN	1/1864	Desertion	nr*	NN2182
3 Hvy. Art.	Pvt. Fee Baker	21	TN	11/1863	TN	12/1863	Desertion	TN	NN2182
3 Hvy. Art.	Sgt. Peter Welch	23	PA	12/1863	TN	4/1864	Desertion	nr*	NN2174
3 Hvy. Art.	Pvt. Wesley Thompson	21	TN	12/1863	TN	1/1864	Innocent	nr*	LL2457
3 Hvy. Art.	Pvt. Henry Thompson	21	NC	6/1863	MS	12/1863	Desertion	nr*	LL2457
3 Hvy. Art.	Pvt. William Rice	23	NC	7/1863	TN	3/1864	Desertion	nr*	LL2457
3 Hvy. Art.	Pvt. Emanuel Blackworth	30	TN	7/1863	TN	7/1863	Desertion	TN	LL2457
3 Hvy. Art.	Pvt. William Hall	22	MS	6/1863	TN	2/1864	Desertion	nr*	NN2657
3 Hvy. Art.	Pvt. Humphrey Stokes	24	MS	11/1863	TN	1/1864	Desertion	TN	NN2657
3 Hvy. Art.	Pvt. William Johnson	21	TN	12/1863	TN	2/1864	Desertion	TN	LL2594
3 Hvy. Art.	Pvt. Henry A. Groves	24	TN	12/1863	TN	5/1864	Desertion	TN	LL2594
3 Hvy. Art.	Pvt. Isham Cook	25	SC	3/1864	TN	4/1864	AWOL	nr*	NN2926 LL2739
3 Hvy. Art.	Pvt. Allen Guy	21	MS	3/1864	TN	6/1864	Desertion	TN	LL3188 OO330

(continued)

Regiment	Rank, Name, and Alias(es)	Age	Birth State	Date Enlisted	State Enlisted In	State Left Camp	Date Left Camp	Crime Convicted Of	State of Imprisonment	Court File(s)
3 Hvy. Art.	Sgt. Elijah Allen	39	SC	12/1863	TN	TN	1/1864	Desertion	TN	MM1965 OO552 MM1866
3 Hvy. Art.	Pvt. George Washington	22	MS	1/1865	TN	TN	2/1866	Desertion	TN	MM3824 MM3787
3 Hvy. Art.	Pvt. Julius Douglass (aka Duglas)	37	TN	9/1864	TN	TN	2/1866	Desertion	nr*	MM3824 MM3787
3 Hvy. Art.	Pvt. George Dare	25	NC	7/1863	TN	TN	2/1865	AWOL	nr*	MM2043 MM2021 OO809
3 Hvy. Art.	Pvt. Robert Young	29	SC	12/1863	TN	TN	6/1864	Desertion	TN	MM2334 OO1159
3 Hvy. Art.	Pvt. Charles Lewis	28	nr*	7/1863	TN	TN	11/1863	Desertion	MO	MM2327 OO1186
3 Hvy. Art.	Cpl. Edward Norfeet	24	MS	6/1863	TN	TN	5/1865	Innocent	nr*	MM2477
3 Hvy. Art.	Pvt. Charles Ball	19	LA	10/1864	IL	MO	11/1864	Desertion	TN	MM2634 OO1263
3 Hvy. Art.	Pvt. Isaac Allen	18	MS	12/1863	TN	TN	4/1864	AWOL	nr*	MM2629 MM2602
3 Hvy. Art.	Pvt. Isham Cook	25	SC	3/1864	TN	TN	8/1864	Desertion	nr*	MM3191
3 Hvy. Art.	Pvt. Allen Summers	28	LA	12/1863	MS	TN	nr*	AWOL	nr*	MM3754
3 Hvy. Art.	Pvt. Isham Barr	33	TN	1/1865	TN	TN	12/1865	Desertion	nr*	MM3754
3 Hvy. Art.	Pvt. James Boniface	18	TN	3/1865	TN	TN	9/1865	Desertion	nr*	MM3885
3 Hvy. Art.	Pvt. John Sheely	26	MS	3/1865	TN	TN	2/1866	Desertion	nr*	MM3885
3 Inf.	Mus. Richard Smith	19	PA	6/1863	PA	PA	8/1863	Desertion	FL	LL1256
3 Inf.	Pvt. George Peach	nr*	nr*	6/1863	PA	PA	9/1863	Desertion	FL	LL1256
3 Inf.	Pvt. George W. Bagwell	30	NY	7/1863	PA	SC	9/1863	Desertion	SC	NN1041 LL1256

Unit	Name	Age	Origin	Date	Residence	Charge	State	File
3 Inf.	Pvt. Theodore Christie	21	IN	7/1863	PA	8/1863	Desertion	SC	LL1395
3 Inf.	Pvt. Chena (aka Chana) Hays	24	PA	6/1863	PA	8/1863	Desertion	FL	LL1880
3 Inf.	Pvt. Alford Watkins	nr*	nr*	2/1864	TN	AL	3/1864	Desertion	nr*	LL1892 NN1677
3 Inf.	Pvt. Galloway Hatch	20	AL	5/1864	TN	6/1864	Desertion	nr*	LL2284
3 Inf.	Pvt. Lewis Waller	nr*	nr*	nr*	nr*	MO	nr*	AWOL	nr*	LL3012
30 Inf.	Pvt. Tilman Wood	nr*	nr*	nr*	nr*	nr*	Innocent	nr*	NN1325
30 Inf.	Pvt. John H. Gray	52	MD	3/1864	MD	PA	2/1865	Desertion	nr*	MM3140 MM2982
31 Inf.	Pvt. William H. Portland	23	NY	1/1864	CT	CT	2/1864	Desertion	FL	NN2905
31 Inf.	Rec. George Austin	21	LA	8/1864	DC	DC	nr*	AWOL	nr*	LL2961
31 Inf.	Pvt. George Wilton	19	Canada	8/1864	NY	VA	1/1865	Desertion	VA	NN3775
31 Inf.	Pvt. Frederick Hill	32	VA	nr*	LA	VA	5/1864	Desertion	FL	MM3123
32 Inf.	Pvt. Charles Wilson	26	PA	2/1864	PA	PA	4/1864	Desertion	FL	NN3048
32 Inf.	Pvt. Simeon Wilhelm (aka Wilhulm)	20	NJ	2/1864	NJ	PA	3/1863	AWOL	nr*	NN2445
32 Inf.	Pvt. Benjamin Lyon (aka Lyons)	31	PA	2/1864	PA	PA	3/1864	Desertion	nr*	LL2600
32 Inf.	Pvt. John H. Conner	25	nr*	2/1864	NJ	PA	4/1864	Desertion	FL	LL2600
32 Inf.	Pvt. Charles Bostic (aka Bostic)	23	PA	2/1864	PA	PA	3/1864	Desertion	FL	MM1833
32 Inf.	Pvt. William H. Harden	39	VA	10/1864	DC	VA	11/1864	Desertion	nr*	LL9284
32 Inf.	Pvt. John Miller	19	NY	3/1864	NJ	SC	12/1864	Desertion	FL	NN3772 OO401
32 Inf.	Pvt. William McNeill	23	GA	10/1864	DC	SC	3/1865	AWOL	FL	MM2140

(*continued*)

Regiment	Rank, Name, and Alias(es)	Age	Birth State	Date Enlisted	State Enlisted In	State Left Camp	Date Left Camp	Crime Convicted Of	State of Imprisonment	Court File(s)
32 Inf.	Pvt. Malachai Wilson	20	DE	3/1864	PA	SC	nr*	Desertion	nr*	MM2676 OO1287
33 Inf.	Pvt. James Brown	18	SC	4/1863	SC	SC	8/1863	Desertion	SC	LL1808
33 Inf.	Pvt. Robert Simmons	33	SC	11/1862	SC	SC	3/1863	Desertion	GA	NN2105
33 Inf.	Pvt. Frank Hagens	24	FL	2/1863	SC	SC	nr*	Desertion	SC	MM3401
34 Inf.	Pvt. Charles Adams	37	FL	8/1864	SC	FL	4/1864	Desertion	nr*	NN2788
34 Inf.	Pvt. Robert Humbert	29	VA	10/1864	VA	DC	12/1864	Desertion	nr*	LL3036
34 Inf.	Pvt. Joseph Smith	21	VA	1/1865	VA	FL	7/1865	Desertion	nr*	MM3122
35 Inf.	Pvt. John Henry	nr*	nr*	nr*	nr*	MS	6/1865	Desertion	NY	MM2944 MM2912
35 Inf.	Pvt. Lewis Bass	21	NC	5/1863	NC	SC	8/1865	AWOL	nr*	MM3196 MM2965
35 Inf.	Pvt. Orange Page	20	NC	5/1863	NC	SC	7/1865	Desertion	SC	MM2955
35 Inf.	Pvt. John Orr	30	GA	4/1865	SC	SC	8/1865	Desertion	SC	MM3401
36 Inf.	Pvt. Alonzo Marshall	18	VA	10/1863	VA	VA	8/1864	Desertion	VA	NN3191
36 Inf.	Pvt. James Smith	23	VA	6/1864	MD	VA	9/1864	Desertion	nr*	NN3191
37 Inf.	Pvt. Richard Merrick	23	NC	3/1865	NC	NC	10/1865	Innocent	NC	MM3447
37 Inf.	Pvt. William Freeman	20	NC	3/1865	NC	NC	3/1865	AWOL	nr*	MM3849
37 Inf.	Pvt. John Royle	23	MD	3/1865	VA	VA	2/1866	Desertion	VA	MM3920
38 Inf.	Sgt. Daniel Watts	19	PA	9/1864	VA	VA	10/1864	Desertion	VA	NN3347
38 Inf.	Pvt. Charles Smith	21	Canada	3/1865	NY	TX	9/1865	Desertion	FL	MM3510
39 Inf.	Pvt. Malcar (aka Mack) Johnson	22	MD	3/1864	MD	MD	1864	AWOL	nr*	LL3033

39 Inf.	Pvt. James Johnson	nr*	nr*	nr*	nr*	VA	AWOL	nr*	LL3906
39 Inf.	Pvt. John W. Goldsboro (aka Goldsborogh)	26	MD	3/1864	3/1864	PA	Desertion	nr*	LL3138
39 Inf.	Rec. Greenberry Barkus	18	VA	7/1864	8/1864	DC	Desertion	nr*	LL2976
39 Inf.	Pvt. Charles Smartboy	18	PA	7/1864	4/1865	MD	Desertion	NC	MM2961 MM2982 MM3140
39 Inf.	Pvt. John W. Bordley	19	VA	7/1864	8/1865	MD	Desertion	NC	MM2982 MM3140
4 Cav.	Pvt. Oscar Miller	nr*	nr*	10/1863	2/1864	LA	Desertion	FL	NN2077 LL2194 OO150
4 Cav.	Pvt. Joseph Backus	25	nr*	4/1864	4/1864	LA	Desertion	LA	LL2744
4 Cav.	Pvt. Alexander Armstead	23	nr*	8/1863	11/1863	LA	Desertion	LA	MM3104
4 Cav.	Pvt. Francis Davenport	19	PA	11/1863	7/1865	LA	Desertion	LA	MM3104
4 Cav.	Pvt. Frank (aka Franklin Loveless)	45	nr*	8/1863	10/1864	LA	Desertion	LA	MM3104
4 Cav.	Pvt. Pleasant McNeil (aka McNeal)	24	MS	4/1865	7/1865	LA	Desertion	LA	MM3104
4 Cav.	Pvt. Edward Mitchell (aka Mitchel)	23	nr*	8/1863	7/1865	LA	Desertion	LA	MM3104
4 Cav.	Bglr. Carroll Parro (aka Parre)	nr*	nr*	10/1863	8/1865	LA	Desertion	FL	MM3347
4 Cav.	Pvt. Sidney Washington	32	LA	4/1865	5/1864	LA	Desertion	LA & FL	MM3347
4 Cav.	Pvt. Charles Hadley	27	MO	4/1865	7/1865	LA	Desertion	FL	MM3561
4 Hvy. Art.	Pvt. General Johnson	21	TN	8/1863	9/1863	KY	Desertion	KY	nr*

(continued)

Regiment	Rank, Name, and Alias(es)	Age	Birth State	Date Enlisted	State Enlisted In	State Left Camp	Date Left Camp	Crime Convicted Of	State of Imprisonment	Court File(s)
4 Hvy. Art.	Pvt. Jack Tilman	17	IL	10/1863	IL	KY	12/1863	Desertion	KY	nr*
4 Hvy. Art.	Sgt. William Curtis	20	nr*	6/1863	IL	KY	8/1863	Desertion	KY	nr*
4 Hvy. Art.	Pvt. Thomas Ringold	25	KY	6/1863	KY	KY	9/1863	Desertion	nr*	NN2350 LL2365 LL2690 LL3174
4 Hvy. Art.	Pvt. Joseph Dodd	18	KY	12/1863	KY	KY	12/1863	AWOL	nr*	nr*
4 Hvy. Art.	Pvt. David Turner	33	TN	10/1863	TN	KY	5/1864	Desertion	KY	MM2476
4 Hvy. Art.	Pvt. David Haines	20	TN	12/1864	KY	KY	5/1865	Desertion	nr*	MM2636
4 Hvy. Art.	Pvt. Henry Tinder	22	VA	12/1863	KY	KY	12/1863	Desertion	KY	MM2990
4 Hvy. Art.	Pvt. William Owens	18	VA	8/1863	KY	KY	11/1863	Desertion	KY	MM3311
40 Inf.	Pvt. Abraham Clayton	18	NC	4/1865	TN	TN	4/1865	Desertion	TN	MM3340 MM3535
40 Inf.	Pvt. Noah Foster	23	NC	4/1865	TN	TN	4/1865	Desertion	TN	MM3340 MM3535
40 Inf.	Pvt. Isaac Garrison	34	NC	4/1865	TN	TN	4/1865	Desertion	TN	MM3340 MM3535
40 Inf.	Pvt. Marsh Glover	18	SC	4/1865	TN	TN	4/1865	Desertion	TN	MM3340 MM3535
40 Inf.	Pvt. Samuel Murphy	17	NC	4/1865	TN	TN	6/1865	Desertion	TN	MM3340 MM3535
40 Inf.	Pvt. Mills Walker	35	NC	4/1865	TN	TN	7/1865	Desertion	TN	MM3340 MM3535
41 Inf.	Pvt. Uriah (aka Urias) Montgomery	25	MS	10/1864	PA	PA	12/1864	Desertion	NY	LL2832
41 Inf.	Pvt. Hill Hough (aka Hodge)	21	GA	9/1864	PA	PA	10/1864	Desertion	nr*	NN2913

Unit	Name	Age						
42 Inf.	Rec. Marion Gregory	22	NC	9/1864	TN	Desertion	nr*	OO1489
42 Inf.	Pvt. Isaac Wheeler	29	VA	6/1864	TN	Desertion	nr*	MM3339
42 Inf.	Pvt. Robert Hall	18	AL	10/1864	TN	Desertion	AL	MM3446
42 Inf.	Pvt. Charles Putnam	18	GA	11/1864	TN	Desertion	AL	MM3735
43 Inf.	Pvt. David Butler	21	DE	4/1864	PA	Desertion	nr*	LL2148
43 Inf.	Cpl. George Edwards	22	SC	3/1865	PA	AWOL	nr*	LL2618
43 Inf.	Pvt. John Alexander	36	KY	4/1864	VA	Desertion	FL	NN2706
43 Inf.	Pvt. Alexander Gardner	40	KY	5/1864	PA	Innocent	nr*	NN2706
43 Inf.	Pvt. Alexander Holland	18	PA	3/1864	PA	Desertion	nr*	MM1773
43 Inf.	Pvt. George Marshall	25	KY	3/1864	VA	Desertion	nr*	MM1829
44 Inf.	Pvt. Edward Price	23	KY	6/1864	PA	Desertion	nr*	MM3446
45 Inf.	Pvt. Arthur Freeman	21	NJ	6/1864	AL	Desertion	DE	NN2979
45 Inf.	Pvt. Richard G. Jackson	37	NJ	5/1864	PA	Desertion	nr*	LL2968
45 Inf.	Pvt. William Williams	18	VA	7/1864	NJ	Desertion	nr*	LL2979
45 Inf.	Pvt. Isaac Wilson	23	VA	7/1864	WV	Desertion	VA	LL3045
45 Inf.	Pvt. Charles H. Brown	25	MD	7/1863	PA	AWOL	nr*	LL3192
45 Inf.	Pvt. Arthur Freeman	21	NJ	6/1864	PA	Desertion	DE	MM2987
46 Inf.	Pvt. Israel Taylor	38	SC	4/1863	DC	Desertion	nr*	NN3666
46 Inf.	Pvt. John Smith	35	MS	12/1864	AR	Desertion	FL	MM2025
47 Inf.	Pvt. Augustus Harrison	36	MS	5/1863	MO	Desertion	nr*	LL1565
47 Inf.	Sgt. Henry E. Hall	nr*	nr*	5/1863	LA	Desertion	nr*	LL1565
47 Inf.	Pvt. Samuel Gordon	nr*	nr*	nr*	LA	Desertion	nr*	LL2477
47 Inf.	Pvt. Amos Bell	23	LA	5/1863	nr*	Desertion	MS	NN3559

(continued)

Regiment	Rank, Name, and Alias(es)	Age	Birth State	Date Enlisted	State Enlisted In	State Left Camp	Date Left Camp	Crime Convicted Of	State of Imprisonment	Court File(s)
47 Inf.	Pvt. William Davis	25	nr*	5/1863	LA	LA	8/1863	Desertion	nr*	NN3670
47 Inf.	Pvt. Lewis Turk	30	VA	2/1864	MS	MS	4/1864	Desertion	MS	MM1615
49 Inf.	Pvt. Archer Bohard	27	MS	5/1863	MS	LA	12/1863	Innocent	nr*	MM2195
49 Inf.	Pvt. Samuel Rinearson	18	MS	10/1864	MO	MS	1/1865	Desertion	nr*	MM2195
49 Inf.	Pvt. James Martin	37	MS	5/1863	MS	MS	7/1865	Desertion	nr*	MM3138
5 MA Cavalry	Pvt. James Williams	19	KY	9/1864	KY	VA	10/1864	Desertion	nr*	NN2593
5 MA Cavalry	Pvt. William Leva (aka Levir)	22	PA	1/1864	MA	PA	4/1864	Desertion	NY	NN2638 NN2611
5 MA Cavalry	Pvt. John Sweetman	21	Canada	12/1864	MA	MD	1/1865	Desertion	nr*	LL3033
5 MA Cavalry	Pvt. Richard Motley	23	VA	12/1864	MA	MD	12/1864	Desertion	nr*	LL3088 NN3347
5 Cav.	Pvt. George Bell	20	KY	6/1864	KY	DC	nr*	Desertion	nr*	LL3138
5 Cav.	Pvt. Daniel Benton (aka Burton)	40	KY	9/1864	KY	KY	12/1864	AWOL	KY	MM2850
5 Cav.	Pvt. John Christopher	18	KY	9/1864	KY	KY	3/1865	Desertion	nr*	MM3372
5 Hvy. Art.	Pvt. Napoleon Bonaparre	22	MS	8/1863	MS	MS	nr*	AWOL	nr*	NN358
5 Hvy. Art.	Pvt. Spencer Watson	29	GA	8/1863	MS	MS	8/1863	Desertion	MS	NN372
5 Hvy. Art.	Pvt. James Johnson	22	MS	12/1863	MS	MS	12/1863	Desertion	nr*	LL1565
5 Hvy. Art.	Pvt. Henry Johnson	30	MS	5/1863	LA	MS	9/1863	Innocent	nr*	LL1565

5 Hvy. Art.	Pvt. Simpson William (aka Williams) (aka William Simpson) (aka William Simson)	28	KY	12/1864	MS	MS	Desertion	nr*	LL1734 LL2677
5 Hvy. Art.	Pvt. John Adams	24	KY	12/1863	MS	MS	Desertion	nr*	NN3506 NN3255 NN3031 LL2819 MM1902
5 Hvy. Art.	Pvt. Samuel Jones	20	MS	7/1864	MS	MS	Desertion	MS	NN2713 LL2657
5 Hvy. Art.	Pvt. Willis Latham (aka Lanthan)	33	KY	10/1863	MS	MS	Desertion	MS	NN3179
5 Hvy. Art.	Pvt. John Willis	nr*	nr*	8/1864	MS	MS	Innocent	nr*	LL2776
5 Hvy. Art.	Pvt. Isaac Powell	36	MO	3/1864	MS	MS	Desertion	nr*	LL2772
5 Hvy. Art.	Pvt. Osborn (aka Osborne) Jackson	30	MS	1/1864	MS	MS	Desertion	nr*	LL2774 LL2819 MM1902 NN3031
5 Hvy. Art.	Pvt. John Gray	36	SC	6/1864	MS	MS	Desertion	nr*	LL2772 LL2774 LL2819 MM1902 NN3031
5 Hvy. Art.	Pvt. Anthony Lennon	23	MS	11/1863	MS	MS	Desertion	MS	LL2772 LL2774 LL2819 MM1902 MM3031
5 Hvy. Art.	Pvt. Page Collins	37	MS	1/1865	MS	MS	AWOL	nr*	NN3179
5 Hvy. Art.	Pvt. Charles Halum (aka Hallum)	24	GA	1/1865	MS	MS	AWOL	nr*	MM1905

(*continued*)

Regiment	Rank, Name, and Alias(es)	Age	Birth State	Date Enlisted	State Enlisted In	State Left Camp	Date Left Camp	Crime Convicted Of	State of Imprisonment	Court File(s)
5 Hvy. Art.	Pvt. Isaac (aka Isdore) Young	27	MS	11/1863	MS	MS	1/1864	Desertion	nr*	MM2195
5 Hvy. Art.	Pvt. Emanuel White	25	MS	11/1863	MS	MS	12/1863	Desertion	FL	MM2195
5 Hvy. Art.	Pvt. Eli Griffin	22	MS	1/1865	MS	MS	2/1865	Desertion	TN	MM3533
5 Hvy. Art.	Pvt. Jerry Williams	20	KY	8/1863	MS	MS	8/1865	Desertion	nr*	MM3535
50 Inf.	Lt. Joseph Meyers	33	nr*	7/1863	MS	TN	11/1863	Desertion	nr*	LL1565
50 Inf.	Pvt. Shack Williams	25	LA	7/1863	MS	MS	nr*	AWOL	nr*	NN1246
50 Inf.	Pvt. Elijah Washington	25	MS	7/1863	MS	MS	8/1863	Desertion	MS & FL	MM1518
50 Inf.	Pvt. Cain (aka Caine) Griffin	23	MS	1/1865	MS	MS	2/1865	Desertion	nr*	MM3058
50 Inf.	Pvt. Stephen Granton	30	MS	5/1864	MS	MS	4/1864	Desertion	nr*	MM3058
50 Inf.	Pvt. Adam Works	26	MS	3/1864	MS	MS	4/1864	Desertion	nr*	MM3058
50 Inf.	Pvt. Wiley Southerland (aka Miley Sutherland)	19	MS	3/1864	MS	MS	4/1864	Desertion	nr*	MM3058
50 Inf.	Pvt. David Sutherland	22	MS	3/1864	MS	MS	3/1864	Desertion	nr*	MM3058
51 Inf.	Pvt. Thomas Riley	25	SC	3/1864	MS	LA	7/1864	Desertion	IL	NN3282
52 Inf.	Pvt. Taylor Williams	18	MS	7/1863	MS	MS	8/1863	AWOL	nr*	LL1565
52 Inf.	Pvt. Thomas Haycoff	18	MS	7/1863	MS	MS	8/1863	Desertion	nr*	LL1565
52 Inf.	Pvt. Philip Green	22	MS	11/1863	nr*	MS	12/1863	Desertion	nr*	LL1565
52 Inf.	Pvt. James Brown	17	MS	7/1863	MS	MS	nr*	AWOL	nr*	LL1565

52 Inf.	Pvt. Mose Germain	16	MS	7/1863	MS	8/1863	Desertion	nr*	LL1734
52 Inf.	Pvt. Henry Jones	20	LA	7/1863	MS	2/1863	Desertion	nr*	LL1734
52 Inf.	Pvt. Tilman Dixon	21	MS	7/1863	MS	8/1863	Desertion	nr*	NN1437
52 Inf.	Pvt. Warthum Banks	nr*	nr*	nr*	MS	nr*	Desertion	nr*	LL2772
52 Inf.	Pvt. Isaac Bruner	22	VA	3/1864	MS	2/1865	Desertion	MS	LL2774 LL2819 MM1902 NN3031 MM2382 OO1220
53 Inf.	Pvt. John Mitchell	20	MS	6/1863	LA	11/1863	Desertion	nr*	NN2350 LL2365 LL2690
53 Inf.	Pvt. William Hilman (aka Hillman) (aka William Middleton) (aka William Midelton)	23	LA	9/1863	MS	3/1864	AWOL	nr*	LL2477
53 Inf.	Pvt. Robert Haymor (aka Haymore)	28	MS	6/1863	MS	5/1864	Desertion	nr*	LL2774 LL2819 MM1902 NN3031 NN3255
53 Inf.	Pvt. Ned Thompson	45	MS	11/1863	MS	3/1864	Desertion	nr*	LL2772
53 Inf.	Pvt. John Chase	22	LA	11/1863	MS	3/1864	Desertion	nr*	LL2774 LL2819 MM1902 NN3031 LL2772
53 Inf.	Pvt. Allen Ross	22	MS	6/1863	MS	6/1863	AWOL	nr*	LL2774 LL2819 MM1902 NN3031 MM2195 OO1220
53 Inf.	Pvt. Samuel Lowry	24	nr*	9/1863	LA	8/1865	Desertion	nr*	MM3646

(continued)

Regiment	Rank, Name, and Alias(es)	Age	Birth State	Date Enlisted	State Enlisted In	State Left Camp	Date Left Camp	Crime Convicted Of	State of Imprisonment	Court File(s)
53 Inf.	Pvt. Granderson Lum	25	MS	12/1863	MS	MS	5/1865	Desertion	nr*	MM3569
54 MA Inf.	Pvt. John Benson	30	nr*	3/1863	MA	MA	4/1863	Desertion	MA	NN19
54 MA Inf.	Pvt. Webster Wilson	24	PA	3/1863	MA	MA	4/1863	Desertion	nr*	LL1256
54 MA Inf.	Pvt. Benjamin Derrick	36	NY	4/1863	MA	SC	5/1865	AWOL	SC	MM2457 MM2438
54 MA Inf.	Pvt. William F. Freeman (aka William T. Freeman)	25	PA	4/1863	MA	SC	5/1865	AWOL	nr*	MM2457 MM2438
54 MA Inf.	Pvt. Joseph W. Reed	23	NH	12/1863	MA	SC	3/1865	Desertion	nr*	MM2498
54 MA Inf.	Pvt. Jacob Ballard	29	PA	3/1863	MA	SC	6/1865	Desertion	SC	MM2551
54 Inf.	Pvt. Charles Harris	24	VA	12/1863	AR	AR	2/1864	Desertion	AR	LL2014 NN3808
54 Inf.	Pvt. Nelson Collier (aka Colier)	25	NC	12/1863	AR	AR	4/1864	Desertion	OH	NN2826 NN2841 NN2718
54 Inf.	Pvt. Francis Myers	nr*	nr*	nr*	nr*	VA	nr*	AWOL	nr*	LL2683
54 Inf.	Pvt. Simon Johnson	23	VA	12/1863	AR	AR	nr*	Desertion	nr*	MM2505 MM2483
54 Inf.	Cpl. Stephen Duke	22	AL	8/1863	AR	AR	9/1863	Desertion	OH	MM3747
55 MA Inf.	Pvt. Isaiah Price	24	OH	11/1863	MA	NY	2/1864	Desertion	FL	NN3122
55 MA Inf.	Pvt. Alfred E. Pelette	nr*	nr*	nr*	nr*	SC	1864	Desertion	SC	MM2239
55 MA Inf.	Pvt. Joseph Brown	18	PA	6/1863	PA	SC	3/1865	Desertion	FL	MM2239
55 Inf.	Pvt. John Hogan	22	AL	6/1863	MS	MS	6/1863	AWOL	nr*	NN477 NN413
55 Inf.	Pvt. Ned Neil	22	TN	6/1863	MS	MS	7/1863	Desertion	nr*	LL1188

55 Inf.	Sgt. Frank Douglass	24	TN	6/1864	MS	7/1864	Innocent	nr*	NN2926 LL2739
56 Inf.	Rec. Ned Lake	20	MS	2/1864	MS	3/1864	Desertion	FL	MM1967
56 Inf.	Pvt. Reuben Hall	28	MO	6/1863	MO	12/1865	Desertion	FL	MM3891
57 Inf.	Pvt. Mauser (aka Monroe) Pennington	19	MS	nr*	nr*	12/1863	Desertion	IL	LL2601
57 Inf.	Pvt. Mathew Perkins	22	TN	12/1863	AR	12/1863	Desertion	IL	LL2735
57 Inf.	Pvt. Nelson Pennington	22	AR	12/1863	AR	12/1863	Desertion	IL	LL2736
57 Inf.	Pvt. Lee Pennington	20	MS	12/1863	AR	12/1863	Desertion	IL	LL2735
57 Inf.	Pvt. Daniel Pennington	24	MS	12/1863	AR	12/1863	Desertion	IL	LL2735
57 Inf.	Pvt. Randolph Irwin	21	VA	11/1863	AR	3/1864	Desertion	nr*	LL2735
57 Inf.	Pvt. Gilbert Hicks	20	TN	12/1863	AR	5/1864	Desertion	AR	LL2735
57 Inf.	Pvt. Jefferson Pennington	nr*	nr*	nr*	nr*	nr*	Innocent	nr*	LL2767
57 Inf.	Pvt. Anthony Booth	25	TN	12/1863	TN	3/1864	Desertion	nr*	LL2767
57 Inf.	Pvt. James Jones	20	KY	12/1863	AR	11/1864	Desertion	AR	LL3210 OO209
57 Inf.	Pvt. Peter Harris	34	AL	2/1865	AR	nr*	AWOL	nr*	MM2035
57 Inf.	Pvt. Cornelius Augustus (aka Augustuss)	20	NC	12/1864	AR	3/1865	Desertion	AR	MM2483 MM2505
57 Inf.	Pvt. William Burden	29	VA	12/1863	AR	6/1865	AWOL	nr*	MM3730
58 Inf.	Pvt. Major Adolph	21	VA	8/1863	MS	9/1863	Desertion	MS	NN2729
58 Inf.	Pvt. Dennis Smith	19	VA	8/1863	MS	9/1863	Desertion	MS	NN2729
58 Inf.	Pvt. Blasker Hening (aka Herring)	18	MS	3/1864	MS	7/1865	AWOL	nr*	MM2881

(continued)

Regiment	Rank, Name, and Alias(es)	Age	Birth State	Date Enlisted	State Enlisted In	State Left Camp	Date Left Camp	Crime Convicted Of	State of Imprisonment	Court File(s)
58 Inf.	Pvt. Bradford Hening (aka Herring)	25	KY	3/1864	MS	MS	7/1865	AWOL	MS	MM2881
58 Inf.	Pvt. Nelson Hening (aka Herring)	18	AL	3/1864	MS	MS	7/1865	AWOL	MS	MM2881
58 Inf.	Pvt. Nathan Wright	21	MS	8/1863	MS	MS	10/1863	Desertion	nr*	MM3325
58 Inf.	Pvt. James Wright	24	MS	8/1863	MS	MS	10/1863	Desertion	nr*	MM3325
58 Inf.	Pvt. George Wright	28	MS	8/1863	MS	MS	10/1863	Desertion	nr*	MM3325
58 Inf.	Pvt. Richard Ware	19	MS	8/1863	MS	MS	9/1863	Desertion	MS	MM3325
58 Inf.	Pvt. William Thomas	20	nr*	8/1863	MS	MS	9/1863	Desertion	nr*	MM3570
58 Inf.	Pvt. Winston Lee	24	nr*	9/1863	MS	MS	10/1863	Desertion	nr*	MM3570
58 Inf.	Pvt. Henry Hutchins	27	MS	8/1863	MS	MS	10/1863	Desertion	nr*	MM3570
59 Inf.	Pvt. Samuel Davis	18	TN	5/1863	TN	TN	6/1863	Innocent	nr*	LL1260
59 Inf.	Pvt. Henry Sykes	22	MS	6/1863	TN	TN	7/1863	Desertion	nr*	LL1870
59 Inf.	Pvt. Jordan (aka Jordon) Henson	31	GA	5/1863	TN	TN	8/1863	Desertion	nr*	LL1765
59 Inf.	Pvt. George Jackson	nr*	nr*	nr*	nr*	TN	nr*	Desertion	nr*	LL2284
59 Inf.	Pvt. Aaron Jones	18	TN	7/1863	TN	TN	9/1863	Desertion	TN	NN2657
59 Inf.	Pvt. Mason Jones	22	TN	6/1863	TN	TN	9/1863	Desertion	TN	NN2657
59 Inf.	Pvt. Randal Williams	29	TN	6/1863	TN	TN	9/1863	Desertion	TN	NN2657
59 Inf.	Pvt. Joseph Garret	21	AL	5/1863	TN	TN	10/1864	Desertion	nr*	MM1677 MM1672

59 Inf.	Pvt. Edward Allen	18	MS	3/1864	TN	nr*	Desertion	nr*	MM1866
59 Inf.	Pvt. Henry Smith	18	MS	5/1863	TN	TN	Desertion	TN	MM3191
59 Inf.	Pvt. Robert Matox	nr*	nr*	nr*	nr*	TN	Desertion	TN	MM3455
6 Cav.	Pvt. William Butts	20	KY	9/1864	KY	KY	Desertion	KY	MM2969
6 Cav.	Pvt. Green Gentry	18	KY	nr*	KY	KY	Desertion	nr*	MM2969
6 Cav.	Pvt. Vincent Granger	18	KY	9/1864	KY	KY	Desertion	KY	MM2969
6 Cav.	Pvt. William Hampton	29	KY	9/1864	KY	KY	Desertion	KY	MM2969
6 Cav.	Pvt. Abraham Coombs (aka Combs)	20	KY	9/1864	KY	KY	Desertion	KY	MM3031
6 Cav.	Pvt. George Washington	22	KY	9/1864	KY	KY	Desertion	KY	MM3031
6 Cav.	Pvt. Henry Williams	19	KY	1/1865	KY	KY	Desertion	nr*	MM3372
6 Hvy. Art.	Pvt. John Adams	nr*	nr*	nr*	nr*	nr*	Desertion	nr*	LL2772 LL2774
6 Hvy. Art.	Pvt. George Shorter	18	MS	1/1864	MS	MS	Desertion	nr*	LL3205 OO439 MM1562
6 Hvy. Art.	Pvt. Stanton Winchester	21	MS	1/1864	MS	MS	Desertion	FL	MM2062
6 Hvy. Art.	Pvt. John Pine (aka Price)	22	AR	1/1865	MS	MS	Desertion	FL	MM2062
6 Hvy. Art.	Pvt. Harris Spurr	20	MS	2/1864	MS	MS	AWOL	MS	MM3325
6 Hvy. Art.	Pvt. Fieldings Gordon (aka Gordins)	30	MS	1/1864	LA	LA	AWOL	nr*	MM3325
6 Hvy. Art.	Pvt. Henry Griffin	18	MS	12/1863	LA	LA	Desertion	nr*	MM3325
6 Hvy. Art.	Pvt. Fleming (aka Flemming) Falkins	25	MS	1/1864	MS	MS	Desertion	nr*	MM3484 MM3483
6 Inf.	Pvt. William Lewis	22	DE	8/1863	PA	PA	AWOL	nr*	OO84

(continued)

Regiment	Rank, Name, and Alias(es)	Age	Birth State	Date Enlisted	State Enlisted In	State Left Camp	Date Left Camp	Crime Convicted Of	State of Imprisonment	Court File(s)
6 Inf.	Pvt. Andrew Boulden	nr*	nr*	8/1863	PA	PA	9/1863	Desertion	nr*	LL1074
6 Inf.	Pvt. George Cooper	22	NJ	9/1863	PA	PA	10/1863	Desertion	nr*	OO84
6 Inf.	Pvt. Levi Leboo	26	PA	8/1863	PA	PA	10/1863	Desertion	VA	NN1259
6 Inf.	Pvt. Richard Young	nr*	nr*	nr*	nr*	VA	2/1864	Desertion	nr*	NN1259
6 Inf.	Pvt. George Book	28	PA	8/1863	PA	nr*	nr*	AWOL	nr*	OO84
6 Inf.	Pvt. Alfred Washington	24	VA	7/1863	PA	PA	10/1863	Desertion	VA	NN1667
6 Inf.	Pvt. John Crawford	21	AL	7/1863	PA	VA	12/1864	AWOL	nr*	LL3033
6 Inf.	Rec. William H. Fillmore	21	MI	9/1864	NY	nr*	4/1865	Desertion	NY	MM1843
6 Inf.	Pvt. Thomas Bush	23	DC	7/1863	PA	VA	9/1864	Desertion	nr*	MM3226
61 Inf.	Pvt. Henry Hunt	16	TN	6/1863	TN	TN	2/1864	Innocent	TN	LL1765
61 Inf.	Mus. Charles Brown	20	TN	8/1863	TN	TN	6/1864	Desertion	IL	LL2699 LL2856
61 Inf.	Pvt. David Prince	21	SC	6/1863	TN	TN	4/1864	Desertion	IL	LL2699 LL2856
64 Inf.	Pvt. Joseph Ball	32	MS	11/1863	MS	MS	4/1864	Desertion	nr*	MM2833
65 Inf.	Cpl. James Switzer	20	MO	12/1863	MO	LA	2/1866	Desertion	MS	MM3917
66 Inf.	Pvt. Benjamin Green	19	MS	12/1863	MS	MS	2/1864	Desertion	nr*	NN2489
66 Inf.	Pvt. Richard Edmington	40	NC	1/1864	LA	LA	1/1864	Desertion	nr*	NN2489
66 Inf.	Pvt. Ennis Thompson	20	MS	1/1864	MS	LA	3/1864	Innocent	nr*	NN2489
66 Inf.	Pvt. Mitchell Robinson	28	MS	2/1864	MS	MS	2/1864	AWOL	nr*	NN2489
66 Inf.	Pvt. Charles McLann (aka McLain)	18	KY	12/1863	MS	MS	3/1864	Desertion	TN	NN2785 MM1974 LL2676

66 Inf.	Pvt. Isaac Wallen	41	VA	1/1864	MS	LA	8/1864	Innocent	nr*	LL3210
66 Inf.	Pvt. Robert Fitzhugh	30	VA	12/1863	MS	MS	3/1864	Desertion	nr*	MM2195
66 Inf.	Pvt. Burgess Rollins (aka Burgess Rollin)	20	VA	12/1864	MS	MS	9/1865	AWOL	nr*	MM3325
66 Inf.	Pvt. Levi Kelsey	29	MS	12/1863	MS	MS	10/1865	Desertion	nr*	MM3484 MM3483
68 Inf.	Pvt. William Winthrop	18	MO	3/1864	MO	TN	10/1864	Desertion	TN	LL3188 OO330
7 Hvy. Art.	Pvt. Samuel Booker	22	nr*	10/1863	KY	KY	11/1863	Desertion	KY	nr*
7 Hvy. Art.	Pvt. Martin Coffee (aka Morton Caffee)	30	nr*	7/1863	MS	MS	10/1863	Desertion	TN	NN1939
7 Hvy. Art.	Pvt. Crawford Wilcox	31	NC	4/1864	TN	TN	6/1864	Desertion	nr*	NN2241
7 Hvy. Art.	Pvt. Charles Baltimore	23	nr*	2/1863	LA	LA	8/1864	Desertion	FL	LL2998 NN3471
7 Hvy. Art.	Pvt. John Perkins	nr*	nr*	nr*	nr*	MS	6/1865	Innocent	nr*	NN3181 NN3577
7 Hvy. Art.	Pvt. Samuel Levy	nr*	nr*	nr*	nr*	TN	nr*	Innocent	nr*	NN3181 NN3577
70 Inf.	Pvt. Flemming Johnson	45	VA	9/1864	LA	MS	10/1864	Desertion	nr*	MM2062
70 Inf.	Pvt. Thomas Jefferson	18	LA	5/1864	LA	MS	3/1865	Desertion	MS	MM2062
70 Inf.	Pvt. Henry Hayfer	38	KY	12/1864	MS	MS	4/1865	Desertion	MS	MM3057
70 Inf.	Pvt. Prince Robinson	45	LA	4/1864	MS	MS	nr*	Desertion	nr*	MM2881
72 Inf.	Pvt. Moses Snell	21	KY	1/1865	OH	KY	4/1865	Desertion	KY	MM2643
72 Inf.	Pvt. John Fraland (aka Fralem and Freeland)	19	PA	1/1865	OH	KY	4/1865	Desertion	nr*	MM2643
73 Inf.	Cpl. John Johnson	22	nr*	9/1862	LA	LA	7/1863	Desertion	nr*	LL3106
73 Inf.	Mus. Warren Hamilton	17	nr*	12/1863	LA	LA	4/1864	Desertion	nr*	LL3106
73 Inf.	Pvt. Alcide Joseph	20	LA	8/1862	LA	LA	8/1863	Desertion	nr*	LL3106

(continued)

Regiment	Rank, Name, and Alias(es)	Age	Birth State	Date Enlisted	State Enlisted In	State Left Camp	Date Left Camp	Crime Convicted Of	State of Imprisonment	Court File(s)
73 Inf.	Pvt. Edward (aka Edouard) Joseph	22	nr*	9/1862	LA	LA	4/1864	Desertion	nr*	LL3106
73 Inf.	Pvt. Francis Esquiano	23	nr*	9/1862	LA	LA	9/1863	Desertion	nr*	LL3106
73 Inf.	Pvt. Pierre Hilain (aka Helaire)	30	nr*	9/1862	LA	LA	12/1863	Desertion	nr*	LL3106
73 Inf.	Pvt. August Anderson	19	nr*	8/1862	LA	LA	10/1863	Desertion	nr*	LL3106
73 Inf.	Pvt. Henry Barnes (aka Barns)	18	VA	9/1862	LA	LA	5/1864	Desertion	nr*	LL3106
73 Inf.	Pvt. Henry Clay	30	nr*	9/1862	LA	LA	3/1864	Desertion	nr*	LL3106
73 Inf.	Pvt. Sylvester John	nr*	nr*	9/1862	LA	LA	nr*	Desertion	nr*	LL3106
73 Inf.	Pvt. Joseph Debar	nr*	nr*	12/1862	LA	LA	9/1863	Desertion	nr*	LL3106
73 Inf.	Pvt. Washington Jefferson	28	nr*	9/1862	LA	LA	8/1864	Innocent	nr*	NN3575
73 Inf.	Pvt. Joseph Norbert	35	LA	9/1862	LA	LA	9/1863	Desertion	nr*	NN3575
73 Inf.	Pvt. Matthew (aka Mathieu and Mathew) Tinely (aka Tensley)	28	nr*	9/1862	LA	LA	4/1864	Innocent	nr*	NN3575
73 Inf.	Cpl. Louis Lafond (aka Lafon)	34	LA	8/1862	LA	LA	10/1863	Desertion	nr*	LL3106
73 Inf.	Pvt. Jack Thompson	30	nr*	9/1862	LA	TN	5/1864	Desertion	nr*	LL3106
73 Inf.	Pvt. John Nelson	18	nr*	9/1862	LA	LA	10/1862	Desertion	nr*	LL3106

73 Inf.	Pvt. John Major	31	nr*	9/1862	LA	LA	4/1864	AWOL	nr*	LL3106
73 Inf.	Pvt. Pierre Lieuchet (aka Luchette)	35	nr*	9/1862	LA	LA	4/1864	Desertion	FL	LL3106
73 Inf.	Pvt. Edward Madison	nr*	nr*	1/1863	LA	LA	12/1863	Desertion	nr*	LL3106
73 Inf.	Pvt. Octave Laveau	20	nr*	9/1862	LA	LA	4/1864	Desertion	nr*	LL3106
73 Inf.	Pvt. Joseph Raney	nr*	nr*	11/1862	LA	LA	6/1864	Desertion	nr*	LL3106
73 Inf.	Pvt. Anthony Primbo (aka Primbow)	24	nr*	9/1862	LA	LA	5/1864	Desertion	FL	LL3106
73 Inf.	Pvt. Vincent Roubert (aka Robert)	40	nr*	9/1862	LA	LA	4/1864	Desertion	nr*	LL3106
73 Inf.	Sgt. Philip (aka Philipp) Sabatier	nr*	nr*	9/1862	LA	LA	5/1863	Desertion	FL	LL3106
73 Inf.	Sgt. Gustave Laurent	43	LA	8/1862	LA	LA	5/1864	AWOL	nr*	LL3106
73 Inf.	Mus. William A. Robertson	24	nr*	9/1862	LA	LA	2/1863	Desertion	nr*	LL3218
74 Inf.	Cpl. Joseph Manuel	nr*	nr*	nr*	nr*	nr*	nr*	Desertion	nr*	MM2724 OO1316
74 Inf.	Pvt. John Allen	40	nr*	10/1862	LA	LA	7/1865	AWOL	LA	MM2792
75 Inf.	Mus. Marshall Cassimo (aka Marshal Casmine)	19	LA	11/1863	LA	LA	4/1864	Desertion	nr*	LL3106
75 Inf.	Pvt. Joseph Rolen (aka Rolend)	27	LA	11/1862	LA	LA	5/1864	AWOL	nr*	NN3575
75 Inf.	Pvt. Joseph Sylvester	28	LA	11/1862	LA	LA	1/1863	Innocent	nr*	MM2059
75 Inf.	Pvt. Robert Braxton	20	VA	1/1865	DC	LA	11/1864	Desertion	nr*	MM2791 MM2808

(*continued*)

Regiment	Rank, Name, and Alias(es)	Age	Birth State	Date Enlisted	State Enlisted In	State Left Camp	Date Left Camp	Crime Convicted Of	State of Imprisonment	Court File(s)
76 Inf.	Pvt. Jim Hagan	20	nr*	2/1863	LA	LA	2/1865	Desertion	nr*	LL2628
77 Inf.	Pvt. Allan George	nr*	nr*	9/1862	LA	nr*	10/1863	Desertion	LA	LL1673
77 Inf.	Pvt. Albert Delong (aka Delany)	nr*	nr*	2/1863	LA	LA	2/1864	Desertion	FL	LL1943
77 Inf.	Pvt. Cornelius Anderson	23	LA	2/1865	LA	LA	6/1865	AWOL	LA	MM3115
77 Inf.	Pvt. Benjamin F. Butler	nr*	nr*	6/1863	LA	LA	6/1865	Desertion	LA	MM3115
77 Inf.	Mus. Leonce Couturie (aka Leon Conturie)	16	LA	12/1864	LA	LA	7/1865	Desertion	LA	MM3102 MM3115
79 Inf.	Pvt. George Mack	27	nr*	10/1863	AR	AR	4/1864	Desertion	nr*	MM2035
79 Inf.	Pvt. George True	24	AL	8/1862	KS	KS	3/1863	Desertion	nr*	MM2035
8 Inf.	Pvt. Hannibal Davis	21	PA	9/1863	PA	PA	10/1863	Desertion	nr*	LL2549
8 Inf.	Pvt. William H. Smith	20	NY	9/1863	PA	PA	12/1863	Desertion	nr*	NN2913
8 Inf.	Pvt. Timothy Coggins	42	PA	9/1861	PA	PA	11/1864	Desertion	DC	NN3477
80 Inf.	Pvt. Abraham Givens	26	LA	6/1863	LA	LA	5/1865	Desertion	LA	MM2635
80 Inf.	Pvt. Jesse Cooper	25	nr*	6/1863	LA	LA	10/1865	Desertion	nr*	MM3924
81 Inf.	Cpl. Alfred Parker	35	nr*	8/1863	LA	LA	11/1863	AWOL	nr*	NN1587
81 Inf.	Pvt. George Thompson	25	nr*	5/1863	LA	LA	5/1864	Desertion	nr*	MM2103
81 Inf.	Pvt. Charles Batice	21	nr*	5/1863	LA	LA	10/1865	Desertion	nr*	MM3373
81 Inf.	Pvt. Edward Barlow	nr*	nr*	1/1864	nr*	LA	10/1865	Desertion	MS	MM3634
81 Inf.	Pvt. Isaac Rhoddy	23	LA	nr*	LA	LA	8/1864	Desertion	FL	MM3634

81 Inf.	Pvt. Victor Du Varris	27	nr*	10/1863	LA	2/1866	Desertion	MS	MM3734
81 Inf.	Pvt. Louis Merrin	19	LA	3/1864	LA	5/1866	AWOL	MS	MM3917
81 Inf.	Pvt. Samuel Galloway	nr*	nr*	nr*	LA	1/1865	Desertion	MS	MM3962 MM3961
81 Inf.	Pvt. Gustave Alexon	nr*	nr*	10/1864	LA	1/1866	Desertion	MS	MM3961
82 Inf.	Pvt. Alexander Jontine (aka Joutine)	37	nr*	5/1863	LA	4/1864	Desertion	nr*	NN1587
82 Inf.	Pvt. Scott Robinson	21	VA	8/1863	FL	7/1864	Desertion	FL	LL2675
82 Inf.	Cpl. Thomas Phillips	25	nr*	5/1863	LA	4/1864	Innocent	nr*	NN3832
83 Inf.	Pvt. John Cole	25	nr*	7/1863	AR	8/1864	Desertion	nr*	MM2437
83 Inf. (old)	Cpl. Alexander Kuhn	nr*	nr*	7/1863	MS	12/1863	AWOL	nr*	NN1455 NN1554
83 Inf. (old)	Pvt. Andrew Lane	25	nr*	7/1863	LA	12/1863	AWOL	nr*	NN1455 NN1554
83 Inf. (old)	Sgt. David Lane (aka Laine)	27	nr*	7/1863	LA	12/1863	Desertion	nr*	NN1455 NN1554
84 Inf.	Pvt. George Banks	25	MS	2/1864	LA	5/1864	Desertion	FL	LL3150
88 Inf.	Pvt. Isham Barr	33	TN	1/1865	TN	3/1865	Desertion	TN	MM2602
9 Inf.	Pvt. James Williams	nr*	nr*	nr*	nr*	nr*	Innocent	nr*	NN1502
90 Inf.	Sgt. Richard Johnson (aka Johnston)	18	MS	10/1863	LA	6/1864	Desertion	LA	NN1887
91 Inf.	Sgt. Henry Lavign (aka Lavigne)	nr*	nr*	8/1863	LA	9/1863	Desertion	MS & FL	LL1673
91 Inf.	Pvt. Louis Romain	nr*	nr*	9/1862	LA	9/1863	AWOL	nr*	LL1673
91 Inf.	Pvt. Edgard Leon	nr*	nr*	9/1862	LA	9/1863	Desertion	MS	LL1673

(*continued*)

Regiment	Rank, Name, and Alias(es)	Age	Birth State	Date Enlisted	State Enlisted In	State Left Camp	Date Left Camp	Crime Convicted Of	State of Imprisonment	Court File(s)
92 Inf.	Pvt. George Washington	26	VA	10/1863	LA	LA	11/1863	Desertion	FL	LL1612 LL1613
93 Inf.	Pvt. James Braxton	44	nr*	11/1863	LA	LA	12/1863	Desertion	nr*	NN2960
93 Inf.	Pvt. Victor Willis	31	nr*	11/1863	LA	LA	12/1863	Desertion	nr*	NN2960
95 Inf.	Pvt. John Handy	25	nr*	5/1863	LA	LA	6/1863	Desertion	FL	LL2201
96 Inf.	Pvt. George Allen	nr*	nr*	9/1862	nr*	LA	8/1864	Desertion	LA	MM3347
97 Inf.	Pvt. Augustine Turibo	nr*	nr*	nr*	nr*	nr*	nr*	Desertion	nr*	NN3461
97 Inf.	Pvt. George Bradly	23	LA	8/1864	LA	AL	10/1865	Desertion	AL	MM3370
98 Inf.	Sgt. James Lane	26	LA	11/1863	LA	LA	3/1864	Desertion	nr*	LL2221
98 Inf.	Pvt. Nelson Lane	23	nr*	11/1863	LA	LA	3/1864	Desertion	nr*	NN2960
98 Inf.	Pvt. Jacob Marshall	32	nr*	11/1863	LA	LA	12/1863	Desertion	FL	MM2059
98 Inf.	Pvt. Hugh Doyle	24	LA	8/1863	LA	LA	10/1863	Desertion	nr*	MM2059
98 Inf.	Pvt. William Allen	20	LA	8/1864	LA	LA	10/1864	Desertion	FL	MM2059
98 Inf.	Pvt. William Gray	21	nr*	8/1863	LA	LA	6/1864	Desertion	nr*	MM3373
99 Inf.	Pvt. Charles Williams	22	nr*	8/1863	LA	LA	2/1864	Desertion	FL	LL1612 LL1613
99 Inf.	Cpl. Ephraim Williams	18	LA	8/1863	LA	LA	9/1863	Desertion	MS	LL1623
99 Inf.	Cpl. John Johnson	39	MD	8/1863	LA	LA	10/1863	Desertion	MS	LL1623
99 Inf.	Pvt. John Wright	23	KY	8/1863	LA	LA	10/1863	Desertion	MS	LL1623
99 Inf.	Pvt. George Landers	nr*	nr*	nr*	nr*	VA	nr*	Desertion	nr*	LL1623
Inf.	Rec. George Taylor	nr*	nr*	nr*	nr*	VA	nr*	Desertion	nr*	LL2895

Inf.	Pvt. James Wilson	nr*	nr*	nr*	nr*	nr*	AWOL	nr*	LL2793
Inf.	Rec. Smith Hazel	26	NY	10/1864	VA	10/1864	Desertion	VA	LL2947
Inf.	Rec. James Smith	nr*	nr*	nr*	VA	nr*	Desertion	nr*	LL2961
Inf.	Rec. John W. Jacobs	23	VA	nr*	MD	nr*	Desertion	nr*	LL2895
Inf.	Rec. David Lee	27	MO	6/1864	VA	8/1864	Desertion	nr*	LL2991
Inf.	Rec. Henry Jackson	21	Canada	8/1864	VA	nr*	Desertion	nr*	LL2900
Inf.	Rec. Thomas Snowden	nr*	nr*	nr*	MD	10/1864	Desertion	nr*	LL2992
Inf.	Pvt. Sandy Curry	nr*	nr*	nr*	MD	nr*	Desertion	nr*	LL3046
Inf.	Rec. George Williams	nr*	nr*	nr*	MD	nr*	Desertion	nr*	LL2028
Inf.	Rec. John Carroll	nr*	nr*	nr*	VA	nr*	Desertion	nr*	LL3045
Inf.	Rec. Chalkey Rixon (aka Rinson)	20	PA	12/1864	DE	nr*	Desertion	nr*	LL3045
Inf.	Rec. James K. Cook	28	VA	8/1864	MD	11/1864	AWOL	nr*	LL3096
Inf.	Rec. Benjamin Green	nr*	nr*	9/1863	DC	nr*	Desertion	nr*	LL2988
Inf.	Rec. George Batry	nr*	nr*	nr*	VA	nr*	Desertion	nr*	LL3077
Inf.	Rec. Henry Dickson	nr*	nr*	nr*	MD	nr*	Desertion	nr*	LL3077
Inf.	Rec. George White	nr*	nr*	nr*	VA	nr*	AWOL	nr*	LL3075
Inf.	Rec. George Stone	nr*	nr*	nr*	VA	nr*	AWOL	nr*	LL2982

Notes

INTRODUCTION

1. Thomas W. Knox, *Camp-Fire and Cotton-Field: Southern Adventure in Time of War, Life with the Union Armies, and Residence on a Louisiana Plantation* (New York: Blelock, 1865), 435. Thomas Wallace Knox did not name the soldier or the regiment, but the soldier most likely served in the Eleventh Louisiana, which was later redesignated the Forty-Ninth United States Colored Infantry (or USCI), because the regiment had served at Milliken's Bend before being moved upriver to Waterproof. Although it is possible Knox referred to the Ninth Louisiana Infantry (African Descent), as it also defended Milliken's Bend and later traveled to Waterproof, it is most plausible that the soldier served in the Eleventh because the regiment was camped at Waterproof during a two-month expedition (January and February 1864) while the Ninth only participated in a skirmish at Waterproof on April 15, 1864. In addition to the extent of service, it is also more likely Knox visited the Eleventh because members of the regiment staged a mutiny in the summer of 1864 due to poor treatment. This suggests that dissent was not only prominent within the regiment, but the men were also willing to act on their dissatisfaction, both rebelling and decamping. David D. Porter, *The Naval History of the Civil War* (New York: Sherman, 1886), 555; John D. Winters, *The Civil War in Louisiana* (1963; repr., Baton Rouge: Louisiana State University Press, 1991), 323–334; Linda Barnickel, *Milliken's Bend: A Civil War Battle in History and Memory* (Baton Rouge: Louisiana State University Press, 2013), 154–155. Recruiters for the regiment also impressed enslaved men, perhaps contributing to the soldiers' disenchantment. William A. Dobak, *Freedom by the Sword: The U.S. Colored Troops, 1862–1867* (Washington, DC: Center of Military History United States Army, 2011), 175.
2. Knox, *Camp-Fire and Cotton-Field*, 433–434.
3. Thomas Wentworth Higginson, a colonel leading formerly enslaved Carolinians, articulated this point following a raid he led in February 1863. US Department of

War, *The War of the Rebellion: A Compilation of the Official Records of the Union and Confederate Armies* (Washington, DC: Government Printing Office, 1880–1901) (hereafter cited as OR), ser. 1, vol. 14, 198.
4. "The Fight at Milliken's Bend," *Harper's Weekly*, July 4, 1863. *Men of Color, to Arms! Now or Never!* (Philadelphia: n.p., 1863). Richard Lowe, "Battle on the Levee: The Fight at Milliken's Bend," in *Black Soldiers in Blue: African American Troops in the Civil War Era*, ed. John David Smith (Chapel Hill: University of North Carolina Press, 2002), 108, 116–124; Barnickel, *Milliken's Bend*, 85, 96, 103–104; Martha M. Bigelow, "The Significance of Milliken's Bend in the Civil War," *Journal of Negro History* 45, no. 3 (July 1960), 161–162.
5. Knox, *Camp-Fire and Cotton-Field*, 433–434.
6. As late as 1865, soldiers of the Eleventh decamped. Private Samuel Rinearsen decamped Vicksburg, and Private James Martin absconded from Yazoo City. Samuel Rinearsen, Court-Martial File MM2195, Record Group 153, National Archives Building, Washington, DC. (Hereafter the court-martial file of the soldiers will be cited.) Samuel Rinearsen Compiled Military Service Record, Record Group 94, National Archives, Washington, DC (hereafter cited as CMSR). James Martin, Court-Martial File MM3138. James Martin CMSR. Record Book Relating to Prisoners at Dry Tortugas, Florida, 1863–1871 (hereafter cited as Dry Tortugas Record Book), Records of the Adjutant General's Office, 1762–1984, Record Group 94, National Archives, line 1480 .
7. William Wells Brown, *Negro in American Rebellion: His Heroism and His Fidelity* (1867; repr., Boston: A. G. Brown, 1880); Frank A. Rollin, *Life and Public Services of Martin R. Delany* (Boston: Lee and Shepard, 1868); James T. Wilson, *The Black Phalanx: African American Soldiers in the War of Independence, the War of 1812, and the Civil War* (1887; repr., New York: De Capo, 1994); George Washington Williams, *A History of the Negro Troops in the War of the Rebellion* (1887; repr., New York: Fordham University Press, 2012). For the place of Black soldiers in wartime activists' perspectives, see Carole Emberton, *Beyond Redemption: Race, Violence, and the American South after the Civil War* (Chicago: University of Chicago Press, 2013), esp. 104.
8. For a comprehensive overview of the scholarship, see Joseph P. Reidy, "The Black Military Experience," in *The Cambridge History of the American Civil War, Vol. 3: Affairs of the People*, ed. Aaron Sheehan-Dean (New York: Cambridge University Press, 2019), 220–241. James M. McPherson, *Drawn with the Sword: Reflections on the American Civil War* (New York: Oxford University Press, 1996), 99–109; Gary W. Gallagher, *Causes Won, Lost, and Forgotten: How Hollywood and Popular Art Shape What We Know about the Civil War* (Chapel Hill: University of North Carolina Press, 2008), 92–95.
9. Eric Foner, *Reconstruction: America's Unfinished Revolution, 1863–1877* (New York: Harper & Row, 1988), 55, 166–167, 372–373; Eric Foner, *The Story of American Freedom* (New York: W. W. Norton, 1998), 101; Steven Hahn, "Forging

Freedom," in *The Routledge History of Slavery*, ed. Gad Heuman and Trevor Burnard (New York: Routledge, 2011), 298–313, esp. 304; Gregory P. Downs and Kate Masur, "Introduction: Echoes of War: Rethinking the Post–Civil War Governance and Politics," in *The World the Civil War Made*, ed. Gregory P. Downs and Kate Masur (Chapel Hill: University of North Carolina Press, 2015), 8, 11.

10. For discussions of the process of emancipation among civilians, see Jim Downs, *Sick from Freedom: African-American Illness and Suffering during the Civil War and Reconstruction* (New York: Oxford University Press, 2012), 13; Adam Rothman, *Beyond Freedom's Reach: A Kidnapping in the Twilight of Slavery* (Cambridge, MA: Harvard University Press, 2015), 7–10; Chandra Manning, *Troubled Refuge: Struggling for Freedom in the Civil War* (New York: Knopf, 2016), 26; Amy Murrell Taylor, *Embattled Freedom: Journeys through the Civil War's Slave Refugee Camps* (Chapel Hill: University of North Carolina Press, 2018), 17; Joseph P. Reidy, *Illusions of Emancipation: The Pursuit of Freedom and Equality in the Twilight of Slavery* (Chapel Hill: University of North Carolina Press, 2019), 20; Yael A. Sternhell, "Emancipation and War," in *The Cambridge History of the American Civil War, Vol. 3: Affairs of the People*, ed. Aaron Sheehan-Dean (New York: Cambridge University Press, 2019), 194; Thavolia Glymph, *The Women's Fight: The Civil War's Battles for Home, Freedom, and Nation* (Chapel Hill: University of North Carolina Press, 2020), 107–118, 221–242; Carole Emberton, *To Walk About in Freedom: The Long Emancipation of Priscilla Joyner* (New York: W. W. Norton, 2022), xiii–xxiv. For the discussion of the process of emancipation on a decades-long timeline, see Ira Berlin, *The Long Emancipation: The Demise of Slavery in the United States* (Cambridge, MA: Harvard University Press, 2015), esp. 8–9, 12–18, 21–27; Patrick Rael, *Eighty-Eight Years: The Long Death of Slavery in the United States, 1777–1865* (Athens: University of Georgia Press, 2015), esp. 2, 19–26. For reflections on such revisions to the story of freedom during the Civil War, see Carole Emberton, "Unwriting the Freedom Narrative: A Review Essay," *Journal of Southern History* 82, no. 2 (May 2016), 377–394; David W. Blight, Gregory P. Downs, and Jim Downs, Introduction to *Beyond Freedom: Disrupting the History of Emancipation*, ed. David W. Blight and Jim Downs (Athens: University of Georgia Press, 2017), 4–5.

11. Although officers often deemed them "deserters" and their actions unlawful, *Freedom Soldiers* does not refer to formerly enslaved men who decamped as "deserters." It refrains from perpetuating the notion that such individuals' actions were necessarily criminal. It instead recognizes that the men entered the army during the process of emancipation and that they decamped, or took "leaves of freedom," to secure key elements of their liberation denied by the US Army. By this logic, the men were "enlisted freedom seekers" who decamped, not "runaways" or "deserters." If the men were tried or convicted for desertion, qualifiers are added to refer to their place within the military justice system. For similar reasons, the book avoids "slave," using instead "enslaved" person to describe those who had been

enslaved at the time of their enlistment. When determining if a Black soldier had been enslaved at enlistment, the records are not always clear, but the status of the men referred to as "enlisted freedom seekers" (and the like) has been confirmed within the primary sources, including diaries, letters, government reports, courts-martial transcripts, and especially compiled military service records. For discussions especially informing decisions on language, see P. Gabrielle Foreman et al., "Writing about Slavery? Teaching about Slavery? This Might Help," Community-sourced document, accessed October 19, 2022, https://docs.google.com/document/d/1A4TEdDgYslX-hlKezLodMIM71My3KTN0zxRv0IQTOQs/mobilebasic; Jeffrey R. Kerr-Ritchie, *Freedom's Seekers: Essays on Comparative Emancipation* (Baton Rouge: Louisiana State University Press, 2013), xxi.

12. OR, ser. 3, vol. 5, 670. Scholars dispute the rate of desertion among white soldiers on both sides of the Civil War, so for the purposes of comparison, the range historians have advanced has been used. Ella Lonn, *Desertion during the Civil War* (1928; repr., Lincoln, NE: Bison Books, 1998), 29–30, 149–150; Bessie Martin, *A Rich Man's War, a Poor Man's Fight: Desertion of Alabama Troops from the Confederate Army* (1932; repr., Tuscaloosa: University of Alabama Press, 2003), 73–74; Mark A. Weitz, *A Higher Duty: Desertion among Georgia Troops during the Civil War* (Lincoln: University of Nebraska Press, 2005), 7; Aaron Sheehan-Dean, *Why Confederates Fought: Family and Nation in Civil War Virginia* (Chapel Hill: University of North Carolina Press, 2007), 227n17; Peter S. Carmichael, *The War for the Common Soldier: How Men Thought, Fought, and Survived in Civil War Armies* (Chapel Hill: University of North Carolina Press, 2018), 177.

13. For soldiers tried and their rate of conviction, see the Appendix, which draws on records held at the National Archives in Washington, DC.

14. For the reasoning behind desertion and its significance most important to this interpretation, see especially the exegeses offered by William Blair in *Virginia's Private War: Feeding Body and Soul in the Confederacy, 1861–1865* (New York: Oxford University Press, 1998), 60–61; Joseph T. Glatthaar, *General Lee's Army: From Victory to Collapse* (New York: Free Press, 2008), 408–420, 440; and Carmichael, *War for the Common Soldier*, 175–177. For previous examinations of Black deserters, see Andrew L. Slap, "The Loyal Deserters: African American Soldiers and Community in Civil War Memphis," in *Weirding the Civil War: Stories from the Civil War's Ragged Edges*, ed. Stephen Berry II (Athens: University of Georgia Press, 2011), 234–248; Jonathan Lande, "Trials of Freedom: African American Deserters during the U.S. Civil War," *Journal of Social History* 43, no. 3 (Spring 2016): 703–705; and Eric Mathisen, *The Loyal Republic: Traitors, Slaves, and the Remaking of Citizenship in Civil War America* (Chapel Hill: University of North Carolina Press, 2018), 110–112.

15. For further detail on the interpretation of sources here, see Jonathan Lande, "Richard Wright's Civil War Cipher," *Process: A Blog for American History*, February 14, 2023, https://www.processhistory.org/lande-richard-wrights-civil-war-cipher/.

16. Peter Way, "'black service . . . white money': The Peculiar Institution of Military Labor in the British Army during the Seven Years' War," in *Workers across the Americas: The Transnational Turn in Labor History*, ed. Leon Fink (New York: Oxford University Press, 2011), 57–79; Erik-Jan Zürcher, "Understanding Changes in Military Recruitment and Employment Worldwide," in *Fighting for a Living: A Comparative Study of Military Labour, 1500–2000*, ed. Erik-Jan Zürcher (Amsterdam: Amsterdam University Press, 2014), 11–41; John A. Lynn, "The Evolution of Army Style in the Modern West, 800–2000," *International History Review* 18, no. 3 (August 1996): 505–545.
17. Edward M. Coffman, *The Old Army: A Portrait of the American Army in Peacetime, 1784–1898* (New York: Oxford University Press, 1986), 15–21, 139–140, 144–145, 155–157; Autumn Hope McGrath, "'An army of working-men': Military Labor and the Construction of American Empire, 1865–1915," PhD diss., University of Pennsylvania, 2016. David Montgomery, *Citizen Worker: The Experience of Workers in the United States with Democracy and the Free Market during the Nineteenth Century* (New York: Cambridge University Press, 1993), 36–37.
18. Roy P. Basler, ed., *Collected Works of Abraham Lincoln*, 8 vols. (New Brunswick, NJ: Rutgers University Press, 1953), 6:445.
19. Bell Irvin Wiley, *The Life of Billy Yank: The Common Soldier of the Union* (1952; repr., Baton Rouge: Louisiana State University Press, 1993), 288; James M. McPherson, *For Cause and Comrades: Why Men Fought in the Civil War* (New York: Oxford University Press, 1997), 48; Stephen Berry II, *All That Makes a Man: Love and Ambition in the Civil War South* (New York: Oxford University Press, 2003), 176–177.
20. On labor on Confederate fortifications or within Rebel camps, see Blair, *Virginia's Private War*, 42, 121–122; Anne J. Bailey, *Invisible Soldiers: Ethnicity in the Civil War* (Athens: University of Georgia Press, 2006), 53; Jaime Amanda Martinez, *Confederate Slave Impressment in the Upper South* (Chapel Hill: University of North Carolina Press, 2013), 18–97; Colin Edward Woodward, *Marching Masters: Slavery, Race, and the Confederate Army during the Civil War* (Charlottesville: University of Virginia Press, 2014), 55–103; Glenn David Brasher, *The Peninsula Campaign and the Necessity of Emancipation: African Americans and the Fight for Freedom* (Chapel Hill: University of North Carolina Press, 2012), 28–33; Kevin M. Levin, *Searching for Black Confederates: The Civil War's Most Persistent Myth* (Chapel Hill: University of North Carolina Press, 2019), 12–99.
21. Basler, ed., *Collected Works of Abraham Lincoln*, 6:30. Andrew F. Lang, *In the Wake of War: Military Occupation, Emancipation, and Civil War America* (Baton Rouge: Louisiana State University Press, 2017), 130. Alexander Porter CMSR; Porter quoted in Elizabeth A. Regosin and Donald R. Shaffer, *Voices of Emancipation: Understanding Slavery, the Civil War, and Reconstruction through the U.S. Pension Bureau Files* (New York: New York University Press, 2008), 68. Hubbard Pryor CMSR; commander quoted in Dobak, *Freedom by the Sword*, 272.

For the excessive labor in the USCT, see OR, ser. 1, vol. 28, pt. 1, 328–331; OR, ser. 1, vol. 41, pt. 2, 566; Carmichael, *War for the Common Soldier*, 143.

22. "Story of an Escaped Slave," *Harper's Weekly*, July 2, 1864. Dobak, *Freedom by the Sword*, 12; Ronald S. Coddington, *African American Faces of the Civil War: An Album* (Baltimore: Johns Hopkins University Press, 2012), 123–128. For a similar set of images, see "A Typical Negro," *Harper's Weekly*, July 4, 1863. The analysis regarding the transition from enslaved laborer to war worker within wartime images here builds on the interpretations of such images and the transformative power of military service by Carole Emberton and Sarah Jones Weicksel. Emberton, *Beyond Redemption*, 103–104; Sarah Jones Weicksel, "To Look like Men of War: Visual Transformation Narratives of African American Union Soldiers," *Clio: Women, Gender, History*, no. 40 (July 2014), esp. 127–130. On uniform's power for USCT soldiers, see also Shae Smith Cox, *The Fabric of Civil War Society* (Baton Rouge: Louisiana State University Press, 2024), 79–86, 127–136. For the provenance of the images in "A Typical Negro," see David Silkenat, "'A Typical Negro': Gordon Peter, Vincent Colyer, and the Story Behind Slavery's Most Famous Photograph," *American Nineteenth Century History* 15, no. 2 (2014): 169–186.

23. W. E. B. Du Bois, *Black Reconstruction in America, 1860–1880* (1935; repr., New York: Free Press, 1998), 55–83; Stephanie McCurry, *Confederate Reckoning: Power and Politics in the Civil War South* (Cambridge, MA: Harvard University Press, 2010), 259; Mark A. Lause, *Free Labor: The Civil War and the Making of an American Working Class* (Urbana: University of Illinois Press, 2015), 55–67.

24. Mary Cochran Diary, undated entry, Filson Historical Society, Louisville, KY. Willie Lee Rose, *Rehearsal for Reconstruction: The Port Royal Experiment* (New York: Oxford University Press, 1976), 63–85, 174–176, 209, 298–313; Lawrence N. Powell, *New Masters: Northern Planters during the Civil War and Reconstruction* (New Haven, CT: Yale University Press, 1980), 97–122; Louis S. Gerteis, *From Contraband to Freedman: Federal Policy toward Southern Blacks, 1861–1865* (Westport, CT: Greenwood, 1973), 167; Julie Saville, *The Work of Reconstruction: From Slave to Wage Laborer in South Carolina 1860–1870* (New York: Cambridge University Press, 1994), 12, 16–24; Amy Dru Stanley, *From Bondage to Contract: Wage Labor, Marriage, and the Market in the Age of Slave Emancipation* (New York: Cambridge University Press, 1998), 2–56; Robert J. Steinfield, *Coercion, Contract, and Free Labor in the Nineteenth Century* (New York: Cambridge University Press, 2001), 267. For the right to quit, see Gerteis, *From Contraband to Freedman*, 112; Jacqueline Jones, *Labor of Love, Labor of Sorrow: Black Women, Work, and the Family from Slavery to the Present* (New York: Oxford University Press, 1985), 52–53; Philip S. Foner and Ronald L. Lewis, eds., *Black Workers: A Documentary History from Colonial Times to the Present* (Philadelphia: Temple University Press, 1989), 14; Tera W. Hunter, *To 'Joy My Freedom: Southern Black Women's Lives and Labors after the Civil War* (Cambridge, MA: Harvard University Press, 1997), 28; Caitlin Rosenthal,

Accounting for Slavery: Masters and Management (Cambridge, MA: Harvard University Press, 2018), 160, 263n9.

25. Dudley Taylor Cornish, *The Sable Arm: Black Troops in the Union Army, 1861–1865* (1956; repr., Lawrence: University Press of Kansas, 1987), 181–196; James McPherson, *The Negro's Civil War: How American Negroes Felt and Acted during the War for the Union* (New York: Vintage, 1965), 99–110, 193–204; Ira Berlin, Joseph P. Reidy, and Leslie S. Rowland, eds., *Freedom: Series II: The Black Military Experience: A Documentary History of Emancipation, 1861–1867* (New York: Cambridge University Press, 1983), 362–405; Joseph T. Glatthaar, *Forged in Battle: The Civil War Alliance of Black Soldiers and White Officers* (Baton Rouge: Louisiana State University Press, 1990), 81–98, 169–206; Donald Yacovone, "The Pay Crisis," in *Hope and Glory: Essays on the Legacy of the 54th Massachusetts Regiment*, ed. Martin H. Blatt, Thomas J. Brown, and Donald Yacovone (Amherst: University of Massachusetts Press, 2001), 38–42; Howard C. Westwood, *Black Troops, White Commanders, and Freedmen during the Civil War* (Carbondale: Southern Illinois University Press, 2002), 125–167; Christian G. Samito, *Becoming American under Fire: Irish Americans, African Americans, and the Politics of Citizenship during the Civil War Era* (Ithaca, NY: Cornell University Press, 2009), 77–102; Stephen Kantrowitz, *More Than Freedom: Fighting for Black Citizenship in a White Republic, 1829–1889* (New York: Penguin, 2012), 175–305; Brian Taylor, *Fighting for Citizenship: Black Northerners and the Debate over Military Service in the Civil War* (Chapel Hill: University of North Carolina Press, 2020), 103–125.

26. For analysis of the differences between Black men from the North and from the South this intervention draws upon, see Joseph P. Reidy, "Armed Slaves and the Struggles for Republican Liberty in the U.S. Civil War," in *Arming Slaves: From Classical Times to the Modern Age*, ed. Christopher Leslie Brown and Philip D. Morgan (New Haven, CT: Yale University Press, 2006), 274–292.

27. For analyses on the emphasis placed on the violent overthrow of slavery by abolitionists and historians, see Edward E. Baptist, "The Absent Subject: African American Masculinity and Forced Migration to the Antebellum Plantation Frontier," in *New Studies in the History of American Slavery*, ed. Edward E. Baptist and Stephanie M. H. Camp (Athens: University of Georgia Press, 2006), 137–138; David Stefan Doddington, *Contesting Slave Masculinity in the American South* (New York: Cambridge University Press, 2018), 6, 20–35.

28. Stephanie M. H. Camp, *Closer to Freedom: Enslaved Women and Everyday Resistance in the Plantation South* (Chapel Hill: University of North Carolina Press, 2004), 61–91; Sylviane A. Diouf, *Slavery's Exiles: The Story of the American Maroons* (New York: New York University Press, 2014), 73–85; Sergio A. Lussana, *My Brother Slaves: Friendship, Masculinity, and Resistance in the Antebellum South* (Lexington: University Press of Kentucky, 2016), 9–10, 45–67.

29. Laura F. Edwards, *The People and Their Peace: Legal Culture and the Transformation of Inequality in the Post-Revolutionary South* (Chapel Hill: University of North

Carolina Press, 2009), 121–131. Kimberly M. Welch, *Black Litigants in the Antebellum American South* (Chapel Hill: University of North Carolina Press, 2018), 13, 27–33. Lea VanderVelde, *Redemption Songs: Suing for Freedom before Dred Scott* (New York: Oxford University Press, 2014), 9; Kelly M. Kennington, *In the Shadow of Dred Scott: St. Louis Freedom Suits and the Legal Culture of Slavery in Antebellum America* (Athens: University of Georgia Press, 2017), 68–76; Anne Twitty, *Before Dred Scott: Slavery and Legal Culture in the American Confluence, 1787–1857* (New York: Cambridge University Press, 2016), 77–79, 96–119; Loren Schweninger, *Appealing for Liberty: Freedom Suits in the South* (New York: Oxford University Press, 2018), 44; W. Caleb McDaniel, *Sweet Taste of Liberty: A True Story of Slavery and Restitution in America* (New York: Oxford University Press, 2019). Susan Eva O'Donovan, "Universities of Social and Political Change: Slaves in Jail in Antebellum America," in *Buried Lives: Incarcerated in Early America*, ed. Michelle Lise Tarter and Richard Bell (Athens: University of Georgia Press, 2012), 125–140. For Black southern civilians repurposing legal endeavors to shape freedom and redefine the social order with their legal efforts during the Civil War and Reconstruction, see Laura F. Edwards, "Reconstruction and the History of Governance," in *The World the Civil War Made*, ed. Gregory P. Downs and Kate Masur (Chapel Hill: University of North Carolina Press, 2015), 33.
30. Carmichael, *War for the Common Soldier*, 24.
31. For the most succinct articulation of this, see Joseph T. Glatthaar, "Black Glory: The African-American Role in Union Victory," in *Why the Confederacy Lost*, ed. Gabor S. Boritt (New York: Oxford University Press, 1992), 152–162.
32. Russell Duncan, ed., *Blue-Eyed Child of Fortune: The Civil War Letters of Colonel Robert Gould Shaw* (Athens: University of Georgia Press, 1992), 360.
33. "Adjutant General Thomas Addressing the Negroes on the Duties of Freedom," *Harper's Weekly*, November 14, 1863. For the theory of the state institutions and their policies as an accumulation of actors informing my interpretation of the USCT here, see Theda Skocpol, "Bring the State Back In: Strategies of Analysis in Current Research," in *Bring the State Back In*, ed. Peter B. Evans, Dietrich Rusehmeyer, and Theda Skocpol (New York: Cambridge University Press, 1985), 21.
34. On the relationship between desertion and soldiers' backgrounds influencing this interpretation, see esp. Lonn, *Desertion during the Civil War*, esp. 134; Carmichael, *War for the Common Soldier*, esp. 175–177. For similar connections made by historians of soldiers outside the United States, see Zürcher, "Understanding Changes in Military Recruitment and Employment Worldwide," 40–41.

CHAPTER 1

1. Soldiers of both the First Arkansas Infantry (African Descent) (later the Forty-Sixth United States Colored Infantry) and First Michigan Colored Infantry (later the 102nd United States Colored Infantry) marched to versions of this song. Sojourner

Truth, writing on behalf of the Michiganders, and Captain Lindley Miller of the First Arkansas claimed authorship of the song. Sojourner Truth, *Narrative of Sojourner Truth: A Bondswoman of Olden Time* . . . (Battle Creek, MI: Review and Herald Officer, 1884), 126; Lindley Miller, *Song of the First of Arkansas . . . Written by Captain Lindley Miller, of the First Arkansas Colored Regiment* (Philadelphia: Supervisory Committee for Recruiting Colored Regiments, 1864). For a discussion of the song's origin, see David Walls, "Marching Song of the First Arkansas Colored Regiment: A Contested Attribution," *Arkansas Historical Quarterly* 64, no. 4 (Winter 2007): 401–421; John Stauffer and Benjamin Soskis, *The Battle Hymn of the Republic: A Biography of the Song That Marches On* (New York: Oxford University Press, 2013), 58–62.

2. Thomas Wentworth Higginson, *Army Life in a Black Regiment* (Boston: Fields, Osgood, 1870), 41, 57, 197–222; William E. Barton, "Hymns of the Slave and the Freedman," in *Old Plantation Hymns: A Collection of Hitherto Unpublished Melodies of the Slave and the Freedman, with Historical and Descriptive Notes* (New York: Lamson, Wolffe, 1899), 25–29; Eileen Southern, *The Music of Black Americans: A History* (New York: W. W. Norton, 1997), 210–212; Keith P. Wilson, *Campfires of Freedom: The Camp Life of Black Soldiers during the Civil War* (Kent, OH: Kent State University Press, 2002), 148; Johair Jabir, *Conjuring Freedom: Music and Masculinity in the Civil War's "Gospel Army"* (Columbus: Ohio State University Press, 2017), 2–3, 12–13. For the importance of marching songs, see Gary W. Gallagher, *The Union War* (Cambridge, MA: Harvard University Press, 2011), 153.

3. "A Visit to Fort Sumter," *Harper's Weekly*, March 18, 1865. Stauffer and Soskis, *Battle Hymn of the Republic*, 58–62, 68–69; Douglas R. Egerton, *Thunder at the Gates: The Black Civil War Regiments That Redeemed America* (New York: Basic Books, 2016), 95; Gordon C. Rhea, *Stephen A. Swails: Black Freedom Fighter in the Civil War and Reconstruction* (Baton Rouge: Louisiana State University Press, 2021), 23, 83; Dean Calbreath, *The Sergeant: The Incredible Life of Nicholas Said: Son of an African General, Slave of the Ottomans, Free Man Under the Tsars, Hero of the Union Army* (New York: Pegasus, 2023), 192; Edda L. Fields-Black, *Combee: Harriet Tubman, the Combahee River Raid, and Black Freedom during the Civil War* (New York: Oxford University Press, 2024), 254, 268–269; Manisha Sinha, *The Rise and Fall of the Second American Republic: Reconstruction, 1860–1920* (New York: Liveright, 2024), 18.

4. Samuel Chapman Armstrong recorded the song "The Enlisted Soldiers," which was quoted in Thomas P. Fenner, Frederic G. Rathbun, and Bessie Cleaveland, *Cabin and Plantation Songs as Sung by the Hampton Students*, 3rd ed. (New York: G. P. Putnam's Sons, 1901), 145. Edith Armstrong Talbot, *Samuel Chapman Armstrong: A Biographical Sketch* (New York: Doubleday, Page, 1904), 106.

5. Charles B. Fox, an officer of the Fifty-Fourth Massachusetts Infantry, recorded the song "All Hail." Quoted in Wilson, *Campfires of Freedom*, 217.

6. Truth, *Narrative of Sojourner Truth*, 126; Miller, *Song of the First of Arkansas*.

7. William H. Robinson, *From Log Cabin to the Pulpit, or, Fifteen Years in Slavery*, 3rd ed. (Eau Claire, WI: Ames H. Tifft, 1913), 96. Bobby L. Lovett, "The Negro's Civil War in Tennessee, 1861–1865," *Journal of Negro History* 61, no. 1 (January 1976): 37.
8. For the consequences of the invasion of the US Army on slavery, see the relationship between emancipation events and the spreading of the US Army southward at Edward L. Ayers and Scott Nesbit, "Visualizing Emancipation," Digital Scholarship Lab, University of Richmond, https://dsl.richmond.edu/emancipation/. For the influence of the US Army on the slave trade specifically, see Robert K. D. Colby, *An Unholy Traffic: Slave Trading in the Civil War South* (New York: Oxford University Press, 2024), 61–76.
9. William Goodale to children, November 3, 1864, William Goodale Papers, Massachusetts Historical Society. Kristopher A. Teters, *Practical Liberators: Union Officers in the Western Theater during the Civil War* (Chapel Hill: University of North Carolina Press, 2018), 47–58, 79, 103–104, 133–152. Matthew Fox-Amato, *Exposing Slavery: Photography, Human Bondage, and the Birth of Modern Visual America* (New York: Oxford University Press, 2019), 160–214.
10. Charlotte Forten, "Life on the Sea Islands," *Atlantic Monthly*, May 1864, 593.
11. Rose, *Rehearsal for Reconstruction*, 15–16, 29–31, 65–101; Eric Foner, *Free Soil, Free Labor, Free Men: The Ideology of the Republican Party before the Civil War* (1970; repr., New York: Oxford University Press, 1995), 297; George M. Fredrickson, *The Black Image in the White Mind* (New York: Harper & Row, 1971), 94, 102–107; Gerteis, *From Contraband to Freedman*, 28–29; Thomas C. Holt, "'An Empire over the Mind': Emancipation, Race, and Ideology in the British West Indies and the American South," in *Region, Race, and Reconstruction: Essays in Honor of C. Vann Woodward*, ed. J. Morgan Kousser and James M. McPherson (New York: Oxford University Press, 1982), 287–289; Paul D. Escott *"What Shall We Do with the Negro?": Lincoln, White Racism, and Civil War America* (Charlottesville: University of Virginia Press, 2009), 29–68; Ibram X. Kendi, *Stamped from the Beginning: The Definitive History of Racist Ideas in America* (New York: Nation, 2016), 168; John Cimprich, *Navigating Liberty: Black Refugees and Antislavery Reformers in the Civil War South* (Baton Rouge: Louisiana State University Press, 2023), 9–11. Reformer quoted in Rose, *Rehearsal for Reconstruction*, 41.
12. Rose, *Rehearsal for Reconstruction*, 63–85, 174–176, 209, 298–313; Powell, *New Masters*, 97–122; Gerteis, *From Contraband to Freedman*, 167; Saville, *Work of Reconstruction*, 12, 16–24. For conflict over the meaning of free labor specifically, see Jonathan A. Glickstein, *Concepts of Free Labor in Antebellum America* (New Haven, CT: Yale University Press, 1991), 2, 11–16.
13. David Herbert Donald, *Lincoln* (New York: Simon & Schuster, 1995), 259–294. Mark Grimsley, *The Hard Hand of War: Union Military Policy toward Southern Civilians, 1861–1865* (New York: Cambridge University Press, 1995), 95.
14. Foner, *Free Labor, Free Soil, Free Men*, xx–xxi, 296. Daniel W. Howe, *The Political Culture of the American Whigs* (Chicago: University of Chicago Press, 1979), 131;

Thomas Brown, *Politics and Statesmanship: Essays on the American Whig Party* (New York: Columbia University Press, 1985), 48, 120, 179.

15. Heather C. Richardson, *The Greatest Nation of the Earth: Republican Economic Policies during the Civil War* (Cambridge, MA: Harvard University Press, 1997), 209, 217–240. John G. Sproat, "Blueprint for Radical Reconstruction," *Journal of Southern History* 23, no. 57 (February 1957): 33; Rose, *Rehearsal for Reconstruction*, 38; Fredrickson, *Black Image in the White Mind*, 102–107; Gerteis, *From Contraband to Freedman*, 5; Brasher, *Peninsula Campaign and the Necessity of Emancipation*, 132, 145–146, 191–205. Elizabeth R. Varon, *Armies of Deliverance: A New History of the Civil War* (New York: Oxford University Press, 2019), 200–201, 235, 298, 267.
16. Basler, ed., *Collected Works of Abraham Lincoln*, 7:23. Ibid., 5:433–436. Ibid., 6:28–30. Grimsley, *The Hard Hand of War*, 120, 141.
17. Taylor, *Fighting for Citizenship*, 17–65.
18. Mark S. Schantz, *Awaiting the Heavenly Country: The Civil War and America's Culture of Death* (Ithaca, NY: Cornell University Press, 2008), 86–87, 98–123; Stephen G. Hall, *A Faithful Account of the Race: African American Historical Writing in Nineteenth-Century America* (Chapel Hill: University of North Carolina Press, 2009), 94–104; Jonathan Lande, "The Black Badge of Courage: The Politics of Recording Black Union Army Service and the Militarization of Black History in the Civil War's Aftermath," *Journal of American Ethnic History* 42, no. 1 (January 2023): 8–15. Cornish, *Sable Arm*, 6, 18. McPherson, *Negro's Civil War*, 19–20. For Black leaders' role in recruitment, see J. Matthew Gallman, *Defining Duty in the Civil War: Personal Choice, Popular Culture, and the Union Home Front* (Chapel Hill: University of North Carolina Press, 2015), 223–50; Taylor, *Fighting for Citizenship*, 40–96. For the shift to violence among Black abolitionists, see Kellie Carter Jackson, *Force and Freedom: Black Abolitionists and the Politics of Violence* (Philadelphia: University of Pennsylvania Press, 2019), esp. 7–9.
19. Frederick Douglass to Edwin Stanton, July 31, 1863, folder 1, Tracy Collection, Connecticut Historical Society, Hartford. Frank J. Cirillo, *The Abolitionist Civil War: Immediatists and the Struggle to Transform the* Union (Baton Rouge: Louisiana State University Press, 2023), 16, 29, 66–67, 77–78, 138, 150, 164–165, 171–172, 201–202. David W. Blight, *Frederick Douglass: The Prophet of Freedom* (New York: Simon and Schuster, 2018), 337. David W. Blight, *Frederick Douglass' Civil War: Keeping Faith in Jubilee* (Baton Rouge: Louisiana State University Press, 1989), 148, 160.
20. *Douglass' Monthly*, April 1863.
21. Thavolia Glymph, "Rose's War and the Gendered Politics of a Slave Insurgency in the Civil War," *Journal of the Civil War Era* 3 (December 2013): 501–532; Amy Dru Stanley, "Instead of Waiting for the Thirteenth Amendment: The War Power, Slave Marriage, and Inviolate Human Rights," *American Historical Review* 115 (June 2010): 732–765; Taylor, *Embattled Freedom*, 125–129; Glymph, *Women's Fight*, 88–118, 226; Stephanie McCurry, *Women's War: Fighting and Surviving the American Civil War* (Cambridge, MA: Harvard University Press, 2019), 63–123.

Stephen Kantrowitz, "Fighting Like Men: Civil War Dilemmas of Abolitionist Manhood," in *Battle Scars: Gender and Sexuality in the American Civil War*, ed. Catherine Clinton and Nina Silber (New York: Oxford University Press, 2006), 19–40; A. Kristen Foster, "'We Are Men!' Frederick Douglass and the Fault Lines of Gendered Citizenship," *Journal of the Civil War Era* 1, no. 2 (June 2011): 143–175.

22. Truth, *Narrative of Sojourner Truth*, 126. Nell Irvin Painter, *Sojourner Truth: A Life, a Symbol* (New York: W. W. Norton & Company, 1996), 182–184. Martha S. Jones, *All Bound Up Together: The Woman Question in African American Public Culture, 1830–1900* (Chapel Hill: University of North Carolina Press, 2007), 125–132, 135–136; Jason H. Silverman, "Mary Ann Shadd and the Search for Equality," in *Black Leaders of the Nineteenth Century*, ed. Leon Litwack and August Meier (Urbana: University of Illinois Press, 1988), 97; Holly A. Pinheiro, "Gendered Rhetoric and Black Civil War Military Recruiting," *American Nineteenth-Century History* 20, no. 3 (December 2019): 273–291.

23. Lewis Douglass to Helen Amelia Loguen Douglass, March 3, 1863, box 3, folder 57; April 15, 1863, box 3, folder 58, Walter O. Evans Collection of Frederick Douglass and Douglass Family Papers, Beinecke Library, Yale University, New Haven, CT. Egerton, *Thunder at the Gates*, 80.

24. Lewis Douglass to Helen Amelia Loguen Douglass, May 9, 1863, box 3, folder 59, Walter O. Evans Collection of Frederick Douglass and Douglass Family Papers, Beinecke Library, Yale University, New Haven, CT.

25. Lewis Douglass to Helen Amelia Loguen Douglass, May 20, 1863, box 3, folder 60, Walter O. Evans Collection of Frederick Douglass and Douglass Family Papers, Beinecke Library, Yale University, New Haven, CT.

26. William Seraile, *Angels of Mercy: White Women and the History of New York's Colored Orphan Asylum* (New York: Fordham University Press, 2011), 65–68. Virginia M. Adams, ed., *On the Altar of Freedom: A Black Soldier's Civil War Letters from the Front* (Amherst: University of Massachusetts Press, 1991), 4. Jeffrey W. Bolster, *Black Jacks: African American Seamen in the Age of Sail* (Cambridge, MA: Harvard University Press, 1997); David S. Cecelski, *The Waterman's Song: Slavery and Freedom in Maritime North Carolina* (Chapel Hill: University of North Carolina Press, 2001).

27. Egerton, *Thunder at the Gates*, 21–25; Brown quoted on ibid., 73. Ezra Greenspan, *William Wells Brown: An African American Life* (New York: W. W. Norton & Company, 2014), 367. Luis F. Emilio, *A Brave Black Regiment: The History of the Fifty-Fourth Regiment of Massachusetts Volunteer Infantry 1863–1865* (1891; repr., New York: Da Capo Press, 1995), 9; Russell Duncan, *Where Death and Glory Meet: Colonel Robert Gould Shaw and the 54th Massachusetts Infantry* (Athens: University of Georgia Press, 1999), 61–63; Earl F. Mulderink III, *New Bedford's Civil War* (New York: Fordham University Press, 2012), 99–118.

28. OR, ser. 3, vol. 5, 138. For population, see Berlin, Reidy, and Rowland, eds., *Black Military Experience*, 87–88.

29. J. M. M'Kim, "The Freed Blacks of South Carolina. Letter from J. M. M'Kim to Stephen Colwell, Esq., Chairman of the Port Royal Relief Committee, July 24, 1862," in *The Freedmen of South Carolina: An Address Delivered by J. Miller M'Kim in Sansom Hall, July 9th, 1862. Together with a Letter from the Same to Stephen Colwell, Esq., Chairman of the Port Royal Relief Committee* (Philadelphia: Willis P. Hazard, 1862), 19.
30. Manning, *Troubled Refuge*, 8, 26, 214–215; Mathisen, *Loyal Republic*, 3, 90.
31. Joseph Mark Califf, *Record of the Services of the Seventh Regiment, U.S. Colored Troops from September, 1863 to November, 1866* (Providence, RI: E. L. Freeman, 1878), 10. Ervin L. Jordan Jr., *Black Confederates and Afro-Yankees in Civil War Virginia* (Charlottesville: University of Virginia Press, 1995), 266–267.
32. Archibald C. Sutherland to Reuben Thomas Durrett, May 24, 1867, box 25, folder 1, Reuben Thomas Durrett Papers, Filson Historical Society, Louisville, KY. Enslavers like Sam's captor knew well the possibility of Black Kentuckians absconding. For the flight of enslaved men in the region, for example, see John Y. Owens to Reuben Thomas Durrett, September 10, 1866, box 25, folder 1, Reuben Thomas Durrett Papers, Filson Historical Society, Louisville, KY. Eli H. Stone to Stephen J. Stone, February 14, 1864; Eli H. Stone to Stephen J. Stone, February 29, 1864, both in box 6, folder 63, Eli Huston Brown Papers, Filson Historical Society, Louisville, KY. Elizabeth D. Leonard, *Slaves, Slaveholders, and a Kentucky Community's Struggle toward Freedom* (Lexington: University Press of Kentucky, 2019), 25–26, 40–45.
33. Henry Clay Bruce, *The New Man: Twenty-Nine Years a Slave, Twenty-Nine Years a Free Man* (York, PA: F. Anstadt & Sons, 1895), 107.
34. Benjamin Rush Plumley, September 4, 1863, Gilder Lehrman Collection, New York. For similar sentiments, see OR, ser. 3, vol. 3, 1141. Rose, *Rehearsal for Reconstruction*, 191. Okon Edet Uya, *From Slavery to Public Service: Robert Smalls, 1839–1915* (New York: Oxford University Press, 1971), 19. Further up the coast in North Carolina, Abraham Galloway assisted the effort as well, but not before he demanded certain guarantees from the government, including the protection of soldiers' families, in exchange for service. See David S. Cecelski, *The Fire of Freedom: Abraham Galloway and the Slaves' Civil War* (Chapel Hill: University of North Carolina Press, 2012), 83–98.
35. Eric Foner, "Rights and the Constitution in Black Life during the Civil War and Reconstruction," *Journal of American History* 74, no. 3 (December 1987): 880; Eric Foner, *Reconstruction*, 8–10; Laura F. Edwards, *A Legal History of the Civil War and Reconstruction: A Nation of Rights* (New York: Cambridge University Press, 2015), 95; Gregory P. Downs, *After Appomattox: Military Occupation and the Ends of War* (Cambridge, MA: Harvard University Press, 2015), 40–67; Chandra Manning, *Troubled Refuge*, 8–12, 205–206. Foner, *Reconstruction*, 7–11; Steven Hahn, *A Nation under Our Feet: Black Political Struggles in the Rural South from Slavery to the Great Migration* (Cambridge, MA: Harvard University Press, 2003), 96; Christopher James Bonner, *Remaking the Republic: Black Politics and the*

Creation of American Citizenship (Philadelphia: University of Pennsylvania Press, 2020), 170.

36. Saville, *Work of Reconstruction*, 2–4; Williams, *Help Me to Find My People*, 139–168; Heather Andrea Williams, *Self-Taught: African American Education in Slavery and Freedom* (Chapel Hill: University of North Carolina Press, 2005); Foner, *Story of American Freedom*, 101; Kidada E. Williams, *They Left Great Marks on Me: African American Testimonies of Racial Violence from Emancipation to World War I* (New York: New York University Press, 2012). Gary Kynoch, "Terrible Dilemmas: Black Enlistment in the Union Army during the American Civil War," *Slavery and Abolition* 18, no. 2 (August 1997): 109, 111–112; Samito, *Becoming American under Fire*, 170–171; Mathisen, *Loyal Republic*, 90; Eric Foner, *The Second Founding: How the Civil War and Reconstruction Remade the Constitution* (New York: W. W. Norton, 2019), 16; Warren Eugene Milteer Jr., *Beyond Slavery's Shadow: Free People of Color in the South* (Chapel Hill: University of North Carolina Press, 2021), 235–242; Cimprich, *Navigating Liberty*, 104–109.

37. OR, ser. 3, vol. 5, 138.

38. Stephen Gano Burbridge to the Adjutant General, February 23, 1865, Gilder Lehrman, New York. Thomas E. Bramlette to Stephen Gano Burbridge, March 14, 1864; Robert J. Breckinridge to Stephen Gano Burbridge, March 26, 1864; Stephen Gano Burbridge to Thomas E. Bramlette, June 16, 1864; Stephen Gano Burbridge Papers, Filson Historical Society, Louisville, KY.

39. Winthrop D. Jordan, *White over Black: American Attitudes toward the Negro, 1550–1812* (Chapel Hill: University of North Carolina Press, 1968), 378–400; Charles B. Dew, *Apostles of Disunion: Southern Secession Commissioners and the Causes of the Civil War* (Charlottesville: University of Virginia Press, 2001), 40–41, 57, 78–79; Blair, *Virginia's Private War*, 29, 46; Elizabeth Fox-Genovese and Eugene D. Genovese, *The Mind of the Master Class: History and Faith in the Southern Slaveholders' Worldview* (New York: Cambridge University Press, 2005), 38–39.

40. S. S. Nichols, *Conservative Essays, Legal and Political* (Philadelphia: J. B. Lippincott, 1863), 214. S. S. Nichols, *Conservative Essays, Legal and Political*, Second Series (Philadelphia: J. B. Lippincott, 1865), 149. Adalbert Volck, "Writing the Emancipation Proclamation," Porter & Coates [reproduction], 1886, Maury A. Bromsen Collection of Confederate Etchings, John Hay Library, Brown University.

41. Paper quoted in Michael Vorenberg, *The Emancipation Proclamation: A Brief History with Documents* (Boston: Bedford Books of St. Martin, 2010), 74. Jean H. Baker, *Affairs of Party: The Political Culture of Northern Democrats in the Mid-Nineteenth Century* (New York: Fordham University Press, 1998), 212–258; Escott, *Worst Passions of Human Nature*, 31–49, 97–100, 125, 133, 152–158. Jennifer Weber, *Copperheads: The Rise and Fall of Lincoln's Opponents in the North* (New York: Oxford University Press, 2006), 63–65; Adam I. P. Smith, *The Stormy Present: Conservatism and the Problem of Slavery in Northern Politics, 1846–1865* (Chapel Hill: University

of North Carolina Press, 2017), 192–199, 209. Rose, *Rehearsal for Reconstruction*, 38; Jordan, *White over Black*, 378–401; Fredrickson, *Black Image in the White Mind*, 8–9, 69; Edward Bartlett Rugemer, *The Problem of Emancipation: The Caribbean Roots of the American Civil War* (Baton Rouge: Louisiana State University Press, 2008), 209; Escott, "What Shall We Do with the Negro?" 47–49; Paul D. Escott, *The Worst Passions of Human Nature: White Supremacy in the Civil War North* (Charlottesville: University of Virginia Press, 2020), 83, 125–133. See also the speech from Representative John Law, a Democrat from Indiana, during the debate over the Second Confiscation Act. Marion Mills Miller, ed., *Great Debates in American History*, 14 vols. (New York: Current Literature Publication, 1913), 6:207. For the consequence of such rhetoric, see Peter H. Clark, *The Black Brigade of Cincinnati: Being a Report of Its Labors and a Muster-Roll of Its Members; Together with Various Orders, Speeches, etc., Relating to It* (Cincinnati: Joseph B. Boyd, 1864), 5; Thomas A. Cheek, *A Sketch of the History of the Colored Race in the United States, and a Reminiscence of Slavery* (Peoria, IL: n.p., 1873), 12; Escott, "What Shall We Do with the Negro?" xvii, 42–43.

42. Rugemer, *Problem of Emancipation*, 9; James Poskett, *Materials of the Mind: Phrenology, Race, and the Global History of Science, 1815–1920* (Chicago: University of Chicago Press, 2019); Michael Sappol, *A Traffic of Dead Bodies: Anatomy and Embodied Social Identity in Nineteenth-Century America* (Princeton, NJ: Princeton University Press, 2002).

43. Jordan, *White over Black*, 380–387; Fredrickson, *Black Image in the White Mind*, 39; Edward Rugemer, *Problem of Emancipation*, 9. L. Maria Child, *The Right Way, the Safe Way, Proved by Emancipation in the British West Indies and Elsewhere* (New York: n.p., 1863), 3, 8, 86, 93. John G. Whittier, "The Proclamation," *Atlantic Monthly*, February 1864, 240–241.

44. *Congressional Globe*, 37th Congress, 3rd Session, 570–571, 600–602 (1863). Ira Berlin, Barbara J. Fields, Thavolia Glymph, Joseph P. Reidy, and Leslie Rowland, eds., *Freedom: A Documentary History of Emancipation, 1861–1867, Series 1*, Vol. 1: *The Destruction of Slavery* (New York: Cambridge University Press), 124. Jordan, *White over Black*, 104–114, 380; T. Cole Jones, *Captives of Liberty: Prisoners of War and the Politics of Vengeance in the American Revolution* (Philadelphia: University of Pennsylvania Press, 2020), 178, 197.

45. *Congressional Globe*, 37th Congress, 3rd Session, Appendix, 92 (1863).

46. Ibid., 607 (1863). See also the speech of John Hutchins (Ohio) in ibid., 605–607 (1863).

47. Ibid., 631–632 (1863).

48. *Congressional Globe*, 37th Congress, 3rd Session, Appendix, 88 (1863).

49. John Fabian Witt, *Lincoln's Code: The Laws of War in American History* (New York: Free Press, 2012), 217–218, 236–240. For Black southerners' strategic use of violence, see Aaron Sheehan-Dean, *The Calculus of Violence: How Americans Fought the Civil War* (Cambridge, MA: Harvard University Press, 2018), 169–179.

228 *Notes to pages 26–31*

50. *Congressional Globe*, 37th Congress, 3rd Session, 695, 924–925, 1307 (1863).
51. OR, ser. 3, vol. 2, 28. OR, ser. 1, vol. 14, 377–378. Rose, *Rehearsal for Reconstruction*, 152–153, 190–191; Cornish, *Sable Arm*, 80. OR, ser. 1, vol. 14, 341; Rose, *Rehearsal for Reconstruction*, 144–150, 194; Edward A. Miller Jr., *Lincoln's Abolitionist General: The Biography of David Hunter* (Columbia: University of South Carolina Press, 1997), 97, 105.
52. Higginson, *Army Life in a Black Regiment*, 2. Rose, *Rehearsal for Reconstruction*, 152–154, 176–181, 193; Howard N. Meyer, *Colonel of the Black Regiment: The Life of Thomas Wentworth Higginson* (New York: W. W. Norton, 1967), 189–191, 201–204; Stephen V. Ash, *Firebrand of Liberty: The Story of Two Black Regiments That Changed the Course of the Civil War* (New York: W. W. Norton, 2008), 52–53.
53. Ash, *Firebrand of Liberty*, 199–204, quotation on 200; Meyer, *Colonel of the Black Regiment*, 226–227; Ira Berlin, Thavolia Glymph, Steven F. Miller, Joseph P. Reidy, Leslie S. Rowland, and Julie Saville, *Freedom: A Documentary History of Emancipation, 1861–1867, Series 1*, Vol. 3: *The Wartime Genesis of Free Labor: The Lower South* (New York: Cambridge University Press, 1990), 99; Emberton, *Beyond Redemption*, 112–113.
54. John Weiss, *Will the Blacks Fight?* (United States: n.p., ca. 1862).
55. Review of Augustin Colchin's *The Results of Emancipation*, *Atlantic Monthly*, March 1863, 397. Escott, *Worst Passions of Human Nature*, 53–76, 126–127.
56. "The Effects of the Proclamation," *Harper's Weekly*, February 21, 1863, 119. "Our Colored Troops in Louisiana," *Harper's Weekly*, February 28, 1863, 143. For the influence of *Harper's Weekly*, see Gallagher, *Union War*, 18–19, 22, 44, 72.
57. OR, ser. 3, vol. 3, 73–74; Berlin et al., *Wartime Genesis of Free Labor*, ser. 1, vol. 3, 254; Rose, *Rehearsal for Reconstruction*, 209–210, 231, 238; Emberton, *Beyond Redemption*, 113.
58. OR, ser. 3, vol. 3, 442, 444, 449; Sproat, "Blueprint for Radical Reconstruction," 33–37; Rose, *Rehearsal for Reconstruction*, 239; Gerteis, *From Contraband to Freedman*, 34–35; Emberton, *Beyond Redemption*, 113.
59. Thomas Wentworth Higginson, "Leaves of an Officer's Journal: A White Officer Recounts His Experience as Colonel of the First Black Regiment," *Atlantic Monthly*, December 1864; Christopher Looby, ed., Introduction to *The Complete Civil War Journal and Selected Letters of Thomas Wentworth Higginson* (Chicago: University of Chicago Press, 2000), 12; OR, ser. 3, vol. 3, 435; Rose, *Rehearsal for Reconstruction*, 238; Meyer, *Colonel of the Black Regiment*, 82, 215; Fredrickson, *Black Image in the White Mind*, 170–171; Emberton, *Beyond Redemption*, 113–116. For an analysis of specific characteristics of soldiers predicated on race and a direct comparison of Black soldiers to children, see Stephen B. Brague, "Notes on Colored Troops and Military Colonies on Southern Soil" (New York: n.p., 1863).
60. OR, ser. 3, vol. 3, 439; *Preliminary Report Touching on the Condition and Management of Emancipated Refugees; Made to the Secretary of War, by the American Freedmen's Inquiry Commission, June 30, 1863* (New York: John F. Trow, 1863), 18;

Fredrickson, *Black Image in the White Mind*, 168; Emberton, *Beyond Redemption*, 113–116.

61. *Congressional Globe*, 37th Congress, 3rd Session, 572 (1863); ibid., 599 (1863). John F. Marszalek, *Sherman: A Soldier's Passion for Order* (Carbondale: Southern Illinois University Press, 2007), 271; Brooks D. Simpson, *Sherman's Civil War: Selected Correspondence of William T. Sherman, 1860–1865* (Chapel Hill: University of North Carolina Press, 1999), 699. Berlin, Reidy, and Rowland, eds., *Black Military Experience*, 20, 304–309; Glatthaar, *Forged in Battle*, 35. New York Union League Club, *Report of the Committee on Volunteering* (New York: Club House, 1864), 16.

62. Russell F. Weigley, *History of the United States Army*, enlarged ed. (Bloomington: Indiana University Press, 1984), 212–215.

63. OR, ser. 3, vol. 3, 215. Cornish, *Sable Arm*, 129–131. Similar civilian reformers participated in the formation of the United States Colored Troops and stressed the selection of officers in Massachusetts, Pennsylvania, New York, and New Orleans. Richard Hallowell to John Forbes, January 30, 1863, letter in Norwood Penrose Hallowell Scrapbook 2, Norwood Penrose Hallowell Papers, Massachusetts Historical Society, Boston; Keith Wilson, "Thomas Webster and the 'Free Military School for Applicants for Commands of Colored Troops,'" *Civil War History* 29, no. 2 (June 1983): 101–122; James G. Hollandsworth Jr., *The Louisiana Native Guards: The Black Military Experience during the Civil War* (Baton Rouge: Louisiana State University Press, 1998), 45, 85.

64. J. W. Adams, *Letter to the Honorable Secretary of War: On the Examination of Field Officers for Colored Troops* (New York: John F. Trow, 1863), 17. Basler, ed., *Collected Works of Abraham Lincoln*, 7:11. For an examiner's review of exam material, see William Henry Thayer, October 12, 1863, in Letters of William Henry Thayer, Rauner Library, Dartmouth College, Hanover, NH. See also J. M. Mickley, *The Forty-Third Regiment United States Colored Troops* (Gettysburg, PA: J. E. Wible, 1866), 84. For commanders' opinions on officer elections, see Andrew S. Bledsoe, *Citizen-Officers: The Union and Confederate Volunteer Junior Officer Corps in the American Civil War* (Baton Rouge: Louisiana State University Press, 2015), 13, 32.

65. OR, ser. 3, vol. 3, 1114. "Free Military School for Applicants for Command of Colored Troops" (Philadelphia: King & Baird, 1863), 8; "Free Military School for Applicants for Command of Colored Troops," 2nd ed. (Philadelphia: King & Baird, 1864), 11; Berlin, Reidy, and Rowland, eds., *Black Military Experience*, 408; Glatthaar, *Forged in Battle*, 38, 42–48; Wilson, "Thomas Webster and the 'Free Military School for Applicants for Commands of Colored Troops,'" 120; Hollandsworth, *Louisiana Native Guards*, 85; Dobak, *Freedom by the Sword*, 15–16; Zachery A. Fry, *A Republic in the Ranks: Loyalty and Dissent in the Army of the Potomac* (Chapel Hill: University of North Carolina Press, 2020), 136–138; Brian P. Luskey, *Men Is Cheap: Exposing the Frauds of Free Labor in Civil War America* (Chapel Hill: University of North Carolina Press, 2020), 24, 139–140, 173–174. See also Paul D. Renard, "The Selection and Preparation of White Officers for the

Command of Black Troops in the American Civil War: A Study of the 41st and 100th U.S. Colored Infantry," PhD diss., Virginia Tech University, 2006.
66. Charles Henry Coxe to Frank Coxe, September 23, 1863, folder 1, Charles Henry Coxe Letters, Historical Society of Pennsylvania, Philadelphia.
67. Owen Lovejoy to Stanton, January 19, 1863, Tracy Collection, Connecticut Historical Society, Hartford. William G. Jackaberry to Charles Sumner, March 26, 1863, Tracy Collection, Connecticut Historical Society, Hartford. Fredrickson, *Black Image in the White Mind*, 171; Lorien Foote, *The Gentlemen and the Roughs: Violence, Honor, and Manhood in the Union Army* (New York: New York University Press, 2010), 120–121. Robert F. Engs and Corey M. Brooks, eds., *Their Patriotic Duty: The Civil War Letters of the Evans Family of Brown County, Ohio* (New York: Fordham University Press, 2007), 143–147. Calvin Symmes Mixter Diary, entries from January 27, March 3–4, 14, August 29, September 7, October 21, 1863, Gilder Lehrman Collection, New York; Calvin Symmes Mixter [listed as "Mixten" in file] CMSR; Dobak, *Freedom by the Sword*, 14–19. Henry Harrison Brown to Mother, February 5, 1864, Henry Harrison Brown Papers, Connecticut Historical Society, Hartford; Reid Mitchell, *Civil War Soldiers: Their Expectations and Their Experiences* (New York: Viking, 1988), 91, 103–107; Glatthaar, *Forged in Battle*, 17–18; Fry, *Republic in the Ranks*, 3–4, 83; Kanisorn Wongsrichanalai, *Northern Character: College-Educated New Englanders, Honor, Nationalism, and Leadership in the Civil War Era* (New York: Fordham University Press, 2016), 113–136. Berlin, Reidy, and Rowland, eds., *Black Military Experience*, 408; Martin W. Öfele, *German-Speaking Officers in the U.S. Colored Troops, 1863–1867* (Gainesville: University Press of Florida, 2003), 141; Kelly D. Mezurek, *For Their Own Cause: The 27th United States Colored Troops* (Kent, OH: Kent State University Press, 2016), 88, 191.
68. Whiting quoted in Henry O'Reilly, *First Organization of Colored Troops in the State of New York, to Aid in Suppressing the Slaveholders' Rebellion* (New York: Baker and Godwin, 1864), 4.
69. OR, ser. 3, vol. 3, 435.

CHAPTER 2

1. Alexander H. Newton, *Out of the Briars: An Autobiography and Sketch of the Twenty-Ninth Regiment Connecticut Volunteers* (Philadelphia: A. M. E. Book Concern, 1910), 74.
2. White soldier quoted in Berry, *All That Makes a Man*, 176–177. "A Letter from a Soldier," *Christian Recorder*, July 9, 1864.
3. Quoted in C. M. Tyler, *Memorials of Lieut. George H. Walcott, Late of the 30th U.S. Colored Troops* (Boston: Massachusetts Sabbath-School Society, 1865), 35. Bledsoe, *Citizen-Officers*, 1–6, 13–59; Ricardo A. Herrera, *For Liberty and the Republic: The*

American Citizen as Soldier, 1775–1861 (New York: New York University Press, 2015), 1–26; Lang, *In the Wake of War*, 2–8, 15, 30–35, 61–67.

4. Quoted in Hamlin Garland, "Grant at the Outbreak of the War," *McClure's Magazine* 9, no. 1 (May–October 1897): 604; Ron Chernow, *Grant* (New York: Penguin, 2017), 128.
5. Quoted in Bell Irvin Wiley, *The Life of Billy Yank: The Common Soldier of the Union* (1952; repr., Baton Rouge: Louisiana State University Press, 1993), 45–65; Carmichael, *War for the Common Soldier*, 20–61, 244.
6. Duncan, ed., *Blue-Eyed Child of Fortune*, 297. On the power of uniforms to soldiers' transformation, see Weicksel, "To Look like Men of War," 124–38; Carmichael, *War for the Common Soldier*, 20; Cox, *Fabric of Civil War Society*, 79–86.
7. Sharon A. Roger Hepburn, ed., *Private No More: The Civil War Letters of John Lovejoy, 102nd United States Colored Infantry* (Athens: University of Georgia Press, 2023), 59. For restrictions, see also ibid., 55.
8. Edwin S. Redkey, ed., *A Grand Army of Black Men: Letters from African-American Soldiers in the Union Army 1861–1865* (New York: Cambridge University Press, 1992), 77.
9. Terrence J. Winschel, ed., *The Civil War Diary of a Common Soldier, William Wiley of the 77th Illinois Infantry* (Baton Rouge: Louisiana State University Press, 2001), 15. Weigley, *History of the United States Army*, 231.
10. Wiley, *Life of Billy Yank*, 49–50; Coffman, *Old Army*, 157.
11. [Silas Casey], *U.S. Infantry Tactics, for the Instruction, Exercise, and Manœuvers, of the Soldier, a Company, Line of Skirmishers, and Battalion; for the Use of the Colored Troops of the United States Infantry* (New York: D. Van Nostrand, 1863). Duncan, ed., *Blue-Eyed Child of Fortune*, 317. Glatthaar, *Forged in Battle*, 99–120.
12. Robert Cowden, *A Brief Sketch of the Organization and Services of the Fifty-Ninth Regiment of the United States Colored Infantry and Biographical Sketches* (Dayton, OH: United Brethren Publishing House, 1883), 46; Berlin, Reidy, and Rowland, eds., *Black Military Experience*, 75. William Woodlin Diary, September 26, 1864, Gilder Lehrman Collection, New York. Bob Luke and John David Smith, *Soldiering for Freedom: How the Union Army Recruited, Trained, and Deployed the U.S. Colored Troops* (Baltimore: Johns Hopkins University Press, 2014), 66–68, quotation on 67.
13. "Negroes as Soldiers," *Harper's Weekly*, March 14, 1863, 174.
14. Glatthaar, *Forged in Battle*, 182. Emberton, *Beyond Redemption*, 104.
15. Lawrence Van Alstyne, *Diary of an Enlisted Man* (New Haven, CT: Tuttle, Morehouse and Taylor, 1910), 206–207. Norwood P. Hallowell, *The Negro as a Soldier in the War of the Rebellion* (Boston: Little, Brown, 1892), 10–11.
16. Ambrose Bierce, "Two Military Executions," in *The Civil War Short Stories of Ambrose Bierce* (Lincoln: University of Nebraska Press, 1988), 120–121.
17. Bledsoe, *Citizen-Officers*, 75–76; Carmichael, *War for the Common Soldier*, 24.

18. Steven J. Ramold, *Baring the Iron Hand: Discipline in the Union Army* (DeKalb: Northern Illinois University Press, 2009), 341–364; Bledsoe, *Citizen-Officers*, 75–76; Carmichael, *War for the Common Soldier*, 180.
19. John D. Billings, *Hardtack and Coffee, or The Unwritten Story of Army Life* (1887; repr., Lincoln: University of Nebraska Press, 1993), 146.
20. Soldier's Certificate No. 254,987, Samuel Dixon, Company B, First Pennsylvania Light Artillery, Civil War Pension Files, Records of the Department of Veterans Affairs, Record Group 15, National Archives Building, Washington, DC.
21. Robert Gould Shaw to Charles F. Morse, June 3, 1863, Robert Gould Shaw Papers, Massachusetts Historical Society, Boston. See also Russell Duncan, ed., *Blue-Eyed Child of Fortune*, 378. Looby, ed., *Complete Civil War Journal and Selected Letters of Thomas Wentworth Higginson*, 158–159; OR, ser. 3, vol. 4, 226–227. Hallowell, *Negro as a Soldier in the War of the Rebellion*, 9. Duncan, *Where Death and Glory Meet*, 63, 55–57.
22. Stephen V. Benet, *A Treatise on Military Law and the Practice of the Courts-Martial* (New York: n.p., 1862), 167.
23. Isaac Little to Sallie Little, October 23, 1862, Isaac Little Papers, Filson Historical Society, Louisville, KY.
24. Jeremiah Leek, Court-Martial File LL1405. Burl Barrett, Court-Martial Files NN2804 and NN2879. Moses Troyer Anderson Diary, April 28, 1864, folder 18, box 3, Frank Anderson Papers, Rauner Library, Dartmouth College, Hanover, NH. Similarly, the army required commissioned officers convicted of cowardice to be condemned in his hometown newspapers. Article 84 of the Articles of War, *Revised Army Regulations*, 498. Billings, *Hardtack and Coffee*, 155–156; James I. Robertson Jr., *Soldiers Blue and Gray* (Columbia: University of South Carolina Press, 1989), 132–136; Ramold, *Baring the Iron Hand*, 364–383.
25. Engs and Brooks, eds., *Their Patriotic Duty*, 263–264. Ramold, *Baring the Iron Hand*, 345.
26. Samuel Watson Van Nuys Diary, June 10, 1863, Diary No. 4: May 11, 1863, to October 16, 1863, Gilder Lehrman Collection, New York, New York. Benet, *Treatise on Military Law and the Practice of the Courts-Martial*, 167–168; Ramold, *Baring the Iron Hand*, 369; Steven J. Ramold, "We Have No Right to Shoot Them: Military Executions in the Union Army," *Journal of America's Military Past* 33, no. 3 (Spring/Summer 2008): 44–48; Billings, *Hardtack and Coffee*, 157; Wiley, *Life of Billy Yank*, 207–208. John Knight to Brother and Sister, July 23, 1863, in *Civil War Letters of John Knight, First Lieutenant, 7th Iowa Infantry*, compiled by Lucy E. Brown (Oak Park: State of Illinois, Daughters of the American Revolution, 1940).
27. Charles M. Maxim to Mother, April 12, 1864, Charles M. Maxim Papers, Clements Library, University of Michigan, Ann Arbor. See also Henry Grimes Marshall to Mary A. Marshall, November 9, 1863, box 17, Henry Grimes Marshall Papers, Clements Library, University of Michigan, Ann Arbor.

28. George W. Buswell Journal, June 11, 1864, Journal C, George W. Buswell Papers, Huntington Library, San Marino.
29. "The Army of the Potomac: Execution of Three Deserters," *Harper's Weekly*, August 8, 1863, 509.
30. Julia Taft Bayne, *Tad Lincoln's Father* (Boston: Little, Brown, 1931), 132.
31. Mitchell, *Civil War Soldiers*, 17; Reid Mitchell, *The Vacant Chair: The Northern Soldier Leaves Home* (New York: Oxford University Press, 1993), 43; Bledsoe, *Citizen-Officers*, 87, 92–93; Fry, *Republic in the Ranks*, 5.
32. Foote, *Gentlemen and the Roughs*, 20; Bledsoe, *Citizen-Officers*, 4–6; Lang, *In the Wake of War*, 15–16, 61–67.
33. Gallagher, *Union War*, 44. Fredrickson, *Black Image in the White Mind*, 168; Michael Vorenberg, *Final Freedom: The Civil War, the Abolition of Slavery, and the Thirteenth Amendment* (New York: Cambridge University Press, 2001), 161; Escott, *Worst Passions of Human Nature*, 6, 77–89, 125–133, 158. Rose, *Rehearsal for Reconstruction*, 29.
34. Cowden, *Brief Sketch of the Organization and Services of the Fifty-Ninth Regiment of the United States Colored Infantry and Biographical Sketches*, 44–47. Fredrickson, *Black Image in the White Mind*, 171; Rose, *Rehearsal for Reconstruction*, 194.
35. Hallowell, *Negro as a Soldier in the War of the Rebellion*, 9. Thomas Wentworth Higginson, "Leaves from an Officer's Journal: A White Civil War Officer Recounts His Experience as Colonel of the First Black Regiment," *Atlantic Monthly* (December 1864). Higginson, *Army Life in a Black Regiment*, 10. George W. Buswell Journal, February 15, 1864, Journal B, George W. Buswell Papers, Huntington Library, San Marino. Leon F. Litwack, *Been in the Storm So Long: The Aftermath of Slavery* (New York: Vintage, 1979), 68; Meyer, *Colonel of the Black Regiment*, 209; Glatthaar, *Forged in Battle*, 100–101; Wilson, *Campfires of Freedom*, 16–38; Luke and Smith, *Soldiering for Freedom*, 70–72; Lorien Foote, *Rites of Retaliation: Civilization, Soldiers, and Campaigns in the American Civil War* (Chapel Hill: University of North Carolina Press, 2021), 73.
36. Henry Harrison Brown to his parents, March 31, 1864, Henry H. Brown Letters and Diaries, Connecticut Historical Society, Hartford. See also the beliefs and subsequent discipline of the well-known Colonel Robert Gould Shaw. Duncan, ed., *Blue-Eyed Child of Fortune*, 308, 313; Duncan, *Where Death and Glory Meet*, 63, 55–57. Glatthaar, *Forged in Battle*, 81–97.
37. Charles Fox to Thomas B. Fox, January 28, 1864, Charles Barnard Fox Papers, Massachusetts Historical Society, Boston.
38. William Woodlin Diary, December 5, 1863, April 20, 1864, Gilder Lehrman Collection, New York, New York. Berlin, Reidy, and Rowland, eds., *Black Military Experience*, 618–619. Ronald E. Butchart, *Schooling the Freed People: Teaching, Learning, and the Struggle for Black Freedom, 1861–1876* (Chapel Hill: University of North Carolina Press, 2010), 52–119. Dudley Taylor Cornish, "The Union Army as a School for Negroes," *Journal of Negro History* 39, no. 4 (October 1852), 379–380;

John W. Blassingame, "The Union Army as an Educational Institution for Negroes, 1862–1865," *Journal of Negro Education* 34, no. 2 (Spring 1865), 152–159; Glatthaar, *Forged in Battle*, 226; Manning, *Troubled Refuge*, 5; Williams, *Self-Taught*, 45–66.

39. David C. Rankin, ed., *Diary of a Christian Soldier: Rufus Kinsley and the Civil War* (New York: Cambridge University Press, 2003), 109, 148. Rufus Kinsley CMSR.

40. W. W. Gardner, General Order Number 21, June 2, 1865, Gilder Lehrman Collection, New York, New York. See also Benjamin C. Lincoln to Isadora Frances Whitman, July 18, 1863, box 52, Benjamin C. Lincoln Papers, Clements Library, University of Michigan, Ann Arbor; George Tate, July 28, 1865, 1865 Diary, George Tate Papers, Huntington Library, San Marino; Cowden, *Brief Sketch of the Organization and Services of the Fifty-Ninth Regiment of the United States Colored Infantry and Biographical Sketches*, 60.

41. William Elgin Journal, February 20, 1864, Clements Library, University of Michigan, Ann Arbor.

42. Berlin, Reidy, and Rowland, eds., *Black Military Experience*, 623–624.

43. Robert Steinfield, *The Invention of Free Labor: The Employment Relations and American Law and Culture, 1350–1870* (Chapel Hill: University of North Carolina Press, 1991), 101, 122–133; Gerteis, *From Contraband to Freedman*, 59, 72–79, 154; Stanley, *From Bondage to Contract*, 17–21; Eric Foner, "The Meaning of Freedom in the Age of Emancipation," *Journal of American History* 81, no. 2 (September 1994), 448–449. *New York Tribune*, July 10, 1864; August 12, 1864. See also letters in the *Evening Post*, February 14, 1864, and *New York Times*, January 22, 1864.

44. Looby, ed., *Complete Civil War Journal and Selected Letters of Thomas Wentworth Higginson*, 217. Duncan, ed., *Blue-Eyed Child of Fortune*, 366. Officers quoted in Susie King Taylor, *A Black Woman's Civil War Memoirs: Reminiscences of My Life in Camp with the 33rd U.S. Colored Troops, Late 1st South Carolina Volunteers*, ed. Patricia W. Romero and Willie Lee Rose (New York: Markus Wiener, 1988), 42. For further articulations along these lines, see also Charles Fox to Father, April 23, 1864, Charles B. Fox Papers, Massachusetts Historical Society, Boston. For the discrepancies on pay, see OR, ser. 3, vol. 3, 250–252, 404–405, 420.

45. Brown, *Negro in American Rebellion*, 252; McPherson, *Negro's Civil War*, 205; Berlin, Reidy, and Rowland, eds., *Black Military Experience*, 28; Westwood, *Black Troops, White Commanders, and Freedmen during the Civil War*, 138, 125; Glatthaar, *Forged in Battle*, 169–175; Yacovone, "Pay Crisis," 43–44; Webb B. Garrison, *Mutiny in the Civil War* (Shippensburg, PA: White Mane, 2000), 3–11; Samito, *Becoming American under Fire*, 96–98; John David Smith, *Lincoln and the U.S. Colored Troops* (Carbondale: Southern Illinois University Press, 2013), 69–71; and Carmichael, *War for the Common Soldier*, 55–57.

46. William Walker, Court-Martial File MM1320. Mary Ryan, *Civic Wars: Democracy and Public Life in the American City during the Nineteenth Century* (Berkeley: University of California Press, 1998), 38–43; Shane White, "'It

was a Proud Day': African Americans, Festivals, and Parades in the North, 1741–1834," *Journal of American History* 81, no. 1 (June 1994), 49.

47. Hallowell, *Negro as a Soldier in the War of the Rebellion*, 42. Noah Andre Trudeau, ed., *Voices of the 55th: Letters from the 55th Massachusetts Volunteers, 1861–1865* (Dayton, OH: Morningside, 1996), 154.

48. Adams quoted in Worthington Chauncey Ford, *A Cycle of Adams Letters, 1861–1865*, 2 vols. (Boston: Houghton Mifflin, 1920), 1:131, 2:217–218. Wongsrichanalai, *Northern Character*, 133; Cornish, "Union Army as a School for Negroes," 379–380.

49. Glatthaar, *Forged in Battle*, 108.

50. Coffman, *Old Army*, 15–21, 139–140, 144–145, 155–157; Gallagher, *Union War*, 124.

51. Quoted in Wiley, *Life of Billy Yank*, 288; Anson W. Bristol CMSR.

52. Wiley, *Life of Billy Yank*, 288; James M. McPherson, *For Cause and Comrades: Why Men Fought in the Civil War* (New York: Oxford University Press, 1997), 48; Berry, *All That Makes a Man*, 176–177.

53. Drew Gilpin Faust, *This Republic of Suffering: Death and the American Civil War* (New York: Vintage, 2008), xii–xvii, 6–13, 27–28; Michael C. C. Adams, *Living Hell: The Dark Side of the Civil War* (Baltimore: Johns Hopkins University Press, 2014), 60–74, 103–104, 115, 125.

54. Isaac Little to Sallie Little, September 16, 1863, Isaac Little Papers, Filson Historical Society, Louisville, KY.

55. Louis P. Masur, *Rites of Execution: Capital Punishment and the Transformation of American Culture, 1776–1865* (New York: Oxford University Press, 1989), 26–27, 39–41, 47, 96–68, 105. Gerald F. Linderman, *Embattled Courage: The Experience of Combat in the American Civil War* (New York: Free Press, 1987), 56–58, 175–177; Robertson, *Soldiers Blue and Gray*, 136; Ramold, *Baring the Iron Hand*, 372–382.

56. Calvin Symmes Mixter Diary, entry from August 29, 1863, Gilder Lehrman Collection, New York, New York.

57. Linderman, *Embattled Courage*, 58, 175–177; martial disciplinarian quoted in ibid., 175; Carmichael, *War for the Common Soldier*, 224.

58. Bleak soldier quoted in Lesley J. Gordon, *A Broken Regiment: The 16th Connecticut's Civil War* (Baton Rouge: Louisiana State University Press, 2014), 110. Ramold, "We Have No Right to Shoot Them," 44.

59. Leon F. Litwack, *North of Slavery: The Negro in the Free States, 1790–1860* (Chicago: University of Chicago Press, 1961), 100–104, 159; Elizabeth Stordeur Pryor, *Colored Travelers: Mobility and the Fight for Citizenship before the Civil War* (Chapel Hill: University of North Carolina Press, 2016), 77–78, 91–92.

60. Blair, *Virginia's Private War*, 42, 121–122; Bailey, *Invisible Soldiers*, 53; Martinez, *Confederate Slave Impressment in the Upper South*, 18–97; Woodward, *Marching Masters*, 55–103; Brasher, *The Peninsula Campaign and the Necessity of Emancipation*, 28–33; Levin, *Searching for Black Confederates*, 12–99. Basler, ed., *Collected Works of Abraham Lincoln*, 6:30. Lang, *In the Wake of War*, 130. For labor in the USCT, see

OR, ser. 1, vol. 28, pt. 1, 328–331; OR, ser. 1, vol. 41, pt. 2, 566; Carmichael, *War for the Common Soldier*, 143.
61. Berlin, Reidy, and Rowland, eds., *Black Military Experience*, 501–502.
62. Benjamin C. Lincoln to Isadora Frances Whitman, November 5, 1863, box 55, Benjamin C. Lincoln Papers, Clements Library, University of Michigan, Ann Arbor
63. "From the Front," *Christian Recorder*, January 28, 1865.
64. Trudeau, ed., *Voices of the 55th*, 113–114.
65. Ibid.
66. Donald Yacovone, ed., *Freedom's Journey: African American Voices of the Civil War* (Chicago: Lawrence Hill, 2004), 156–159.
67. Charles Merritt, Court-Martial File NN2479. Pierpont C. Turner CMSR.
68. Ira Berlin, Joseph P. Reidy, and Leslie S. Rowland, eds., *Freedom's Soldiers: The Black Military Experience in the Civil War* (New York: Cambridge University Press, 1998), 110.
69. James Oakes, *The Ruling Race: A History of American Slaveholders* (New York: Knopf, 1982), 154–159.
70. OR, ser. 1, vol. 26, 457–479, quotation on 474. Harrington, "The Fort Jackson Mutiny," 420–431. Glatthaar, *Forged in Battle*, 114–115, 222–223; Westwood, *Black Troops, White Commanders, and Freedmen during the Civil War*, 142–166; John F. Fannin, "The Jacksonville Mutiny of 1865," *Florida Historical Quarterly* 88, no. 3 (Winter 2010): 368–396; Samito, *Becoming American under Fire*, 77–102; Foote, *Gentlemen and the Roughs*, 160–165; Lande, "Disciplining Freedom," 286–319.
71. Wallace Baker CMSR; Wallace Baker, Court-Martial LL2112; Egerton, *Thunder at the Gates*, 234–235; Yacovone, "Pay Crisis," 45–47.
72. Baker, Court-Martial File LL2112.
73. Trudeau, ed., *Voices of the 55th*, 224, 113.
74. Thomas R. R. Cobb, *An Inquiry into the Law of Negro Slavery in the United States of America* (Philadelphia: T. and J. W. Johnson, 1858), 266. Daniel Flanigan, "The Criminal Law of Slavery and Freedom, 1800–1868," PhD diss., Rice University, 1973, 21; Norrece T. Jones Jr., *Born a Child of Freedom, Yet a Slave: Mechanisms of Control and Strategies of Resistance in Antebellum South Carolina* (Hanover, NH: Wesleyan University Press, 1990), 2, 8, 91–92, 181–182, 187; Camp, *Closer to Freedom*, 66–68. Edward L. Ayers, *Vengeance and Justice: Crime and Punishment in the 19th-Century American South* (New York: Oxford University Press, 1984), 136; Thomas D. Morris, *Southern Slavery and the Law, 1619–1860* (Chapel Hill: University of North Carolina Press, 1996), 268–271; Winthrop D. Jordan, *Tumult and Silence at Second Creek: An Inquiry into a Civil War Slave Conspiracy* (Baton Rouge: Louisiana State University Press, 1993), 260. For the mass executions of rebels and its meaning, see Douglas R. Egerton, *Gabriel's Rebellion: The Virginia Slave Conspiracies of 1800 and 1802* (Chapel Hill: University of North Carolina Press, 1993), ix, 139–141; Jordan, *Tumult and Silence at Second Creek*, 317, 323. Stephen B. Oates, *The Fires of Jubilee: Nat Turner's Fierce Rebellion* (New York: Harper & Row, 1975), 114;

Daina Ramey Berry, *The Price for Their Pound of Flesh: The Value of the Enslaved, from Womb to Grave, in the Building of a Nation* (Boston: Beacon, 2017), 91–109, 152–174.

75. Trudeau, ed., *Voices of the 55th*, 225, 113.
76. Berlin, Reidy, and Rowland, eds., *Black Military Experience*, 467–468.
77. "War Letters of Charles P. Bowditch," *Proceedings of the Massachusetts Historical Society* 57 (October 1923): 444.
78. "A Soldier's Letter," *Christian Recorder*, July 9, 1864. Aleck Williams CMSR; Aleck Williams, Courts-Martial File LL2113. Richard M. Reid, *Freedom for Themselves: North Carolina's Black Soldiers in the Civil War* (Chapel Hill: University of North Carolina Press, 2008), 32. For a similar reaction to an officer, see the case of Kentucky-born private John Higgins. John Higgins, Court-Martial File OO1429; John Higgins, CMSR; Berlin, Reidy, and Rowland, eds., *Black Military Experience*, 475–476; Dry Tortugas Record Book, line 1686.
79. Christian A. Fleetwood to Dr. James Hall, June 8, 1965, Carter G. Woodson Papers, Library of Congress.
80. Ulysses S. Grant, *The Personal Memoirs of Ulysses S. Grant: The Complete Annotated Edition*, ed. John F. Marszalek (1885; repr., Cambridge, MA: Harvard University Press, 2017), 376–377; Westwood, *Black Troops, White Commanders, and Freedmen during the Civil War*, 21–36; Barnickel, *Milliken's Bend*, xiv. Benjamin Quarles, *The Negro in the Civil War* (1953; repr., Boston: De Capo Press, 1989), 224; Cornish, *Sable Arm*, 144–154; Glatthaar, *Forged in Battle*, 135, 153–154, 165–168; Noah Andre Trudeau, *Like Men of War: Black Troops in the Civil War, 1862–1865* (Boston: Little, Brown, 1998), 87. Marcus Rediker, *The* Amistad *Rebellion: An Atlantic Odyssey of Slavery and Freedom* (New York: Viking, 2012), 159–163.
81. Donald R. Shaffer, *After the Glory: The Struggles of Black Civil War Veterans* (Lawrence: University Press of Kansas, 2004), 67–70, 169–188; Barbara A. Gannon, *The Won Cause: Black and White Comradeship in the Grand Army of the Republic* (Chapel Hill: University of North Carolina Press, 2011), 58, 72–76, 100, 112–118; Elizabeth R. Varon, "Joseph T. Wilson's *The Black Phalanx:* African American Patriotism and the Won Cause," in *Civil War Writing: New Perspectives on Iconic Texts*, ed. Gary W. Gallagher and Stephen Cushman (Baton Rouge: Louisiana State University Press, 2019), 13–41; Lande, "Black Badge of Courage," 5–42.

CHAPTER 3

1. Napoleon Bonaparte CMSR; Napoleon Bonaparte, Court-Martial File NN358.
2. Berlin, Reidy, and Rowland, eds., *Black Military Experience*, 656–732; Jim Cullen, "'I's a Man Now': Gender and African American Men," in *Divided Houses: Gender and the Civil War*, ed. Catherine Clinton and Nina Silber (New York: Oxford University Press, 1992), 76–96; James Oliver Horton, "Defending the Manhood of the Race: The Crisis of Citizenship in Black Boston at Midcentury," in *Hope and*

Glory: Essays on the Legacy of the 54th Massachusetts Regiment, ed. Martin H. Blatt, Thomas J. Brown, and Donald Yacovone (Amherst: University of Massachusetts Press, 2001), 7–20; Hahn, *Nation under Our Feet*, 169; Shaffer, *After the Glory*, 1–5; Williams, *Help Me to Find My People*, 139–188; Tera W. Hunter, *Bound in Wedlock: Slave and Free Black Marriage in the Nineteenth Century* (Cambridge, MA: Harvard University Press, 2017), 123–231; Reidy, *Illusions of Emancipation*, 229; Libra R. Hilde, *Slavery, Fatherhood, and Paternal Duty in African American Communities over the Long Nineteenth Century* (Chapel Hill: University of North Carolina Press, 2020), 227–252.

3. OR, ser. 3, vol. 5, 670. For the rate of desertion among white soldiers, see Lonn, *Desertion during the Civil War*, 29–30, 149–150; Martin, *A Rich Man's War, a Poor Man's Fight*, 73–74; Weitz, *A Higher Duty*, 7; Sheehan-Dean, *Why Confederates Fought*, 227n17.

4. James H. Edmondson, "Desertion in the American Army during the American Revolution," PhD diss., Louisiana State University, 1971, esp. 99–136; Coffman, *Old Army*, 21, 193–195, quotation on 193; Weigley, *History of the United States Army*, 168.

5. OR, ser. 3, vol. 5, 677; OR, ser. 1, vol. 28, 329; Lonn, *Desertion during the Civil War*, 150; Carmichael, *War for the Common Soldier*, 177–180.

6. Alexis de Tocqueville, *Democracy in America*, trans. Henry Reeve (1835; repr., New York: Knopf, 1945), 271. On colonists' difficulties in the military and with its discipline bolstering de Tocqueville's observations, see Charles Royster, *A Revolutionary People at War: The Continental Army and American Character, 1775–1783* (Chapel Hill: University of North Carolina Press, 1980), and Fred Anderson, *A People's Army: Massachusetts Soldiers and Society in the Seven Years' War* (Chapel Hill: University of North Carolina, 1984).

7. Lonn, *Desertion during the Civil War*, 134. Lonn referred here to the US Army, though she identified that the reasons for desertion ran parallel because "the combatants on both sides were, after all, one people." Ibid., 127. See also Martin, *A Rich Man's War, a Poor Man's Fight*, 73–74. Ibid., 72–73, 78–91, 108–114, 121–155. Blair, *Virginia's Private War*, 60, 64, 88–89, 131; Armstead L. Robinson, *Bitter Fruits of Bondage: The Demise of Slavery and the Collapse of the Confederacy, 1861–1865* (Charlottesville: University of Virginia Press, 2005), 8–10, 156–162; Sheehan-Dean, *Why Confederates Fought*, 4, 90–96; Glatthaar, *General Lee's Army*, 411; Joan E. Cashin, "Deserters, Civilians, and Draft Resistance in the North," in *The War Was You and Me: Civilians in the American Civil War*, ed. Joan E. Cashin (Princeton, NJ: Princeton University Press, 2002), 262–285; Mark A. Weitz, *More Damning Than Slaughter: Desertion in the Confederate Army* (Lincoln: University of Nebraska Press, 2008); Jonathan W. White, *Emancipation, the Union Army, and the Reelection of Abraham Lincoln* (Baton Rouge: Louisiana State University Press, 2014), 78–81; Carmichael, *War for the Common Soldier*, 176, 225–227.

8. OR, ser. 3, vol. 5, 670; Lonn, *Desertion during the Civil War*, 149. Gallman, *Defining Duty in the Civil War*, 223–250; Taylor, *Fighting for Citizenship*, 40–96.

9. For letters on injustice, see Redkey, ed., *Grand Army of Black Men*. Kate Masur, *An Example for All the Land: Emancipation and the Struggle over Equality in Washington, D.C.* (Chapel Hill: University of North Carolina Press, 2010), 44.
10. Adams, ed., *On the Altar of Freedom*, 119.
11. Cornish, *Sable Arm*, 181–196; McPherson, *Negro's Civil War*, 99–110, 193–204; Glatthaar, *Forged in Battle*, 81–98, 169–206; Yacovone, "Pay Crisis," 38–42; Westwood, *Black Troops, White Commanders, and Freedmen during the Civil War*, 125–167; Kantrowitz, *More Than Freedom*, 175–305; Smith, *Lincoln and the U.S. Colored Troops*, 69–71; Taylor, *Fighting for Citizenship*, 112.
12. Berlin, Reidy, and Rowland, eds., *Black Military Experience*, 401–402. Taylor, *Fighting for Citizenship*, 103–107.
13. Berlin, Reidy, and Rowland, eds., *Black Military Experience*, 112.
14. Slap, "Loyal Deserters," 234–248; Mathisen, *Loyal Republic*, 110–112.
15. *Douglass' Monthly*, January 1863.
16. Harrington, "Fort Jackson Mutiny," 429; Glatthaar, *Forged in Battle*, 114–115, 222–223; Westwood, *Black Troops, White Commanders, and Freedmen during the Civil War*, 142–166; Fannin, "Jacksonville Mutiny of 1865," 368–396; Samito, *Becoming American under Fire*, 77–102; Foote, *Gentlemen and the Roughs*, 160–165; Dobak, *Freedom by the Sword*, 96–97, 112–113; Wilson, *Campfires of Freedom*, 204–205; Lande, "Disciplining Freedom," 286–319; Jonathan Lande, "Mutiny in the Civil War," *Civil War Monitor* 9 (March 2019): 54–65, 77; Crystal N. Feimster, "Rape and Mutiny at Fort Jackson: Black Laundresses Testify in Civil War Louisiana," *Labor* 19, no. 1 (March 2022): 18–22. For the political education Black northerners would share with Black southerners during their service in the USCT, see Foner, *Reconstruction*, 7–11; Hahn, *A Nation under Our Feet*, 96; Bonner, *Remaking the Republic*, 170.
17. Basler, ed., *Collected Works of Abraham Lincoln*, 7:500. Lincoln quoted his previous letter. For the original iteration on Black soldiers' motives, see ibid., 6:409.
18. J. H. Greene, *Reminiscences of the War: Bivouacs, Marches, Skirmishes, and Battles* (Medina, OH: Gazette Print, 1886), 61–62.
19. For prewar flight by the enslaved, see esp. Peter H. Wood, *Black Majority: Negroes in Colonial South Carolina from 1670 through the Stono Rebellion* (New York: W. W. Norton, 1974), 239–268; John Hope Franklin and Loren Schweninger, *Runaway Slaves: Rebels on the Plantation* (New York: Oxford University Press, 1999), 2, 291; Camp, *Closer to Freedom*, 117–138; Diouf, *Slavery's Exiles*, 2–10, 89; Yael A. Sternhell, *Routes of War: The World of Movement in the Confederate South* (Cambridge, MA: Harvard University Press, 2012), 93–100; Andrew Delbanco, *The War before the War: Fugitive Slaves and the Struggle for America's Soul from the Revolution to the Civil War* (New York: Penguin, 2018), 2.
20. Miller, *Lincoln's Abolitionist General*, 97–105.
21. OR, ser. 1, vol. 14, 1020.
22. Recruiter quoted in Rose, *Rehearsal for Reconstruction*, 145.

23. OR, ser. 1, vol. 14, 341. Ira Berlin, Barbara J. Fields, Steven F. Miller, Joseph P. Reidy, and Leslie Rowland, *Free at Last: A Documentary History of Slavery, Freedom, and the Civil War* (New York: New Press, 1992), 46–48; Rose, *Rehearsal for Reconstruction*, 146. Miller, *Lincoln's Abolitionist General*, 97–105; Trudeau, *Like Men of War*, 109; Manning, *Troubled Refuge*, 91–92, 188.
24. Higginson, *Army Life in a Black Regiment*, 273. Fields-Black, *Combee*, 208–210, 238, 255. For enslaved southerners' apprehension of the US Army during the Combahee River Raid, see ibid., 371–374.
25. David Donald, ed., *Inside Lincoln's Cabinet: The Civil War Diaries of Salmon P. Chase* (New York: Longmans, Green, 1954), 96.
26. Rose, *Rehearsal for Reconstruction*, 188–191.
27. Elizabeth Ware Pearson, ed., *Letters from Port Royal, Written at the Time of the Civil War* (Boston: W. B. Clarke, 1906), 96.
28. Higginson, *Army Life in a Black Regiment*, 43. For Higginson's affirmation that drafts led to desertions, see Higginson, *Army Life in a Black Regiment*, 224.
29. Robert Simmons CMSR; Robert Simmons, Court-Martial File LL1808.
30. James Brown [Thirty-Third USCI] CMSR; James Brown, Court-Martial File NN2205.
31. Higginson, *Army Life in a Black Regiment*, 43.
32. Downs, *Sick from Freedom*, 26–28; Glymph, *Women's Fight*, 103, 114–116, 224; Kelly Houston Jones, "Making Their Place on the South's Ragged Edge: USCT Women and Place in Little Rock, Arkansas," in *Southern Black Women and Their Struggle for Freedom during the Civil War and Reconstruction*, ed. Karen Cook Bell (New York: Cambridge University Press, 2024), 121–135.
33. Michael Burlingame and John R. Turner Ettlinger, eds., *Inside Lincoln's White House: The Complete Civil War Diary of John Hay* (Carbondale: Southern Illinois University Press, 1997), 57.
34. Mary Thacher Higginson, ed., *The Letters and Journals of Thomas Wentworth Higginson, 1846–1906* (New York: Houghton Mifflin, 1921), 178, 189–190. Stanley Howard, *Border War: Fighting over Slavery before the Civil War* (Chapel Hill: University of North Carolina Press, 2010), 173, 193. Duncan, ed., *Blue-Eyed Child of Fortune*, 362, 378.
35. Pearson, ed., *Letters from Port Royal*, 188, 236–240, quotation on 240. Rose, *Rehearsal for Reconstruction*, 236–237, 268–269.
36. Doddington, *Contesting Slave Masculinity in the American South*, 89–126; Hilde, *Slavery, Fatherhood, and Paternal Duty in African American Communities over the Long Nineteenth Century*, 69, 82–87, 92–96.
37. "Conversations with General Thomas," undated newspaper clipping in John O. Sargent Scrapbook, John O. Sargent Papers, Massachusetts Historical Society, Boston; Eggleston, *President Lincoln's Recruiter*, 18; Glatthaar, *Forged in Battle*, 35; Luke and Smith, *Soldiering for Freedom*, 55–59. William M. Parkinson [Forty-Seventh USCI] CMSR; Parkinson quoted in Dobak, *Freedom by the Sword*, 175–176.

38. Henry E. Hall, Court-Martial File LL1565; Henry E. Hall CMSR.
39. Linderman, *Embattled Courage*, 115–117.
40. OR, ser. 3, vol. 5, 669. Margaret Humphreys, *Intensely Human: The Health of the Black Soldier in the American Civil War* (Baltimore: Johns Hopkins University Press, 2008), xviii; Leslie A. Schwalm, *Medicine, Science and Making Race in Civil War America* (Chapel Hill: University of North Carolina Press, 2023), 15–17.
41. Samuel Ferguson Jayne to Charlotte Elizabeth Jayne, July 3–5, 1864, folder 1, Jayne Papers, Clements Library, University of Michigan, Ann Arbor. Black northerners also expressed reservations about visiting US Army hospitals. See, for example, Hepburn, ed., *Private No More*, 101, 106.
42. Kathryn Shively Meier, *Nature's Civil War: Common Soldiers and the Environment in 1862 Virginia* (Chapel Hill: University of North Carolina Press, 2013), 22–24, 126–141.
43. Henry E. Hall, Court-Martial File LL1565; Henry E. Hall CMSR.
44. Sharla M. Fett, *Working Cures: Healing, Health, and Power on Southern Slave Plantations* (Chapel Hill: University of North Carolina Press, 2002), 33, 112–118, 143–188, 173–177.
45. Burt G. Wilder CMSR. Richard M. Reid, ed., *Practicing Medicine in a Black Regiment: The Civil War Diary of Burt G. Wilder, 55th Massachusetts* (Amherst: University of Massachusetts Press, 2010), 69–70, 75, 76, 183, 184.
46. Enoch W. Robbins CMSR; "Home from the War," *Harper's Weekly*, June 13, 1863. See also *Harper's Weekly*, January 23, 1864. Billings, *Hardtack and Coffee*, 211–212; Wiley, *Life of Billy Yank*, 292; Robertson, *Soldiers Blue and Gray*, 79–80; Ramold, *Baring the Iron Hand*, 224–225.
47. Richard Johnson (aka Johnston) CMSR; Richard Johnson, Court-Martial File NN1887; Dry Tortugas Record Book, line 1014. Other soldiers communicated similar sentiments in the last years of fighting. See Galloway Hatch, Court-Martial File LL2284; Galloway Hatch CMSR; William Simpson, Court-Martial File LL1734; William Simpson was listed as William Simson and Simpson Williams in CMSR. See also the case of James Lane, Court-Martial File LL2221; James Lane CMSR.
48. Spencer Watson, Court-Martial File NN372; Spencer Watson CMSR. Colonel Herman Lieb of the Fifth United States Colored Heavy Artillery sought to prevent desertions from camp in the fall and winter of 1864 by supplying soldiers with the means to build cabins and raise gardens for families nearby. Wilson, *Campfires of Freedom*, 189–191.
49. Mary F. Berry, "Negro Troops in Blue and Gray: The Louisiana Native Guards, 1861–1863," *Louisiana History: The Journal of the Louisiana Historical Association* 8, no. 2 (Spring 1967): 185–189; Roland C. McConnell, "Louisiana's Black Military History, 1729–1861," in *Louisiana's Black Heritage*, ed. Robert R. MacDonald, John R. Kemp, and Edward F. Haas (New Orleans: Louisiana State Museum, 1979), 46–61; Hollandsworth, *Louisiana Native Guards*, 20, 30, 98. OR, ser. 1, vol. 26, pt. 1, 685–686; Lawrence Lee Hewitt, "An Ironic Route to Glory: Louisiana's Native

Guards at Port Hudson," in *Black Soldiers in Blue: African American Troops in the Civil War Era*, ed. John David Smith (Chapel Hill: University of North Carolina Press, 2002), 82. Stephen J. Ochs, *A Black Patriot and a White Priest: André Cailloux and Claude Paschal Maistre in Civil War New Orleans* (Baton Rouge: Louisiana State University Press, 2006), 81, 92–94, 139–159, 205–206, officers' quotation on 210. Private Henry Wright of the Third United States Colored Heavy Artillery also fled to care for family, affirming the officers' conjecture further up the Mississippi River. Standing trial in Tennessee after decamping on April 12, 1864, Wright said, "I only went away for a few days to see my mother and was afraid to go back. So I went and staid with the Cavalry until they arrested me." Henry Wright, Court-Martial File NN2174; Henry Wright CMSR.

50. Surgeon quoted in Joseph Norbert CMSR; Joseph Norbert, Court-Martial File NN3575; Anthony Primbow, Court-Martial File LL3106, folder 2; Anthony Primbow CMSR.

51. Ochs, *Black Patriot*, 215. Leonel McCarty, Court-Martial File LL3106, folder 2; Leonel McCarty CMSR. John James Cage CMSR. In the text, "Lionel Macarty" is used because that was how Macarty signed his name. In the notes, "Leonel McCarty" is retained for reference since the US government archived Macarty as "Leonel McCarty."

52. McCarty, Court-Martial File LL3106, folder 2; McCarty CMSR. Prison letter located in CMSR. Dry Tortugas Record Book, line 1235. Glymph, *Women's Fight*, 114–116, 224.

53. Duncan, ed., *Blue-Eyed Child of Fortune*, 378.

54. "A Negro's Views on Negro Troops," *Boston Journal*, March 17, 1864, in Scrapbook Vol. 2 (1863–1867), box 2, folder 31, Norwood Penrose Hallowell Papers, Massachusetts Historical Society, Boston. Trudeau, *Like Men of War*, 72–73; Dobak, *Freedom by the Sword*, 40–47; OR, ser. 1, vol. 14, 466. Hardtime White, CMSR; Fields-Black, *Combee*, 431. White's pension record stated that he was hanged, Edda Fields-Black wrote, but White may have in fact survived. His service record said that he was "probably to be found [at] St. Helena," and he apparently returned to duty because, according to his service record, he was mustered out February 28, 1866. Charles Adams, Court-Martial File NN2788; Robert Humbert, Court-Martial File LL3036; Joseph Smith, Court-Martial File MM3122; Charles Adams CMSR; Robert Humbert CMSR; Joseph Smith CMSR; Hector Fields CMSR; Fields-Black, *Combee*, 431, 450, 502–503. OR, ser. 3, vol. 4, 226–227.

55. Cowden, *A Brief Sketch of the Organization and Services of the Fifty-Ninth Regiment of the United States Colored Infantry and Biographical Sketches*, 38–40. On impressment, see Glatthaar, *Forged in Battle*, 72–76, 81–91; Berlin et al., *Free at Last*, 46–48; Miller, *Lincoln's Abolitionist General*, 99–101; Trudeau, *Like Men of War*, 109; Manning, *Troubled Refuge*, 91–92.

56. Crawford Wilcox, Court-Martial File NN2241, RG153; Crawford Wilcox CMSR. OR, ser. 3, vol. 5, 138.

57. Louis Hughes, *Thirty Years a Slave: From Bondage to Freedom* (Milwaukee: South Side Printing, 1897), 155–156.
58. Wilcox, Court-Martial File NN2241; Wilcox CMSR. OR, ser. 3, vol. 5, 677; Ramold, *Baring the Iron Hand*, 219. Jeffrey N. Lash, *A Politician Turned General: The Civil War Career of Stephen Augustus Hurlbut* (Kent, OH: Kent State University Press, 2003), 108–109, 141–142.
59. Wilcox CMSR. "Forrest's Raid into Memphis—Rebel Attack on the Irving Prison," *Harper's Weekly*, September 10, 1864.
60. Hepburn, ed., *Private No More*, 92–93.
61. Henry Harrison Brown to his parents, May 29, 1865, folder 15, Henry Harrison Brown Papers, Connecticut Historical Society, Hartford.
62. Billings, *Hardtack & Coffee*, 146.
63. Rollin Burgess, Court-Martial File MM3325; Rollin Burgess (aka Burgess Rollin) CMSR.

CHAPTER 4

1. James Brown CMSR. James Brown, Court-Martial File LL1565.
2. Benet, *Treatise on Military Law and the Practice of the Courts-Martial*, 29–30.
3. Ibid., 8–9.
4. Articles 64 through 93 of the Articles of War, *Revised United States Army Regulations of 1861 with an Appendix Containing the Changes and Laws Affecting Army Regulations and Articles of War to June 25, 1863* (Washington, DC: Government Printing Office, 1863), 495–500. For an analysis of the Articles of War in relation to the broader strategic goals of the war, see Witt, *Lincoln's Code*.
5. Article 38 in the 1861 version and Articles 64 through 93 in the revised section. *Revised United States Army Regulations of 1861*, 125–127, 495–500. OR, ser. 1, vol. 4, 340; OR, ser. 1, vol. 5, 584.
6. Benet, *Treatise on Military Law and the Practice of the Courts-Martial*, 50, 59–80; Levi S. Graybill 1865 Diary, May 31, 1865, Levi S. Graybill Papers, Huntington Library, San Marino; Ramold, *Baring the Iron Hand*, 317, 321.
7. Henry Coppée, *Field Manual of Courts-Martial* (Philadelphia: J. B. Lippincott, 1864), 53. Ramold, *Baring the Iron Hand*, 320. For references to the role of jurors, see Benet, *Treatise on Military Law and the Practice of the Courts-Martial*, 22, 59, 158, 300, 316.
8. Luis F. Emilio to Isa Emilio, March 4, 1864, Luis F. Emilio Papers, Massachusetts Historical Society, Boston.
9. George Bliss, February 1864 Correspondence, George N. Bliss Papers, Rhode Island Historical Society, Providence.
10. J. Hoff, "Manner of Setting Up a Court-Martial," in *A Treatise on Martial Law, and Courts-Martial: As Practised in the United States of America* (Charleston: n.p., 1809), 187; Coppée, *Field Manual of Courts-Martial*, 21–23.

11. Channing Richards Diary, August 14, 1862, Channing Richards Papers, Filson Historical Society, Louisville, KY.
12. Wilfrid Prist, *William Blackstone: Law and Letters in the Eighteenth Century* (New York: Oxford University Press, 2008), 117. Francis S. Drake, *Dictionary of American Biography, including Men of the Time* . . . (Boston: James R. Osgood, 1872), 262. William Chetwood De Hart, *Observations of Military Law and the Constitution and Practice of Courts-Martial, with Summary of the Law of Evidence as Applicable to Military Trials* (New York: D. Appleton, 1863).
13. Benet, *Treatise on Military Law and the Practice of the Courts-Martial*, 59–65, 96–118; De Hart, *Observations of Military Law and the Constitution and Practice of Courts-Martial*, 308–314. William Winthrop, *Digest of Opinions of the Judge Advocate General* (Washington, DC: Government Printing Office, 1865), 70–72; Coppée, *Field Manual of Courts-Martial*, 26–33; Ramold, *Baring the Iron Hand*, 318–322. *Revised United States Army Regulations of 1861*, 125–126. Order to Emilio, May 24, 1864; Luis Emilio Diary, June 2, 1864–1865; Isabel Emilio to Luis F. Emilio, April 3, 1864, Luis F. Emilio Papers, Massachusetts Historical Society, Boston.
14. Thomas Brooks Fairleigh Diary, January 8 and 9, 1864, Filson Historical Society, Louisville, KY.
15. Article 38 in the 1861 version and Articles 64 through 93 in the revised section. *Revised United States Army Regulations of 1861*, 125–127, 495–500. Stansfield, "History of the Judge Advocate General's Department United States Army," 219–237. Eugene R. Fidell, *Military Justice: A Very Short Introduction* (New York: Oxford University Press, 2016), 27–41; Christopher Bray, *Court-Martial: How Military Justice Has Shaped America from the Revolution to 9/11 and Beyond* (New York: W. W. Norton, 2016), xiii–xiv, 8–9; Sheehan-Dean, *Calculus of Violence*, 242–245; Joshua E. Kastenberg, *Law in War, War as Law: Brigadier General Joseph Holt and the Judge Advocate General's Department in the Civil War and Early Reconstruction, 1861–1865* (Durham, NC: Carolina Academic Press, 2011), 59. Ramold, *Baring the Iron Hand*, 4–5, 12–15, 21; George James Stansfield, "A History of the Judge Advocate General's Department United States Army," *Military Affairs* 9, no. 3 (Autumn 1945): 219–237; David A. Schlueter, "The Military Justice System Conundrum: Justice or Discipline?," *Military Law Review* 215 (Spring 2013): 23.
16. George N. Bliss to Gerald [illegible], March 11; October 25, 1863, George N. Bliss Papers, Rhode Island Historical Society, Providence.
17. Benjamin C. Lincoln to Isadora Frances Whitman, November 2, 1864, box 56, Benjamin C. Lincoln Papers, Clements Library, University of Michigan, Ann Arbor.
18. Coppée, *Field Manual of Courts-Martial*, 57–58. For similar sentiments, see Benet, *Treatise on Military Law and the Practice of the Courts-Martial*, 126, 61.
19. Benet, *Treatise on Military Law and the Practice of the Courts-Martial*, 126, 20, 7. During the war, Benet updated the 1862 volume, publishing editions in 1863, 1864, 1866, and 1868.

Notes to pages 86–87

20. Foote, *Gentlemen and the Roughs*, 45–65, 122–126, 135–143; Witt, *Lincoln's Code*, 252–292; Sheehan-Dean, *Calculus of Violence*, 40–41, 79–81, 235–246; Kastenberg, *Law in War, War as Law*, 117; White, *Emancipation, the Union Army, and the Reelection of Abraham Lincoln*, 55; Kenneth W. Noe, "The Arrest and Court-Martial of Captain George Dobson," in *Weirding the Civil War: Stories from the Civil War's Ragged Edges*, ed. Stephen W. Berry II (Athens: University of Georgia Press, 2011), 262.
21. Ramold, *Baring the Iron Hand*, 302, 315, 326–328. Kastenberg, *Law in War, War as Law*, 43. *Revised United States Army Regulations of 1861*, 125.
22. Charles Barnard Fox, *The Record of Service of the Fifty-Fifth Massachusetts Regiment* (Cambridge, MA: John Wilson and Son, 1908), 114. Leonard, *Slaves, Slaveholders, and a Kentucky Community's Struggle toward Freedom*, 22–24; Elizabeth D. Leonard, *Lincoln's Forgotten Ally: Judge Advocate General Joseph Holt of Kentucky* (Chapel Hill: University of North Carolina Press, 2011), 174–176. For examples of overturned cases of Black soldiers, see Thomas Carmichael, Court-Martial File OO1786; Abram Barnes, Court-Martial File OO1786. James Williams, Court-Martial File NN1502; Thomas Seymore, Court-Martial File NN1502; Lewis Beeler, Court-Martial File NN1502.
23. Berlin, Reidy, and Rowland, eds., *Black Military Experience*, 433–442. Samito, *Becoming American under Fire*, 4, 80, 84–86. On justice within the courts-martial for Black men, see also Glatthaar, *Forged in Battle*, 118–119; Ramold, *Baring the Iron Hand*, 333.
24. On the importance of Black judges to Black defendants, African American jurist Damon J. Keith, former judge of the United States Court of Appeals for the Sixth Circuit, stated that trusting those passing judgment because they share experiences promotes "the feeling that everybody will be treated fairly." Linn Washington, ed., *Black Judges on Justice: Perspectives from the Bench* (New York: New Press, 1994), 124. For assessments of the legal system informing the interpretation here, see Sheri Lynn Johnson, "Black Innocence and the White Jury," *Michigan Law Review* 83, no. 7 (June 1985): 1611–1708; Samuel H. Pillsbury, "Emotional Justice: Moralizing the Passions of Criminal Punishment," *Cornell Law Review* 74, no. 4 (May 1989): 655–710; Jennifer L. Eberhardt, Phillip A. Goff, Valerie J. Purdie, and Paul G. Davies, "Seeing Black: Race, Crime, and Visual Processing," *Journal of Personality and Social Psychology* 87, no. 6 (2004): 876–893. Rebecca C. Hetey and Jennifer L. Eberhardt, "Racial Disparities in Incarceration Increase Acceptance of Punitive Policies," *Psychological Science* 25, no. 10 (October 2014): 1949–1954.
25. Article 38 in the 1861 version and Articles 64 through 93 in the revised section. *Revised United States Army Regulations of 1861*, 125–127, 495–500. Stansfield, "History of the Judge Advocate General's Department United States Army," 219–237.

26. Coppée, *Field Manual of Courts-Martial*, 57–58. J. G. Rosengarten, "Obituary Notice of Henry Coppée, LL.D.," *Proceedings of the American Philosophical Society* 34, no. 149 (1895): 357–361.
27. Higginson, *Army Life in a Black Regiment*, 65–66.
28. Gallagher, *Union War*. For the relationship between the Union motivation and the US Constitution, see specifically Ibid., 34, 46–73. For reverence of the founding document, see Michael Vorenberg, "Bringing the Constitution Back In: Amendment, Innovation, and Popular Democracy during the Civil War Era," in *The Democratic Experiment: New Directions in American Political History*, ed. Meg Jacobs, William J. Novak, and Julian E. Zelizer (Princeton, NJ: Princeton University Press, 2003), 120–144.
29. Grant quoted in Garland, "Grant at the Outbreak of the War," 406. Michael Burlingame, *Abraham Lincoln: A Life*, 2 vols. (Baltimore: Johns Hopkins University Press, 2008), 2:492–495; P. S. Ruckman Jr. and David Kincaid, "Inside Lincoln's Clemency Decision Making," *Presidential Studies Quarterly* 29, no. 1 (March 1999): 84–99.
30. Higginson quoted in Meyer, *Colonel of the Black Regiment*, 29. Looby, ed., *Complete Civil War Journal*, 166, 182. Ramold, *Baring the Iron Hand*, 302, 315; Wiley, *Life of Billy Yank*, 209–210.
31. Benjamin C. Lincoln to Isadora Frances Whitman, March 3, 1863, box 52, Benjamin C. Lincoln Papers, Clements Library, University of Michigan, Ann Arbor.
32. Naham W. Daniels [aka Nathan W. Daniels] CMSR. Nathan W. Daniels Diary, Vol. 1, August 26 and 27, 1863, Library of Congress. Daniels deemed emancipation a "grand idea" and praised the army's push to expand the regiments of enslaved men, writing that the "Gov't has at last awoke to the efficacy of such organization." March 29 and April 27, 1863, in ibid.
33. Gideon R. Viars to Mother, July 2, 1864, Viars Family Papers, Filson Historical Society, Louisville, KY.
34. *The Liberator*, October 4, 1864. Glatthaar, *Forged in Battle*, 176. In this, "Sergeant" echoed activists down through history who have remarked on the discrimination within state, federal, and military legal systems stemming from the dearth of Black jurists. This includes Thurgood Marshall, who investigated the courts-martial trials of Black soldiers in the twentieth century. See Washington, ed., *Black Judges on Justice*, 47, 71–73, 83, 103, 119, 124, 132, 147, 240, 247–250. Mark V. Tushnet, ed., *Thurgood Marshall: His Speeches, Writings, Arguments, Opinions, and Reminiscences* (Chicago: University of Chicago Press, 2001), 135.
35. Donald Yacovone, ed., *A Voice of Thunder: The Civil War Letters of George E. Stephens* (Urbana: University of Illinois Press, 1997), 223.
36. Ibid., 299.
37. Ibid.
38. Thomas D. Morris, *Southern Slavery and the Law, 1619–1860* (Chapel Hill: University of North Carolina Press 1996), 21–29, 35–36. Jordan, *Tumult and Silence at Second*

Creek, 202, 323; A. Leon Higginbotham Jr., *Shades of Freedom: Racial Politics and the Presumptions of American Legal Process* (New York: Oxford University Press, 1996), 26, 41; Michael S. Hindus, "Black Justice under White Law: Criminal Prosecutions of Blacks in Antebellum South Carolina," *Journal of American History* 63, no. 3 (December 1976): 575–599; Michael S. Hindus, *Prison and Plantation: Crime, Justice, and Authority in Massachusetts and South Carolina, 1767–1878* (Chapel Hill: University of North Carolina Press, 2019), 129–161. A. E. Keir Nash, "Fairness and Formalism in the Trials of Blacks in the State Supreme Court of the Old South," *Virginia Law Review* 56, no. 1 (February 1970): 64–100; A. E. Keir Nash, "Reason of Slavery: Understanding the Judicial Role in the Peculiar Institution," *Vanderbilt Law Review* 32, no. 1 (January 1979): 7–218; Daniel Flanigan, "Criminal Procedure in the Slave Trials in the Antebellum South," *Journal of Southern History* 40, no. 4 (November 1974): 537–564; Ayers, *Vengeance and Justice*, 134–136; Arthur F. Howington, *What Saveth the Law: The Treatment of Slaves and Free Blacks in the State and Local Courts of Tennessee* (New York: Garland, 1986); Daniel J. Flanigan, *The Criminal Law of Slavery and Freedom, 1800–1868* (New York: Garland, 1987). Edwards, *People and Their Peace*, 121–131; Kennington, *In the Shadow of Dred Scott*, 134–141; Welch, *Black Litigants*, 40–41, 46, 62–63. Judith Kelleher Schafer, *Slavery, the Civil Law, and the Supreme Court of Louisiana* (Baton Rouge: Louisiana State University Press, 1994), 224–234; Judith Kelleher Schafer, *Becoming Free, Remaining Free: Manumission and Enslavement in New Orleans, 1846–1862* (Baton Rouge: Louisiana State University Press, 2003), 45–58; Kennington, *In the Shadow of Dred Scott*, 127; Welch, *Black Litigants*, 168–176; Schweninger, *Appealing for Liberty*, 44. For the foundation of chattel slavery in the South, see Morris, *Southern Slavery and the Law*, 37–57.

39. Moses Smith CMSR; Moses Smith, Court-Martial File LL1811. Helen E. Brown, *John Freeman and His Family* (Boston: American Tract Society, 1864), 22; William Elgin Journal, September 27, 1864, Clements Library, University of Michigan, Ann Arbor; William L. Richter, *Overreached on All Sides: The Freedmen's Bureau Administrators in Texas, 1865–1868* (College Station: Texas A&M University Press, 1991), 23; Stanley, *From Bondage to Contract*, 37; McDaniel, *Sweet Taste of Liberty*, 172.

40. Anderson, *A People's Army*, 168–195; Bernard Bailyn, *Ideological Origins of the American Revolution* (Cambridge, MA: Harvard University Press, 1967), 61–63, 281–284; Gordon S. Wood, *Radicalism of the American Revolution* (New York: Vintage, 1993), 215–220. Bledsoe, *Citizen-Officers*, 1–6; Herrera, *For Liberty and the Republic*, 1–26; Lang, *In the Wake of War*, 2–8, 15, 30–35, 61–67.

41. Edward L. Ayers, "Loyalty and America's Civil War," lecture presented at the Forty-Ninth Annual Fortenbaugh Memorial Lecture, Gettysburg College, Gettysburg, PA, 2010 (pamphlet, Gettysburg College), 8; Carmichael, *War for the Common Soldier*, 183, 189. William A. Blair, *With Malice toward Some: Treason and Loyalty in the Civil War Era* (Chapel Hill: University of North Carolina Press, 2014), 232.

42. Thompson quoted in Mark E. Neely, *Lincoln and the Triumph of the Nation: Constitutional Conflict in the American Civil War* (Chapel Hill: University of North Carolina Press, 2011), 130. Zürcher, "Understanding Changes in Military Recruitment and Employment Worldwide," 17. Thompson's observation pointed to a knowledge of contracts during the era that was not attained through the study of law or employment practices but rather was common among freeborn Americans. For contracts in a constitutional context, see James W. Ely Jr., *The Contract Clause: A Constitutional History* (Lawrence: University Press of Kansas, 2016).

43. Steinfeld, *Invention of Free Labor*, 101, 122–133; Christopher L. Tomlins, *Law, Labor, and Ideology in the Early American Republic* (New York: Cambridge University Press, 1993), 227–231; Montgomery, *Citizen Worker*, 36–37; Stanley, *From Bondage to Contract*, 17–21; Foner, "Meaning of Freedom in the Age of Emancipation," 448–449. For the place of free labor in Republican politics, see esp. Foner, *Free Soil, Free Labor, Free Men*, 11–39, 73–102; Daniel Walker Howe, *Making the American Self: Jonathan Edwards to Abraham Lincoln* (New York: Oxford University Press, 2009), 145–146.

44. James M. McPherson, *Battle Cry of Freedom: The Civil War Era* (New York: Oxford University Press, 1989), 322.

45. Blair, *Virginia's Private War*, 60, 64, 88–89, 131; Sheehan-Dean, *Why Confederates Fought*, 47–51, 189; Glatthaar, *General Lee's Army*, 411; White, *Emancipation, the Union Army, and the Reelection of Abraham Lincoln*, 78–81.

46. See circular provided to soldiers from Office of the Judge Advocate in the Department of the Gulf, folder 14, box 9, Charles Winthrop Lowell Papers, Historical Society of Pennsylvania, Philadelphia.

47. *Revised United States Army Regulations of 1861*, 130–131.

48. Ibid., 132, 521.

49. Ibid., 130–132, 521.

50. Daniel Burton [aka Benton] CMSR. Burton's service record also includes a claim by his former enslaver for compensation. Burton would later decamp, claiming his wife had become sick. Daniel Burton, Court-Martial File MM2850.

51. Charles Rash, Court-Martial File II821. Winthrop, *Digest of Opinions of the Judge Advocate General of the Army*, 4, 41–43. On Judge Advocate General Joseph Holt's construction of the digest based on wartime cases, see Leonard, *Lincoln's Forgotten Ally*, 182.

52. Charles Evans, Court-Martial File KK354; Jacob Yeagar, Court-Martial File LL159; Neely, *Lincoln and the Triumph of the Nation*, 167–183. Lincoln encountered a question regarding an underage soldier on September 19, 1861, asking Winfield Scott if Almon Baker, an enlisted man under age eighteen, should be released from service after his father, who had not provided consent, requested it. In response, Scott cited an act of Congress from September 28, 1850, and released Almon from service on account of Almon's age. Basler, ed., *Collected Works of Abraham Lincoln*, 4:529. For the contracting of children within armies, see Frances M. Clarke and

Rebecca Jo Plant, *Of Age: Boy Soldiers and Military Power in the Civil War Era* (New York: Oxford University Press, 2023), 231–235.

53. Steinfeld, *Coercion, Contract, and Free Labor in the Nineteenth Century*, 42, 45, 50, 83, 234, 290, 305.
54. Basler, ed., *Collected Works of Abraham Lincoln*, 6:266.
55. Article 21, *Revised United States Army Regulations of 1861*, 489. Ibid., 29–30, 503. Thomas P. Lowry, "Research Note: New Access to a Civil War Resource," *Civil War History* 49, no. 1 (March 2003): 56. Officers in the Confederate ranks similarly used the courts-martial to enforce discipline on deserting men. Kevin Conley Ruffin, "Civil War Desertion from a Black Belt Regiment: An Examination of the 44th Virginia Infantry," in *The Edge of the South: Life in Nineteenth-Century Virginia*, ed. Edward L. Ayers and John C. Willis (Charlottesville: University of Virginia Press, 1991), 94–95.
56. Robert Winn CMSR. Robert Winn to Martha Winn, January 12, 1863; December 27, 1863; February 25, 1864; June 18, 1864; December 24, 1864; July 13, 1864; June 29, 1864; October 26, 1864; December 29, 1864; May 26, 1865, Winn-Cook Family Papers, Filson Historical Society, Louisville, KY.
57. James W. Greary, *We Need Men: The Union Draft in the Civil War* (DeKalb: Northern Illinois University Press, 1991), 49–77.
58. Joseph W. Edwards, Court-Martial File NN745. John L. Phillips, Court-Martial File NN745. Joseph W. Edwards CMSR. John L. Phillips CMSR. For cases of white draftees, see James Coombs, Court-Martial File LL1088; Edward Gilleland, Court-Martial File LL1199. For evasion more broadly, see Greary, *We Need Men*, 97–102.
59. See Appendix. Lowry, "Research Note," 56. Lowry states that 95 percent of all men were convicted of absence without leave, but he does not state whether convictions of those men charged with desertion were convictions specifically of desertion or were also of absence without leave. Reviewing the cases and compiled military service records of alleged Black deserters shows that 81 percent of the Black soldiers charged with desertion were convicted of desertion and 15 percent were convicted of absence without leave. Ultimately, then, 96 of those charged with desertion were convicted.
60. See Appendix.
61. Following the trial of Private Ennis Thompson of the Fourth Mississippi Infantry (African Descent) (later the Sixty-Sixth USCI) for desertion, Major General John P. Hawkins affirmed in a review of the case the importance of forms and oaths to convicting soldiers as guidance to future judge advocates, exposing the continuity between the trials of white and Black deserters. Ennis Thompson CMSR. Ennis Thompson, Court-Martial File NN2489.
62. Mose Germain, Court-Martial LL1734; Mose Germain CMSR.
63. Stanley, *From Bondage to Contract*, 3. Dylan Penningroth, *Claims of Kinfolk: African American Property and Community in the Nineteenth-Century South* (Chapel Hill: University of North Carolina Press, 2003), 45–80. Kennington, *In the Shadow*

of Dred Scott, 127; Welch, *Black Litigants*, 168–176; Schweninger, *Appealing for Liberty*, 44.
64. Mose Germain, Court-Martial LL1734; Mose Germain CMSR.
65. Mose Germain, Court-Martial LL1734; Mose Germain CMSR.
66. John Mitchell CMSR; John Mitchell, Court-Martial Files NN2350, LL2365, and LL2690. Doddington, *Contesting Slave Masculinity in the American South*, 89–126. Thomas C. Buchanan, *Black Life on the Mississippi: Slaves, Free Blacks, and the Western Steamboat World* (Chapel Hill: University of North Carolina Press, 2004); Bolster, *Black Jacks*; Cecelski, *Waterman's Song*.
67. Mitchell CMSR; Mitchell, Court-Martial Files NN2350, LL2365, and LL2690.
68. Mitchell CMSR; Mitchell, Court-Martial Files NN2350, LL2365, and LL2690. *List of U.S. Soldiers Executed by the United States Military Authorities during the Late War*, 10–11. William L. Burton, *Melting Pot Soldiers: The Union's Ethnic Regiments*, 2nd ed. (New York: Fordham University Press, 1998), 130–131.
69. William Middleton, Court-Martial File LL2477; Robert Haymor, Court-Martial File LL2774; Ned Thompson, Court-Martial File LL2772; John Chase, Court-Martial File LL2772; Alan Ross, Court-Martial File MM2195.
70. See Appendix.
71. Eustis (aka Gustav) Glover, Court-Martial File LL2284; Eustis (aka Gustav) Glover CMSR.
72. Allen Guy CMSR; Allen Guy, Court-Martial File LL3188.

CHAPTER 5

1. Abraham Coombs (aka Combs), Court-Martial File MM3031; Abraham Coombs (aka Combs) CMSR.
2. Benet, *Treatise on Military Law and the Practice of the Courts-Martial*, 65, 126.
3. Berlin, Reidy, and Rowland, eds., *Black Military Experience*, 433–442; Glatthaar, *Forged in Battle*, 118–119; Samito, *Becoming American under Fire*, 84–86; Jonathan W. White, "Martial Law and the Expansion of Civil Liberties during the Civil War," in Ex Parte *Milligan Reconsidered: Race and Civil Liberties from the Lincoln Administration to the War on Terror*, ed. Stewart L. Winger and Jonathan W. White (Lawrence: University Press of Kansas, 2020), 52–72; Kate Masur, *Until Justice Be Done: America's First Civil Rights Movement from the Revolution to Reconstruction* (New York: W. W. Norton, 2021), 290–291; Jonathan W. White, ed., *To Address You as My Friend: African Americans' Letters to Abraham Lincoln* (Chapel Hill: University of North Carolina Press, 2021), 136–137.
4. Christian G. Samito, "The Intersection between Military Justice and Equal Rights: Mutinies, Courts-Martial, and Black Civil War Soldiers," *Civil War History* 53, no. 2 (June 2007), 174–177, 202; Samito, *Becoming American under Fire*, 79–87.
5. George Brown, Court-Martial File II821.
6. Joseph Rundall, Court-Martial File II821.

Notes to pages 111–116   251

7. Henry Hall, *Cayuga in the Field, a Record of the 19th N.Y. Volunteers, and the 3d New York Artillery* (Auburn, NY: n.p., 1873), 18, 30.
8. George Brown, Court-Martial File II821; Joseph Rundall, Court-Martial File II821; Stephen Briggs, Court-Martial File II821; James S. Betts, Court-Martial File II821; Allen Kilburn, Court-Martial File II821; John Coleman, Court-Martial File II821; Charles Rash, Court-Martial File II821; Theodore Goff, Court-Martial File II821; John Smagg, Court-Martial File II821.
9. John Murphy, Court-Martial File II650. George W. Bagwell, Court-Martial File LL1041; George W. Bagwell CMSR.
10. Charles Wilson CMSR; Charles Wilson, Court-Martial File NN3048. Henry Bennett, Court-Martial File II663. Thomas Stanley, Court-Martial File II870. See also Thomas F. Riley, Court-Martial File II566; George Holzman, Court-Martial File II641. Neely, *Lincoln and the Triumph of the Nation*, 167–183.
11. Jerome B. Ray CMSR; Jerome B. Ray, Court-Martial File MM1916.
12. Edwards, *People and Their Peace*, 121–131; Kennington, *In the Shadow of Dred Scott*, 7, 134–141; Welch, *Black Litigants*, 40–41, 46, 62–63. Schafer, *Slavery, the Civil Law, and the Supreme Court of Louisiana*, 224–234; Schafer, *Becoming Free, Remaining Free*, 45–58. For similar efforts among the enslaved of New England, see Jared Ross Hardesty, *Unfreedom: Slavery and Dependence in Eighteenth-Century Boston* (New York: New York University Press, 2016), 136–144. On contracts during slavery, see Kennington, *In the Shadow of Dred Scott*, 127; Welch, *Black Litigants*, 168–176; Schweninger, *Appealing for Liberty*, 44.
13. Although the extent of knowledge transmission of judicial strategies among the enslaved eludes the historical record, Kelly Kennington pointed out that evidence hints at a sharing of legal arguments and strategies within enslaved communities. The continuity between Black legal knowledge before, during, and after the war has been further supported by scholarship of the immediate aftermath of the war, which has shown that Black southerners demonstrated a nuanced understanding of the law. Kennington, *In the Shadow of Dred Scott*, 29. Edwards, *A Legal History of the Civil War and Reconstruction*, 129. Melissa Milewski, *Litigating across the Color Line: Civil Cases between Black and White Southerners from the End of Slavery to Civil Rights* (New York: Oxford University Press, 2018), 22, 69, 102, 174.
14. Paris White CMSR. Paris White, Court-Martial File NN516.
15. William Owens CMSR; Williams Owens, Court-Martial File MM3311. Margaret Humphreys, *Marrow of Tragedy: The Health Crisis of the American Civil War* (Baltimore: Johns Hopkins University Press, 2013), 26, 199; Humphreys, *Intensely Human*, xiii; Meier, *Nature's Civil War*, 127.
16. John Hope Franklin, ed., *The Diary of James T. Ayers: Civil War Recruiter* (1947; repr., Baton Rouge: Louisiana State University Press, 1999), 19–21.
17. Henry Tinder CMSR; Henry Tinder, Court-Martial File MM2990. See also the case of Private Silas Ellis, who told the court he had been persuaded to leave without offering further details. Silas Ellis, Court-Martial File MM3917.

18. Wesley Ball, Court-Martial File MM3031; Wesley Ball CMSR. Berlin, Reidy, and Rowland, eds., *Black Military Experience*, 435–436; White, *To Address You as My Friend*, 136–162.
19. See Appendix. *List of U.S. Soldiers Executed by the United States Military Authorities during the Late War.* Ramold, *Baring the Iron Hand*, 253, 328. In analyses of the military justice system, Robert Alotta and Steven Ramold found the official list of executed soldiers to be inaccurate. Ramold concluded that the true number of executed soldiers will remain elusive indefinitely because of shoddy record-keeping. Robert I. Alotta, *Civil War Justice: Union Army Executions under Lincoln* (Shippensburg, PA: White Mane, 1989), 202–209; Ramold, *Baring the Iron Hand*, 439n241.
20. Bell Irvin Wiley, *Life of Johnny Reb: The Common Soldier of the Confederacy* (1943; repr., Baton Rouge: Louisiana State University Press, 2008), 151–173; Wiley, *Life of Billy Yank*, 153–191; Robertson, *Soldiers Blue and Gray*, 81–101.
21. Isaac Little to Sallie Little, October 23, 1862, Isaac Little Papers, Filson Historical Society, Louisville, KY.
22. Lewis Morgan CMSR; Lewis Morgan Court-Martial file LL2139. William Gillum, CMSR; William Gillum, Court-Martial File LL2898.
23. Christopher Hager, *Word by Word: Emancipation and the Act of Writing* (Cambridge, MA: Harvard University Press, 2013), 20. This interpretation draws on analyses of stories among the enslaved by scholars, including Lawrence W. Levine, *Black Culture and Black Consciousness: Afro-American Folk Thought from Slavery to Freedom* (1977; repr., New York: Oxford University Press, 2007), 3–133; Walter Johnson, *Soul by Soul: Life inside the Antebellum Slave Market* (Cambridge, MA: Harvard University Press, 2000), 46–47, 59, 69–75, 126–130, 162–164, 170–171; Berry, *Price for Their Pound of Flesh*, 61–67, 92–93. For the role of narrative and stories within the law, see Edwards, *People and Their Peace*, 121–131; Kennington, *In the Shadow of Dred Scott*, 134–141; Welch, *Black Litigants*, 12, 27, 40–41, 46, 62–63. Black southerners also used their storytelling abilities in the North; they dissuaded white people of the prejudicial belief that all Black people lied by offering narratives as evidence of their truthfulness. Ann Fabian, *The Unvarnished Truth: Personal Narratives in Nineteenth-Century America* (Berkeley: University of California Press, 2000), 85, 99.
24. For the use of descriptive lists to convict accused Black deserters, see, for example: John W. Butler, Court-Martial File LL1406; John W. Butler CMSR; Henry C. Ramsey, Court-Martial Files MM3832, LL1406; and Thomas Pruden, Court-Martial File OO368.
25. James Pennington, *The Fugitive Blacksmith; or, Events in the History of James W. C. Pennington . . .* (London: Charles Gilpin, 1849), xii.
26. Philip S. Foner, ed., *The Life and Writings of Frederick Douglass*, 5 vols. (New York: International Publishers, 1950), 2:236.
27. Stephanie E. Smallwood, *Saltwater Slavery: A Middle Passage from Africa to American Diaspora* (Cambridge, MA: Harvard University Press, 2007), 98;

Saidiya Hartman, *Lose Your Mother: A Journey along the Atlantic Slave Route* (New York: Farrar, Straus and Giroux, 2008), 17.

28. Johnson, *Soul by Soul*, 58; Berry, *Price for Their Pound of Flesh*, 12–13, 41, 84.
29. Graham Russell Gao Hodges and Alan Edward Brown, eds., *"Pretends to Be Free": Runaway Slave Advertisements from Colonial and Revolutionary New York and New Jersey* (1994; repr. New York: Fordham University Press, 2019), xxv, xxxi–xxxii.
30. Rosenthal, *Accounting for Slavery*, 50–83, 86–98; Caitlin Rosenthal, "Numbers for the Innumerate: Everyday Arithmetic and Atlantic Capitalism," *Technology and Culture* 58, no. 2 (June 2017): 529–544.
31. Pennington, *Fugitive Blacksmith*, xii.
32. Stanley, *From Bondage to Contract*, 90–93.
33. For analyses of the law and of paper influencing the interpretation here, see Colin Dayan, *The Law Is a White Dog: How Legal Rituals Make and Unmake Persons* (Princeton, NJ: Princeton University Press, 2011), xi–xii, 4, 32; Suzanne Daly, "Belligerent Instruments: The Documentary Violence of 'Bleak House,'" *Studies in the Novel* 47, no. 1 (Spring 2015): 20–42; Martha S. Jones, *Birthright Citizens: A History of Race and Rights in Antebellum America* (New York: Cambridge University Press, 2018), 118, 126.
34. Anderson Phillips, Court-Martial File LL3213; Anderson Phillips CMSR. Dobak, *Freedom by the Sword*, 278–280; Christopher M. Rein, *Alabamians in Blue: Freedmen, Unionists, and the Civil War in the Cotton State* (Baton Rouge: Louisiana State University Press, 2019), 170–172.
35. Nelson Wright CMSR; Nelson Wright, Court-Martial File NN2147. Former Mississippi laborer Private Henry Sykes of the First Tennessee Infantry (African Descent) (later the Fifty-Ninth USCI) echoed Wright, remarking in his defense that he left his regiment July 3, 1863, and joined another regiment to be with his brother. Henry Sykes CMSR; Henry Sykes, Court-Martial File LL1870.
36. Stephen Jones CMSR; Stephen Jones, Court-Martial File MM3339. On the enslavement of USCT soldiers, see Colby, *Unholy Traffic*, 160–162, 171–173, 193, 209–211.
37. Ira Berlin, Thavolia Glymph, Steven F. Miller, Joseph P. Reidy, Leslie S. Rowland, and Julie Saville, eds., *Freedom: A Documentary History of Emancipation, 1861–1867, Series 1,* Volume 3: *The Wartime Genesis of Free Labor: The Lower South* (New York: Cambridge University Press, 1990), 219, 239.
38. Ibid., 414, 419.
39. Nathaniel P. Banks, *Emancipated Labor in Louisiana* (n.p., 1864), 7, 24–25. Gerteis, *From Contraband to Freedman*, 38, 59, 72–79, 122–124, 154; Foner, *Reconstruction*, 55–56; Sproat, "Blueprint for Radical Reconstruction," 29–30; Rose, *Rehearsal for Reconstruction*, 191; Saville, *Work of Reconstruction*, 12; Luskey, *Men Is Cheap*, 48–55, 67, 163–165.
40. Berlin, Reidy, and Rowland, eds., *Black Military Experience*, 388, 402.
41. Eli Graham, Court-Martial File NN2174; Eli Graham CMSR. For a similar argument, see Hardin Perkins, Court-Martial File NN2174; Hardin Perkins CMSR.

42. Alexander Gardner CMSR.
43. Gardner CMSR. Alexander Gardner, Court-Martial File NN2706. Offering a similar defense, Black Philadelphian Private James Harris, said, "I was intoxicated when I was enlisted and was taken advantage of while *Intoxicated* I had no Intentions of Deserting." James Harris, Court-Martial File NN2604.
44. Lonn, *Desertion during the Civil War*, 227. William Seraile, *New York's Black Regiments during the Civil War* (New York: Routledge, 2001), 35–40. *Harper's Weekly*, January 23, 1864.
45. Carol Wilson, *Freedom at Risk: The Kidnapping of Free Blacks in America, 1780–1865* (Lexington: University Press of Kentucky, 1994), 6. Ira Berlin, Introduction to Solomon Northup, *Twelve Years a Slave: Narrative of Solomon Northup* (1853; repr., New York: Penguin, 2013), xxxiv. Jonathan Daniel Wells, *Blind No More: African American Resistance, Free-Soil Politics, and the Coming of the Civil War* (Athens: University of Georgia Press, 2019), 71–73, 94–95.
46. Welch, *Black Litigants*, 63.
47. Alexander Gardner, Court-Martial File NN2706.
48. Andrew Thompson CMSR; Thompson, Court-Martial File LL2900.
49. Solomon Fuquay CMSR; Solomon Fuquay, Court-Martial Files MM3810 and MM1916.
50. Fuquay CMSR; Fuquay, Court-Martial Files MM3810 and MM1916. Rein, *Alabamians in Blue*, 138–139. For other soldiers who constructed defenses by pointing to their impressment or for whom the question of coercion during enlistment arose, see Emmanuel Blackworth, Court-Martial File LL2457; Daniel Fuquay, Court-Martial Files MM3810, MM1916; Marion Gregory, Court-Martial File OO1489.
51. Edmond Johnson CMSR. McPherson, *Battle Cry of Freedom*, 825; Dobak, *Freedom by the Sword*, 278–280; Rein, *Alabamians in Blue*, 170–172.
52. Letter in Johnson CMSR.
53. Johnson CMSR; Edmond Johnson, Court-Martial File OO1489. For other prisoners of war charged with desertion and pointing to their captivity to win their cases, see Nathan Potter, Court-Martial File MM3191; Albert McGee, Court-Martial File OO1489; Spencer Simpson, Court-Martial File OO1489.
54. George Tate, September 9, 1865, 1865 Diary, George Tate Papers, Huntington Library, San Marino.

CHAPTER 6

1. Charles Baltimore [Tenth USCHA] CMSR. The regiment went through several redesignations, including the Tenth USCHA and finally the Eleventh USCHA (new), but because Baltimore was tried when the regiment was designated the Seventh USCHA, Seventh USCHA is used in the text. Board of Artillery Officers, *Instruction for Field Artillery* (Philadelphia: J. B. Lippincott, 1861), 4.

2. Charles Baltimore, Court-Martial Files, folder 1, LL2998 and NN3471. J. Richard Sherikel, Bethlyn McCloskey, and Betsy Swanson, "Nomination Form: Fort Livingston," March 28, 1974, National Register of Historic Places Inventory, National Park Service, 3. Dry Tortugas Record Book, line 1215. Edwin C. Bearss, "Historical Structure Report, Historical Data Section, Fort Jefferson: 1846–1898," (Monroe County, FL: National Monument Printing, 1983), 3–10, 44–45, 181–194, 231; Thomas Reid, *America's Fortress: A History of Fort Jefferson, Dry Tortugas, Florida* (Gainesville: University Press of Florida, 2006), 50–51, 68, 75.
3. Warner, *Generals in Blue*, 67–68. Grant, *Personal Memoirs of Ulysses S. Grant*, 745–776.
4. Baltimore's letter is marked 1865, but he misdated the letter. The special order commanding his release was sent on March 29, 1865, and the prison record book states that he left April 8, 1865. Baltimore, CMSR. Dry Tortugas Record Book, line 1215.
5. Ramold, *Baring the Iron Hand*, 253, 333, 344–383.
6. Angela M. Zombek, *Penitentiaries, Punishment, and Military Prisons* (Kent, OH: Kent State University Press, 2018), 1–21. Coffman, *Old Army*, 376–377; Bray, *Court-Martial*, xiii–xiv; Sheehan-Dean, *Calculus of Violence*, 242–245.
7. Joshua Kastenberg, "A Sesquicentennial Historic Analysis of *Dynes v. Hoover* and the Supreme Court's Bow to Military Necessity: From Its Relationship to *Dred Scott v. Sandford* to Its Contemporary Influence," *University of Memphis Law Review* 39, no. 3 (Spring 2009): 617–624; Zombek, *Penitentiaries, Punishment, and Military Prisons*, 17.
8. OR, ser. 2, vol. 3, 621–631.
9. Zombek, *Penitentiaries, Punishment, and Military Prisons*, 80–100.
10. Isaac Little to Sallie Little, December 7, 1862, Isaac Little Papers, Filson Historical Society, Louisville, KY. Gideon R. Viars to sister, May 19, 1864, Viars Family Papers, Filson Historical Society, Louisville, KY. Robertson, *Soldiers Blue and Gray*, 135. Lonnie R. Speer, *Portals to Hell: Military Prisons of the Civil War* (Mechanicsburg, PA: Stackpole, 1997), 9–10. Ramold, *Baring the Iron Hand*, 30–39, 333; Stansfield, "History of the Judge Advocate General's Department United States Army," 219–237. On sentences, see also Benjamin Lincoln to Isadora Frances Whitman, March 26, 1863, box 52, Benjamin C. Lincoln Papers, Clements Library, University of Michigan, Ann Arbor.
11. Basler, ed., *Collected Works of Abraham Lincoln*, 8:300.
12. See Appendix.
13. For other soldiers sentenced to serve in the regimental guardhouse, see William Lewis, Court-Martial Files OO84 and NN2350; Thomas Ringold, Court-Martial Files LL2365 and LL2690; George Marshall, Court-Martial File MM1829.
14. Spencer Watson, Court-Martial File NN372; Spencer Watson CMSR. Lewis Turk, Court-Martial File MM1615; Lewis Turk CMSR. Dry Tortugas Record Book, lines 308, 315–316, 350, 377, 386, 388, 392. Henry Williams, Court-Martial File NN643; John Lomax, Court-Martial File NN643; Henry Williams CMSR;

John Lomax CMSR; Levi Leboo, Court-Martial NN1259; Levi Leboo CMSR; Alfred Washington, Court-Martial File NN1667; Alfred Washington CMSR; Richard Smith, Court-Martial File LL1256; Richard Smith CMSR; William Lucas, Court-Martial File NN2457; William Lucas CMSR; Charles Wilson, Court-Martial File NN3048; Charles Wilson CMSR; Eustis (aka Gustav) Glover, Court-Martial File LL2284; Eustis (aka Gustav) Glover CMSR; James Palmer, Court-Martial File NN2158; James Palmer CMSR; John Gray, Court-Martial File MM2982; John Gray CMSR; Charles Smartboy, Court-Martial File MM2982; Charles Smartboy CMSR; John Bordley, Court-Martial File MM3140; John Bordley CMSR.

15. Theodore Christie, Court-Martial File LL1395; Theodore Christie CMSR; George W. Bagwell, Court-Martial Files NN1041 and LL1256; George Bagwell CMSR; Ephraim Williams, Court-Martial File LL1623; Ephraim Williams CMSR; Robert Carr, Court-Martial Files NN2828 and NN2785; Robert Carr CMSR; Charles McLain (aka McLann), Court-Martial File LL2676; Charles McLain (aka McLann) CMSR.

16. William Johnson (aka Johnston), Court-Martial File LL2983; William Johnson (aka Johnston) CMSR; James Harris, Court-Martial File NN2604; James Harris CMSR; Thomas Clark, Court-Martial Files LL2621 and LL2616; Thomas Clark CMSR; Ned Wilson, Court-Martial File MM2799; Ned Wilson CMSR.

17. Richard Merrick, Court-Martial File MM3447; Richard Merrick CMSR; Henry Brown, Court-Martial File MM3226; Henry Brown CMSR; George Washington, Court-Martial File MM3031; George Washington CMSR.

18. Edward Allen, Court-Martial Files NN3470 and NN3007; Edward Allen CMSR; David Washington, Court-Martial Files LL2783 and NN2705; David Washington CMSR; Samuel Jeffers, Court-Martial Files LL2783 and NN–2705; Samuel Jeffers CMSR; Richard Johnson (aka Johnston), Court-Martial File NN1887; Richard Johnson (aka Johnston) CMSR; Jacob Ballard, Court-Martial File MM2551; Jacob Ballard CMSR; James Clark, Court-Martial File OO1785; James Clark CMSR; Lande, "Mutiny in the Civil War," 54–65, 77.

19. Timothy Coggins, Court-Martial File NN3477; Timothy Coggins CMSR; Charles Brown, Court-Martial File LL2699; Charles Brown CMSR; David Prince, Court-Martial File LL2856; David Prince CMSR; Monroe (aka Mauser) Pennington, Court-Martial File LL2601; Monroe (aka Mauser) Pennington CMSR.

20. John Henry, Court-Martial Files MM2944 and MM2912; John Henry CMSR; Tero Ashmo, Court-Martial File MM2810; Tero Ashmo CMSR; William Levir (aka Leva), Court-Martial Files NN2638 and NN2611; William Levir (aka Leva) CMSR; William (aka Jacob) Stafford (aka Fillmore), Court-Martial File MM1843; William (aka Jacob) Stafford (aka Fillmore) CMSR. John Nelson, Court-Martial File NN3806; John Nelson CMSR; Stephen Duke, Court-Martial File MM3747; Stephen Duke CMSR.

21. McPherson, *Battle Cry of Freedom*, 791–793, 802–803; William Best Hesseltine, *Civil War Prisons: A Study in War Psychology* (Columbus: Ohio State University Press, 1998), 2; Ramold, *Baring the Iron Hand*, 349–351.
22. Basler, ed., *Collected Works of Abraham Lincoln*, 6:357.
23. Benet, *Treatise on Military Law and the Practice of the Courts-Martial*, 143–144; Ramold, *Baring the Iron Hand*, 322–328. Leonard, *Lincoln's Forgotten Ally*, 190.
24. Holt quoted in Burlingame, *Abraham Lincoln*, 2:493. Bell Irvin Wiley, "Billy Yank and Abraham Lincoln," *Abraham Lincoln Quarterly* 6 (March 1950): 106; Zombek, *Penitentiaries, Punishment, and Military Prisons*, 123.
25. White, *To Address You as My Friend*, 9. Donald, *Lincoln*, 311; Benjamin Quarles, *Lincoln and the Negro* (1962; repr., New York: De Capo, 1990), 182; David Silkenat and John Barr, " 'Serving the Lord and Abe Lincoln's Spirit': Lincoln and Memory in the WPA Narratives," *Lincoln Herald* 115 (2013): 75–97.
26. Angelina E. G. Weld, "Speech of Angelina E. G. Weld," in *History of Pennsylvania Hall, Which Was Destroyed by a Mob, on the 17th of May, 1838* (Philadelphia: Merrihew and Gunn, 1838), 126. Susan Zaeske, *Signatures of Citizenship: Petitioning, Antislavery, and Women's Political Identity* (Chapel Hill: University of North Carolina Press, 2003). For petition's origins, see Edmund S. Morgan, *Inventing the People: The Rise of Popular Sovereignty in England and America* (New York: W. W. Norton, 1989), 223–239.
27. Benjamin Quarles, *Black Abolitionists* (New York: Oxford University Press, 1969), 92; Nicholas P. Wood "A 'Class of Citizens': The Earliest Black Petitioners to Congress and Their Quaker Allies," *William and Mary Quarterly* 74, no. 1 (January 2017): 109–144; Sarah L. H. Gronningsater, "Practicing Formal Politics without the Vote: Black New Yorkers in the Aftermath of 1821," in *Revolutions and Reconstructions: Black Politics in the Long Nineteenth Century*, ed. Van Gosse and David Waldstreicher (Philadelphia: University of Pennsylvania Press, 2020), 116–138; Masur, *Until Justice Be Done*, 81–118; White, *To Address You as My Friend*, 5.
28. Alfred J. Bloor to Charles Sumner, June 3, 1863, Abraham Lincoln Papers, Library of Congress. Basler, ed., *Collected Works of Abraham Lincoln*, 6:244, 248. A portion of the letter is quoted in Basler, ed., *Collected Works of Abraham Lincoln*, 6:248n1. Basler also notes that no record of the soldiers exists after Lincoln stayed the execution. No further record of them has been located; they do not appear in the official list of executed soldiers. *List of U.S. Soldiers Executed by the United States Military Authorities during the Late War*, 6–7. Making a similar plea, Private William J. Nelson, Twenty-Seventh USCI, argued that he had been cheated out of his bounty, implying that his promised pay had not been delivered. Berlin, Reidy, and Rowland, eds., *Black Military Experience*, 112.
29. Basler, ed., *Collected Works of Abraham Lincoln*, 6:280; 400; 475, 488. Ibid., 6:472.
30. Ibid., 6:266–267.

31. Berlin, Reidy, and Rowland, eds., *Black Military Experience*, 435–456, 477; White, *To Address You as My Friend*, 136–162.
32. Isaiah Price, Court-Martial File NN3122; Isaiah Price CMSR.
33. White, *To Address You as My Friend*, 155–156. Price CMSR. Dry Tortugas Record Book, line 1334.
34. Jonathan Lande, "'Prisoners with Undaunted Patriotism': Incarcerated Black Soldiers and Battles of Citizenship in Military Prisons during the Civil War," *Civil War History* 68, no. 3 (September 2022): 240–242. For broader lessons in how to engage the state informing the interpretation here, see Gregory P. Downs, *Declarations of Dependence: The Long Reconstruction of Popular Politics in the South, 1861–1908* (Chapel Hill: University of North Carolina Press, 2011), 1–2, 45.
35. For the developing relationship between Black southerners and the state, see Foner, "Rights and the Constitution in Black Life during the Civil War and Reconstruction," 864–885; Foner, *Reconstruction*, 8–10; Samito, *Becoming American under Fire*, 170–171; Manning, *Troubled Refuge*, 8–26, 205–208; Mathisen, *Loyal Republic*, 90; Foner, *Second Founding*, 16; Dale Kretz, *Administering Freedom: The State of Emancipation after the Freedmen's Bureau* (Chapel Hill: University of North Carolina Press, 2022), 2–11.
36. The interpretation of the men's strategy draws on the prewar legal strategy deployed by enslaved men and women who, as historian Laura Edwards argued, established their reputations within communities to participate in southern courtrooms. Edwards, *People and Their Peace*, 112–113. See also Kennington, *In the Shadow of Dred Scott*, 135; Welch, *Black Litigants*, 65. Melissa Milewski showed that these practices continued during and after Reconstruction; the wartime legal battles therefore linked pre- and postwar activism. Milewski, *Litigating across the Color Line*, 22, 38–39, 69, 102, 174.
37. John Handy, Court-Martial File LL2201; John Handy CMSR. Fred H. Harrington, *Fighting Politician: Major General N. P. Banks* (Philadelphia: University of Pennsylvania Press, 1948), 47; Hollandsworth, *Louisiana Native Guards*, 43–45.
38. John Handy CMSR. Rose, *Rehearsal for Reconstruction*, 22–31, 101; Fredrickson, *Black Image in the White Mind*, 94, 102–107; Escott, *"What Shall We Do with the Negro?,"* 29–60; Kendi, *Stamped from the Beginning*, 168.
39. John Johnson CMSR; John Johnson, Court-Martial File LL1632; Dry Tortugas Record Book, line 466; White, *To Address You as My Friend*, 140–142.
40. Nettie Mudd, ed., *The Life of Dr. Samuel A. Mudd* (New York: Neale Publishing, 1906), 115; Evan A. Kutzler, *Living by Inches: The Smells, Sounds, Tastes, and Feeling of Captivity in Civil War Prisons* (Chapel Hill: University of North Carolina Press, 2019), 45, 75–82; Reid, *America's Fortress*, 57.
41. John Johnson CMSR; John Johnson, Court-Martial File LL1632; Dry Tortugas Record Book, line 466; White, *To Address You as My Friend*, 140–142.

Notes to pages 146–147

42. David Washington CMSR. Glatthaar, *Forged in Battle*, 109–117, 180, 222–223. David Washington, Court-Martial File LL2378. Benet, *Treatise on Military Law and the Practice of the Courts-Martial*, 120–121.
43. Berlin, Reidy, and Rowland, eds., *Black Military Experience*, 455; White, *To Address You as My Friend*, 152. For similar arguments made by soldiers convicted of mutiny, see Sergeant William Mayo's case: Mayo D. Williams, Court-Martial File NN3832; Berlin, Reidy, and Rowland, eds., *Black Military Experience*, 453–454; William Mayo CMSR; Dry Tortugas Record Book, line 1212. See also the cases of and letter from sixteen soldiers of the Forty-Ninth USCI: Street Humphrey, Washington Fountaine (aka Fontine), Giles Simms (aka Sims), Frank Watson, Thomas Johnson, Evans (Eavens) County, Albert (aka Alfred) Rodgers, James Martin, Samuel Smith, Peter Anderson, Harrison Fields, Price Warfield, Adam Qualls, Willis Henry, Albert Francis, Jefferson Cotterall, William Johnson, George Owens, Hector Marbly, and Charles Bill, Courts-Martial Files NN2350, LL2365, and LL2690; Street Humphrey CMSR; Washington Fountaine (aka Fontine) CMSR; Giles Simms (aka Sims) CMSR; Frank Watson CMSR; Thomas Johnson CMSR; Evans (Eavens) County CMSR; Albert (aka Alfred) Rodgers CMSR; James Martin CMSR; Samuel Smith CMSR; Peter Anderson CMSR; Harrison Fields CMSR; Price Warfield CMSR; Adam Qualls CMSR; Willis Henry CMSR; Albert Francis CMSR; William Johnson CMSR; George Owens CMSR; Hector Marbly CMSR; Charles Bill CMSR; Berlin, Reidy, and Rowland, eds., *Black Military Experience*, 459–460.
44. This interpretation stems from Garrett Felber's analysis of courtroom battles waged by members of the Nation of Islam who turned questions of Black criminality in courtrooms into discussions of police brutality. Garrett Felber, *Those Who Know Don't Say: The Nation of Islam, the Black Freedom Movement, and the Carceral State* (Chapel Hill: University of North Carolina Press, 2020), 85–119. For a similar argument, see John Miller's letter to the Philadelphia governor Andrew Curtain. John Miller CMSR; Dry Tortugas Record Book, line 1706; Berlin, Reidy, and Rowland, eds., *Black Military Experience*, 473–474.
45. For other appeals to Lincoln by Black soldiers convicted of mutiny based on character, see the cases of Private Franklin Smith and Sergeant Adam Laws. Frank Smith, Court-Martial File LL2394; Franklin Smith CMSR; White, *To Address You as My Friend*, 142–144, 150–151.
46. David Washington CMSR. Berlin, Reidy, and Rowland, eds., *Black Military Experience*, 455. For the relationship between the Republican campaign to sustain the war effort and soldiers' support for the Republican-led war, see Gienapp, ed., *Civil War and Reconstruction*, 275–276; White, *Emancipation, the Union Army, and the Reelection of Abraham Lincoln*, 55, 78–81, 91–96; John H. Matsui, *The First Republican Army: The Army of Virginia and the Radicalization of the Civil War* (Charlottesville: University of Virginia Press, 2016), 92–111; Fry, *Republic in*

the Ranks, 80–98, 155. Burlingame, *Abraham Lincoln*, 2:492–495; Ruckman and Kincaid, "Inside Lincoln's Clemency Decision Making," 84–99. OR, ser. 2, vol. 4, 57; OR, ser. 2, vol. 4, 673; OR, ser. 2, vol. 5, 75–76; OR, ser. 2, vol. 5, 564–565; Louis S. Gerteis, *Civil War St. Louis* (Lawrence: University Press of Kansas, 2001), 171, 187–195.

47. For Black southerners' reaction to violence during Reconstruction generally, see Foner, "Rights and the Constitution in Black Life during the Civil War and Reconstruction," 881; Williams, *They Left Great Marks on Me*, 6–7, 19–25.

48. Chandra Manning, *What This Cruel War Was Over: Soldiers, Slavery, and the Civil War* (New York: Knopf, 2007), 21–22, 216–229; Foner, *Second Founding*, 42, 185; Matsui, *First Republican Army*, 3, 92; Varon, *Armies of Deliverance*, 200–201, 235–236, 298; Fry, *Republic in the Ranks*, 3, 46–98.

49. Fredrickson, *Black Image in the White Mind*, 46. Foner, *Free Soil, Free Labor, Free Men*, 296; Richardson, *Greatest Nation of the Earth*, 221–227, 229–234; Steven Joseph Ross, "Freed Soil, Freed Labor, Freed Men: John Eaton and the Davis Bend Experiment," *Journal of Southern History* 44 (May 1978): 213–232; Stanley, *From Bondage to Contract*, 35–36.

50. Hunter, *Bound in Wedlock*, 134–135, 138, 153; Foner, *Second Founding*, 44, 182; Stephen M. Frank, *Life with Father: Parenthood and Masculinity in the Nineteenth-Century American North* (Baltimore: Johns Hopkins University Press, 1998), 62–64, 141–144. Hunter, *Bound in Wedlock*, 26–84; Reidy, *Illusions of Emancipation*, 229; Hilde, *Slavery, Fatherhood, and Paternal Duty in African American Communities over the Long Nineteenth Century*, 12, 69, 76–87; Fields-Black, *Combee*, 447–449, 473–474.

51. Roosa is listed as "Rosa" in a service record and court-martial record, but "Roosa" is used in the text because that was how he signed his letter to Lincoln. Samuel Roosa CMSR (which says, "See Rosa, Samuel"); Jack Morris CMSR. Samuel Rosa, Court-Martial Files NN3056 and LL2816. Jack Morris, Court-Martial File LL3106. Berlin, Reidy, and Rowland, eds., *Black Military Experience*, 477.

52. "General Ullman on the Employment of Negro Troops" from New Orleans on June 10, 1863, General Orders No. 7, newspaper clipping from John O. Sargent Papers, Massachusetts Historical Society, Boston. Dobak, *Freedom by the Sword*, 113.

53. Jack Morris CMSR; Dry Tortugas Record Book, line 1231.

54. Isham Barr, Court-Martial Files MM2606 and MM3754; Isham Barr [Eighty-eighth USCI] CMSR.

55. Isham Barr [Eighty-Eighth USCI] CMSR. Hunter, *Bound in Wedlock*, 26–84; Hilde, *Slavery, Fatherhood, and Paternal Duty in African American Communities over the Long Nineteenth Century*, 12, 69, 76–87; Shaffer, *After the Glory*, 22. Isham Barr, Court-Martial Files MM2606 and MM3754; Isham Barr [Eighty-Eighth USCI] CMSR. Isham Barr [Third USCHA] CMSR. Barr, Court-Martial Files MM2606 and MM3754.

56. Stephen V. Ash, *A Massacre in Memphis: The Race Riot That Shook the Nation One Year after the Civil War* (New York: Hill & Wang, 2013), 1; Downs, *After Appomattox*, 5–6, 32, 40–97, 247–249. Barr [Third USCHA] CMSR; Barr [Eighty-Eighth USCI] CMSR. Barr, Courts-Martial Files MM2606 and MM3754. Hunter, *Bound in Wedlock*, 123–138. For a similar argument by a Black inmate of Fort Jefferson convicted of mutiny, among other charges, see John Higgins's case in Berlin, Reidy, and Rowland, eds., *Black Military Experience*, 475–476; John Higgins CMSR; Dry Tortugas Record Book, line 1686.

57. Elizabeth R. Varon, *Appomattox: Victory, Defeat, and Freedom at the End of the Civil War* (New York: Oxford University Press, 2014), 94–100, 139; Sheehan-Dean, *Calculus of Violence*, 166–179, 343.

58. Barr [Third USCHA] CMSR.

59. Ash, *Massacre in Memphis*, 15–16; Hannah Rosen, *Terror in the Heart of Freedom: Citizenship, Sexual Violence, and the Meaning of Race in the Postemancipation South* (Chapel Hill: University of North Carolina Press, 2009), 3–83, 274n45. Barr [Third USCHA] CMSR. For a similar argument in South Carolina, see James Clark's response to incarceration in Lande, "Mutiny in the Civil War," 54–65, 77.

60. James Gilbert Ryan, "The Memphis Riots of 1866: Terror in a Black Community during Reconstruction," *Journal of Negro History* 62 (July 1977): 248–249; Kevin R. Hardwick, "'Your Old Father Abe Lincoln Is Dead and Damned': Black Soldiers and the Memphis Race Riot of 1866," *Journal of Social History* 27 (Autumn 1993): 109–128; Rosen, *Terror in the Heart of Freedom*, 23–83.

61. Eric Foner, "Rights and the Constitution in Black Life during the Civil War and Reconstruction," 880; Edwards, *Legal History of the Civil War and Reconstruction*, 95; Downs, *After Appomattox*, 40–67; Milewski, *Litigating across the Color Line*, 38–39. For Black activists' influence on the Fourteenth Amendment, see Jones, *Birthright Citizens*, 1–12; Foner, *Second Founding*, 8–11; Bonner, *Remaking the Republic*, 6–8; Masur, *Until Justice Be Done*, xvi–xx.

CONCLUSION

1. Joseph Williams CMSR. Robert E. Lester, ed., *Records of U.S. Colored Troops: Part 1: Letters Related to Recruitment of African Americans, 1863–1865* (Bethesda, MD: UPA Collection from LexisNexis, 2005), roll 3.

2. Cowden, *Brief Sketch of the Organization and Services of the Fifty-Ninth Regiment of the United States Colored Infantry and Biographical Sketches*, 44.

3. Engs and Brooks, eds., *Their Patriotic Duty*, 158. Patriarch quoted on ibid., 153. Cowden, *Brief Sketch of the Organization and Services of the Fifty-Ninth Regiment of the United States Colored Infantry and Biographical Sketches*, 46–47; Dobak, *Freedom by the Sword*, 21.

4. Colonel quoted in Dobak, *Freedom by the Sword*, 209–213.
5. Thomas E. Parson, *Work for Giants: The Campaign and Battle of Tupelo/Harrisburg, Mississippi, June–July 1864* (Kent, OH: Kent State University Press, 2014), 2, 23–25, 55. Colby, *Unholy Traffic*, 160–162.
6. Cowden, *Brief Sketch of the Organization and Services of the Fifty-Ninth Regiment of the United States Colored Infantry and Biographical Sketches*, 38–40.
7. Samuel Davis CMSR; Samuel Davis, Court-Martial File LL1260.
8. Engs and Brooks, eds., *Their Patriotic Duty*, 158.
9. Cowden, *Brief Sketch of the Organization and Services of the Fifty-Ninth Regiment of the United States Colored Infantry and Biographical Sketches*, 90.
10. Engs and Brooks, eds., *Their Patriotic Duty*, 161. Davis CMSR; Davis, Court-Martial File LL1260.
11. Downs, *Sick from Freedom*, 4; Humphreys, *Intensely Human*, xiii.
12. Cowden, *Brief Sketch of the Organization and Services of the Fifty-Ninth Regiment of the United States Colored Infantry and Biographical Sketches*, 48. Fett, *Working Cures*, 30–33.
13. Dobak, *Freedom by the Sword*, 474. Lester, ed., *Records of U.S. Colored Troops*, roll 3.
14. Department of the Interior, Bureau of Pensions, *Laws of the United States Governing the Granting of Army and Navy Pensions Together with Regulations Relating Thereto* (Washington, DC: Government Printing Office, 1916), 101.
15. Lester, ed., *Records of U.S. Colored Troops*, roll 3. Alleged deserter Hector Fields and his attorney made a similar argument in 1890. Fields-Black, *Combee*, 502–503.
16. Shaffer, *After the Glory*, 122–128; Regosin and Shaffer, *Voices of Emancipation*, 3–4; Fields-Black, *Combee*, 495–518.
17. Hillard Johnson CMSR. Lester, ed., *Records of U.S. Colored Troops*, roll 3.
18. Du Bois, *Black Reconstruction*, 30.
19. Kirk Savage, *Standing Soldiers: Race, War, and Monument in Nineteenth-Century America* (Princeton, NJ: Princeton University Press, 1997), 52–128; Blight, *Race and Reunion*, 18, 92–95, 103–104, 132–135, 168–170, 193–197, 301; Shaffer, *After the Glory*, 169–188; Gannon, *Won Cause*, 58, 72, 76, 100, 112, 118, 125, 166, 174, 193; William Blair, *Cities of the Dead: Contesting the Memory of the Civil War in the South, 1865–1914* (Chapel Hill: University of North Carolina Press, 2004), 23–76; Kathleen Ann Clark, *Defining Moments: African American Commemoration and Political Culture in the South, 1863–1913* (Chapel Hill: University of North Carolina Press, 2005), 13–55; Leslie A. Schwalm, *Emancipation's Diaspora: Race and Reconstruction in the Upper Midwest* (Chapel Hill: University of North Carolina Press, 2009), 219–264; Janney, *Remembering the Civil War*, 4, 7, 75, 87–91, 105–117, 211–227, 342; Robert J. Cook, *Civil War Memories: Contesting the Past in the United States since 1865* (Baltimore: Johns Hopkins University Press, 2017), 77–85; John A. Casey Jr., *New Men: Reconstructing the Image of the Veteran in Late-Nineteenth Century American Literature and Culture* (New York: Fordham University Press, 2015), 13–62.

20. Richard Wright, *Black Boy: A Record of Childhood and Youth* (Stockholm: A/B Ljus Förlag, 1946), 123. Hazel Rowley, *Richard Wright: The Life and Times* (New York: Henry Holt, 2001), 3–4.
21. Paul Laurence Dunbar, *Majors and Minors: Poems* (Toledo, OH: Hadley and Hadley, 1895), 39. Henrietta Cordelia Ray, *Poems* (New York: Grafton Press, 1910), 88. "Prof. Washington's Address" [at Shaw Memorial Unveiling], newspaper clipping in Norwood Penrose Howell Scrapbook, vol. 3, Norwood Penrose Howell Papers, Massachusetts Historical Society, Boston. Booker T. Washington, N. B. Wood, and Fannie Barrier Williams, *A New Negro for a New Century* (Chicago: American Publishing House, 1900), 260–286.
22. Herbert Aptheker, ed., *The Correspondence of W. E. B. Du Bois*, 3 vols. (Amherst: University of Massachusetts Press, 1973), 3:126, 128. For his historical assessment, see Du Bois, *Black Reconstruction in America*, esp. 104, 110.
23. Patricia G. Davis, *Laying Claim: African American Cultural Memory and Southern Identity* (Tuscaloosa: University of Alabama Press, 2016), 34.
24. "Whose Heritage? Public Symbols of the Confederacy," Southern Poverty Law Center, February 1, 2019, https://www.splcenter.org/20190201/whose-heritage-public-symbols-confederacy#executive-summary.
25. Barack Obama, "Remarks by the President at the Dedication of the National Museum of African American History and Culture," September 24, 2016, https://obamawhitehouse.archives.gov/the-press-office/2016/09/24/remarks-president-dedication-national-museum-african-american-history.
26. For recent and exceptional contributions discussing Black soldiers' heroism, see Rhea, *Black Freedom Fighter*, esp. 56–68; R. Isabela Morales, *Happy Dreams of Liberty: An American Family in Slavery and Freedom* (New York: Oxford University Press, 2022), 121–125; Fields-Black, *Combee*, esp. 272, 345, 397, 418; Sinha, *Rise and Fall of the Second American Republic*, esp. 15–22.

Bibliography

MANUSCRIPT COLLECTIONS

Beinecke Library, Yale University, New Haven, CT
    Walter O. Evans Collection of Frederick Douglass and Douglass Family Papers
Boston Atheneum, Boston, MA
    Broadsides Collection
William L. Clements Library, University of Michigan, Ann Arbor, MI
    African American History Collection
    Edward F. Cahill Collection
    Civil War Collection
    Henry Clinton Papers
    John S. Corliss Papers
    District of Carrollton (LA) Letters
    Levi B. Downs Papers
    William Elgin Journal
    Thomas Hall Diary
    Charles Otto Henthorn Papers
    Samuel Ferguson Jayne Papers
    Langstroth Family Papers
    Benjamin C. Lincoln Papers
    Henry Grimes Marshall Papers
    Charles M. Maxim Papers
    Charlie and John Moore Papers
    United Sons of Salem Benevolent Society Minute Book
Connecticut Historical Society, Hartford, CT
    African American Collection
    Orra B. Bailey Letters
    Charles Barbour Papers
    Henry E. Blakeslee Letters

Henry Harrison Brown Letters
William F. Buckingham Letters
Civil War Collection
Joseph Orin Cross Letters
Frederick Douglass Letters
James William Eldridge Diary
Ralph Waldo Emerson Letters
Reese B. Gwillim Diary
William Robert Harmount Papers
Lewis Hazzard Letters
Nathanial N. Hubbard Letters
William L. Norton Letters
Primus Family Papers
Joseph Alfred Scoville Letters
William Henry Simons Letters
Tracy Collection
Gideon Welles Letterbooks

Filson Historical Society, Louisville, KY
Theodore Allen Diaries
Stephen Gano Burbridge Papers
Bush Family Papers
Thomas Brooks Fairleigh Diary
Mary Cochran Diary
Reuben Thomas Durrett Papers
Eli Huston Brown Papers
Henry S. Manning Papers
Channing Richards Papers
Viars Family Papers
Winn-Cook Papers

Gilder Lehrman Collection, New York, NY
William A. Allison Letters
Nathaniel Prentiss Banks Letters
John A. Bogert Letters
Broadsides Collection
Stephen G. Burbridge Letters
Civil War Posters, 1861–1865
Charles M. Coit Letters
Christian Fleetwood Letters
Francis H. Fletcher Letters
Ulysses S. Grant Letters
Edward W. Hincks Letters
William H. Holly Letters

David Hunter Letters
Witter H. Johnston Letters
Robert M. King Letters
Abraham Lincoln Letters
Joseph M. Maitland Letters
Morris N. Oviatt Diary
John Owen Letters
Heber Painter Letters
William A. Smith Letters
Samuel Watson Van Nuys Papers
William P. Woodlin Diary

John Hay Library, Brown University, Providence, RI
    Maury A. Bromsen Collection of Confederate Etchings

Historical Society of Pennsylvania, Philadelphia, PA
    Abraham Barker Collection
    Butler Family Papers
    McAllister Small Collection

Houghton Library, Harvard University, Cambridge, MA
    Thomas Wentworth Higginson Papers

Huntington Library, San Marino, CA
    Lewis N. T. Allen Papers
    Charles Atkin Letters
    John B. Burrud Papers
    George W. Buswell Papers
    James Monro Forbes Papers
    Levi S. Graybill Papers
    Thomas Sumner Greene Papers
    James Haggerty Diaries and Sketchbook
    Jonathan B. Labrant Papers
    Jay T. Last Collection of Military Prints and Ephemera
    Francis Lieber Papers
    Luther Osborn Papers
    Manley Ebenezer Rice Papers
    George Tate Papers
    William S. Trask Journal

Library of Congress, Washington, DC
    African American Pamphlet Collection
    Nathan W. Daniels Diary
    Abraham Lincoln Papers
    Alfred Whital Stern Collection of Lincolniana
    Carter G. Woodson Papers

Massachusetts Historical Society, Boston, MA
    Edward Atkinson Papers
    Charles Francis Adams Papers
    John A. Andrew Papers
    Benjamin Butler Collection
    DeGrasse-Howard Papers
    Luis F. Emilio Papers
    Charles B. Fox Papers
    Warren Goodale Papers
    Norwood P. Hallowell Papers
    Henry Hedge Papers
    James Family Papers
    Kinsley Papers
    Amos Adams Lawrence Papers
    Lee Family Papers
    H. H. Mitchell Papers
    James A. Munroe Papers
    John Owen, Jr., Papers
    John O. Sargent Papers
    Robert Gould Shaw Letters
    Vendig Collection
    Wolcott Family Civil War Carte de Visite Album
    Records of the Association of Officers of the Fifty-fifth Massachusetts Volunteer Infantry
National Archives and Records Administration, Washington, DC
    Record Group 15, Records of the Department of Veterans Affairs
    Record Group 94, Records of the Adjutant General's Office
    Record Group 110, Records of the Provost Marshal General's Bureau (Civil War)
    Record Group 153, Records of the Office of the Judge Advocate General (Army)
    Record Group 393, Records of United States Army Continental Commands
New-York Historical Society, New York, NY
    William Cullen Bryant Papers
    John Alexander Archibald Campbell Papers
    Civil War Collection
    Charles Willoughby Dayton Papers
    Dryer Family Papers
    Frey Family Papers
    Thomas Wentworth Higginson Letters
    Lyon Family Papers
    Naval History Society Collection
    New Orleans Diary
    George Ward Nichols Papers

Printed Collections
    Emily Satterlee Letters
    Robert Gould Shaw Letters
    Slavery Collection
    Mary Ann Watkins Papers
Newberry Library, Chicago, IL
    John Knight Letters
Rauner Library, Dartmouth College, Hanover, NH
    Frank Anderson Papers
    Ziba C. Barton Letters
    Calvin M. Burbank Letters
    Grenville Clark Collection of Civil War Papers
    Joseph Messer Clough Letters
    Oren Colby Letters
    Perley F. Dodge Letters
    Samuel A. Duncan Letters
    Claude Goings Civil War Papers
    Agnes and M. Lafayette Gordon Papers
    Leander Harris Letters
    Jared P. Hubbard Papers
    William P. Kelly Family Papers
    Edward Lathem Papers
    George Augustus Marden Letters
    Elias Cummings Mather Civil War Papers
    John McCoy Family Papers
    Reuben Mussey Papers
    Rufus Patten Papers
    Albert M. Putnam Letters
    Calvin Shedd Papers
    Ira Stockbridge Diaries
    William Henry Thayer Letters
    William H. Tupper Papers
    Ransom R. Wheeler Letters
    E. D. Woodbury Diaries
    Andrew Hale Young Letters
Rhode Island Historical Society, Providence, RI
    Joshua Addeman Papers
    Bacon Family Papers
    Phanuel Euclid Bishop Diary
    George Bliss Papers
    Civil War Military Records
    Hagadorn-Welles Family Papers

North Kingston Town Records Collection
Rhode Island Association of Freedmen Records
George Sherman Papers
Soldiers and Sailors Historical Society Records
Nelson Viall Papers
Schomburg Center for Research in Black Culture, New York, NY
    John V. De Grasse Portrait Collection
    Christian A. Fleetwood Collection
    Christian A. Fleetwood Portrait Collection
    Thomas W. Higginson Portrait Collection
    Orpheus C. Kerr Papers
    Military Collection
    John Payne Civil War Collection
    Henry M. Turner Portrait Collection
Virginia Tech, Blacksburg, VA
    Henry Goddard Thomas Letters
    US Army Civil War Courts-Martial Database

NEWSPAPERS AND PERIODICALS

American Phrenological Journal and Life Illustrated (NY)
Atlantic Monthly (DC)
Boston Journal
Brooklyn Eagle (NY)
Chicago Tribune
Christian Recorder (PA)
Colored American (DC)
Congressional Globe (DC)
Daily Gazette (Janesville, WS)
Douglass' Monthly (NY)
Forney's War Press (PA)
Frederick Douglass' Paper (NY)
Harper's New Monthly Magazine (NY)
The Liberator (MA)
McClure's Magazine (NY)
National Era (DC)
National Intelligencer (DC)
Newark Daily Advertiser (NJ)
Newark Daily Mercury (NJ)
Newport Daily News (RI)
New York Evening Post

New York Herald
New York Times
New York Tribune
New York World
North American (Philadelphia)
Philadelphia Inquirer
Providence Journal (RI)
Provincial Freeman (Toronto, CA)
The Times (London, UK)
Weekly Anglo-African (NY)

CONTEMPORARY DOCUMENTS

Government Publications

Adjutant General's Office, *Index of General Orders, 1864*. 7 vols. Washington, DC: Government Printing Office, 1865.

Bureau of Pensions, Department of the Interior. *Laws of the United States Governing the Granting of Army and Navy Pensions Together with Regulations Relating Thereto*. Washington, DC: Government Printing Office, 1916.

Lester, Robert E., ed. *Records of U.S. Colored Troops: Part 1: Letters Related to Recruitment of African Americans, 1863–1865*. Bethesda, MD: UPA Collection from LexisNexis, 2005.

Message of the President of the United States to the Two Houses of Congress at the Commencement of the Second Session of the Thirty-Seventh Congress. Washington, DC: Government Printing Office, 1861.

Preliminary Report Touching on the Condition and Management of Emancipated Refugees; Made to the Secretary of War, by the American Freedmen's Inquiry Commission, June 30, 1863. New York: n.p., 1863.

Revised United States Army Regulations of 1861 with an Appendix Containing the Changes and Laws Affecting Army Regulations and Articles of War to June 25, 1863. Washington, DC: Government Printing Office, 1863.

US War Department. *The War of the Rebellion: A Compilation of the Official Records of the Union and Confederate Armies*. Washington, DC: Government Printing Office, 1880–1901.

Winthrop, William. *Digest of Opinions of the Judge Advocate General*. Washington, DC: Washington Government Printing Office, 1865.

Diaries, Letters, and Memoirs

Adams, J. W. *Letter to the Honorable Secretary of War: On the Examination of Field Officers for Colored Troops*. New York: John F. Trow, 1863.

Adams, Virginia M., ed. *On the Altar of Freedom: A Black Soldier's Civil War Letters from the Front.* Amherst: University of Massachusetts Press, 1991.

Banks, Nathaniel P. *Emancipated Labor in Louisiana.* N.p., 1864.

Barton, William E. *Old Plantation Hymns: A Collection of Hitherto Unpublished Melodies of the Slave and the Freedman, with Historical and Descriptive Notes.* New York: Lamson, Wolffe, 1899.

Basler, Roy P., ed. *Collected Works of Abraham Lincoln.* 8 vols. New Brunswick, NJ: Rutgers University Press, 1953.

Bayne, Julia Taft. *Tad Lincoln's Father.* Boston: Little, Brown, 1931.

Berlin, Ira, Barbara J. Fields, Thavolia Glymph, Joseph P. Reidy, and Leslie S. Rowland, eds. *Freedom: Series 1,* Volume 1: *The Destruction of Slavery: A Documentary History of Emancipation, 1861–1867.* New York: Cambridge University Press, 1986.

Berlin, Ira, Thavolia Glymph, Steven F. Miller, Joseph P. Reidy, Leslie S. Rowland, and Julie Saville. *Freedom: A Documentary History of Emancipation, 1861–1867, Series 1,* Volume 3: *The Wartime Genesis of Free Labor: The Lower South.* New York: Cambridge University Press, 1990.

Berlin, Ira, Joseph P. Reidy, and Leslie S. Rowland, eds. *Freedom: Series II,* Volume 1: *The Black Military Experience: A Documentary History of Emancipation, 1861–1867.* New York: Cambridge University Press, 1983.

Berlin, Ira, Joseph P. Reidy, and Leslie S. Rowland, eds. *Freedom's Soldiers: The Black Military Experience in the Civil War.* New York: Cambridge University Press, 1998.

Billings, John D. *Hardtack and Coffee, or the Unwritten Story of Army Life.* 1887. Reprint, Lincoln: University of Nebraska Press, 1993.

Blackett, Richard J. M., ed. *Thomas Morris Chester, Black Civil War Correspondent: His Dispatches from the Virginia Front.* Baton Rouge: Louisiana State University Press, 1989.

Blassingame, John W., ed. *Slave Testimony: Two Centuries of Letters, Speeches, Interviews and Autobiographies.* Baton Rouge: Louisiana State University Press, 1977.

Brown, Lucy E., comp. *Civil War Letters of John Knight, First Lieutenant, 7th Iowa Infantry.* Oak Park: State of Illinois, Daughters of the American Revolution, 1940.

Bruce, Henry Clay. *The New Man: Twenty-Nine Years a Slave, Twenty-Nine Years a Free Man.* York, PA: F. Anstadt & Sons, 1895.

Burlingame, Michael, and John R. Turner Ettlinger, eds. *Inside Lincoln's White House: The Complete Civil War Diary of John Hay.* Carbondale: Southern Illinois University Press, 1997.

Califf, Joseph Mark. *Record of the Services of the Seventh Regiment, U.S. Colored Troops from September, 1863 to November, 1866.* Providence, RI: E. L. Freeman, 1878.

Cheek, Thomas A. *A Sketch of the History of the Colored Race in the United States, and a Reminiscence of Slavery.* Peoria, IL: n.p., 1873.

Clark, Peter H. *The Black Brigade of Cincinnati: Being a Report of Its Labors and a Muster-Roll of Its Members; Together with Various Orders, Speeches, etc., Relating to It.* Cincinnati: Joseph B. Boyd, 1864.

Cowden, Robert. *A Brief Sketch of the Organization and Services of the Fifty-Ninth Regiment of the United States Colored Infantry and Biographical Sketches*. Dayton, OH: United Brethren Publishing House, 1883.

Donald, David, ed. *Inside Lincoln's Cabinet: The Civil War Diaries of Salmon P. Chase*. New York: Longmans, Green, 1954.

Douglass, Frederick. *My Bondage and My Freedom*. New York: Miller, Orton and Mulligan, 1855.

Douglass, Frederick. *Narrative of the Life of Frederick Douglass, An American Slave*. Boston: Anti-Slavery Office, 1845.

Duncan, Russell, ed. *Blue-Eyed Child of Fortune: The Civil War Letters of Colonel Robert Gould Shaw*. Athens: University of Georgia Press, 1992.

Emilio, Luis F. *A Brave Black Regiment: The History of the Fifty-Fourth Regiment of Massachusetts Volunteer Infantry 1863–1865*. 1891. Reprint, New York: Da Capo Press, 1995.

Engs, Robert F., and Corey M. Brooks, eds. *Their Patriotic Duty: The Civil War Letters of the Evans Family of Brown County, Ohio*. New York: Fordham University Press, 2007.

Fenner, Thomas P., Frederic G. Rathbun, and Bessie Cleaveland. *Cabin and Plantation Songs as Sung by the Hampton Students*. 3rd edition. New York: G. P. Putnam's Sons, 1901.

Fields, Barbara J., Steven F. Miller, Joseph P. Reidy, Rowland, and Ira Berlin, eds. *Free at Last: A Documentary History of Slavery, Freedom, and the Civil War*. New York: New Press, 1992.

Foner, Philip S., ed. *The Life and Writings of Frederick Douglass*. 5 vols. New York: International Publishers, 1950.

Ford, Worthington Chauncey, ed. *A Cycle of Adams Letters, 1861–1865*. 2 vols. Boston: Houghton Mifflin, 1920.

Fox, Charles Barnard. *Record of the Service of the Fifty-Fifth Regiment of Massachusetts Volunteer Infantry*. Cambridge, MA: J. Wilson and Son, 1868.

Franklin, John Hope, ed. *The Diary of James T. Ayers: Civil War Recruiter*. Baton Rouge: Louisiana State University Press, 1999.

Gilmore, James R. *Personal Recollections of Abraham Lincoln and the Civil War*. Boston: L. C. Page, 1898.

Grant, Ulysses S. *The Personal Memoirs of Ulysses S. Grant: The Complete Annotated Edition*. Edited by John F. Marszalek. First published in 2 vols. in 1885 and 1886 by Charles L. Webster (New York). Reprint, Cambridge, MA: Harvard University Press, 2017.

Greene, J. H. *Reminiscences of the War: Bivouacs, Marches, Skirmishes, and Battles*. Medina, OH: Gazette Print, 1886.

Hall, Henry. *Cayuga in the Field, a Record of the 19th N.Y. Volunteers, and the 3d New York Artillery*. Auburn, NY: n.p., 1873.

Hallowell, Norwood P. *The Negro as a Soldier in the War of the Rebellion.* Boston: Little, Brown, 1892.

Hepburn, Sharon A. Roger, ed. *Private No More: The Civil War Letters of John Lovejoy, 102nd United States Colored Infantry.* Athens: University of Georgia Press, 2023.

Higginson, Mary Thacher, ed. *The Letters and Journals of Thomas Wentworth Higginson, 1846–1906.* New York: Houghton Mifflin, 1921.

Higginson, Thomas Wentworth. *Army Life in a Black Regiment.* Boston: Fields, Osgood, 1870.

King Taylor, Susie. *A Black Woman's Civil War Memoirs: Reminiscences of My Life in Camp with the 33rd U.S. Colored Troops, Late 1st South Carolina Volunteers.* Edited by Patricia W. Romero and Willie Lee Rose. New York: Markus Wiener, 1988.

Knox, Thomas. *Camp-Fire and Cotton-Field: Southern Adventure in Time of War, Life with the Union Armies, and Residence on a Louisiana Plantation.* New York: Blelock, 1865.

Looby, Christopher, ed. *The Complete Civil War Journal and Selected Letters of Thomas Wentworth Higginson.* Chicago: University of Chicago Press, 1999.

Macintosh, James T., ed. Vol. 2 of *The Papers of Jefferson Davis: June 1841–July 1846.* Baton Rouge: Louisiana State University Press, 1974.

Marrs, Elijah P. *Life and History of the Rev. Elijah P. Marrs.* Louisville, KY: Bradley & Gilbert, 1885.

Mickley, J. M. *The Forty-Third Regiment United States Colored Troops.* Gettysburg, PA: J. E. Wible, 1866.

M'Kim, J. M. *"The Freedmen of South Carolina: An Address Delivered by J. Miller M'Kim in Sansom Hall, July 9th, 1862." Together with a Letter from the Same to Stephen Colwell, Esq., Chairman of the Port Royal Relief Committee.* Philadelphia: Willis P. Hazard, 1862.

Mudd, Nettie, ed. *The Life of Dr. Samuel A. Mudd.* New York: Neale Publishing, 1906.

Newton, Alexander Herritage. *Out of the Briars; an Autobiography and Sketch of the Twenty-Ninth Regiment, Connecticut Volunteers.* Philadelphia: A. M. E. Book Concern, 1910.

Nolin, Kelly. "The Civil War Letters of J. O. Cross, Twenty-Ninth Connecticut Volunteer Infantry (Colored)." *Connecticut Historical Society Bulletin* 60 (Summer/Fall 1995): 211–235.

Northup, Solomon. *Twelve Years a Slave.* Auburn, NY: Derby and Miller, 1853.

Northup, Solomon. *Twelve Years a Slave: Narrative of Solomon Northup.* 1853. Reprinted with a foreword by Steven McQueen, an introduction by Ira Berlin, and an afterword by Henry Louis Gates. Jr. New York: Penguin, 2013.

Pearson, Elizabeth Ware, ed. *Letters from Port Royal Written at the Time of the Civil War.* Boston: W. B. Clarke, 1906.

Pennington, James. *The Fugitive Blacksmith; or, Events in the History of James W. C. Pennington, Pastor of a Presbyterian Church, New York, Formerly a Slave in the State of Maryland, United States.* London: Charles Gilpin, 1849.

Porter, David D. *The Naval History of the Civil War*. New York: Sherman, 1886.

Rankin, David C., ed. *Diary of a Christian Soldier: Rufus Kinsley and the Civil War*. New York: Cambridge University Press, 2003.

Rauscher, Frank J. *Music on the March, 1862–65, with the Army of Potomac, 114th Regt. P. V., Collis Zouaves*. Philadelphia: William F. Fell, 1892.

Redkey, Edwin S., ed. *A Grand Army of Black Men: Letters from African-American Soldiers in the Union Army 1861–1865*. New York: Cambridge University Press, 1992.

Reid, Richard M., ed. *Practicing Medicine in a Black Regiment: The Civil War Diary of Burt G. Wilder, 55th Massachusetts*. Amherst: University of Massachusetts Press, 2010.

Rhodes, Robert Hunt, ed. *All for the Union: The Civil War Diary and Letters of Elisha Hunt Rhodes*. New York: Orion Books, 1985.

Robinson, William H. *From Log Cabin to the Pulpit, or, Fifteen Years in Slavery*. 3rd edition. Eau Claire, WI: Ames H. Tifft, 1913.

Simon, John Y., ed. *The Papers of Ulysses S. Grant*. 31 vols. Carbondale: Southern Illinois University Press, 1969.

Sparks, David S. ed. *Inside Lincoln's Army: The Diary of Marsena Rudolph Patrick, Provost Marshal General, Army of the Potomac*. New York: Thomas Yoscloff, 1964.

Stein, A. H., and Nathan Goff. *History of the Thirty-Seventh Regt. U.S.C. Infantry: From Its Organization in the Winter of 1863 and '64, to the Present Time, with List of Names of All Officers and Enlisted Men Who Have Ever Belonged to the Regiment, and Remarks Attached to Each Name, Noting All Changes, Such as Promotions, Transfers, Discharges, Deaths, Etc.: Brevet Brig. Gen. Nathan Goff, Jr., Commanding*. Philadelphia: King & Baird, 1866.

Trudeau, Noah Andre, ed. *Voices of the 55th: Letters from the 55th Massachusetts Volunteers, 1861–1865*. Dayton, OH: Morningside, 1996.

Truth, Sojourner. *Narrative of Sojourner Truth: A Bondswoman of Olden Time*. Battle Creek, MI: Review and Herald Office, 1884.

Tushnet, Mark V., ed. *Thurgood Marshall: His Speeches, Writings, Arguments, Opinions, and Reminiscences*. Chicago: University of Chicago Press, 2001.

Tyler, C. M. *Memorials of Lieut. George H. Walcott, Late of the 30th U. S. Colored Troops*. Boston: Massachusetts Sabbath-School Society, 1865.

Van Alstyne, Lawrence. *Diary of an Enlisted Man*. New Haven, CT: Tuttle, Morehouse & Taylor, 1910.

White, Jonathan W., ed. *To Address You as My Friend: African Americas' Letters to Abraham Lincoln*. Chapel Hill: University of North Carolina Press, 2021.

Williams, George Washington. *A History of the Negro Troops in the War of Rebellion, 1861–1865*. 1887. Reprinted with an Introduction by John David Smith. New York: Fordham University Press, 2012.

Wilson, James T. *The Black Phalanx: African American Soldiers in the War of Independence, the War of 1812, and the Civil War.* 1887. Reprinted with foreword by Dudley Taylor Cornish, New York: De Capo, 1994.

Winschel, Terrence J., ed. *The Civil War Diary of a Common Soldier, William Wiley of the 77th Illinois Infantry.* Baton Rouge: Louisiana State University Press, 2001.

The Works of Charles Sumner. 15 vols. Boston: Lee and Shepard, 1870–1883.

Yacovone, Donald, ed. *Freedom's Journey: African American Voices of the Civil War.* Chicago: Lawrence Hill, 2004.

Yacovone, Donald, ed. *A Voice of Thunder: The Civil War Letters of George E. Stephens.* Urbana: University of Illinois Press, 1997.

Novels and Tracts

Bierce, Ambrose. *The Civil War Short Stories of Ambrose Bierce.* Lincoln: University of Nebraska Press, 1988.

Benet, Stephen V. *A Treatise on Military Law and the Practice of the Courts-Martial.* New York: n.p., 1862.

Brown, Helen E. *John Freeman and His Family.* Boston: American Tract Society, 1864.

[Casey, Silas.] *U.S. Infantry Tactics, for the Instruction, Exercise, and Manœuvers of the Soldier, a Company, Line of Skirmishers, and Battalion; for the Use of the Colored Troops of the United States Infantry.* New York: D. Van Nostrand, 1863.

Child, L. Maria. *The Right Way, The Safe Way, Proved by Emancipation in the British West Indies and Elsewhere.* New York: n.p., 1863.

Cobb, Thomas R. R. *An Inquiry into the Law of Negro Slavery in the United States of America.* Philadelphia: T. and J. W. Johnson, 1858.

Coppée, Henry. *Field Manual of Courts-Martial.* Philadelphia: J. B. Lippincott, 1864.

De Hart, William Chetwood. *Observations of Military Law and the Constitution and Practice of Courts-Martial, with Summary of the Law of Evidence as Applicable to Military Trials.* New York: D. Appleton, 1863.

Dunbar, Paul Laurence. *Majors and Minors: Poems.* Toledo, OH: Hadley and Hadley, 1895.

Garnet, Henry Highland. *Walker's Appeal, with a Brief Sketch of His Life. And Also Garnet's Address to the Slaves of the United States of America.* New York: J. H. Tobitt, 1848.

Hoff, J. *A Treatise on Martial Law, and Courts-Martial: As Practised in the United States of America.* Charleston: n.p., 1809.

Nichols, S. S. *Conservative Essays, Legal and Political.* Philadelphia: J. B. Lippincott, 1863.

Nichols, S. S. *Conservative Essays, Legal and Political.* Second Series. Philadelphia: J. B. Lippincott, 1865.

Ray, Henrietta Cordelia. *Poems.* New York: Grafton Press, 1910.

Tocqueville, Alexis de. *Democracy in America.* 1835. Translated by Henry Reeve. New York: Knopf, 1945.

Washington, Booker T., N. B. Wood, and Fannie Barrier Williams. *A New Negro for a New Century*. Chicago: American Publishing House, 1900.

Wright, Richard. *Black Boy: A Record of Childhood and Youth*. Stockholm: A/B Ljus Förlag, 1946.

Broadsides, Pamphlets, and Speeches

Board of Artillery Officers. *Instruction for Field Artillery*. Philadelphia: J. B. Lippincott, 1861.

Brague, Stephen B. *Notes on Colored Troops and Military Colonies on Southern Soil*. New York, 1863.

History of Pennsylvania Hall, Which Was Destroyed by a Mob, on the 17th of May, 1838. Philadelphia: Merrihew and Gunn, 1838.

Kelley, William D., Frederick Douglass, and Anna E. Dickinson. *Addresses of the Hon. W. D. Kelley, Miss Anna E. Dickinson, and Mr. Frederick Douglass, at a Mass Meeting Held at National Hall, Philadelphia, July 6, 1863, for the Promotion of Colored Enlistments*. Philadelphia: n.p., 1863.

Lee, Charles Henry. *The Judge Advocate's Vade Mecum: Embracing a General View of Military Law, and the Practice before Courts Martial, with an Epitome of the Law of Evidence, as Applicable to Military Trials*. Cincinnati: J. B. Boyd, 1864.

Leland, Charles Godfrey. *Ye Book of Copperheads*. Philadelphia: Frederick Leypoldt, 1863.

Men of Color, to Arms! Now or Never! Philadelphia: n.p., 1863.

Miller, Lindley. *Song of the First of Arkansas . . . Written by Captain Lindley Miller, of the First Arkansas Colored Regiment*. Philadelphia: Supervisory Committee for Recruiting Colored Regiments, 1864.

Miller, Marion Mills, ed. *Great Debates in American History*. 14 vols. New York: Current Literature, 1913.

Obama, Barack. "Remarks by the President at the Dedication of the National Museum of African American History and Culture." September 24, 2016. https://obamawhitehouse.archives.gov/the-press-office/2016/09/24/remarks-president-dedication-national-museum-african-american-history.

O'Rielly, Henry. *First Organization of Colored Troops in the State of New York, to Aid in Suppressing the Slaveholders' Rebellion*. New York: Baker & Godwin, 1864.

Portman, Arthur B. *A Few of the Reasons for Recruiting Our Black Army*. Boston, 1863.

Report of the Supervisory Committee for Recruiting Colored Regiments. Philadelphia: King & Baird, 1864.

Taggart, John H. *Free Military School for Applicants for Commands of Colored Troops*. Philadelphia: King & Baird, 1864.

Ullmann, Daniel. *Address by Daniel Ullmann, L.L.D., before the Soldier's and Sailor's Union of the State of New York, on the Organization of Colored Troops and the*

Regeneration of the South, Delivered at Albany, February 5, 1868. Washington, DC: Great Republic Office, 1868.

Union League Club. *Report of the Committee on Volunteering; Presented October 13th, 1864*. New York, 1864.

Weiss, John. *Will the Blacks Fight?* United States: n.p., ca. 1862.

SECONDARY WORKS

Adams, Michael C. C. *Living Hell: The Dark Side of the Civil War*. Baltimore: Johns Hopkins University Press, 2014.

Alotta, Robert I. *Civil War Justice: Union Army Executions under Lincoln*. Shippensburg, PA: White Mane, 1989.

Anderson, Fred. *A People's Army: Massachusetts Soldiers and Society in the Seven Years' War*. Chapel Hill: University of North Carolina, 1984.

Aptheker, Herbert, ed. *The Correspondence of W. E. B. Du Bois*. 3 vols. Amherst: University of Massachusetts, 1973.

Ash, Stephen V. *Firebrand of Liberty: The Story of Two Black Regiments That Changed the Course of the Civil War*. New York: W. W. Norton, 2008.

Ash, Stephen V. *A Massacre in Memphis: The Race Riot That Shook the Nation One Year after the Civil War*. New York: Hill & Wang, 2013.

Ayers, Edward L. "Loyalty and America's Civil War." Lecture presented at the Forty-Ninth Annual Fortenbaugh Memorial Lecture, Gettysburg College, Gettysburg, PA, 2010.

Ayers, Edward L. *Vengeance and Justice: Crime and Punishment in the 19th-Century American South*. New York: Oxford University Press, 1984.

Ayers, Edward L., and Scott Nesbit. "Visualizing Emancipation." Digital Scholarship Lab. University of Richmond. https://dsl.richmond.edu/emancipation/.

Ayers, Edward L., and John C. Willis. *The Edge of the South: Life in Nineteenth-Century Virginia*. Charlottesville: University of Virginia Press, 1991.

Bailey, Anne J. *Invisible Soldiers: Ethnicity in the Civil War*. Athens: University of Georgia Press, 2006.

Bailyn, Bernard. *Ideological Origins of the American Revolution*. Cambridge, MA: Harvard University Press, 1967.

Baker, Jean H. *Affairs of Party: The Political Culture of Northern Democrats in the Mid-Nineteenth Century*. New York: Fordham University Press, 1998.

Baker, Jean H. "Mary Todd Lincoln: Biography as Social History." *Register-Kentucky Historical Society* 86, no. 3 (Summer 1988): 203–215.

Baptist, Edward E., and Stephanie M. H. Camp, eds. *New Studies in the History of American Slavery*. Athens: University of Georgia Press, 2006.

Barnett, James. "Bounty Jumpers of Indiana." *Civil War History* 4, no. 4 (December 1958): 429–436.

Barnickel, Linda. *Milliken's Bend: A Civil War Battle in History and Memory*. Baton Rouge: Louisiana State University Press, 2013.

Bearss, Edwin C. "Historical Structure Report, Historical Data Section, Fort Jefferson: 1846–1898." Monroe County, FL: National Monument Printing, 1983.

Berlin, Ira. *The Long Emancipation: The Demise of Slavery in the United States*. Cambridge, MA: Harvard University Press, 2015.

Berlin, Ira, Barbara J. Fields, Steven F. Miller, Joseph P. Reidy, and Leslie S. Rowland. *Slaves No More: Three Essays on Emancipation and the Civil War*. New York: Cambridge University Press, 1992.

Berlin, Isaiah. *Four Essays on Liberty*. New York: Oxford University Press, 1990.

Berry, Daina Ramey. *The Price for Their Pound of Flesh: The Value of the Enslaved, from Womb to Grave, in the Building of a Nation*. Boston: Beacon Press, 2017.

Berry, Mary Frances. *Military Necessity and Civil Rights Policy: Black Citizenship and the Constitution, 1861–1868*. Port Washington, NY: Kennikat Press, 1977.

Berry, Mary Frances. "Negro Troops in Blue and Gray: The Louisiana Native Guards, 1861–1863." *Louisiana History: The Journal of the Louisiana Historical Association* 8, no. 2 (Spring 1967): 165–190.

Berry, Stephen, II. *All That Makes a Man: Love and Ambition in the Civil War South*. New York: Oxford University Press, 2003.

Berry, Stephen, II, ed. *Weirding the Civil War: Stories from the Civil War's Ragged Edges*. Athens: University of Georgia Press, 2011.

Bigelow, Martha M. "The Significance of Milliken's Bend in the Civil War." *Journal of Negro History* 45, no. 3 (July 1960): 156–163.

Blair, William A. *Cities of the Dead: Contesting the Memory of the Civil War in the South, 1865–1914*. Chapel Hill: University of North Carolina Press, 2004.

Blair, William A. *With Malice toward Some: Treason and Loyalty in the Civil War Era*. Chapel Hill: University of North Carolina Press, 2014.

Blair, William A. *Virginia's Private War: Feeding Body and Soul in the Confederacy, 1861–1865*. New York: Oxford University Press, 1998.

Blassingame, John W. "The Union Army as an Educational Institution for Negroes, 1861–1875." *Journal of Negro Education* 34, no. 2 (Spring 1965): 152–159.

Blatt, Martin H., Thomas J. Brown, and Donald Yacovone, eds. *Hope & Glory: Essays on the Legacy of the 54th Massachusetts Regiment*. Amherst: University of Massachusetts Press, 2009.

Bledsoe, Andrew S. *Citizen-Officers: The Union and Confederate Volunteer Junior Officer Corps in the American Civil War*. Baton Rouge: Louisiana State University Press, 2015.

Blight, David W. *Frederick Douglass: The Prophet of Freedom*. New York: Simon and Schuster, 2018.

Blight, David W. *Frederick Douglass' Civil War: Keeping Faith in Jubilee*. Baton Rouge: Louisiana State University Press, 1989.

Blight, David W. *Race and Reunion: The American Civil War in American Memory*. Cambridge, MA: Harvard University Press, 2001.

Blight, David W., and Jim Downs, eds. *Beyond Freedom: Disrupting the History of Emancipation*. Athens: University of Georgia Press, 2017.

Bolster, W. Jeffrey. *Black Jacks: African American Seamen in the Age of Sail*. Cambridge, MA: Harvard University Press, 1997.

Bonner, Christopher James. *Remaking the Republic: Black Politics and the Creation of American Citizenship*. Philadelphia: University of Pennsylvania Press, 2020.

Brasher, Glenn David. *The Peninsula Campaign and the Necessity of Emancipation: African Americans and the Fight for Freedom*. Chapel Hill: University of North Carolina Press, 2012.

Bray, Christopher. *Court-Martial: How Military Justice Has Shaped America from the Revolution to 9/11 and Beyond*. New York: W. W. Norton, 2016.

Brown, Christopher Leslie, and Philip D. Morgan, ed. *Arming Slaves: From Classical Times to the Modern Age*. New Haven, CT: Yale University Press, 2006.

Brown, Thomas. *Politics and Statesmanship: Essays on the American Whig Party*. New York: Columbia University Press, 1985.

Brown, William Wells. *Negro in American Rebellion: His Heroism & His Fidelity*. Boston: A. G. Brown, 1880.

Buchanan, Thomas C. *Black Life on the Mississippi: Slaves, Free Blacks, and the Western Steamboat World*. Chapel Hill: University of North Carolina Press, 2004.

Burlingame, Michael. *Abraham Lincoln: A Life*. 2 vols. Baltimore: Johns Hopkins University Press, 2008.

Burton, William L. *Melting Pot Soldiers: The Union's Ethnic Regiments*. 2nd edition. New York: Fordham University Press, 1998.

Butchart, Ronald E. *Schooling the Freed People: Teaching, Learning, and the Struggle for Black Freedom, 1861–1876*. Chapel Hill: University of North Carolina Press, 2010.

Calbreath, Dean. *The Sergeant: The Incredible Life of Nicholas Said: Son of an African General, Slave of the Ottomans, Free Man Under the Tsars, Hero of the Union Army*. New York: Pegasus, 2023.

Camp, Stephanie M. H. *Closer to Freedom: Enslaved Women and Everyday Resistance in the Plantation South*. Chapel Hill: University of North Carolina Press, 2004.

Carmichael, Peter S. *The War for the Common Soldier: How Men Thought, Fought, and Survived in Civil War Armies*. Chapel Hill: University of North Carolina Press, 2018.

Carter Jackson, Kellie. *Force and Freedom: Black Abolitionists and the Politics of Violence*. Philadelphia: University of Pennsylvania Press, 2019.

Casey, John A., Jr. *New Men: Reconstructing the Image of the Veteran in Late-Nineteenth Century American Literature and Culture*. New York: Fordham University Press, 2015.

Cashin, Joan, ed. *The War Was You and Me: Civilians in the American Civil War*. Princeton, NJ: Princeton University Press, 2002.

Cecelski, David S. *The Fire of Freedom: Abraham Galloway and the Slaves' Civil War*. Chapel Hill: University of North Carolina Press, 2012.

Cecelski, David S. *The Waterman's Song: Slavery and Freedom in Maritime North Carolina*. Chapel Hill: University of North Carolina Press, 2001.

Chernow, Ron. *Grant*. New York: Penguin, 2017.

Cimprich, John. *Navigating Liberty: Black Refugees and Antislavery Reformers in the Civil War South*. Baton Rouge: Louisiana State University Press, 2023.

Cirillo, Frank J. *The Abolitionist Civil War: Immediatists and the Struggle to Transform the Union*. Baton Rouge: Louisiana State University Press, 2023.

Clark, Kathleen Ann. *Defining Moments: African American Commemoration and Political Culture in the South, 1863–1913*. Chapel Hill: University of North Carolina Press, 2005.

Clarke, Frances M., and Rebecca Jo Plant. *Of Age: Boy Soldiers and Military Power in the Civil War Era*. New York: Oxford University Press, 2023.

Coddington, Ronald S. *African American Faces of the Civil War: An Album*. Baltimore: Johns Hopkins University Press, 2012.

Coffman, Edward M. *The Old Army: A Portrait of the American Army in Peacetime, 1784–1898*. New York: Oxford University Press, 1986.

Colby, Robert K. D. *An Unholy Traffic: Slave Trading in the Civil War South*. New York: Oxford University Press, 2024.

Cook, Robert J. *Civil War Memories: Contesting the Past in the United States since 1865*. Baltimore: Johns Hopkins University Press, 2017.

Cook Bell, Karen, ed. *Southern Black Women and Their Struggle for Freedom during the Civil War and Reconstruction*. New York: Cambridge University Press, 2024.

Cornish, Dudley Taylor. *The Sable Arm: Black Troops in the Union Army, 1861–1865*. 1956. Reprint, Lawrence: University Press of Kansas, 1987.

Cornish, Dudley Taylor. "The Union Army as a School for Negroes." *Journal of Negro History* 37, no. 4 (October 1952): 368–382.

Cox, Shae Smith. *The Fabric of Civil War Society*. Baton Rouge: Louisiana State University Press, 2024.

Daly, Suzanne. "Belligerent Instruments: The Documentary Violence of 'Bleak House.'" *Studies in the Novel* 47, no. 1 (Spring 2015): 20–42.

Davis, Patricia G. *Laying Claim: African American Cultural Memory and Southern Identity*. Tuscaloosa: University of Alabama Press, 2016.

Dayan, Colin, *The Law Is a White Dog: How Legal Rituals Make and Unmake Persons*. Princeton, NJ: Princeton University Press, 2011.

Delbanco, Andrew. *The War before the War: Fugitive Slaves and the Struggle for America's Soul from the Revolution to the Civil War*. New York: Penguin, 2018.

Delgado, Richard, and Jean Stefancic, eds. *Critical Race Theory: An Introduction*. 3rd edition. New York: New York University Press, 2017.

Dew, Charles B. *Apostles of Disunion: Southern Secession Commissioners and the Causes of the Civil War*. Charlottesville: University of Virginia Press, 2001.

Diouf, Sylviane A. *Slavery's Exiles: The Story of the American Maroons*. New York: New York University Press, 2014.

Dobak, William A. *Freedom by the Sword: The U.S. Colored Troops, 1862–1867*. Washington, DC: Center of Military History United States Army, 2011.
Doddington, David Stefan. *Contesting Slave Masculinity in the American South*. New York: Cambridge University Press, 2018.
Donald, David Herbert. *Charles Sumner and the Coming of the Civil War*. New York: Knopf, 1960.
Donald, David Herbert. *Lincoln*. New York: Simon and Schuster, 1995.
Downs, Gregory P. *After Appomattox: Military Occupation and the Ends of War*. Cambridge, MA: Harvard University Press, 2015.
Downs, Gregory P. *Declarations of Dependence: The Long Reconstruction of Popular Politics in the South, 1861–1908*. Chapel Hill: University of North Carolina Press, 2011.
Downs, Gregory P., and Kate Masur, eds. *The World the Civil War Made*. Chapel Hill: University of North Carolina Press, 2015.
Downs, Jim. *Sick from Freedom: African-American Illness and Suffering during the Civil War and Reconstruction*. New York: Oxford University Press, 2012.
Drake, Francis S. *Dictionary of American Biography, including Men of the Time*. Boston: James R. Osgood, 1872.
Du Bois, W. E. B. *Black Reconstruction in America, 1860–1880*. First published in 1935 by Harcourt, Brace (New York). Reprint, New York: Free Press, 1998.
Duncan, Russell. *Where Death and Glory Meet: Colonel Robert Gould Shaw and the 54th Massachusetts Infantry*. Athens: University of Georgia Press, 1999.
Eberhardt, Jennifer L., Phillip A. Goff, Valerie J. Purdie, and Paul G. Davies. "Seeing Black: Race, Crime, and Visual Processing." *Journal of Personality and Social Psychology* 87, no. 6 (2004): 876–893.
Edmondson, James H. "Desertion in the American Army during the American Revolution." PhD diss., Louisiana State University, 1971.
Edwards, Laura F. *A Legal History of the Civil War and Reconstruction: A Nation of Rights*. New York: Cambridge University Press, 2015.
Edwards, Laura F. *The People and Their Peace: Legal Culture and the Transformation of Inequality in the Post-Revolutionary South*. Chapel Hill: University of North Carolina Press, 2009.
Egerton, Douglas R. *Gabriel's Rebellion: The Virginia Slave Conspiracies of 1800 and 1802*. Chapel Hill: University of North Carolina Press, 1993.
Egerton, Douglas R. *Thunder at the Gates: The Black Civil War Regiments That Redeemed America*. New York: Basic Books, 2016.
Eggleston, Michael A. *President Lincoln's Recruiter: General Lorenzo Thomas and the United States Colored Troops in the Civil War*. Jefferson: McFarland, 2013.
Ely, James W., Jr. *The Contract Clause: A Constitutional History*. Lawrence: University Press of Kansas, 2016.
Emberton, Carole. *Beyond Redemption: Race, Violence, and the American South after the Civil War*. Chicago: University of Chicago Press, 2013.

Emberton, Carole. "'Only Murder Makes Men': Reconsidering the Black Military Experience." *Journal of the Civil War Era* 2, no. 3 (September 2012): 369–393.

Emberton, Carole. "Unwriting the Freedom Narrative: A Review Essay." *Journal of Southern History* 82, no. 2 (May 2016): 377–394.

Emberton, Carole. *To Walk About in Freedom: The Long Emancipation of Priscilla Joyner.* New York: W. W. Norton, 2022.

Escott, Paul D. *"What Shall We Do with the Negro?": Lincoln, White Racism, and Civil War America.* Charlottesville: University of Virginia Press, 2009.

Escott, Paul D. *The Worst Passions of Human Nature: White Supremacy in the Civil War North.* Charlottesville: University of Virginia Press, 2020.

Evans, Peter B., Dietrich Rusehmeyer, and Theda Skocpol, eds. *Bring the State Back In.* New York: Cambridge University Press, 1985.

Fabian, Ann. *The Unvarnished Truth: Personal Narratives in Nineteenth-Century America.* Berkeley: University of California Press, 2000.

Fannin, John F. "The Jacksonville Mutiny of 1865." *Florida Historical Quarterly* 88, no. 3 (Winter 2010): 368–396.

Faust, Drew Gilpin. *This Republic of Suffering: Death and the American Civil War.* New York: Vintage, 2008.

Feimster, Crystal N. "Rape and Mutiny at Fort Jackson: Black Laundresses Testify in Civil War Louisiana." *Labor* 19, no. 1 (March 2022): 11–31.

Felber, Garrett. *Those Who Know Don't Say: The Nation of Islam, the Black Freedom Movement, and the Carceral State.* Chapel Hill: University of North Carolina Press, 2020.

Fett, Sharla M. *Working Cures: Healing, Health, and Power on Southern Slave Plantations.* Chapel Hill: University of North Carolina Press, 2002.

Fidell, Eugene R. *Military Justice: A Very Short Introduction.* New York: Oxford University Press, 2016.

Fields-Black, Edda L. *Combee: Harriet Tubman, the Combahee River Raid, and Black Freedom during the Civil War.* New York: Oxford University Press, 2024.

Fink, Leon. *Workers across the Americas: The Transnational Turn in Labor History.* New York: Oxford University Press, 2011.

Finkelman, Paul. *Dred Scott v. Sandford: A Brief History with Documents.* 2nd edition. Boston: Bedford Books of St. Martin, 2016.

Flanigan, Daniel J. *The Criminal Law of Slavery and Freedom, 1800–1868.* New York: Garland, 1987.

Flanigan, Daniel J. "The Criminal Law of Slavery and Freedom, 1800–1868." PhD diss., Rice University, 1973.

Flanigan, Daniel J. "Criminal Procedure in the Slave Trials in the Antebellum South." *Journal of Southern History* 40, no. 4 (November 1974): 537–564.

Foner, Eric. *Free Soil, Free Labor, Free Men: The Ideology of the Republican Party before the Civil War with a New Introductory Essay.* First published in 1970 by Oxford University Press (New York). New York: Oxford University Press, 1995.

Foner, Eric. "The Meaning of Freedom in the Age of Emancipation." *Journal of American History* 81, no. 2 (September 1994): 435–460.

Foner, Eric. *Reconstruction: America's Unfinished Revolution, 1863–1877.* New York: Harper & Row, 1988.

Foner, Eric. "Rights and the Constitution in Black Life during the Civil War and Reconstruction." *Journal of American History* 74, no. 3 (December 1987): 863–883.

Foner, Eric. *The Second Founding: How the Civil War and Reconstruction Remade the Constitution.* New York: W. W. Norton, 2019.

Foner, Eric. *Story of American Freedom.* New York: W. W. Norton, 1998.

Foner, Philip S., and Ronald L. Lewis, eds. *Black Workers: A Documentary History from Colonial Times to the Present.* Philadelphia: Temple University Press, 1989.

Foote, Lorien. *The Gentlemen and the Roughs: Violence, Honor, and Manhood in the Union Army.* New York: New York University Press, 2010.

Foote, Lorien. *Rites of Retaliation: Civilization, Soldiers, and Campaigns in the American Civil War.* Chapel Hill: University of North Carolina Press, 2021.

Forman, P. Gabrielle, et al. "Writing about Slavery? Teaching about Slavery? This Might Help." https://docs.google.com/document/d/1A4TEdDgYslX-hlKezLod MIM71My3KTNozxRvoIQTOQs/mobilebasic.

Foster, A. Kristen. "'We Are Men!' Frederick Douglass and the Fault Lines of Gendered Citizenship." *Journal of the Civil War Era* 1, no. 2 (June 2011): 143–175.

Fox-Amato, Matthew. *Exposing Slavery: Photography, Human Bondage, and the Birth of Modern Visual America.* New York: Oxford University Press, 2019.

Fox-Genovese, Elizabeth, and Eugene D. Genovese. *The Mind of the Master Class: History and Faith in the Southern Slaveholders' Worldview.* New York: Cambridge University Press, 2005.

Frank, Stephen M. *Life with Father: Parenthood and Masculinity in the Nineteenth-Century American North.* Baltimore: Johns Hopkins University Press, 1998.

Franklin, John Hope. *George Washington Williams: A Biography.* Chicago: University of Chicago Press, 1985.

Franklin, John Hope, and Loren Schweninger. *Runaway Slaves: Rebels on the Plantation.* New York: Oxford University Press, 1999.

Fredrickson, George M. *The Black Image in the White Mind.* New York: Harper & Row, 1971.

Fry, Zachery A. *A Republic in the Ranks: Loyalty and Dissent in the Army of the Potomac.* Chapel Hill: University of North Carolina Press, 2020.

Gallagher, Gary W. *Causes Won, Lost, and Forgotten: How Hollywood and Popular Art Shape What We Know about the Civil War.* Chapel Hill: University of North Carolina Press, 2008.

Gallagher, Gary W. *The Union War.* Cambridge, MA: Harvard University Press, 2011.

Gallagher, Gary W., and Stephen Cushman, eds. *Civil War Writing: New Perspectives on Iconic Texts.* Baton Rouge: Louisiana State University Press, 2019.

Gallman, J. Matthew. *Defining Duty in the Civil War: Personal Choice, Popular Culture, and the Union Home Front*. Chapel Hill: University of North Carolina Press, 2015.

Gannon, Barbara A. *The Won Cause: Black and White Comradeship in the Grand Army of the Republic*. Chapel Hill: University of North Carolina Press, 2011.

Garrison, Webb B. *Mutiny in the Civil War*. Shippensburg, PA: White Mane, 2000.

Gerteis, Louis S. *Civil War St. Louis*. Lawrence: University Press of Kansas, 2001.

Gerteis, Louis S. *From Contraband to Freedman: Federal Policy toward Southern Blacks, 1861–1865*. Westport, CT: Greenwood Press, 1973.

Gienapp, William E., ed. *The Civil War and Reconstruction: A Documentary Collection*. New York: W. W. Norton, 2001.

Glatthaar, Joseph T. *Forged in Battle: The Civil War Alliance of Black Soldiers and White Officers*. Baton Rouge: Louisiana State University Press, 1990.

Glatthaar, Joseph T. *General Lee's Army: From Victory to Collapse*. New York: Free Press, 2008.

Glickstein, Jonathan. *Concepts of Free Labor in Antebellum America*. New Haven, CT: Yale University Press, 1991.

Glymph, Thavolia. "Rose's War and the Gendered Politics of a Slave Insurgency in the Civil War." *Journal of the Civil War Era* 3, no. 4 (December 2013): 501–532.

Glymph, Thavolia. *The Women's Fight: The Civil War's Battles for Home, Freedom, and Nation*. Chapel Hill: University of North Carolina Press, 2020.

Gordon, Lesley J. *A Broken Regiment: The 16th Connecticut's Civil War*. Baton Rouge: Louisiana State University Press, 2014.

Gosse, Van, and David Waldstreicher, eds. *Revolutions and Reconstructions: Black Politics in the Long Nineteenth Century*. Philadelphia: University of Pennsylvania Press, 2020.

Greary, James W. *We Need Men: The Union Draft in the Civil War*. DeKalb: Northern Illinois University Press, 1991.

Greenberg, Kenneth S., ed. *Nat Turner: A Slave Rebellion in History and Memory*. New York: Oxford University Press, 2004.

Greenspan, Ezra. *William Wells Brown: An African American Life*. New York: W. W. Norton, 2014.

Grimsley, Mark. *The Hard Hand of War: Union Military Policy toward Southern Civilians, 1861–1865*. New York: Cambridge University Press, 1995.

Gronningsater, Sarah L. H. "'On Behalf of His Race and the Lemmon Slaves': Louis Napoleon, Northern Black Legal Culture, and the Politics of Sectional Crisis." *Journal of the Civil War Era* 7, no. 2 (June 2017): 206–241.

Gross, Ariela Julie. *Double Character: Slavery and Mastery in the Antebellum Southern Courtroom*. Princeton, NJ: Princeton University Press, 2000.

Guelzo, Allen C. *Abraham Lincoln: Redeemer President*. 2nd edition. Grand Rapids: William B. Eerdmans, 2022.

Guelzo, Allen C. *Lincoln's Emancipation Proclamation: The End of Slavery in America*. New York: Simon and Schuster, 2004.

Hadden, Sally E. *Slave Patrols: Law and Violence in Virginia and the Carolinas*. Cambridge, MA: Harvard University Press, 2001.

Hager, Christopher. *Word by Word: Emancipation and the Act of Writing*. Cambridge, MA: Harvard University Press, 2013.

Hahn, Steven. *A Nation under Our Feet: Black Political Struggles in the Rural South from Slavery to the Great Migration*. Cambridge, MA: Harvard University Press, 2003.

Hall, Stephen G. *A Faithful Account of the Race: African American Historical Writing in Nineteenth-Century America*. Chapel Hill: University of North Carolina Press, 2009.

Hallock, Judith Lee. "The Role of Community in Civil War Desertion." *Civil War History* 29, no. 2 (June 1983): 123–134.

Hardesty, Jared Ross. *Unfreedom: Slavery and Dependence in Eighteenth-Century Boston*. New York: New York University Press, 2016.

Hardwick, Kevin R. "'Your Old Father Abe Lincoln Is Dead and Damned': Black Soldiers and the Memphis Race Riot of 1866." *Journal of Social History* 27, no. 1 (Autumn 1993): 109–128.

Harrington, Fred H. *Fighting Politician: Major General N. P. Banks*. Philadelphia: University of Pennsylvania Press, 1970.

Harrington, Fred H. "The Fort Jackson Mutiny." *Journal of Negro History* 27, no. 4 (October 1942): 420–431.

Hartman, Saidiya. *Lose Your Mother: A Journey along the Atlantic Slave Route*. New York: Farrar, Straus and Giroux, 2008.

Hartog, Hendrik. *The Trouble with Minna: A Case of Slavery and Emancipation in the Antebellum North*. Chapel Hill: University of North Carolina Press, 2018.

Herrera, Ricardo A. *For Liberty and the Republic: The American Citizen as Soldier, 1775–1861*. New York: New York University Press, 2015.

Hesseltine, William Best. *Civil War Prisons: A Study in War Psychology*. Columbus: Ohio State University Press, 1998.

Hetey, Rebecca C., and Jennifer L. Eberhardt. "Racial Disparities in Incarceration Increase Acceptance of Punitive Policies." *Psychological Science* 25, no. 10 (October 2014): 1949–1954.

Heuman, Gad, and Trevor Burnard, eds. *The Routledge History of Slavery*. New York: Routledge, 2011.

Higginbotham, A. Leon, Jr. *Shades of Freedom: Racial Politics and the Presumptions of American Legal Process*. New York: Oxford University Press, 1996.

Hild, Matthew, and Keri Leigh Merritt, eds. *Rethinking Southern Labor History: Race, Class, and Power*. Gainesville: University Press of Florida, 2018.

Hilde, Libra R. *Slavery, Fatherhood, and Paternal Duty in African American Communities over the Long Nineteenth Century*. Chapel Hill: University of North Carolina Press, 2020.

Hillman, Elizabeth Lutes. *Defending America: Military Culture and the Cold War Court-Martial*. Princeton, NJ: Princeton University Press, 2005.

Hindus, Michael S. "Black Justice under White Law: Criminal Prosecutions of Blacks in Antebellum South Carolina." *Journal of American History* 63, no. 3 (December 1976): 575–599.

Hindus, Michael S. *Prison and Plantation: Crime, Justice, and Authority in Massachusetts and South Carolina, 1767–1878*. Chapel Hill: University of North Carolina Press, 2019.

Hodges, Graham Russell Gao, and Alan Edward Brown, eds. *"Pretends to Be Free": Runaway Slave Advertisements from Colonial and Revolutionary New York and New Jersey*. 1994. Reprint, New York: Fordham University Press, 2019.

Hollandsworth, James G., Jr. *The Louisiana Native Guards: The Black Military Experience during the Civil War*. Baton Rouge: Louisiana State University Press, 1998.

Howard, Stanley. *Border War: Fighting over Slavery before the Civil War*. Chapel Hill: University of North Carolina Press, 2010.

Howe, Daniel Walker. *Making the American Self: Jonathan Edwards to Abraham Lincoln*. New York: Oxford University Press, 2009.

Howe, Daniel Walker. *The Political Culture of the American Whigs*. Chicago: University of Chicago Press, 1979.

Howington, Arthur F. *What Saveth the Law: The Treatment of Slaves and Free Blacks in the State and Local Courts of Tennessee*. New York: Garland, 1986.

Humphreys, Margaret. *Intensely Human: The Health of the Black Soldier in the American Civil War*. Baltimore: Johns Hopkins University Press, 2008.

Humphreys, Margaret. *Marrow of Tragedy: The Health Crisis of the American Civil War*. Baltimore: Johns Hopkins University Press, 2013.

Hunter, Tera W. *Bound in Wedlock: Slave and Free Black Marriage in the Nineteenth Century*. Cambridge, MA: Harvard University Press, 2017.

Hunter, Tera W. *To 'Joy My Freedom: Southern Black Women's Lives and Labors after the Civil War*. Cambridge, MA: Harvard University Press, 1997.

Jabir, Johair. *Conjuring Freedom: Music and Masculinity, in the Civil War's "Gospel Army."* Columbus: Ohio State University Press, 2017.

Jacobs, Meg, William J. Novak, and Julian E. Zelizer, eds. *The Democratic Experiment: New Directions in American Political History*. Princeton, NJ: Princeton University Press, 2003.

Janney, Caroline E. *Remembering the Civil War: Reunion and the Limits of Reconciliation*. Chapel Hill: University of North Carolina Press, 2013.

Johnson, Sheri Lynn. "Black Innocence and the White Jury." *Michigan Law Review* 83, no. 7 (June 1985): 1611–1708.

Johnson, Walter. *Soul by Soul: Life inside the Antebellum Slave Market*. Cambridge, MA: Harvard University Press, 2000.

Jones, Jacqueline. *Labor of Love, Labor of Sorrow: Black Women, Work, and the Family from Slavery to the Present*. New York: Oxford University Press, 1985.

Jones, Martha S. *All Bound Up Together: The Woman Question in African American Public Culture, 1830–1900*. Chapel Hill: University of North Carolina Press, 2007.

Jones, Martha S. *Birthright Citizens: A History of Race and Rights in Antebellum America*. New York: Cambridge University Press, 2018.

Jones, Norrece T., Jr. *Born a Child of Freedom, Yet a Slave: Mechanisms of Control and Strategies of Resistance in Antebellum South Carolina*. Hanover, NH: Wesleyan University Press, 1990.

Jones, T. Cole. *Captives of Liberty: Prisoners of War and the Politics of Vengeance in the American Revolution*. Philadelphia: University of Pennsylvania Press, 2020.

Jones, Thomas L. "The Union League Club and New York's First Black Regiments in the Civil War." *New York History* 87, no. 3 (Summer 2006): 312–343.

Jordan, Ervin, L., Jr. *Black Confederates and Afro-Yankees in Civil War Virginia*. Charlottesville: University of Virginia Press, 1995.

Jordan, Winthrop D. *Tumult and Silence at Second Creek: An Inquiry into a Civil War Slave Conspiracy*. Baton Rouge: Louisiana State University Press, 1993.

Jordan, Winthrop D. *White over Black: American Attitudes toward the Negro, 1550–1812*. Chapel Hill: University of North Carolina Press, 1968.

Kantrowitz, Stephen. *More Than Freedom: Fighting for Black Citizenship in a White Republic, 1829–1889*. New York: Penguin, 2012.

Kastenberg, Joshua E. *Law in War, War as Law: Brigadier General Joseph Holt and the Judge Advocate General's Department in the Civil War and Early Reconstruction, 1861–1865*. Durham, NC: Carolina Academic Press, 2011.

Kastenberg, Joshua E. "A Sesquicentennial Historic Analysis of *Dynes v. Hoover* and the Supreme Court's Bow to Military Necessity: From Its Relationship to *Dred Scott v. Sandford* to Its Contemporary Influence." *University of Memphis Law Review* 39, no. 3 (Spring 2009): 595–662.

Kelley, Robin D. G. *Race Rebels: Culture, Politics, and the Black Working Class*. New York: Free Press, 1994.

Kelley, Robin D. G. "'We Are Not What We Seem': Rethinking Black Working-Class Opposition in the Jim Crow South." *Journal of American History* 80, no. 1 (June 1993): 75–112.

Kendi, Ibram X. *Stamped from the Beginning: The Definitive History of Racist Ideas in America*. New York: Nation Books, 2016.

Kennington, Kelly M. *In the Shadow of Dred Scott: St. Louis Freedom Suits and the Legal Culture of Slavery in Antebellum America*. Athens: University of Georgia Press, 2017.

Kerr-Ritchie, Jeffrey R. *Freedom's Seekers: Essays on Comparative Emancipation*. Baton Rouge: Louisiana State University Press, 2013.

Kousser, J. Morgan, and James M. McPherson, eds. *Region, Race and Reconstruction: Essays in Honor of C. Vann Woodward*. New York: Oxford University Press, 1982.

Kutzler, Evan A. *Living by Inches: The Smells, Sounds, Tastes, and Feeling of Captivity in Civil War Prisons*. Chapel Hill: University of North Carolina Press, 2019.

Kretz, Dale. *Administering Freedom: The State of Emancipation after the Freedmen's Bureau*. Chapel Hill: University of North Carolina Press, 2022.

Kynoch, Gary. "Terrible Dilemmas: Black Enlistment in the Union Army during the American Civil War." *Slavery and Abolition* 18, no. 2 (August 1997): 104–127.

Lande, Jonathan. "The Black Badge of Courage: The Politics of Recording Black Union Army Service and the Militarization of Black History in the Civil War's Aftermath." *Journal of American Ethnic History* 42, no. 1 (January 2023): 5–42.

Lande, Jonathan. "Disciplining Freedom: Union Army Slave Rebels and Emancipation in the Civil War Courts-Martial." PhD diss., Brown University, 2018.

Lande, Jonathan. "'Lighting Up the Path of Liberty and Justice': Black Abolitionist Fourth of July Celebrations and the Promise of America from the Fugitive Slave Act to the Civil War." *Journal of African American History* 105, no. 3 (Summer 2020): 364–395.

Lande, Jonathan. "Mutiny in the Civil War." *Civil War Monitor* 9 (March 2019): 54–65, 77.

Lande, Jonathan. "Richard Wright's Civil War Cipher." *Process: A Blog for American History*. February 14, 2023. https://www.processhistory.org/lande-richard-wrights-civil-war-cipher/.

Lande, Jonathan. "Trials of Freedom: African American Deserters during the U.S. Civil War." *Journal of Social History* 49, no. 3 (Spring 2016): 693–709.

Lang, Andrew F. *In the Wake of War: Military Occupation, Emancipation, and Civil War America*. Baton Rouge: Louisiana State University Press, 2017.

Lash, Jeffrey N. *A Politician Turned General: The Civil War Career of Stephen Augustus Hurlbut*. Kent, OH: Kent State University Press, 2003.

Lause, Mark A. *Free Labor: The Civil War and the Making of an American Working Class*. Urbana: University of Illinois Press, 2015.

Leonard, Elizabeth D. *Lincoln's Forgotten Ally: Judge Advocate General Joseph Holt of Kentucky*. Chapel Hill: University of North Carolina Press, 2011.

Leonard, Elizabeth D. *Slaves, Slaveholders, and a Kentucky Community's Struggle toward Freedom*. Lexington: University Press of Kentucky, 2019.

Levin, Kevin M. *Searching for Black Confederates: The Civil War's Most Persistent Myth*. Chapel Hill: University of North Carolina Press, 2019.

Levine, Lawrence W. *Black Culture and Black Consciousness: Afro-American Folk Thought from Slavery to Freedom*. 1977. Reprint, New York: Oxford University Press, 2007.

Levine, Peter. "Draft Evasion in the North during the Civil War, 1863–1865." *Journal of American History* 67, no. 4 (March 1981): 816–834.

Linderman, Gerald F. *Embattled Courage: The Experience of Combat in the American Civil War*. New York: Free Press, 1987.

Litwack, Leon F. *Been in the Storm So Long: The Aftermath of Slavery*. New York: Vintage, 1979.

Litwack, Leon F. *North of Slavery: The Negro in the Free States, 1790–1860*. Chicago: University of Chicago Press, 1961.

Litwack, Leon, and August Meier. *Black Leaders of the Nineteenth Century*. Urbana: University of Illinois Press, 1988.

Lonn, Ella. *Desertion during the Civil War*. First published in 1928 by the American Historical Association (Gloucester, MA). Reprint, Lincoln: University of Nebraska Press, 1998.

Lowry, Thomas P. "Research Note: New Access to a Civil War Resource." *Civil War History* 49, no. 1 (March 2003): 52–63.

Luke, Bob, and John David Smith. *Soldiering for Freedom: How the Union Army Recruited, Trained, and Deployed the U.S. Colored Troops*. Baltimore: Johns Hopkins University Press, 2014.

Luskey, Brian P. *Men Is Cheap: Exposing the Frauds of Free Labor in Civil War America*. Chapel Hill: University of North Carolina Press, 2020.

Lussana, Sergio A. *My Brother Slaves: Friendship, Masculinity, and Resistance in the Antebellum South*. Lexington: University Press of Kentucky, 2016.

Lynn, John A. "The Evolution of Army Style in the Modern West, 800–2000." *International History Review* 18, no. 3 (August 1996): 505–545.

MacDonald, Robert R., John R. Kemp, and Edward F. Haas, eds. *Louisiana's Black Heritage*. New Orleans: Louisiana State Museum, 1979.

Manning, Chandra. "The Costs of Emancipation: Panel Comment." Comment delivered at Annual Meeting of the Southern Historical Association, St. Pete Beach, FL, November 5, 2016.

Manning, Chandra. *Troubled Refuge: Struggling for Freedom in the Civil War*. New York: Knopf, 2016.

Manning, Chandra. *What This Cruel War Was Over: Soldiers, Slavery, and the Civil War*. New York: Knopf, 2007.

Marszalek, John F. *Sherman: A Soldier's Passion for Order*. Carbondale: Southern Illinois University Press, 2007.

Martin, Bessie. *A Rich Man's War, a Poor Man's Fight: Desertion of Alabama Troops from the Confederate Army*. 1932. Reprint, Tuscaloosa: University of Alabama Press, 2003.

Martinez, Jaime Amanda. *Confederate Slave Impressment in the Upper South*. Chapel Hill: University of North Carolina Press, 2013.

Marvel, William. *Lincoln's Autocrat: The Life of Edwin Stanton*. Chapel Hill: University of North Carolina Press, 2015.

Marvel, William. *Lincoln's Mercenaries: Economic Motivation among Union Soldiers during the Civil War*. Baton Rouge: Louisiana State University Press, 2018.

Masur, Kate. *An Example for All the Land: Emancipation and the Struggle over Equality in Washington, D.C.* Chapel Hill: University of North Carolina Press, 2010.

Masur, Kate. *Until Justice Be Done: America's First Civil Rights Movement from the Revolution to Reconstruction*. New York: W. W. Norton, 2021.

Masur, Kate. "'A Rare Phenomenon of Philological Vegetation': The Word 'Contraband' and the Meanings of Emancipation in the United States." *Journal of American History* 93, no. 4 (March 2007): 1050–1084.

Mathisen, Eric. *The Loyal Republic: Traitors, Slaves, and the Remaking of Citizenship in Civil War America*. Chapel Hill: University of North Carolina Press, 2018.

Matsui, John H. *The First Republican Army: The Army of Virginia and the Radicalization of the Civil War*. Charlottesville: University of Virginia Press, 2016.

McCarthy, Molly. *The Accidental Diarist: A History of the Daily Planner in America*. Chicago: University of Chicago Press, 2013.

McCurry, Stephanie. *Confederate Reckoning: Power and Politics in the Civil War South*. Cambridge, MA: Harvard University Press, 2010.

McCurry, Stephanie. *Women's War: Fighting and Surviving the American Civil War*. Cambridge, MA: Harvard University Press, 2019.

McDaniel, W. Caleb. *Sweet Taste of Liberty: A True Story of Slavery and Restitution in America*. New York: Oxford University Press, 2019.

McGrath, Autumn Hope. "'An Army of Working-Men': Military Labor and the Construction of American Empire, 1865–1915." PhD diss., University of Pennsylvania, 2016.

McPherson, James M. *Battle Cry of Freedom: The Civil War Era*. New York: Oxford University Press, 1988.

McPherson, James M. *Battle Cry of Freedom: The Civil War Era*. Reprint, New York: Oxford University Press, 2003.

McPherson, James M. *For Cause and Comrades: Why Men Fought in the Civil War*. New York: Oxford University Press, 1997.

McPherson, James M. *Drawn with the Sword: Reflections on the American Civil War*. New York: Oxford University Press, 1996.

McPherson, James M. *The Negro's Civil War: How American Blacks Felt and Acted during the War for the Union*. New York: Vintage, 1965.

Meier, Kathryn Shively. *Nature's Civil War: Common Soldiers and the Environment in 1862 Virginia*. Chapel Hill: University of North Carolina Press, 2013.

Mendez, James G. *A Great Sacrifice: Northern Black Soldiers, Their Families, and the Experience of Civil War*. New York: Fordham University Press, 2019.

Meyer, Howard N. *Colonel of the Black Regiment: The Life of Thomas Wentworth Higginson*. New York: W. W. Norton, 1967.

Mezurek, Kelly D. *For Their Own Cause: The 27th United States Colored Troops*. Kent, OH: Kent State University Press, 2016.

Milewski, Melissa. *Litigating across the Color Line: Civil Cases between Black and White Southerners from the End of Slavery to Civil Rights*. New York: Oxford University Press, 2018.

Miller, Edward A., Jr. *Lincoln's Abolitionist General: The Biography of David Hunter*. Columbia: University of South Carolina Press, 1997.

Milteer, Warren Eugene, Jr. *Beyond Slavery's Shadow: Free People of Color in the South*. Chapel Hill: University of North Carolina Press, 2021.

Mitchell, Reid. *Civil War Soldiers: Their Expectations and Their Experiences*. New York: Viking, 1988.

Mitchell, Reid. *The Vacant Chair: The Northern Soldier Leaves Home*. New York: Oxford University Press, 1993.

Montgomery, David. *Citizen Worker: The Experience of Workers in the United States with Democracy and the Free Market during the Nineteenth Century.* New York: Cambridge University Press, 1993.
Montgomery, David. *Workers' Control in America: Studies in the History of Work, Technology, and Labor Struggles.* New York: Cambridge University Press, 1979.
Morales, R. Isabela. *Happy Dreams of Liberty: An American Family in Slavery and Freedom.* New York: Oxford University Press, 2022.
Morgan, Edmund S. *Inventing the People: The Rise of Popular Sovereignty in England and America.* New York: W. W. Norton, 1989.
Morris, Thomas D. *Southern Slavery and the Law, 1619–1860.* Chapel Hill: University of North Carolina Press, 1996.
Mulderink, Earl F., III. *New Bedford's Civil War.* New York: Fordham University Press, 2012.
Nash, A. E. Keir. "Fairness and Formalism in the Trials of Blacks in the State Supreme Court of the Old South." *Virginia Law Review* 56, no. 1 (February 1970): 64–100.
Nash, A. E. Keir. "Reason of Slavery: Understanding the Judicial Role in the Peculiar Institution." *Vanderbilt Law Review* 32, no. 1 (January 1979): 7–218.
Neely, Mark E. *Lincoln and the Triumph of the Nation: Constitutional Conflict in the American Civil War.* Chapel Hill: University of North Carolina Press, 2011.
Neely, Mark E. *The Last Best Hope of Earth: Abraham Lincoln and the Promise of America.* Cambridge, MA: Harvard University Press, 1993.
Oakes, James. *The Ruling Race: A History of American Slaveholders.* New York: Knopf, 1982.
Oates, Stephen B. *The Fires of Jubilee: Nat Turner's Fierce Rebellion.* New York: Harper & Row, 1975.
Ochs, Stephen J. *A Black Patriot and a White Priest: André Cailloux and Claude Paschal Maistre in Civil War New Orleans.* Baton Rouge: Louisiana State University Press, 2006.
O'Donovan, Susan E. *Becoming Free in the Cotton South.* Cambridge, MA: Harvard University Press, 2009.
Öfele, Martin W. *German-Speaking Officers in the U.S. Colored Troops, 1863–1867.* Gainesville: University Press of Florida, 2003.
Painter, Nell Irvin. *Sojourner Truth: A Life, a Symbol.* New York: W. W. Norton, 1996.
Pargas, Damian Alan. *Freedom Seekers: Fugitive Slaves in North America, 1800–1860.* New York: Cambridge University Press, 2022.
Parson, Thomas E. *Work for Giants: The Campaign and Battle of Tupelo/Harrisburg, Mississippi, June–July 1864.* Kent, OH: Kent State University Press, 2014.
Penningroth, Dylan C. *The Claims of Kinfolk: African American Property and Community in the Nineteenth-Century South.* Chapel Hill: University of North Carolina Press, 2003.
Pillsbury, Samuel H. "Emotional Justice: Moralizing the Passions of Criminal Punishment." *Cornell Law Review* 74, no. 4 (May 1989): 655–710.

Pinheiro, Holly A. "Gendered Rhetoric and Black Civil War Military Recruiting." *American Nineteenth-Century History* 20, no. 3 (December 2019): 273–291.
Poskett, James. *Materials of the Mind: Phrenology, Race, and the Global History of Science, 1815–1920*. Chicago: University of Chicago Press, 2019.
Powell, Lawrence N. *New Masters: Northern Planters during the Civil War and Reconstruction*. New Haven, CT: Yale University Press, 1980.
Prist, Wilfrid. *William Blackstone: Law and Letters in the Eighteenth Century*. New York: Oxford University Press, 2008.
Pryor, Elizabeth Stordeur. *Colored Travelers: Mobility and the Fight for Citizenship before the Civil War*. Chapel Hill: University of North Carolina Press, 2016.
Quarles, Benjamin. *Black Abolitionists*. New York: Oxford University Press, 1969.
Quarles, Benjamin. *Lincoln and the Negro*. First published in 1962 by Oxford University Press (New York). Reprint, New York: De Capo, 1990.
Quarles, Benjamin. *The Negro in the Civil War*. First published in 1953 by Little, Brown (Boston). Reprint, Boston: De Capo Press, 1989.
Rael, Patrick. *Black Identity and Black Protest in the Antebellum North*. Chapel Hill: University of North Carolina Press, 2002.
Rael, Patrick. *Eighty-Eight Years: The Long Death of Slavery in the United States, 1777–1865*. Athens: University of Georgia Press, 2015.
Ramold, Steven J. *Baring the Iron Hand: Discipline in the Union Army*. DeKalb: Northern Illinois University Press, 2009.
Ramold, Steven J. "We Have No Right to Shoot Them: Military Executions in the Union Army." *Journal of America's Military Past* 33, no. 3 (Spring/Summer 2008): 42–66.
Rediker, Marcus. *The Amistad Rebellion: An Atlantic Odyssey of Slavery and Freedom*. New York: Viking, 2012.
Regosin, Elizabeth A., and Donald R. Shaffer. *Voices of Emancipation: Understanding Slavery, the Civil War, and Reconstruction through the U.S. Pension Bureau Files*. New York: New York University Press, 2008.
Reid, Richard M. *Freedom for Themselves: North Carolina's Black Soldiers in the Civil War Era*. Chapel Hill: University of North Carolina Press, 2008.
Reid, Thomas. *America's Fortress: A History of Fort Jefferson, Dry Tortugas, Florida*. Gainesville: University Press of Florida, 2006.
Reidy, Joseph P. *Illusions of Emancipation: The Pursuit of Freedom and Equality in the Twilight of Slavery*. Chapel Hill: University of North Carolina Press, 2019.
Rein, Christopher M. *Alabamians in Blue: Freedmen, Unionists, and the Civil War in the Cotton State*. Baton Rouge: Louisiana State University Press, 2019.
Renard, Paul D. "The Selection and Preparation of White Officers for the Command of Black Troops in the American Civil War: A Study of the 41st and 100th U.S. Colored Infantry." PhD diss., Virginia Tech, 2006.
Rhea, Gordon C. *Stephen A. Swails: Black Freedom Fighter in the Civil War and Reconstruction*. Baton Rouge: Louisiana State University Press, 2021.

Richardson, Heather Cox. *The Greatest Nation of the Earth: Republican Economic Policies during the Civil War* Cambridge, MA: Harvard University Press, 1997.

Richter, William L. *Overreached on All Sides: The Freedmen's Bureau Administrators in Texas, 1865–1868*. College Station: Texas A&M University Press, 1991.

Roberts, Neil. *Freedom as Marronage*. Chicago: University of Chicago Press, 2015.

Robertson, James I., Jr. *Soldiers Blue and Gray*. Columbia: University of South Carolina Press, 1989.

Robinson, Armstead L. *Bitter Fruits of Bondage: The Demise of Slavery and the Collapse of the Confederacy, 1861–1865*. Charlottesville: University of Virginia Press, 2005.

Rollin, Frank A. *Life and Public Services of Martin R. Delany*. Boston: Lee and Shepard, 1868.

Rose, Willie Lee. *Rehearsal for Reconstruction: The Port Royal Experiment*. New York: Oxford University Press, 1976.

Rosen, Hannah. *Terror in the Heart of Freedom: Citizenship, Sexual Violence, and the Meaning of Race in the Postemancipation South*. Chapel Hill: University of North Carolina Press, 2009.

Rosengarten, J. G. "Obituary Notice of Henry Coppée, LL.D." *Proceedings of the American Philosophical Society* 34, no. 149 (1895): 357–361.

Rosenthal, Caitlin. *Accounting for Slavery: Masters and Management*. Cambridge, MA: Harvard University Press, 2018.

Rosenthal, Caitlin. "Numbers for the Innumerate: Everyday Arithmetic and Atlantic Capitalism." *Technology and Culture* 58, no. 2 (June 2017): 529–544.

Ross, Steven Joseph. "Freed Soil, Freed Labor, Freed Men: John Eaton and the Davis Bend Experiment." *Journal of Southern History* 44, no. 2 (May 1978): 213–232.

Rothman, Adam. *Beyond Freedom's Reach: A Kidnapping in the Twilight of Slavery*. Cambridge, MA: Harvard University Press, 2015.

Rowley, Hazel. *Richard Wright: The Life and Times*. New York: Henry Holt, 2001.

Royster, Charles. *A Revolutionary People at War: The Continental Army and American Character, 1775–1783*. Chapel Hill: University of North Carolina Press, 1980.

Ruckman, P. S., Jr., and David Kincaid. "Inside Lincoln's Clemency Decision Making." *Presidential Studies Quarterly* 29, no. 1 (March 1999): 84–99.

Rugemer, Edward Bartlett. *The Problem of Emancipation: The Caribbean Roots of the American Civil War*. Baton Rouge: Louisiana State University Press, 2008.

Ryan, James Gilbert. "The Memphis Riots of 1866: Terror in a Black Community during Reconstruction." *Journal of Negro History* 62 (July 1977): 243–257.

Ryan, Mary. *Civic Wars: Democracy and Public Life in the American City during the Nineteenth Century*. Berkeley: University of California Press, 1998.

Samito, Christian G. *Becoming American under Fire: Irish Americans, African Americans, and the Politics of Citizenship during the Civil War Era*. Ithaca, NY: Cornell University Press, 2009.

Samito, Christian G. "The Intersection between Military Justice and Equal Rights: Mutinies, Courts-Martial, and Black Civil War Soldiers." *Civil War History* 53, no. 2 (June 2007): 170–202.

Sanders, Charles W., Jr. *While in the Hands of My Enemy: Military Prisons of the Civil War*. Baton Rouge: Louisiana State University Press, 2005.

Sandow, Robert M. *Deserter Country: Civil War Opposition in the Pennsylvania Appalachians*. New York: Fordham University Press, 2009.

Sappol, Michael. *A Traffic of Dead Bodies: Anatomy and Embodied Social Identity in Nineteenth-Century America*. Princeton, NJ: Princeton University Press, 2002.

Savage, Kirk. *Standing Soldiers: Race, War, and Monument in Nineteenth-Century America*. Princeton, NJ: Princeton University Press, 1997.

Saville, Julie. *The Work of Reconstruction: From Slave to Wage Laborer in South Carolina 1860–1870*. New York: Cambridge University Press, 1994.

Schafer, Judith Kelleher. *Becoming Free, Remaining Free: Manumission and Enslavement in New Orleans, 1846–1862*. Baton Rouge: Louisiana State University Press, 2003.

Schafer, Judith Kelleher. *Slavery, the Civil Law, and the Supreme Court of Louisiana*. Baton Rouge: Louisiana State University Press, 1994.

Schantz, Mark S. *Awaiting the Heavenly Country: The Civil War and America's Culture of Death*. Ithaca, NY: Cornell University Press, 2008.

Schlueter, David A. "The Military Justice System Conundrum: Justice or Discipline?" *Military Law Review* 215 (Spring 2013): 4–74.

Schwalm, Leslie A. *Emancipation's Diaspora: Race and Reconstruction in the Upper Midwest*. Chapel Hill: University of North Carolina Press, 2009.

Schwalm, Leslie A. *Medicine, Science & Making Race in Civil War America*. Chapel Hill: University of North Carolina Press, 2023.

Schwartz, Thomas F., ed. *"For a Vast Future Also": Essays from the* Journal of the Abraham Lincoln Association. New York: Fordham University Press, 1999.

Schweninger, Loren. *Appealing for Liberty: Freedom Suits in the South*. New York: Oxford University Press, 2018.

Scott, Rebecca J., and Jean M. Hébrard. *Freedom Papers: An Atlantic Odyssey in the Age of Emancipation*. Cambridge, MA: Harvard University Press, 2012.

Seraile, William. *Angels of Mercy: White Women and the History of New York's Colored Orphan Asylum*. New York: Fordham University Press, 2011.

Seraile, William. *New York's Black Regiments during the Civil War*. New York: Routledge, 2011.

Shaffer, Donald R. *After the Glory: The Struggles of Black Civil War Veterans*. Lawrence: University Press of Kansas, 2004.

Sheehan-Dean, Aaron. *The Calculus of Violence: How Americans Fought the Civil War*. Cambridge, MA: Harvard University Press, 2018.

Sheehan-Dean, Aaron. *Why Confederates Fought: Family & Nation in Civil War Virginia*. Chapel Hill: University of North Carolina Press. 2007

Sherikel, J. Richard, Bethlyn McCloskey, and Betsy Swanson. "Nomination Form: Fort Livingston." March 28, 1974. National Register of Historic Places Inventory, National Park Service.

Silkenat, David. "'A Typical Negro': Gordon Peter, Vincent Colyer, and the Story Behind Slavery's Most Famous Photograph." *American Nineteenth Century History* 15, no. 2 (2014): 169–186.

Silkenat, David. *Driven from Home: North Carolina's Civil War Refugee Crisis.* Athens: University of Georgia Press, 2016.

Silkenat, David, and John Barr. "'Serving the Lord and Abe Lincoln's Spirit': Lincoln and Memory in the WPA Narratives." *Lincoln Herald* 115 (2013): 75–97.

Simpson, Brooks D. *Sherman's Civil War: Selected Correspondence of William T. Sherman, 1860–1865.* Chapel Hill: University of North Carolina Press, 1999.

Sinha, Manisha. *The Rise and Fall of the Second American Republic: Reconstruction, 1860–1920.* New York: Liveright, 2024.

Sinha, Manisha. *The Slave's Cause: A History of Abolition.* New Haven, CT: Yale University Press, 2016.

Smallwood, Stephanie. *Saltwater Slavery: A Middle Passage from Africa to American Diaspora.* Cambridge, MA: Harvard University Press, 2007.

Smith, Adam I. P. *The Stormy Present: Conservatism and the Problem of Slavery in Northern Politics, 1846–1865.* Chapel Hill: University of North Carolina Press, 2017.

Smith, John David. *Lincoln and the U.S. Colored Troops.* Carbondale: Southern Illinois University Press, 2013.

Smith, John David, ed. *Black Soldiers in Blue: African American Troops in the Civil War Era.* Chapel Hill: University of North Carolina Press, 2003.

Smith, Michael Thomas. "The Most Desperate Scoundrels Unhung: Bounty Jumpers and Recruitment Fraud in the Civil War North." *American Nineteenth Century* 6, no. 2 (August 2005): 149–172.

Southern, Eileen. *The Music of Black Americans: A History.* New York: W. W. Norton, 1997.

Speer, Lonnie R. *Portals to Hell: Military Prisons of the Civil War.* Mechanicsburg, PA: Stackpole, 1997.

Sproat, John G. "Blueprint for Radical Reconstruction." *Journal of Southern History* 23, no. 1 (February 1957): 25–44.

Spurgeon, Ian Michael. *Soldiers in the Army of Freedom: The 1st Kansas Colored, the Civil War's First African American Combat Unit.* Norman: University of Oklahoma Press, 2014.

Stanley, Amy Dru. *From Bondage to Contract: Wage Labor, Marriage, and the Market in the Age of Slave Emancipation.* New York: Cambridge University Press, 1998.

Stanley, Amy Dru. "Instead of Waiting for the Thirteenth Amendment: The War Power, Slave Marriage, and Inviolate Human Rights." *American Historical Review* 115, no. 3 (June 2010): 732–765.

Stansfield, George James. "A History of the Judge Advocate General's Department United States Army." *Military Affairs* 9, no. 3 (Autumn 1945): 219–237.

Stauffer, John, and Benjamin Soskis. *The Battle Hymn of the Republic: A Biography of the Song That Marches On*. New York: Oxford University Press, 2013.

Steinfeld, Robert J. *Coercion, Contract, and Free Labor in the Nineteenth Century*. New York: Cambridge University Press, 2001.

Steinfeld, Robert J. *The Invention of Free Labor: The Employment Relations and American Law and Culture, 1350–1870*. Chapel Hill: University of North Carolina Press, 1991.

Sternhell, Yael A. *Routes of War: The World of Movement in the Confederate South*. Cambridge, MA: Harvard University Press, 2012.

Stewart, James Brewer. "The Emergence of Racial Modernity and the Rise of the White North, 1790–1840." *Journal of the Early Republic* 18, no. 2 (Summer 1998): 181–217.

Suggs, Christian. *Whispered Consolations: Law and Narrative in African American Life*. Ann Arbor: University of Michigan Press, 2000.

Talbot, Edith Armstrong. *Samuel Chapman Armstrong: A Biographical Sketch*. New York: Doubleday, Page, 1904.

Tarter, Michelle Lise, and Richard Bell, eds. *Buried Lives: Incarcerated in Early America*. Athens: University of Georgia Press, 2012.

Taylor, Amy Murrell. *Embattled Freedom: Journeys through the Civil War's Slave Refugee Camps*. Chapel Hill: University of North Carolina Press, 2018.

Taylor, Brian. *Fighting for Citizenship: Black Northerners and the Debate over Military Service in the Civil War*. Chapel Hill: University of North Carolina Press, 2020.

Teters, Kristopher A. *Practical Liberators: Union Officers in the Western Theater during the Civil War*. Chapel Hill: University of North Carolina Press, 2018.

Thomas, William G. *A Question of Freedom: The Families Who Challenged Slavery from the Nation's Founding to the Civil War*. New Haven, CT: Yale University Press, 2020.

Tomlins, Christopher L. *Law, Labor, and Ideology in the Early American Republic*. New York: Cambridge University Press, 1993.

Trudeau, Noah Andre. *Like Men of War: Black Troops in the Civil War, 1862–1865*. New York: Little, Brown, 1998.

Twitty, Anne. *Before* Dred Scott: *Slavery and Legal Culture in the American Confluence, 1787–1857*. New York: Cambridge University Press, 2016.

Uya, Okon Edet. *From Slavery to Public Service: Robert Smalls, 1839–1915*. New York: Oxford University Press, 1971.

VanderVelde, Lea. *Redemption Songs: Suing for Freedom before* Dred Scott. New York: Oxford University Press, 2014.

Varon, Elizabeth R. *Appomattox: Victory, Defeat, and Freedom at the End of the Civil War*. New York: Oxford University Press, 2014.

Varon, Elizabeth R. *Armies of Deliverance: A New History of the Civil War*. New York: Oxford University Press, 2019.

Vorenberg, Michael. *The Emancipation Proclamation: A Brief History with Documents*. Boston: Bedford Books of St. Martin, 2010.

Vorenberg, Michael. *Final Freedom: The Civil War, the Abolition of Slavery, and the Thirteenth Amendment*. New York: Cambridge University Press, 2001.

Walls, David. "Marching Song of the First Arkansas Colored Regiment: A Contested Attribution." *Arkansas Historical Quarterly* 64, no. 4 (Winter 2007): 401–421.

Warner, Ezra J., Jr. *Generals in Blue: Lives of the Union Commanders*. Baton Rouge: Louisiana State University Press, 1964.

Washington, Linn, ed. *Black Judges on Justice: Perspectives from the Bench*. New York: New Press, 1994.

Washington, Versalle F. *Eagles on Their Buttons: A Black Infantry Regiment in the Civil War*. Columbia: University of Missouri Press, 1999.

Weber, Jennifer L. *Copperheads: The Rise and Fall of Lincoln's Opponents in the North*. New York: Oxford University Press, 2006.

Weicksel, Sarah Jones. "To Look like Men of War: Visual Transformation Narratives of African American Union Soldiers." *Clio: Women, Gender, History*, no. 40 (July 2014): 124–138

Weigley, Russell F. *History of the United States Army*. Enlarged ed. Bloomington: Indiana University Press, 1984.

Weitz, Mark A. *A Higher Duty: Desertion among Georgia Troops during the Civil War*. Lincoln: University of Nebraska Press, 2005.

Weitz, Mark A. *More Damning Than Slaughter: Desertion in the Confederate Army*. Lincoln: University of Nebraska Press, 2008.

Welch, Kimberly M. *Black Litigants in the Antebellum American South*. Chapel Hill: University of North Carolina Press, 2018.

Wells, Jonathan Daniel. *Blind No More: African American Resistance, Free-Soil Politics, and the Coming of the Civil War*. Athens: University of Georgia Press, 2019.

Wells, Tom Henderson. *The Slave Ship Wanderer*. 1967. Reprint, Athens: University of Georgia Press, 2009.

Westwood, Howard. *Black Troops, White Commanders, and Freedmen during the Civil War*. Carbondale: Southern Illinois University Press, 2002.

White, Jonathan W. *Emancipation, the Union Army, and the Reelection of Abraham Lincoln*. Baton Rouge: Louisiana State University Press, 2014.

White, Shane. "'It Was a Proud Day': African Americans, Festivals, and Parades in the North, 1741–1834." *Journal of American History* 81, no. 4 (June 1994): 13–50.

Wiley, Bell Irvin. "Billy Yank and Abraham Lincoln." *Abraham Lincoln Quarterly* 6, no. 2 (March 1950): 103–122.

Wiley, Bell Irvin. *The Life of Billy Yank: The Common Soldier of the Union*. 1952. Reprint, Baton Rouge: Louisiana State University Press, 1993.

Wiley, Bell Irvin. *The Life of Johnny Reb: The Common Soldier of the Confederacy*. 1943. Reprint, Baton Rouge: Louisiana State University Press, 2008.

Williams, David. *I Freed Myself: African American Self-Emancipation in the Civil War Era*. New York: Cambridge University Press, 2014.

Williams, Heather Andrea. *Help Me to Find My People: The African American Search for Family Lost in Slavery.* Chapel Hill: University of North Carolina Press, 2012.

Williams, Heather Andrea. *Self-Taught: African American Education in Slavery and Freedom.* Chapel Hill: University of North Carolina Press, 2005.

Williams, Kidada E. *They Left Great Marks on Me: African American Testimonies of Racial Violence from Emancipation to World War I.* New York: New York University Press, 2012.

Williams, T. Harry. *Lincoln and the Radicals.* Madison: University of Wisconsin Press, 1941.

Wilson, Carol. *Freedom at Risk: The Kidnapping of Free Blacks in America, 1780–1865.* Lexington: University Press of Kentucky, 1994.

Wilson, Keith P. *Campfires of Freedom: The Camp Life of Black Soldiers during the Civil War.* Kent, OH: Kent State University Press, 2002.

Wilson, Keith P. "Thomas Webster and the 'Free Military School for Applicants for Commands of Colored Troops.'" *Civil War History* 29, no. 2 (June 1983): 101–122.

Winger, Stewart L., and Jonathan W. White, eds. *Ex Parte Milligan Reconsidered: Race and Civil Liberties from the Lincoln Administration to the War on Terror.* Lawrence: University Press of Kansas, 2020.

Winters, John D. *The Civil War in Louisiana.* 1963. Reprint, Baton Rouge: Louisiana State University Press, 1991.

Witt, John Fabian. *Lincoln's Code: The Laws of War in American History.* New York: Free Press, 2012.

Wong, Edlie L. *Neither Fugitive nor Free: Atlantic Slavery, Freedom Suits, and the Legal Culture of Travel.* New York: New York University Press, 2009.

Wongsrichanalai, Kanisorn. *Northern Character: College-Educated New Englanders, Honor, Nationalism, and Leadership in the Civil War Era.* New York: Fordham University Press, 2016.

Wood, Gordon S. *The Radicalism of the American Revolution.* New York: Knopf, 1992.

Wood, Peter H. *Black Majority: Negroes in Colonial South Carolina from 1670 through the Stono Rebellion.* New York: W. W. Norton, 1974.

Wood, Nicholas P. "A 'Class of Citizens': The Earliest Black Petitioners to Congress and Their Quaker Allies." *William and Mary Quarterly* 74, no. 1 (January 2017): 109–144.

Woodward, Edward Colin. *Marching Masters: Slavery, Race, and the Confederate Army during the Civil War.* Charlottesville: University of Virginia Press, 2014.

Zaeske, Susan. *Signatures of Citizenship: Petitioning, Antislavery, and Women's Political Identity.* Chapel Hill: University of North Carolina Press, 2003.

Zombek, Angela M. *Penitentiaries, Punishment, and Military Prisons: Familiar Responses to an Extraordinary Crisis during the American Civil War.* Kent, OH: Kent State University Press, 2018.

Zürcher, Erik-Jan, ed. *Fighting for a Living: A Comparative Study of Military Labour, 1500–2000.* Amsterdam: Amsterdam University Press, 2014.

Index

For the benefit of digital users, indexed terms that span two pages (e.g., 52–53) may, on occasion, appear on only one of those pages.

Note: page numbers followed by *f* and *t* refer to figures and tables respectively. Those followed by n refer to notes, with note number.

Adams, Charles, 72–73
Adams, Charles Francis, Jr., 47–48
AFIC. *See* American Freedmen's Inquiry Commission
Alotta, Robert, 252n.19
American Freedmen's Inquiry Commission (AFIC), 30–31
Antietam, Battle of, 18
arming of Black soldiers
   American Freedmen's Inquiry Commission study on, 30–31
   expedition into Florida to test, 28–29
   legislation enabling, 25, 26–27
   white people's fears about, 23–28
Articles of War
   and courts-martial, 82–83
   ignorance of, as desertion trial defense, 104–6, 109, 112–13, 143–46

Bagwell, George, 112
Baker, Almon, 248–49n.52
Baker, Wallace, 53–54
Ball, Wesley, 116–17

Baltimore, Charles, 132–33, 133*f*
Banks, Nathaniel, 31, 141–42, 144*f*
Barbour, James, 57
Barr, Isham, 152–56, 154*f*
Barton, William, 128–30
Bates, Edward, 134–35
Benedict, Augustus, 53
Benet, Stephen V., 86, 110–11
Bennett, Henry, 112–13
Bierce, Ambrose, 39
Black Man, His Antecedents, His Genius, and His Achievements, The (Brown), 89–90
Black northerners
   demands for equal treatment, 58–59
   enlistments, 18–20
   and nineteenth-century tradition of letters to elected officials, 137–38
   number tried for desertion, *vs.* Black southerners, 99–100, 101*t*, 102*t*
   reasons for desertion, 58–60
   views on military discipline, 48–49, 50–52

Black soldiers, 59. *See also* instruction of Black soldiers in skills for free society; pay of Black soldiers
　Black northerners' demands for equal treatment, 58–59
　clothing/uniforms worn by, 1–2, 8f, 36–37
　discouragement about lack of advancement, 54–55
　engagement with state, lessons learned in, 162
　exposure to new diseases, 67
　fear of US Army hospitals, 159
　first regiment formed, 63–64
　freedom promised to, 1, 15–16
　as less hardy, due to slavery, 67
　monuments to, 164–65, 165f
　movies about, 164–65
　as national symbol, 164–65
　opening of US Army to, 6, 18, 27
　political empowerment gained through service, 156–57, 163–64
　pride of soldiers and families in, 163–64
　reasons for enlisting, 161
　reduction in rank for disobedience, 76–77
　reluctance to part from families, 1–2
　and rigid discipline in some units, 159
　tactics of resistance, 60
　total number enlisted, 17
　training of, 19
　Union's acceptance of, 17
　Union's delay in accepting, 1, 15–16
　view of military service as exercise of freedom, 60–61
　white people's concerns about ability to control, 25–26, 44–45
　white people's views on, 158–59
Black southerners. *See also* enslaved persons, former; impressed Black southerners
　enlistment by, 20–21
　number trials for desertion, *vs.* Black northerners, 99–100, 101t, 102t
　reasons for leaves of freedom, 60–61
　views on military discipline, 48–49, 52–53
　women, wartime hardship of, 65
Blackstone's Commentaries on the Laws of England, 85
Bliss, George, 85–86
Bloor, Alfred, 138
Bonaparte, Napoleon, 56
Brice's Crossroads, Battle of, 158–59
Brown, George, 111
Brown, Henry-Harrison, 44, 75–76
Brown, James, 64, 81–82
Brown, John, 24f
Brown, Sussex, 114–15
Brown, William J., 54
Brown, William Wells, 19–20, 89–90
Bureau of Colored Troops, 31–32
Bureau of Refugees, Freedmen, and Abandoned Lands (Freedmen's Bureau), 149–50
Burgess, Rollin, 76–77
Burton, Daniel, 93–95, 94f, 248n.50

Cage, John, 71
Canby, Edward, 127–28, 132–33
Charleston, South Carolina, Black troops' occupation of, 16f
Child, Lydia Maria, 25
Christian Recorder, 59
Cochin, Augustin, 28–29
Conant, Sherman, 52
conduct prejudicial to military order, number tried for, 96–97
Confiscation Act, First (1861), 18
Confiscation Act, Second (1862), 18, 25, 26–27
Congress's debate on arming of Black soldiers, 25–27
contract, military service as, 91–98

courts' favoring of government/
employer in, 91, 96–97, 98
and desertion as contract violation,
91, 96–97
as distinct from ideological motives
for service, 91–92
draft and, 97–98
enforcement of, vs. soldiers'
expectations for justice, 97, 111
establishment of valid contract in
court-martial, 93–97, 94f, 100
maintaining US Army strength as
paramount consideration, 96–97
and nineteenth-century contract
theory, 92–93
soldiers claiming government breaches
of, 92–93, 96–97, 112
Coombs, Abraham, 109
Coppée, Henry, 87–88
Corning, Erastus, 138–39
Cornish, Samuel, 58–59
courts-martial. *See also* contract, military
service as
and all-white jurors, as issue, 87–88
and Articles of War, 82–83
Black soldiers' concerns about, 89–91
Black soldiers' expectations for, 82, 86,
87, 116–17
and Black southerners' experiences of
courts under slavery, 90
and bureaucratic erasure of
humanity, 118–19
call for Black officers to sit on, 89,
245n.24, 246n.34
character of accused as factor in, 86
correction and appeal mechanisms,
86–87, 137
differences from civilian
courts, 85–86
effect of participants'
backgrounds on, 87
equal treatment of Black soldiers in,
81–82, 103–4, 106–7

fairness of, 86–87, 88–89
focus on discipline, not justice, 82, 85–
86, 87–88, 91
legal counsel for defendants, 110–11
and military common law (*lex non
scripta*), 82–83
number tried for conduct prejudicial
to military order, 96–97
officers qualified to sit as jurors
in, 87–88
presiding officers' knowledge of
law, 87–88
public humiliation as
punishment, 90–91
role of judge advocate, 83–84, 85
structure of, 82–83
typical trial, described, 83–84, 84f, 85
white soldiers' expectations for, 82, 86,
87, 88–89
courts-martial trials for desertion. *See
also* defense arguments in trials for
desertion
and contract law applied to drafted
men, 98
conviction rate, 96–97, 116–17
conviction rate for Black *vs.* white
soldiers, 99–100
maintaining US Army strength as
paramount consideration, 96–
97, 106–7
number of southern *vs.* northern
Black soldiers tried for, 99–100,
101*t*, 102*t*
number tried, 96–97
and valid enlistment as contract, 93–
97, 94f, 118
courts-martial trials for leaves of
freedom, 99–108. *See also* defense
arguments in trials for desertion
Black soldiers' awareness of
penalties, 116–17
and criminalization of acts of self-
liberation, 99, 101–2, 106–8

courts-martial trials for leaves of freedom (*cont.*)
  failure to understand Black people's experiences, 87–88, 89, 245n.24
  failure to understand Black southerners' journey to freedom, 81–82
  former enslaved men's disputing of terms of service in, 110
  former slaves' limited knowledge of law and, 81–82, 100, 104–6
  punishments in, as perceived reenslavement, 101–2
  sentences in, 64, 67–68, 69, 72–73, 81, 88–89, 100–2, 104–6, 109, 113, 115, 119–20, 121, 132–33, 134, 143, 146, 150–51, 152
  soldier executed for, 103–4
  soldiers' defenses of, in court, 3–4
Cowden, Robert, 43–44
Cox, Samuel, 31
Crittenden, John, 26

Daniels, Nathan, 88–89
Davis, Samuel, 159
Declaration of the Recruit, 93
defense arguments in trials for desertion
  basis in labor contract law, 111–12, 113
  capture by enemy as, 127–30
  challenging legality of enlistment contracts, 122–25, 126–27
  claimed abduction by bounty brokers, 123–25
  and claiming of status as free men, 117
  contesting of terms of service, 110–11, 113–14
  danger of nearby enemy forces as, 121
  defendant's responsibility for delivering, 110–11
  dishonesty in, 115–16
  disputes of legitimacy of enlistment, 112
  efforts to carve out liberties, 130–31
  efforts to evoke sympathy, 116–18, 130
  family obligations as, 116–21, 130
  former enslaved persons' familiarity with freedom suits and, 113
  and former enslaved persons' knowledge of law, 113, 130, 251n.13
  ignorance and confusion as, 112–13, 115–16
  ignorance of regulations as, 104–6, 109, 119–20, 124–25
  illness as, 109, 114–15, 120–21
  inability to return following leave as, 125–26
  insistence on treatment as person, 119–20, 121
  invoking of prior enslavement as, 113–14, 115–16
  low success rate of, 130–31
  missed transportation as, 112
  and playing-up of Black people's supposed ignorance, 124–25
  pleas for recognition of mitigating circumstances, 110
  and stable family as important benefit for previously enslaved people, 117–18, 120–21
  successful, 124–25
  visions of personal emancipation in, 116–17
De Hart, William Chetwood, 85
Delany, Martin, 58–59
Democrats
  exploitation of white people's fears about emancipation, 24–25, 26–27, 43
  opposition to Black men in US Army, 25–26
desertion. *See also* contract, military service as; courts-martial trials for desertion
  absent without leave as lesser charge, 81, 96, 152

from Confederate Army, 57–58
conviction for, and denial of
pension, 160
executions for, as percentage of total
executions, 116–17
from first Black regiments formed in
Sea Islands, 63–64
necessity of strong penalty for, 96–97
desertion from US Army
conviction rate, 96–97
history of, 57
number tried, 96–97
punishments, 96–97
rate of, 57
reasons for, 57–58, 70
desertion from USCT units. *See also*
leaves of freedom
to avoid unjust punishment, 76–77, 146
Black northerners' reasons for, 58–60
as continuation of journey toward freedom, 161
flight from slave-like work, 5–6
flight to Confederate Army, 76–77
imprisonment for, 74
number tried, and
convicted, 5n.13, 5
rate *vs.* white soldiers, 5
as term, 215–16n.11
total number of, 5, 56–57
desertion from white units
rate of, 5, 56–57
reasons for desertion, 5
discipline, military
absolute submission to authority as
goal, 36, 37
all soldiers' complaints about, 34–35
avoidance of slavery-like punishments
for Black soldiers, 44
Black northerners' views on, 48–49, 50–52
Black soldiers and, 36–39, 38*f*

Black soldiers' resistance to, 161, 162
Black soldiers' revolts against, 52–54
Black southerners' views on, 48–49, 52–53
excessive, failure of early Sea Island
regiments due to, 63–64
as expression of white supremacy,
in Black soldiers' view, 48–49,
50, 51–53
fears of Black soldiers' insurrection
and, 48–49
former enslaved persons' avoidance of,
using tactics used under slavery, 1–2,
3–4, 8–9, 56–57, 60, 61, 63, 162
harshness of, 36–37
and lack of regulations on
punishments, 39–40
as more burdensome for Black
soldiers hoping for freedom and
equality, 35
as necessary for training citizen-soldiers, 35–36, 39
as nullification of emancipation, in
Black soldiers' view, 48–49
public execution of deserters, 40–42, 41*f*
some soldiers' condemnation of, 42
violence and humiliation used to
enforce, 39–40
white soldiers' anger at violent
enforcement, 49
white soldiers' begrudging acceptance
of, 48–50
disease. *See* illness
Diven, Alexander, 26
Dix-Hill Cartel, 137
Douglass, Frederick, 18–19, 118–19
Douglass, Lewis, 19
draft, military service as contract
and, 97–98
Du Bois, W. E. B., 163–64
Dunbar, Paul Laurence, 163–64

Dynes, Frank, 134–35
Dynes vs. Hoover (1857), 134–35

Edwards, Joseph, 98
Edwards, Laura, 258n.36
elected officials, nineteenth-century tradition of letters to, 137–38
Eleventh Louisiana Infantry (African Descent) (later Forty-Ninth USCI)
  and Battle of Milliken's Bend, 1–2, 3*f*
  deserters from, 1, 213n.1, 214n.6
  dissatisfaction of troops in, 213n.1
  soldiers' reluctance to part from families, 1–2
Ellsworth, Thomas, 53
emancipation
  media's calming of fears about, 28–29, 29*f*
  and US Army's hope to shape the unfolding process, 16–17
  US government's adoption of as military strategy, 17
  white's peoples fears about, 23–27, 24*f*
  white supporters of, 25
Emancipation Proclamation
  and Black enlistment, 18–19, 20–23
  and opening of US Army to Black soldiers, 6, 18, 27
Emery, Andre, 146–47
enlistment
  below age of consent, and parental consent, 248–49n.52
  as contract, and documents signed by recruit, 93–97, 94*f*
  Declaration of the Recruit oath in, 93
  underage, documents required for, 96
enlistment of Black men
  increase, after Emancipation Proclamation, 18–19, 20–21
  in North, 18–20
  number, by state, 22*t*
  reasons for, 18–21, 161
  from South, 20–21
enslaved persons
  disruptions behind Confederate lines, 17
  early reluctance to trust Union intentions, 20–21
  escape to Union territory, 1, 17–18
  legal challenges to slavery (freedom suits), 8–9
  participation in courts, 258n.36
  some northerners' abuse of refugees, 17–18
  strategies of resistance, 8–9
  as term, 215–16n.11
  wartime protests against working conditions, 6–8
  work for Confederate Army, 6, 50–51
enslaved persons, former
  as child-like, and need for discipline and education, 9–10, 18, 30, 42, 43–44
  documents required for enlistment, 93–95, 94*f*
  drafting of, and contract law, 97–98
  enlistment, 1
  number tried for desertion, *vs.* Black northerners, 99–100, 101*t*, 102*t*
  and perceived similarity of US Army discipline and slavery, 103–4
  resentment of treatment as child-like, 35
enslaved persons' journey to freedom
  brief success before reassertion of white supremacy, 163
  as complex and protracted, 3–4, 11–12, 15–16, 162–63
  leaves of freedom and, 3–4, 8–12, 56–57, 60, 63, 69, 70, 74, 77, 101–2, 106–8, 161, 162
  US Army service as impediment to, 161–64, 166
  view of military service as a step in, 60–61, 161
  white media's oversimplification of, 4*f*

Evans, Sam, 32–33
execution
   of Black soldiers, Black soldiers' views on, 89–90
   Black soldiers' resentment of, 51
   of deserters, 40–42, 41*f*
   for leaves of freedom, 103–4
   for mutiny, 53–54
   percentage for desertion, 116–17
   of strike leader demanding higher pay, 47
   total number executed, 252n.19
   white soldiers' begrudging acceptance of, 49

family
   Black, Reconstruction goal of remaking, 150–53, 156–57
   stable, as benefit for previously enslaved people, 117–18, 120–21
Fields, Hector, 72–73, 262n.15
Fifth Amendment, 88, 112
Fleetwood, Christian, 54–55
food for Black soldiers, poor quality of, 50–51
Forrest, Nathan Bedford, 127–30, 158–59
Fort Jefferson, prison at, 69, 71–72, 132–33, 133*f*, 139–40, 143–46, 150–51
Fort Pillow, massacre of Black soldiers at, 158–59
Foster, Charles, 31–32
Fox, Charles, 44–45
Freedmen's Bureau, 149–50
freedom, dispute between enslaved persons and white northerners over meaning of, 18, 23. *See also* enslaved persons' journey to freedom
Freedom's Journal, 58–59
free labor practices
   Black soldiers' pay disputes as lessons in, 122
   guidance for Black soldiers in proper forms of labor protest, 46–47
   Reconstruction's imposition in South, 121–22, 149–50
Fuquay, Solomon, 126–27

Gardner, Alexander, 123–25
General Order No. 143, 31–32
Germain, Mose, 100–2
Gillum, William, 117
Glory (1989 film), 2–3, 164–65
Glover, Gustav, 104
Gooding, James Henry, 19–20, 59
Gordon (formerly enslaved Black soldier), 4*f*
Graham, Eli, 122–23
Grant, Ulysses S.
   on courts-martial, 88
   and fall of Vicksburg, 81
   on military discipline, 36
   return from retirement for Civil War, 36
   on success of USCT units, 55
Greene, James Harvey, 60–61
Griffith, James, 41*f*
Guy, Allen, 104–6

Haitian Revolution, and white Americans' fears, 24–25, 26–27
Hall, Henry, 66–68
Hallowell, Norwood, 44
Hamilton, Robert, 126–27
Handy, John, 141–43, 144*f*
Harper's Weekly
   on Battle at Milliken's Bend, 1–2, 3*f*
   on Black soldiers in Charleston, 16*f*
   cartoons on bounty brokers, 124–25
   on emancipation fears, 29, 29*f*
   on execution of deserters, 42
   on training of Black recruits, 37–38, 38*f*
   "Typical Negro, A," 4*f*
   "War in the Southwest, The," 10*f*

Hawkins, John P., 103, 249n.61
Hay, John, 65
Higginson, Thomas Wentworth
  on courts-martial, 87–88
  and desertions by Black soldiers, 64, 65
  expedition into Florida, 28
  on First Contraband regiment, 63–64
  on formerly enslaved persons as childlike, 30, 44
  interview by AFIC, 30
  search for deserters, 65
  on unequal pay for Black soldiers, 46–47
Holt, Joseph, 137, 139–40, 143–47, 150–51
Howe, Samuel Gridley, 30
Humbert, Robert, 72–73
Hunter, David, 63–64

illness
  Black soldiers' exposure to new diseases, 67
  Black soldiers' faking of, 68–69
  Black soldiers' lower hardiness and, 67
  formerly enslaver persons' bad experiences with doctors and, 159–60
  home care for, as standard of the period, 67–68
  leaves of freedom to recover at home from, 66–68, 70–71, 104, 114–15, 143–46, 159, 160
impressed Black southerners
  desertion by, 63–64, 73–75, 159
  seizure as property by Union recruiters, 73–74, 159
injustices suffered by Black soldiers, as grounds for release, in their view, 59–60

instruction of Black soldiers in skills for free-labor society
  American Freedmen's Inquiry Commission study on, 30–31
  and disputed meaning of freedom, 9–10, 23, 33
  guidance in proper labor protest, 46–47
  and limits on scope of emancipation, 42
  paternalistic condescension of, 43
  prioritizing over military role, 46
  US Army literacy schools, 45–46
  US Army's role in, 7f, 9–10, 16–17, 26–28, 30–31, 33, 42, 43–45
  variations in officers' severity in, 44
  and vocational training, 47–48

Jackaberry, William, 32
"John Brown's Body" (song), 15–16, 16f
Johnson, Edmond, 127–30, 129f
Johnson, Hillard, 160
Johnson, John, 143–46
Johnson, Richard, 69
Jones, Stephen, 121
"Journey of a Slave from the Plantation to the Battlefield" (Queen), 62f

Keith, Damon J., 245n.24
Kelley, William, 26
Kennington, Kelly, 251n.13
Kinsley, Rufus, 46
Knox, Thomas W., 1–2, 70, 213n.1

labor activism
  of Black southerners during Civil War, 6–8
  US Army's guidance of Black soldiers in, 46–47
leaves of freedom. *See also* courts-martial trials for leaves of freedom
  in 1863, 63–69
  in 1864–1865, 70–77

Black soldiers' opposition to
  punishment for, 71–72
Black southerners' reasons for, 60–61
by both white and Black soldiers, 77
to care for sick family members,
  69, 120–21
citizen-soldier ethos and, 77
conflict with military discipline, 63, 77
as continuation of mobility practices
  after enslavement ended, 1–2, 3–4,
  8–9, 56–57, 60, 61, 63, 162
convictions for encouraging or aiding,
  71–72, 73f, 150–51
efforts to stem, through harsh
  punishment, 72–73
and enslaved persons' journey to
  freedom, 3–4, 8–12, 56–57, 60, 63,
  69, 70, 74, 77, 101–2, 106–8, 161, 162
to escape slavery-like working
  conditions, 9–10
executions for, 72–73, 103–4
punishment as limited deterrent, 75–
  76, 104
range of reasons for taking, 11–12, 56–
  57, 63, 161
to recover at home from illness, 66–68,
  70–71, 104, 114–15, 143–46, 159, 160
soldiers' failure to 1–2, 3–4, 9–10, 60–
  61, 65–66, 67, 70, see problem with
and struggle for freedom, 3–4, 8–12,
  56–57, 60, 63, 69, 70, 74, 77, 101–2,
  106–8, 162
as term, 61–62, 215–16n.11
US Army's searches for missing
  soldiers, 65, 70–71, 74–75
to visit or support family, 1–2, 11–12,
  56, 65, 109, 116–21, 143, 152
in Western Theater, 65–66, 76–77
Leblanc, Armand, 71
Liberator, The, 89
Lincoln, Abraham
  and Black soldiers' equal pay disputes, 122

decision to undermine slavery, 18
Emancipation Proclamation, 6,
  18, 50–51
and First Contraband
  regiment, 63–64
on freedom as Black soldiers'
  motivation, 60
initial call for recruits, 92–93
initial limiting of Black soldiers to
  noncombat roles, 50–51
on jobless men enlisting by necessity, 5–6
letters received from irate Black
  soldiers, 59
on need for strong desertion
  penalties, 96–97
opening of US Army to Black
  soldiers, 6, 18
petitions from jailed soldiers, 137, 138–
  40, 143–47, 150–51
on prisons for soldiers, 135
sons' play imitating execution of
  deserter, 42
and underage enlistees, 96n.52
understanding view of leaves of
  freedom, 60
on vetting officers for USCT units, 31–32
and white people's fears about
  emancipation, 24–25, 24f
Little, Isaac, 49
Loguen, Helen Amelia, 19
Lovejoy, Elijah, 32
Lovejoy, Owen, 32

Macarty, Lionel, 71–72, 73f
manual labor in US Army
  Black soldiers' resentment of, 50–
    51, 54–55
  disproportionate assignment of Black
    soldiers to, 54
  limiting of Black soldiers' service
    to, 50–51
  white soldiers' dislike of, 49

Margraff, Philip, 138, 257n.28
Maynard, Horace, 31
McKaye, James, 30
media, and emancipation fears, 28–29
Memphis, Reconstruction in, 153–56
Merriam, Henry, 71
Merritt, Charles, 52
Milewski, Melissa, 251n.13
military common law (*lex non scripta*), 82–83
military service, as part of US social contract, 91–92
Milliken's Bend, Battle of, 1–2, 3*f*
Mitchell, John, 102–4
Mixter, Calvin Simms, 32–33
M'Kim, James Miller, 20–21
Montgomery, James, 39–40, 65, 72–73
Morris, Jack, 150–52
Murphy, John, 112
Murray, John Lovejoy, 74–75
mutiny
  Black soldiers' legal defense against charges of, 111
  execution for, 53–54

National Museum of African American History and Culture, 164–65
Nelson, William J., 257n.28
Newton, Alexander, 34–35
Norbert, Joseph, 70–71
Northrup, Solomon, 124–25

Obama, Barack, 164–65
Observations of Military Law and the Constitution and Practice of Courts-Martial (De Hart), 85
officers of US Army
  moral instruction of white soldiers, 42–43
  treatment of white soldiers as family, 42–43

officers of USCT units. *See also* instruction of Black soldiers in skills for free-labor society
  as almost exclusively white northerners, 9–10, 32
  antislavery activists among, 32
  appointment of, *vs.* standard unit elections of leader, 27–28
  debate on qualities needed by, 25
  decision to appoint white officers, 27–28
  paternalistic condescension toward Black soldiers, 43
  racist views of, 32–33, 162
  some less-desirable choices, 31–32
  support for equal pay protests, 47
  three types of, 44–45
  vetting of, 31–33, 162
Owen, Robert Dale, 30
Owens, William, 115, 116

Parkinson, William, 65–66
pay of Black soldiers
  officers' instruction in proper protesting of, 46–47
  protests for equal pay, 46–47, 59
  winning of equal pay, 47
Pennington, James, 118–19
pensions, military
  denial after conviction for desertion, 160
  discrimination in application system, 160
petitions for release by jailed Black soldiers
  claimed cruel treatment by officers, 146–47, 148–49
  claim of desertion through trickery, 142
  claims of labor contract problems, 257n.28

defenses of leaves of freedom in, 133–34, 140, 152–53
emphasis on good character and record in, 141, 142–43
evocation of Reconstruction goal of remaking Black family in, 150–53, 156–57
as form of resistance, 156
ignorance of the law as grounds for, 142–47
insights gained from, 133–34
large number sent, 137
Lincoln and, 137, 138–40, 143–47, 150–51
as motivated by belief in justice, 137
offers to help with Reconstruction, 133–34, 149
offers to help with war, 133–34, 140, 141–49
and political empowerment gained through military service, 156–57
requests for mercy, 139–40
sick family members needing care and, 132–33
successful, 132–33, 142–43
petitions for removal of desertion conviction record, 160
philanthropists, northern, and dispute over meaning of freedom, 18
Phillips, Anderson, 118–20, 121
Phillips, John, 98
Port Hudson, Battle of, 70–71
Porter, Alexander, 6
Price, Isaiah, 139–40
Primbow, Anthony, 70–71
prisons used for soldiers, 132–33, 133f, 134–35
for Black soldiers, 135–37, 136t, 139–40
conditions in, 137
Supreme Court ruling on, 134–35
for white soldiers, 135

Pryor, Hubbard, 6, 7f

Queen, James Fuller, 62f

racial attitudes
Black soldiers' view of military discipline as white supremacy, 48–49
officers' paternalistic condescension toward Black soldiers, 43, 162
white officers hostile to Black rights, 141–42, 152–53
white people's view of enslaved persons as child-like, 9–10, 18, 25–26, 30, 35, 42, 44
Ramold, Steven, 252n.19
Ray, Henrietta Cordelia, 163–64
Ray, Jerome, 113
Reconstruction
Black soldiers' role in, 152, 153–55
disarming of Black soldiers in Memphis, 153–55
eradication of southern society as goal of, 149–50
imposition of free-labor system in South, 121–22, 149–50
incarcerated Black soldiers seeking release to aid with, 133–34, 149
remaking of Black families in mold of white middle class as goal of, 149–50
white southerners' resistance to, 153–56
recruiting of Black soldiers
by Black leaders in North, 18–20
and disputed concepts of freedom, 23
emancipation as incentive in, 21–23
by former enslaved men, 21–23
in South, 21–23

Republicans. *See also* Reconstruction
  and arming Black soldiers, 26–27, 28–31
  decision to admit Black men to US Army, 15–16, 17, 23
  eradication of southern culture as goal of, 18, 149–50
  and free-labor practices, 121–22
  policies of, echoed in Black soldiers' petitions for release, 140, 149, 150, 156–57, 162
  undermining of slavery, 18
  views on Black people, 16–17, 43, 149–50
Results of Emancipation, The (Cochin), 28–29
Richards, Channing, 85
Right Way, The Safe Way, Proved, The (Child), 25
Rivers, Prince, 20–23
Roosa, Samuel, 150–51
Russwurm, John, 58–59

Saxton, Rufus, 28, 64, 65
Scott, Winfield, 248–49n.52
Sea Islands
  First Black regiments formed in, 63–64
  schools for freedpeople on, 18
Shaw, Robert Gould, 39–40, 46–47, 72–73
Sherman, William T., 31, 158–59
Simmons, Robert, 64
Sixth Amendment, and courts-martial, 88
slavery. *See also* enslaved persons
  and bureaucratic erasure of humanity, 118–19
  end of, views of white historians on, 2–3
Smalls, Robert, 21–23
Smith, Caleb, 134–35

Smith, Joseph, 72–73
Smith, Moses, 90–91
songs sung by Black soldiers, 15–16, 16*f*
Spirit of Freedom monument, 164–65, 165*f*
Stanley, Thomas, 112–13
Stanton, Edwin
  and American Freedmen's Inquiry Commission, 30–31
  and choice of commanders for USCT units, 27–28
  complaints received about poor treatment of Black soldiers, 54
  and officers for USCT units, 31–32
  and recruiting of Black soldiers, 25
  and Western Theater, 65–66
Stephens, George, 89–90
Stevens, Thaddeus, 25–27
Stoneman, George, 152–55
stories told by soldiers to evoke sympathy of superiors, 117–18
Sturgis, Samuel, 158–59
Sumner, Charles, 32, 138
Supreme Court, on prisons for soldiers, 134–35

Taylor, Richard, 127–28
temporary absences of Black soldiers. *See* leaves of freedom
Thomas, Lorenzo, 7*f*, 65–66
Thompson, Andrew, 125–26
Thompson, Ennis, 249n.61
Thompson, James, 92
Tinder, Henry, 115–16
Tocqueville, Alexis de, 57–58
Twelve Years a Slave (Northrup), 124–25

Ullman, Daniel, 71–72, 151
United States Colored Troops (USCT). *See also* Black soldiers; officers of USCT
  advocates for Black officers in, 151

Black officers restricted to chaplain or surgeon roles, 31
and Black social contract with federal government, 12, 21–23
and disputed meaning of freedom, 23
early units with Black officers, 31
history of depictions of, 2–3
noncombat labor assignments of, 6
protests against working conditions, 6–8
significance for Black men's liberation, 55
successes of, 55
tensions in, throughout war, 55
tools for resisting unjust treatment, 8–9
unexplored aspects of history, 2–3
units organized by War Department, 31–32
US Army. *See also* courts-martial; desertion from US Army; discipline, military; officers of US Army; United States Colored Troops (USCT)
perceived duty to instruct Black soldiers in skills for free society, 7*f*, 9–10, 16–17, 26–28, 30–31, 33, 42, 43–45
tedium and hard work of life in, 5–6
US Army, Regiments and Batteries
1st Arkansas Infantry (African Descent) (46th USCI), 15n.1
29th Connecticut (Colored) Infantry, 75–76, 113
29th Connecticut Infantry, 34–35, 44
2nd Corps d'Afrique (74th USCI), 46
4th Corps d'Afrique (76th USCI), 53
15th Corps d'Afrique Engineers (99th USCI), 143
1st Corps d'Afrique Infantry (73rd USCI), 70–71, 150–51
18th Corps d'Afrique Infantry (90th USCI), 69
91st Illinois, 142–43
91st Illinois Infantry, 142
84th Indiana Infantry, 49
9th Indiana Infantry, 39
21st Indiana Infantry, 112–13
23rd Iowa Infantry, 3*f*
3rd Kentucky Cavalry, 97
1st Louisiana Engineers (95th USCI), 141–42
8th Louisiana Infantry (African Descent) (47th USCI), 65–66
9th Louisiana Infantry (African Descent), 56
9th Louisiana Infantry (African Descent) (63rd USCI), 3*f*, 213n.1
11th Louisiana Infantry (African Descent) (49th USCI). *See* Eleventh Louisiana Infantry (African Descent) (later Forty-Ninth USCI)
13th Louisiana Infantry (African Descent), 3*f*
1st Louisiana Native Guards (7th USCHA), 132–33
2nd Louisiana Native Guards (74th USCI), 88–89
4th Maryland Volunteers, 138–39
50th Massachusetts Cavalry, 47–48, 139–40
54th Massachusetts Infantry, 221n.5
55th Massachusetts Infantry, 16*f*, 44–45, 47, 52, 53, 59, 139–40
54th Massachusetts Infantry, 19–20, 39–40, 46–47, 59, 72–73, 89–90
1st Michigan Colored Infantry (102nd USCI), 220–21n.1
1st Mississippi Infantry (African Descent) (51st USCI), 3*f*
2nd Mississippi Infantry (African Descent) (52nd USCI), 81, 100

US Army, Regiments and Batteries (*cont.*)
    3rd Mississippi Infantry (African Descent) (52nd USCI), 102–3
    4th Mississippi Infantry (African Descent) (66th USCI), 76–77, 249n.61
    5th New York Infantry, 138
    11th New York Infantry, 112–13
    19th New York Infantry, 111
    146th New York Infantry, 138
    1st North Carolina (Colored) Infantry (35th USCI), 54
    7th Ohio Cavalry, 88–89
    22nd Ohio Infantry, 85
    1st South Carolina (Colored) Infantry (33rd USCI), 28, 44, 46–47, 64, 87–88
    2nd South Carolina (Colored) Infantry (34th USCI), 39–40, 65, 72–73
    3rd South Carolina (Colored) Infantry (21st USCI), 47, 122
    1st Tennessee Infantry (African Descent) (59th USCI), 253n.35
    5th United States Artillery, 112
    3rd United States Colored Cavalry or USCC, 146
    5th USCC, 93–95
    6th USCC, 109
    3rd United States Colored Heavy Artillery or USCHA, 54, 104, 120–21, 123, 152
    4th USCHA, 115
    5th USCHA, 56, 70
    7th USCHA, 73–74
    7th USCHA (1st Louisiana Native Guards), 132–33
    1st United States Colored Infantry or USCI, 125
    3rd USCI, 72–73, 112
    4th USCI, 54–55
    8th USCI, 45
    20th USCI, 50–51, 150–51
    21st USCI, 16*f*
    21st USCI (3rd South Carolina (Colored) Infantry), 47, 122
    27th USCI, 74–75, 117, 257n.28
    35th USCI (1st North Carolina (Colored) Infantry), 54
    31st USCI, 98
    32nd USCI, 50–51, 112
    33rd USCI (1st South Carolina (Colored) Infantry), 28, 44, 46–47, 64, 87–88
    34th USCI (2nd South Carolina (Colored) Infantry), 39–40, 65, 72–73
    43rd USCI, 51, 123–24
    44th USCI, 6
    46th USCI (1st Arkansas Infantry (African Descent)), 220–21n.1
    47th USCI (8th Louisiana Infantry (African Descent)), 65–66
    49th USCI (11th Louisiana Infantry (African Descent)). *See* Eleventh Louisiana Infantry (African Descent) (later Forty-Ninth USCI)
    51st USCI (1st Mississippi Infantry (African Descent)), 3*f*
    52nd USCI (2nd Mississippi Infantry (African Descent)), 81, 100
    52nd USCI (3rd Mississippi Infantry (African Descent)), 102–3
    58th USCI, 6
    59th USCI, 43–44, 158–60
    59th USCI (1st Tennessee Infantry (African Descent)), 253n.35
    63rd USCI (9th Louisiana Infantry (African Descent)), 3*f*, 213n.1
    66th USCI (4th Mississippi Infantry (African Descent)), 76–77, 249n.61

68th USCI, 42, 44
73rd USCI (1st Corps d'Afrique Infantry), 70–71, 150–51
74th USCI (2nd Corps d'Afrique), 46
74th USCI (2nd Louisiana Native Guards), 88–89
76th USCI (4th Corps d'Afrique), 53
88th USCI, 152
90th USCI, 39
90th USCI (18th Corps d'Afrique Infantry), 69
95th USCI (1st Louisiana Engineers), 141–42
99th USCI (15th Corps d'Afrique Engineers), 143
102nd USCI, 74–75
102nd USCI (1st Michigan Colored Infantry), 220–21n.1
110th USCI, 121, 127–30
111th USCI, 118, 126–27
119th USCI, 116–17
8th Wisconsin Infantry, 60–61
USCT. *See* United States Colored Troops

Van Alstyne, Lawrence, 39
Vicksburg guardhouse, 135–37, 146, 148*f*
Volck, Adalbert, 24*f*

Walcott, George, 35–36
Walker, William, 47
Washington, Booker T., 163–64
Washington, David, 146–47
Watson, Spencer, 70
Weekly Anglo-African, 51, 59
Weld, Angelina Grimké, 137–38
White, Hardtime, 72–73, 242n.54
White, Paris, 114–15
Whiting, William, 33
Wilcox, Crawford, 73–74
Wilder, Burt, 68–69
Williams, Aleck, 54
Williams, Fannie Barrier, 163–64
Williams, Joseph, 158–60
Will the Blacks Fight? (Weiss), 28–29
Wilson, Charles, 112
Wilson, Jack, 128–30
Winn, Robert, 97, 101–2
women
  Black southern, wartime hardship of, 65
  inability to serve in military, 18–19
Wright, Nelson, 120–21
Wright, Richard, 163–64